Home Reference Book

Dearborn™
Home Inspection

This publication is designed to provide accurate and authoritative information in regard to the subject matter covered. It is sold with the understanding that the publisher is not engaged in rendering legal, accounting, or other professional service. If legal advice or other expert assistance is required, the services of a competent professional person should be sought.

President: Roy Lipner
Publisher and Director of Distance Learning: Evan M. Butterfield
Senior Development Editor: Laurie McGuire
Content Consultant: Alan Carson
Acting Editorial Production Manager: Daniel Frey
Creative Director: Lucy Jenkins
Graphic Design: Neglia Design Inc.

BIBLIOGRAPHY

	AUTHOR/S	PUBLISHERS
ROOFING		
Roofing Materials Guide	Compilation	National Roofing Contractors Association
The Complete Roofing Handbook	James E. Brumbaugh	Macmillan Publishing Co.
Slate Roofs	National Slate Association	Vermont Structural Slate Company Inc.
Roofs	Maxwell C. Baker	Multiscience Publications Ltd.
NRCA Roofing & Waterproofing Manual	Trade Manual	National Roofing Contractors Association
Residential Asphalt Roofing Manual	Compilation	Asphalt Roofing Manufacturers Assoc.
EXTERIOR		
The Consumer's Stucco Handbook	John Bucholz, P.E.	Plaster Information Center
Technical Notes on Brick Construction	Compilation	Brick Institute of America
STRUCTURE		
Architectural Graphic Standards	Charles George Ramsey/ Harold Reeve Sleeper	John Wiley & Sons
The Handbook of Building Construction	George A. Hool/ Nathan C. Johnson	McGraw-Hill
The New Science of Strong Materials	J.E. Gordon	Pelican
Structures	J.E. Gordon	Plenum Press
Permanent Wood Foundations	Gary J. Gibson	Sure-West Publishing Inc.
Diagnosing & Repairing House Structure Problems	Edgar O. Seaquist	McGraw-Hill
Wood Design Manual	Compilation	Taunton Press
Building Failures, Diagnosis & Avoidance, 2d Ed.	W.H. Ronsom	E. & F. N. Spon, London
Truman's Scientific Guide to Pest Control Operations	Compilation	Edgell Communications
Design of Wood Structures	Donald E. Breyer	McGraw-Hill
Residential Foundations: Design, Behavior, and Repair	Robert Wade Brown	Van Nostrand Reinhold
ELECTRICAL		
Alternating Current Fundamentals	John R. Duff/ Milton Kaufman	Delmar Publishers Inc.
House Wiring Simplified	Floyd M. Mix	Goodheart-Willcox Co. Inc.
American Electricians' Handbook	Terrell Croft/ Wilford Summers	McGraw-Hill
National Electrical Code 1990 Handbook	Compilation	National Fire Protection Association

HEATING/AIR CONDITIONING

The Steam Book	Fluid Handling Division ITT	Wallace Eannace Associates Inc.
Heating, Ventilating & Air Conditioning Library, Volumes I, II & III	James E. Brumbaugh	Macmillan
Home Guide to Plumbing, Heating & Air Conditioning	George Daniels	Harper & Row
Refrigeration & Air Conditioning Technology	Rex Miller	Bennett Publishing Co.
Modern Refrigeration & Air Conditioning	Althouse, Turnquist, & Bracciano	Goodheart-Willcox Co. Inc.
Basic Mechanical Code	Compilation	Building Officials &Code Administrators Intn'l.
Standard Mechanical Code	Compilation	Southern Building Code Congress Intn'l.
Standard Gas Code	Compilation	Southern Building Code Congress Intn'l.
Uniform Mechanical Code	Compilation	International Assoc. of Plumbing & Mechanical Officials & Intn'l. Conference of Building Officials
National Fuel Gas Code/ National Fuel Gas Code Handbook	Compilation	American Gas Association
Fundamentals of Gas Appliance Venting & Ventilation	Compilation	American Gas Association
Principles of Steam Heating	Dan Holohan	Fuel Oil & Oil Heat Magazine
Installation Guide for Residential Hydronic Heating Systems	Compilation	The Hydronics Institute

PLUMBING

Home Guide to Plumbing, Heating & Air Conditioning	George Daniels	Harper & Row
Uniform Plumbing Code Illustrated Training Manual	Compilation	International Assoc. of Plumbing & Mechanical Officials
Basic Plumbing Code	Compilation	Building Officials & Code Administrators Intn'l.
Standard Plumbing Code	Compilation	Southern Building Code Congress Intn'l.
Uniform Plumbing Code	Compilation	International Assoc. of Plumbing & Mechanical Officials

INTERIOR

Fireplace Technology	H. Morstead	Centre for Research & Development in Masonry
Residential Masonry Fireplace & & Chimney Handbook	James E. Amrhein	Masonry Institute of America

GENERAL

Title	Author	Publisher
House Building Regulations Simplified	J.C. Curry/ J.S. Robertson	C Text Research Inc.
Home Maintenance & Repair	Gary D. Branson	Theodore Audel & Co.
Complete Building Construction	John Phelps/ Tom Philbin	Macmillan Publishing Co.
National Construction Estimator	Martin D. Kiley/ Will Moselle	Craftsman Book Company
Fine Homebuilding Magazine	Compilation	Taunton Press
The Old House Journal	Compilation	Old House Journal Corp.
Construction Principles, Materials & Methods	Harold B. Olin	Institute of Financial Education
A Training Manual for Home Inspectors	Alfred L. Alk	ASHI
Preventive Home Maintenance	Compilation	ASHI & the Editors of Consumer Reports
Maintaining Your Home	Compilation	Consumer Reports & ASHI
The ASHI Technical Journal	Periodical	ASHI
The Journal of Light Construction	Periodical	P.O. Box 686 Holmes, P.A. 19043
CABO One and Two Family Dwelling Code	Compilation	Basic/National Building Code
Basic Building Code	Compilation	Building Officials &Code Administrators Intn'l.
Standard Building Code	Compilation	Southern Building Code Congress Intn'l., Inc.
Uniform Building Code	Compilation	International Conference of Building Officials

We extend our thanks to the following contributing authors:

Mr. Dan Friedman
American Home Inspection Service
Poughkeepsie, New York

Mr. Kevin O'Malley
Inspection Training Associates
Oceanside, California

Mr. Richard Malin
Richard D. Malin & Associates
Monroeville, Pennsylvania

ACKNOWLEDGEMENTS AND CREDITS

A. Illustrations

Our thanks to the following contributors are offered for their kind permission to use illustrations in this book.

1. Canada Mortgage and Housing Corporation.

a) Trouble Free Windows, Doors and Skylights.
(NHA 5735 07/87)

b) Canadian Wood Frame House Construction, Metric Edition.
(NHA 5031 07/87)

Roofing, Flashings & Chimneys
Figures: 5, 7, 8.

Structure
Figures: 40.

B. Technical Assistance

We also appreciate the input of the following groups who have provided technical assistance and/or critiques of the manuscript.

1. Canada Mortgage and Housing Corporation.

2. National Research Council of Canada. Institute for Research in Construction.

3. Government of Ontario, Ministry of Housing.

4. Government of Ontario, Ministry of the Environment, Pest Control Division.

5. University of Illinois, Small Homes Council - Building Research Council.

6. Energy, Mines and Resources, Canada.

7. The Canadian Wood Council.

8. Ontario Hydro.

9. The American Society of Home Inspectors.

ROOFING/FLASHINGS/CHIMNEYS   Page

EXTERIOR   Page

STRUCTURE

Page

ELECTRICAL

HEATING

Page

COOLING/HEAT PUMPS

INSULATION   Page

PLUMBING

INTERIOR

Page

1 ROOFING/ FLASHINGS/ CHIMNEYS

TABLE OF CONTENTS   Page

► INTRODUCTION

The primary purpose of a roof is to keep the building and its occupants protected from rain, snow, sun, wind, and all the combinations of these. Roofs may also add to or detract from the appearance of a building. Roofs provide some mechanical protection against falling objects, although anyone who has seen the damage done by a large tree falling on a house, knows their strength is limited. Contrary to what many think, roof coverings are not intended to keep out the cold. The majority of roofs are extremely poor insulators.

► 1.0 ROOFING

Sloped and Flat

There are two main categories of roofing systems: sloped roofs and flat roofs. Sloped roofing systems are not watertight, per se. They shed water much like a pyramid of umbrellas. Flat roofs, on the other hand, are watertight membranes which are designed to be impervious to water penetration. Flat roofing is actually a misnomer as these roofing systems should never be perfectly flat. They

Drainage

should slope enough to allow water to drain properly, since water standing on the roof for long periods of time will accelerate deterioration of the membrane. Good practice includes a secondary drain for flat roofs.

Pitch

Before discussing roofing materials, two common roofing expressions should be defined. The first is "pitch". The pitch of a roof is really the slope of the roof. Convention dictates that the slope is defined as a ratio of rise over run. For uniformity, the run is always defined as twelve feet. Therefore, a six in twelve roof would have a vertical rise of six feet over a horizontal distance of twelve feet.

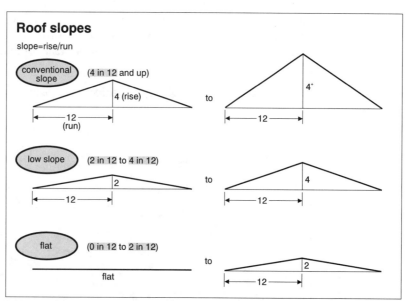

Figure 1. Roof Slope or Pitch

Roofs with a pitch greater than four in twelve are considered conventional roof systems. Roofs with a slope between four in twelve and two in twelve are considered to be low slope roofs, and roofs with a pitch less than two in twelve are considered to be flat roofs.

3

Square

Another common roofing term is "square". A square is a roofer's expression for the amount of material required to cover one hundred square feet. The pitch of the roof and the number of squares are two major factors that roofers consider when pricing a job. Other considerations are the height of the roof above the ground, the complexity of the roof (the number of dormers, chimneys, changes in direction, etc.) and the number of layers of material that are on the roof.

1.1 Asphalt Shingles: Asphalt shingles are the most common roofing material used at present. The shingles consist of asphalt impregnated felt paper, coated with an additional layer of asphalt and covered with granular material. Some manufacturers use fiber glass matting as an alternative to felt paper.

Shingle Weight

Life Expectancy

Asphalt shingles were historically classified by weight. The most common type of shingles used today weigh two hundred and ten pounds per square. They have an average life expectancy of twelve to fifteen years. Heavier asphalt shingles such as 225's (two hundred and twenty-five pounds per square), 235's and even 320's are available. 225's and 235's have an average life expectancy of fifteen to twenty years, while 320's have a life expectancy in excess of twenty-five years.

Today, asphalt shingles are classified by the warranty offered by the manufacturer. They would now be known as 10 year, 15 year, 20 year, 25 year, 30 year or 35 year shingles. The reason for this change was the use of lighter fiber glass matting. Modern shingles are also available in various textures and edge patterns.

Self Sealing Shingles

Since the mid 1960's, most asphalt shingles have been of the self sealing type. A strip of tar is put on the surface of the shingles by the manufacturer. This strip is covered by the shingle installed immediately above. When the sun warms the roof surface, the two shingles stick together. This helps prevent the shingles from being blown off in a wind storm. (Shingles installed in the late fall and winter often do not seal themselves until the next spring.) On older, non-sealing asphalt shingles, a wind storm is often the final blow (no pun intended). The shingles, brittle with age, simply tear off and land in the garden.

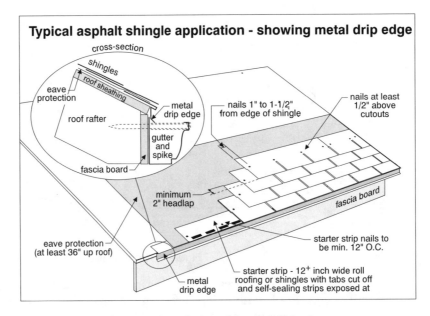

Figure 2. Installation of Asphalt Shingles

Conventional Shingles

Conventional asphalt shingles can be used on a slope as low as four in twelve, using normal techniques. Some roofers use these shingles down to a pitch of two in twelve if the roof is first covered with non-perforated, saturated felt papers. The felt papers must be overlapped by fifty percent and the section at the eaves (from the bottom edge up to twenty-four inches beyond the interior of the exterior wall) must be cemented in place to provide extra protection. Unfortunately, it is impossible to determine, during a visual examination, whether this procedure was undertaken. Many roofing experts feel this is not an ideal approach.

Low Slope Shingles

There are also special low slope shingles which are designed for pitches down to two in twelve. With these shingles, only one third of the shingle is exposed to the weather (as opposed to half of the shingle on a conventional installation) and the shingles are individually cemented in place.

Wear Factors

Regardless of the type of asphalt shingle used, there are two general rules with regard to wear. 1) Sunlight is one of the biggest enemies of asphalt roofs and consequently in many areas the south and west exposures wear out the fastest. (Lighter colored shingles reflect more light and, consequently, last slightly longer.) 2) The steeper the pitch of the roof, the longer the shingles will last.

As asphalt shingles wear, they lose their granular covering. The granular material protects the shingles from ultra-violet light. As it is worn off, the shingles dry out and become brittle. They crack, buckle, and curl. Areas where the granular material has eroded the fastest, wear out first. These may be areas where there is heavy foot traffic, abrasion from tree branches, or erosion from downspouts discharging onto the roof surface.

Premature Blisters

Occasionally, shingles will wear out prematurely due to a manufacturer's defect. Blisters, approximately the size of a dime, form underneath the granular surface and cause raised sections in the shingles. While these are not aesthetically pleasing, they do not affect performance until the granular material wears off in these areas.

Premature Cracking

In some instances, premature cracking and splitting of fiberglass reinforced shingles occurs. This cracking is sometimes noted as early as 6 months into the shingle life. Cracks on the shingles can be in any direction. Cracks lead to reduced shingle life.

1.2 Wood Shingles and Shakes: Wood shingles are machine cut, while wood shakes are hand split or mechanically split. Wood shakes are thicker and have a much more uneven surface. Most wood shingles are cedar; however, some are redwood. Wood shingles can be used on roofs with a pitch as low as four in twelve; however, six in twelve or more is recommended. Wood shingles vary in length between sixteen inches and twenty-four inches. On a good quality installation, no more than one third of the shingle is exposed to the weather.

Life Expectancy

The life expectancy of wood shingles is generally thirty to forty years; however, low quality shingles have been known to deteriorate badly in fifteen to twenty years. The rate of wear depends largely on exposure (the amount of shingle which is exposed to the weather), the pitch (the steeper the better), the grade of shingle (there are three), and the amount of sun and shade. Too much sunlight dehydrates the shingles, causing them to become brittle. This results

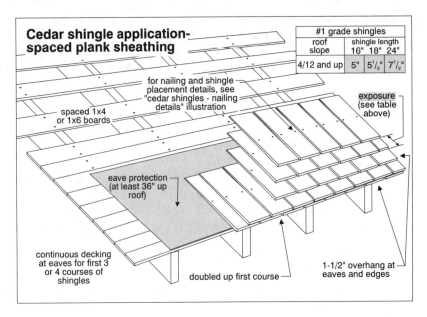

Figure 3. Shingle Application

in splitting and cupping of the shingles. Too much shade and moisture causes rot and moss to grow. Wood shingles and shakes can also suffer mechanical damage from tree branches, foot traffic, snow shovelling, etc.

Another factor which affects the life of wood shingles is their ability to dry quickly. It is preferable to put wood shingles over spaced roof sheathing boards rather than plywood sheets. Some experts say the use of plywood will halve the life of the shingles.

As a general rule, when more than ten to fifteen percent of the roof requires repair, it is best to replace the roof covering.

1.3 Slate Shingles: Slate is a natural material. It is sedimentary rock which is quarried; consequently, the quality can vary. High quality slate roofs have an average life expectancy of sixty to one hundred years. Slate roofs are heavy, weighing three to five times as much as conventional asphalt shingles. A pitch of six in twelve or more is recommended and usually, slates are installed with fifty percent of the slate to the weather.

Wear Factors

While some slates are of low quality and tend to flake and shale, the biggest problem with slate roofs is not the slates themselves, but the nails holding the slates in place. With time, the nails rust and allow the slates to slide out of position. Once one slate has come loose, water penetration accelerates rusting of nails holding other slates in the same vicinity. Therefore, it is imperative to be diligent in the maintenance of an older slate roof. While it is not common practice, slate roofs should be inspected and repaired at least twice annually. Slates which have slipped should be resecured, and slates which have cracked or split as a result of mechanical damage should be replaced. As a general rule of thumb, replacement of the entire roof covering makes sense when more than ten percent of the roof is in need of repair.

A slate roof in perfect condition can still leak under some circumstances. Because of the nature of the material, leakage can occur during periods of wind-blown rain, particularly on slate roofs with a low pitch.

Flashings

Another common problem with slate roofs is that the flashing materials do not last as long as the slates themselves. Flashings, typically made of metal, are used wherever the roof changes direction or meets an obstruction such as a chimney. If the flashings rust, a section of the roof may have to be removed to install a new flashing. This is an expensive and difficult proposition.

Repair Work

Another difficulty with slate roofs is finding qualified people to repair them. Since slate has not been used commonly for the past fifty years, their installation and repair is a vanishing art. Those who do not understand slate roof systems tend to do more damage than good when attempting repairs. There also seems to be a tendency to suggest replacement with a more conventional material that the roofer knows and understands.

1.4 Concrete and Clay Tiles:
These roofing systems are relatively rare; however, concrete tiles are making a comeback. These are high quality roofing systems with life expectancies in the neighborhood of fifty to one hundred years. Like slate, these roofs are heavy, weighing four to five times as much as asphalt shingles. Often, modifications to the roof structure are required if replacing asphalt shingles with concrete.

Concrete and clay tiles can be used on a pitch as low as four in twelve but as with most roofing systems, steeper is better. The amount of overlap (exposure of the tiles) varies depending on the roof system. Systems with a limited overlap are sometimes prone to leakage during wind-blown rains.

Some parts of the USA use the clay or concrete tiles over a built up roof membrane. The tiles are not water tight but provide protection against fire, ultraviolet light and mechanical damage.

Some systems are nailed in place while others use special clips or wire ties. In some regions the tiles are mortared into place.

Wear Factors

Like any brittle roofing system, concrete and clay tiles are subject to mechanical damage, and like any long lasting roof system, the fasteners tend to wear out faster than the tiles. Depending upon the design of the roof system, they can be very difficult to repair.

Because most concrete and clay tiles are not flat, they are more difficult to flash.

1.5 Asbestos Cement Shingles:
Asbestos cement shingles are not very common. They are reasonably high quality and typically last thirty to fifty years. They consist of a mixture of Portland cement and asbestos fiber and require a pitch of three in twelve or more.

Asbestos cement shingles are brittle and are susceptible to mechanical damage. They often discolor and promote the growth of fungus or moss. They are difficult to repair and replacement shingles are hard to obtain.

1.6 Metal Roofs: There are many types of metal roofs. Copper, galvanized steel, pre-painted or coated steel, terne and tin are some of the most common. Most metal roofs (particularly copper) are very expensive systems. Metal roofs can be installed in sheet form or as shingles. Sheets and shingles can be used on sloped roofs; however, flat roofs are only covered in sheets.

Sheet metal roofs can have many different types of seams. Some are soldered while others are folded and crimped in a variety of ways.

Wear Factors   Like any roofing system there are disadvantages; seams can split, or standing seams can get bent. All metal roofs except copper and pre-painted or pre-coated roofs should be painted on a regular basis. Metal roofs should never be covered with tar as moisture trapped below the tar causes accelerated rusting. As a general rule, when one is looking at a tar covered metal roof, one is looking at an inexpensive and short lived repair.

Metal roofs are very difficult to repair, once they have begun to rust and leak. Replacement is the best alternative.

1.7 Corrugated Plastic Roofs: Corrugated plastic is a specialty type of roofing. It is a single ply, translucent roof surface which is generally used over patios and light structures. It should never be used over living areas, as it is not considered to be truly watertight. Corrugated plastic roofs are extremely weak and should never be walked on.

They are generally considered to be low quality roofing systems which are easily damaged, discolor with sunlight and leak at the joints.

1.8 Built-up Roofs: Built-up roofs are commonly called tar and gravel roofs. They are a multi-ply roofing system, consisting of two, three, four or even five plys of roofing felts with a mopping of asphalt (nobody uses coal tar anymore) between layers. A flood coat of asphalt is then applied over the top and covered with gravel to reflect ultra-violet light and protect the roof from mechanical damage. Some roofers use roll roofing rather than gravel to protect the membrane. This is a sacrifice material which may only last five years. Most roofing experts consider this a second choice to gravel.

Pitch   Built-up roofs are designed for flat roof applications and should not be used with a pitch of greater than three in twelve, unless special asphalt is used which will not run when heated by the sun.

Life Expectancy   Two ply built-up roofs have a life expectancy of five to ten years while four-ply roofs normally last fifteen to twenty years. Unfortunately, if the roof has a flood coat of tar and gravel, it is not possible to determine how many plys exist without taking a core sample. It is also difficult to determine the condition of the membrane due to the gravel on top.

Wear Factors   Built-up roofs require a considerable amount of expertise to install properly. If moisture is trapped underneath the membrane or within the layers of the membrane, blisters and bubbles will form and reduce the life expectancy of the roof significantly. A lack of gravel causes rapid deterioration of the roof surface. A condition known as "alligatoring" occurs as the surface breaks down and dehydrates due to exposure to sunlight.

Drainage

Water ponding on a flat roof can shorten the life expectancy by as much as fifty percent. When reroofing, rigid insulation or wood decking can be used to sculpt the roof surface to promote good drainage. As an alternative, under some circumstances, additional drains can be installed. Good practice includes a secondary drain for flat roofs. Drains may be gutters, central drains or scuppers.

Leaks

Because of the construction of built-up roofs, leaks are difficult to isolate and repair. A water stain on a ceiling does not necessarily indicate a leak immediately above. Water can travel a significant distance through the plys of a roof before emerging on the interior.

Because of the complexity of built-up roofs, it is imperative that a reputable roofer, offering a meaningful guarantee, be used.

1.9 Roll Roofing: Roll roofing is sometimes known as selvage roofing. It typically comes in eighteen inch or thirty-six inch wide rolls. It consists of the same material as asphalt shingles (asphalt impregnated felts covered with granules). The surface can be completely covered with granules or only fifty percent covered (designed for two-ply application). The material is most often installed as a single ply with very little overlap.

Life Expectancy

It is considered to be a low quality roof covering with a limited life expectancy of five to ten years. There is an exception to this rule. Sometimes, roll roofing is used to protect a built-up roof covering as an alternative to gravel. Unfortunately, from a visual inspection it is impossible to tell. Modified bitumen roofing (a single ply membrane) can be very similar to roll roofing in appearance. The inspector may not be able to determine the chemical make-up of the roofing material.

Wear Factors

Because roll roofing material is installed in long strips, and because the material expands and contracts with changes in temperature, it tends to buckle or wrinkle. The granular covering breaks down quickly in the wrinkled areas, resulting in localized wear and short life.

The material is used on both sloped roof and flat roof applications. It is sometimes cemented in place but most often it is simply cemented at the seams or nailed at the edges. Often, there is no protection for the nails and leaks occur at these locations.

The material is generally considered to be a handyman type of roof covering.

1.10 Modified Bitumen: Modified bitumen membranes are an alternative to built-up roofs. Polymer-modified asphalt is bonded to fiberglass or polyester reinforcing to form sheets of roofing membrane. Rolls of this rubberized asphalt membrane are typically torched onto the roof, or bonded (mopped in) to the roof with hot asphalt. The surface of the membrane may be protected from ultraviolet rays by a coating of granules, foil, or paint. The sheets are approximately thirty-six inches wide and usually overlap each other by three inches. Modified bitumen roofs may be installed as either a single or double layer system. It is usually not possible to tell how many layers exist on a roof

Life Expectancy

Modified bitumen membranes have only been in use for about twenty years, and their life expectancy is not yet well-defined. A lifespan of fifteen to twenty years seems reasonable, but many roofs have failed sooner.

Wear Factors   Many early failures of modified bitumen roofs have been the result of poor installation. Roofs with ultraviolet protection last longer than those without. Two-ply installations are more durable. Some types of membranes perform better in a cold or a warm climate. There is no way to determine the type during a home inspection.

Since seam failure and installation problems are most common, it is imperative that a good roofer, providing a meaningful guarantee, be used.

1.11 Other Roof Coverings: There are many types of roof coverings on the market today. There are plastic (primarily PVC) and synthetic rubber (elastoneric, EPDM) membranes for flat roofs, hardboard and rubber shingles for sloped roofs, and many more.

With all roofing systems, some basic principles apply. The roof surface should keep the water out. The life expectancy and guarantee should be reasonable. As a general rule, shedding type roofs should have a slope of four in twelve or more. Any roof system which absorbs water (e.g. wood or hardboard) should be installed to permit quick drying.

Asphalt   **1.12 Strip When Reroofing:** While it is better to remove old roofing, an asphalt shingle roof can be installed immediately over one other layer of asphalt shingles, if the layer being covered is relatively smooth and flat. Longer nails must be used. If there are two layers of asphalt shingles on the roof at present, they should be removed prior to adding another layer.

Asphalt shingles are often installed over a single layer of wood shingles or slate shingles; however, the preferred practice is to remove these roof coverings prior to installing asphalt.

Wood   Wood shingles or shakes can be installed over a single layer of asphalt shingles; however, it is preferable to remove existing shingles to allow the wood roof system to breathe. Wood shingles or shakes should never be installed over an existing layer of wood shingles or shakes.

Slate   Slate roofs should never be installed over another layer of roofing. New slate roofs are extremely rare. A new slate roof on a building not designed for slate would likely require structural modifications to contemplate the weight of the roof.

Concrete   Concrete or clay tiles cannot be installed over another roofing system, with the exception of a single layer of asphalt shingles. The roof structure may require modification to handle the additional load.

Asbestos Cement   New asbestos cement shingles are rarely installed. Ideally, existing asbestos cement shingles should be removed prior to installing any other form of roofing material. Because of the asbestos content of the shingles, special provisions must be made for handling and disposing of the material.

Metal   Metal roofs should not be installed over other roofing materials.

Built-Up Roofs   While it is common practice to install new built-up roofs over existing built-up roofing systems, the practice is not advisable. Moisture trapped in the old roofing system will cause premature deterioration of the new membrane.

Single Ply Membranes

While some manufacturers of single ply membranes claim their product can be installed over existing materials, most recommend stripping. Most plastic and synthetic rubber roof membranes are not compatible with asphalt. These should not be installed over built-up roofs.

Corrugated Plastic

Corrugated plastic roofing should not be installed over other roofing materials.

Flashings

1.13 Unusually Vulnerable Areas: The typical vulnerable areas of a roof are where the roof changes direction, or where a change in materials occurs (for example, where the roof meets a chimney or a wall). On a properly installed roof, these areas are flashed. Please refer to 2.0 in this section. Particularly vulnerable areas exist where two or more flashings intersect, for example where a chimney occurs in a valley.

Antennas

In addition to flashings, areas where television antennas and their supporting wires are attached are potential trouble spots.

Low Slope Roofs

As a rule, areas with a low slope tend to be more vulnerable to wear and leakage. If the low slope portion of the roof is covered with asphalt shingles, refer to 1.1 in this section.

Previous Repairs

Areas that have already been repaired are vulnerable. Previous repairs could have been undertaken for a number of reasons; however, in most cases a repair to a roof indicates one of the following: a design problem, defective materials,

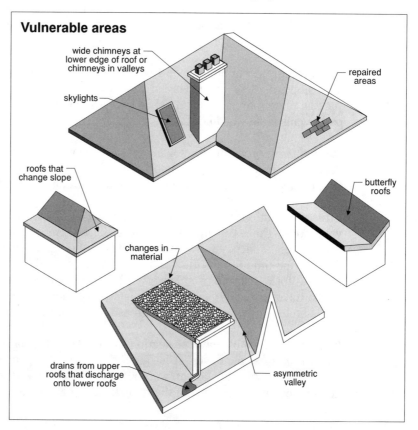

Figure 4. Vulnerable Areas

defective installation, mechanical damage or a roofing system nearing the end of its life.

Low Areas

On sloped roofs, valleys are often required. The valley itself, however, should always have some slope. The lower the slope or pitch of the valley, the more prone it is to leakage. Some roofs are poorly designed with valleys where the base of the valley is flat (horizontal) or nearly flat. These roofs are very prone to leakage and ice damming. Refer to 1.14 in this section.

Low areas on flat roofs pond water. Ponding water will reduce the life expectancy of some flat roofing systems by as much as fifty percent. If the roof is in good condition and is relatively new, modifications are not warranted until replacement is necessary.

Unsuitable Materials

Sometimes, roofing materials which are suitable for one application are used for another. Other times, low quality materials which are simply not suitable at all have been employed. In most cases, corrective action should be undertaken or, at the very least, the area should be monitored.

1.14 High Risk of Ice Damming: Some roofing configurations are more prone to ice damming problems than others. Ice damming occurs when snow and ice collect in a certain area of the roof (often the eaves). Melting snow on the upper portion of the roof cannot drain properly as it is trapped behind the ice dam. See Figure 5. If the dam is large enough and sufficient water collects, it will back up under the shingles and leak into the eaves or worse, into the exterior walls or the building interior.

Ice dams are most common on low slope roofs or roofs which change from a high slope to a low slope. The largest dams tend to form over unheated areas, such as eaves, porches, and attached garages. Ice dams are also common above party walls in attached houses.

Ice damming problems do not necessarily occur every winter. They normally occur after periods of heavy snow fall when day time temperatures are at or slightly above freezing while night time temperatures are below freezing.

Solutions

Effective solutions to ice damming problems are increased attic insulation and ventilation. These two measures reduce the air temperature in the attic so that there is less tendency for snow to melt over the heated portions of the house. Also, at the time of reroofing, eave protection should be provided beneath the shingles for a distance of at least 2-1/2 feet beyond the interior of the exterior walls. Eave protection should be a waterproof membrane. Polyethylene sheeting is no longer accepted in many areas for eave protection.

In extreme climates, eave protection is visible and usually takes the form of metal roofing at the eaves. It is impervious to water penetration and tends to allow snow and ice to slide off the roof. A metal or vinyl drip edge flashing will help protect the lower edge of the roof sheathing and direct water into the gutter.

Avalanche Guards

Metal devices which protrude above roof surfaces (usually on the lower section of roof) are designed to hold snow on the roof and prevent avalanches. These may worsen ice damming conditions.

Heating cables can also be used, however, they are considered to be a less desirable approach. Heating cables must be turned on prior to to the accumulation of snow and ice. In some cases, they can aggravate a situation rather than improve it if they are turned on after the ice dam has formed. Heating cables are not tested during an inspection.

Preventing ice dams with ventilation

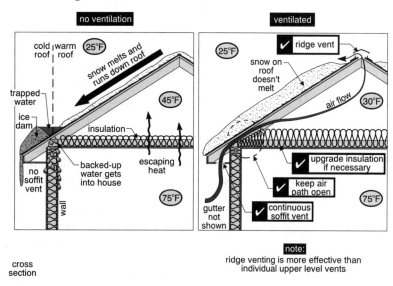

Eave protection against ice dams

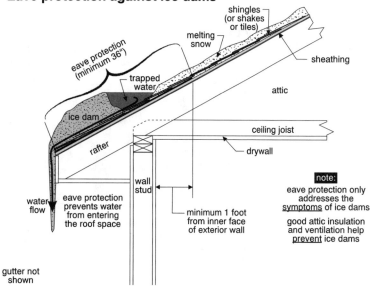

Figure 5. Ice Damming

1.15 Tree branches Touching Roof: Trees should be kept trimmed away from roof and wall surfaces. The abrasive action of branches rubbing against the roof can damage the roof system and shorten its life expectancy.

Tree limbs touching buildings also provide easy access to the home for pests such as squirrels and raccoons.

▶ 2.0 FLASHINGS

Material   Flashings are designed to keep water out. They are used where dissimilar materials meet, where a material changes direction, or at joints in materials. Most flashings are galvanized steel; however, they can also be tin, terne (steel containing copper, coated with a lead-tin alloy), aluminum, or copper. In some cases, lead is used. In specific applications, roll roofing material is used as a flashing. Roll roofing is a material similar to asphalt shingles, except that it comes in rolls, which are either eighteen inches or thirty-six inches wide.

Location   Most flashings are associated with roofs. When a roof line changes direction, a ridge, a valley, or a hip is created. Ridges are horizontal and are found at the highest portion of any given section of a roof. When a roof changes direction in such a way that water will be directed towards that change in direction, a valley is created. When the opposite is true, a hip is created.

2.1 Valley Flashings: Ideally, valley flashings should be constructed of metal; however, most are constructed of roll roofing. In some cases, valley flashings are omitted altogether and the roofing material is bent around the corner. This is not a wise practice. Sometimes a proper valley flashing is installed and then covered with shingles. This is called a closed valley. These may be interwoven or closed cut. Where the flashing is visible, it is known as an open valley. Metal valley flashings are typically twenty-four inches wide; however, the majority of the material cannot be seen, as it is hidden under the shingles. When roll roofing is used, two layers are installed; one being eighteen inches wide, and the other thirty-six inches.

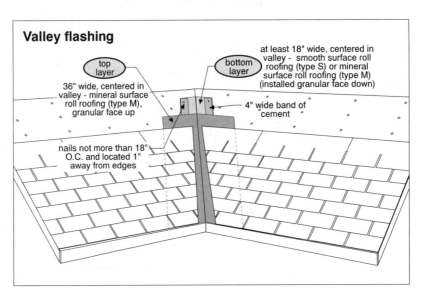

Figure 6. Valley Flashing (Roll Roofing)

Problems   Valleys are particularly weak spots on roofs, as they channel a significant amount of water; therefore, even a small leak can cause considerable damage. The slope of the valley is less than the slope on either side. This causes increased wear on the valley. Sometimes valley flashings stop short of the edge of the roof and allow water to pour into the eaves. Also, the inexperienced tend to walk up valleys when traversing a roof. This damages valley flashings, particularly if they are constructed of roll roofing. If the flashings are not lying flat, they are more prone to damage. Valley flashings are difficult to replace when not replacing the entire roof surface and, consequently, they are often repaired. Even when reroofing, some roofers shingle up to existing valleys and do not replace them. This is not considered good practice.

Low slope   As a general rule, valley flashings on low pitched roofs are more prone to leakage than on steeply pitched roofs. There is also a greater tendency for snow and ice accumulation in low pitched valleys which can result in water backup under the shingles.

Problems can also occur at a valley between a steeply pitched roof and a low pitched roof. Water cascading down the steeply pitched roof can sometimes overshoot the valley and run under the shingles on the lower pitched side. Under some circumstances, special valley flashings have to be created to prevent water from overshooting the valley.

2.2 Hip and Ridge Flashings: When pliable shingles (such as asphalt) are used on the roof, shingles are simply cut and bent over hips and ridges to make them watertight. When the roof shingles are brittle and non-pliable (such as wood shingles, slate, and asbestos cement), metal flashings are often used at the ridges and hips. On some of these roofing systems, the flashing is buried beneath a decorative layer of shingles. In most cases, the condition of hip and ridge flashings is not a major concern, since water is always shed away from these flashings, due to the configuration of the roof. On older roofs such as slate, however, metal flashings rust away and require replacement.

Older metal flashings are often poorly secured and can be blown off in high winds.

2.3 Sloped Roof To Flat Roof Flashings: Many methods are used to flash between sloped and flat roofs (assuming the flat roof is at the bottom of the sloped roof). The principle is always the same - to prevent simple water penetration and to prevent water backing up underneath the shingles, as snow tends to accumulate in this area. Since flat roofs and shingle roofs are often not replaced at the same time, many flashings in this area are poorly installed. The flat roof membrane should extend at least three feet up the sloped roof. Minor building settlement also tends to tear flashings in this location. This is an area which should be carefully monitored.

2.4 Roof To Wall Flashings: Many different flashing configurations are used when a roof intersects a wall. The type of flashing arrangement depends on whether the roof is flat or sloped, and whether the slope is away from the wall, or parallel to the wall. The slope should never be toward the wall. If the roof is flat or slopes away from the wall surface, a simple counter flashing can be installed over the roofing material. A counter flashing is simply a metal skirt which covers the top six inches (roughly) of the roofing material and which is turned up the wall surface. A tight connection between the top of the flashing and the wall is important. This is the most common area of failure.

When a roof slope is parallel to a wall, two sets of flashings are required. Step flashings are installed between each layer of shingles and covered with a counter flashing. Unfortunately during a visual inspection, it is often difficult to determine the presence of step flashings. Sometimes, the siding material acts as a counter flashing.

Counter flashings often pull away from the wall and allow water penetration.

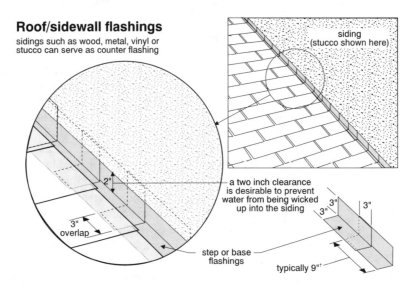

Roof/sidewall flashings

sidings such as wood, metal, vinyl or stucco can serve as counter flashing

siding (stucco shown here)

2"

a two inch clearance is desirable to prevent water from being wicked up into the siding

3"

3"   3"

3" overlap

step or base flashings

typically 9"±

Figure 7. Roof to Wall Flashing

2.5 Chimney Flashings: The flashings used on the sides and downhill portion of the chimney are similar to the wall flashings described above. The portion of a chimney flashing which is most prone to leakage is the portion facing the high section of roofing. (No such section exists if a chimney protrudes through the ridge of a roof.) Water running off a roof hits the high side and must be diverted around the chimney. Therefore, flashings on the high side should be a minimum of six inches in height or one-sixth of the width of

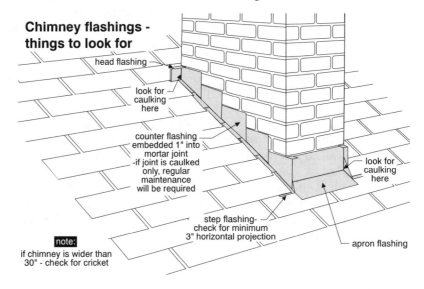

Chimney flashings - things to look for

head flashing

look for caulking here

counter flashing embedded 1" into mortar joint -if joint is caulked only, regular maintenance will be required

look for caulking here

step flashing- check for minimum 3" horizontal projection

apron flashing

note: if chimney is wider than 30" - check for cricket

Figure 8. Chimney Flashings

the chimney, whichever is greater. The flashing should continue up under the shingles to an equal height. When a chimney is more than thirty inches in width, a saddle (or cricket) should be installed behind the chimney to divert water around the chimney. This device is simply a miniature peak roof directing water away from the chimney. They are often missing. There are alternative approaches.

Location

The location of a chimney will dictate how prone it is to flashing leaks. A chimney near the peak of a roof is less prone to water penetration problems than a chimney in a valley or at the bottom of a long section of sloped roof.

Problems

Flashings are often torn, loose, missing, incomplete, rusted, or mechanically damaged by animals.

Roofing cement is often used to correct chimney flashing leaks. This should be considered a short term solution; however, it is sometimes viable if reroofing is to be undertaken within the next few years. At the time, proper chimney flashings can be installed.

2.6 Parapet Wall Flashings: On some houses, the exterior wall of the house protrudes above the roof line. Where the roof meets the wall, flashings are required. These are typical wall/roof flashings (see 2.4) and their design will depend upon whether the roof is sloped or flat. In addition to the wall/roof flashing, a cap flashing should be provided over the top of the parapet wall to prevent water penetration into the wall system.

Parapet wall flashings are often loose, deteriorated or missing altogether.

2.7 Plumbing Stack/Electrical Mast/Exhaust Flue Flashings: A flashing must be provided where a plumbing stack, mast or flue protrudes through a roofing system. These flashings are typically constructed of metal or rubber. On flat roofs, pitch pans are often used. A sheet metal pan around the stack or mast is filled with pitch or tar to a depth of one or two inches. Many experts consider this a poor flashing. Sometimes, condensation forming on the plumbing stack is mistaken for a flashing problem.

Plumbing stack and electrical mast flashings are sometimes torn and often missing (particularly on flat roofs where roofing cement is used as a poor alternative).

2.8 Dormer Flashings: Many types of flashing arrangements are used where dormers intersect the main roof. The type of flashing depends largely upon the dormer shape. The most common flashings are step flashing, which fit between each layer of shingles and extend up the wall surface, and counter flashings which cover the portion of the stepped flashing on the wall surface. Depending upon the configuration of the roof, step flashings are not usually visible. Sometimes, siding material fulfills the role of the counter flashing. If wood siding material is used on a dormer, it should stop approximately two inches above the main roof surface so that rot does not occur.

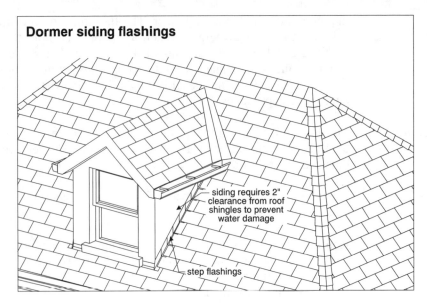

Dormer siding flashings

siding requires 2" clearance from roof shingles to prevent water damage

step flashings

Figure 9. Dormer Flashings

2.9 Skylight Flashings: Skylights should be flashed in a similar method to chimneys. Unfortunately, many skylights are not installed at the same time as the roof and consequently, proper flashing details are omitted. Ideally, a skylight should sit on a curb or box which protrudes at least six inches above the roof surface (unless the skylight comes with a premanufactured flashing assembly). This allows for the installation of proper flashings and limits snow accumulation on the skylight.

*Flush
Skylights*

Some skylights are simply a bubble which is intended to have no flashings. The bubble simply slides under the shingle material on the sides and uphill portion of the skylight. On the downhill side, the skylight overlaps the roofing material. The pitch of the roof, and the distance the skylight projects under the shingles, determines the effectiveness of this arrangement. Generally, this type of skylight is prone to leakage. Replacement with a better quality skylight and flashing system is the best solution.

It is not uncommon for condensation to form on the interior of skylights. This is often mistaken for flashing leakage problems.

2.10 Solarium Flashings: Leakage from solariums often occurs where the glass roof meets the conventional roof or original wall of the house. It is imperative that this area be properly flashed. Leakage also tends to occur where the glass roof meets the glass wall at the eaves of the solarium. Many solarium designs allow water to collect at a moulding or frame at the lower edge of the windows creating the roof. If these components are wood, they invariably rot.

Regardless of the material used, the puddle of water created in this location inevitably leaks through to the interior. Often, design modifications are required to correct a chronic problem. Caulking will work as a short term solution but rebuilding, in whole or in part, is often the only viable long term repair.

As with skylights, water stains from condensation may be difficult to differentiate from water penetration stains.

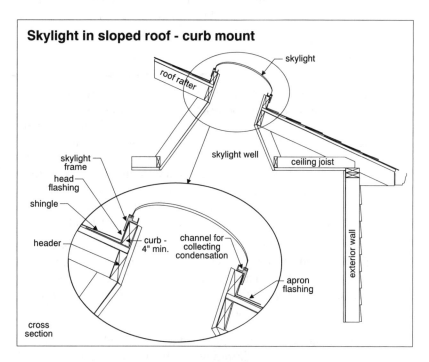

Figure 10. Skylight Flashings

2.11 Drip Edge: This metal flashing is provided along the lower edge of some sloped roofs. It is intended to direct water from the roof edge into the gutters without damaging the fascia or roof sheathing edges. If it is not installed properly, it can cause water damage to the eaves.

2.12 Gravel Stop Flashing: On most flat roofs, a gravel stop flashing is used to terminate the roof membrane at the perimeters. This metal flashing typically has a low profile and performs several functions, including securing and protecting the roof membrane at the edge of the roof, preventing the gravel from sliding off a built-up roof, and forming a drip edge to keep water run off from damaging the wood fascia.

Gravel stop flashings are sometimes loose, rusted or missing altogether. It is common to find the roof membrane lifting from the gravel stop. This can occur due to a poor installation or not properly preparing the metal prior to roofing.

2.13 Roof Vent(s): Flashings are an integral part of most roof vents. The flashing slides under the shingle material on the sides and uphill portion of the vent. On the downhill side, the flashing is exposed, overlapping the roofing material. The amount of overlap of shingles and flashing, as well as the quality of the installation dictates the effectiveness.

3.0 CHIMNEYS

Material

Flues

The most common materials used in chimney construction are masonry and steel. Masonry chimneys can be brick, block or stone and are sometimes stuccoed or parged. In some areas, cement asbestos chimneys are found. Chimneys often have more than one flue. A flue is a separate and distinct channel for the smoke on the inside of the chimney. Each appliance within the house must have a separate flue, with a few exceptions. Two gas furnaces on the same floor within a house can share a common flue, as can a gas furnace and a gas hot water heater on the same level. Some codes allow wood stoves to share flues with gas or oil furnaces, if at the same floor level.

Flue Liners

Some flues are unlined in that there is masonry exposed on the inside of the flue. Unlined chimney flues are most common in houses built before the Second World War. These unlined masonry flues have performed reasonably well for fireplaces and oil-fired furnaces. Gas-fired furnaces, on the other hand, usually require a liner.

Flues can be lined with one of several materials: clay tile, metal, or asbestos cement pipe. For more information on chimney liners, refer to Heating.

Mutual Chimneys

Many attached and row houses share chimneys. One chimney may have one or more flues for each house. Prior to working on a mutual chimney, it is both courteous and prudent to discuss the work with the neighbor first, as often the costs and benefits of the improvements can be shared. Shared flues present a safety concern. This is discussed in Section 8.9 of the Interior chapter.

Removed

Many chimneys which are no longer needed, are removed down to a point below roof level during re-roofing. This eliminates the need to maintain the upper section and eliminates the risk of water leakage through the chimney flashing, a common source of problems. Removal is appropriate as long as nothing which could be used inadvertently is connected to the chimney below.

Partly Removed

Occasionally, abandoned chimneys are knocked down part way, but still protrude above the roof line. In some cases the flue is sealed, with concrete for example. When re-roofing, it is wise to remove the section of the chimney above the roof line to eliminate the necessity of future maintenance and the risk of roof flashing leakage.

Problems   Chimney deterioration is a very common problem. In most cases, water is the culprit. Metal chimneys corrode, and masonry chimneys suffer deterioration to mortar, brick, stucco, et cetera. The source of the water can sometimes be wind driven rain. In many cases, however, the water is condensation within the chimney. One of the by-products of burning fossil fuels is water vapor. As exhaust gases travel up the chimney, they cool, sometimes reaching the dew point, forming condensation. The water droplets are absorbed into masonry chimneys and sit on the interior of metal chimneys. The water droplets are somewhat acidic from products of combustion. This causes corrosion in metal flues and deterioration within masonry flues. Condensation can also damage cement asbestos chimneys over several years. In severe cases, the chimney can be obstructed.

Freeze/Thaw   The problem is compounded in masonry chimneys because of cyclical heating. Chimneys are forever heating up and cooling down, as furnaces, boilers, hot water heaters and fireplaces are only on intermittently. The moisture which has been absorbed into masonry chimneys freezes as the temperature drops. This causes mortar to deteriorate, bricks to spall and parging or stucco to loosen. This is a natural phenomenon with all chimneys, and deterioration over time should be anticipated.

Gap in Liner   Some masonry chimneys are lined with clay tile. The top flue tile should protrude two to four inches beyond the top of the chimney. If the top section of clay tile was too short to protrude, some brick masons simply raised the top tile, leaving a gap between the top two tiles in the flue. A ring of more rapid deterioration normally shows up on the exterior of the chimney, corresponding to the gap in the clay tile liner.

Scaffolding   The amount of deterioration dictates whether chimneys require repair or rebuilding. On tall chimneys or chimneys situated on steeply pitched roofs, it is often necessary to build scaffolding to facilitate proper repairs. This adds to the cost.

3.1 Chimney Cap: The purpose of a chimney cap is to prevent water from penetrating the top of a masonry chimney. The chimney cap should not be confused with the rain caps which sometimes cover the tops of chimney flues to prevent rain water from running down the flues. A chimney cap is usually constructed of concrete; however, some are stone or metal. A good quality cap normally overhangs the sides of the chimney at least one inch to provide some protection for the chimney from water which is dripping off the cap.

Missing   In many cases, a proper cap is not provided. Bricklayers often put a thin coat of mortar over the top of the chimney (exclusive of the flues, of course). With time, this thin layer of mortar cracks and eventually becomes loose. The rate of deterioration to the top of the chimney which does not have a cap depends largely upon the type of masonry used to build the chimney and the quality of the mortar. There are many chimneys that have no cap that do not show signs of deterioration.

Cracked   A cracked cap allows water to penetrate the chimney causing premature deterioration and in northern climates, freeze/thaw damage.

3.2 Brace: Tall chimneys, whether they be masonry or metal, should be braced. The requirements for bracing are not only based on the height of the chimney but also on the width and depth of the chimney.

3.3 Height: Chimneys should be a minimum of three feet above the point of penetration through the roof and two feet higher than anything within ten feet of them. Minor liberties can be taken with this rule when considering single flue metal chimneys for furnaces.

Draft Problems

Chimneys of insufficient height are prone to downdraft problems. Consider a chimney on the leeward side which does not extend above the peak of the roof. On windy days, wind blowing across the roof will tend to follow the roof line. This would result in wind pressure on the top of the chimney. This can cause fireplaces to smoke and products of combustion from furnaces to back up.

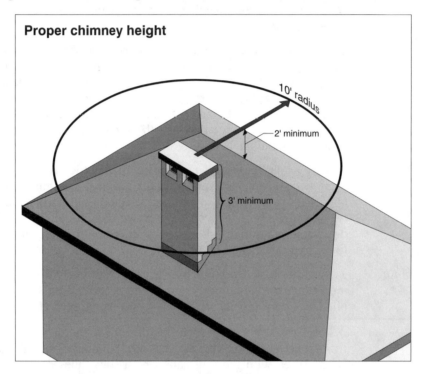

Proper chimney height

10' radius

2' minimum

3' minimum

Figure 11. Chimney Height Above Ridge

The best solution is to extend the chimney upwards. Alternative solutions such as a wind cap or adding glass doors on a fireplace are effective in some cases.

3.4 Vermin Screens: In some neighborhoods, particularly those near park lands or wooded areas, problems are encountered with vermin. Raccoons, birds and squirrels sometimes nest in chimneys to take advantage of their warmth. In these neighborhoods, vermin screens on the top of the chimney flues are advisable.

► 4.0 PROBABILITY OF LEAKAGE

Roofing systems often consist of several different types of flashings and materials. Water leakage may be caused by a number of different factors operating either together or independently. The probability of leakage refers to the chance of leakage occurring within the next year. A low probability does not mean that a roof will not leak within the next year, just that it is less likely to do so than a roof with a high probability of leakage. In some cases, the failure will be significant enough to warrant replacement of the roofing materials. In other cases, minor repairs or improvements are all that are necessary.

Age As roofing materials grow old, they lose their ability to create a weather-tight system. Asphalt shingles can curl and shrink. Built-up roofing dries out and cracks. Wood shingles can do all of these things. Refer to individual material descriptions in Section 1.0 for more information. It is important to note that a new roof is less likely to leak than an old one, but it is still possible.

Installation When roofing systems are not installed properly, the probability of failure increases. Installation defects include exposed fasteners, poor alignment of materials, incorrect materials, and too many layers of roofing.

Manufacturing Defects Defective materials can cause problems with the performance of the roofing system. These defects include cracking or premature aging of the materials. Some defects, such as color variations, are simply cosmetic in nature.

Flashings Flashings are perhaps the most vulnerable areas of the roof, as they represent a seam, or interruption, in the surface of the roof. Refer to Section 2.0.

Design Steep, simple roofs are less likely to develop problems than roofs with a variety of slopes, angles and penetrations. A low-slope design combined with a large roof overhang will make the roof more prone to ice damming, for example.

Weather The most unpredictable factor in predicting leakage is the weather. Often, even a new, perfectly-installed roof will leak under just the right conditions, such as a wind-driven rain from an unusual direction, or a heavy snow following by warmer temperatures and rain.

2
EXTERIOR

► TABLE OF CONTENTS   Page

► INTRODUCTION

The exterior components of a building work together to provide a weathertight skin, if all the parts are doing their job. Protection against intruders, both animal and human, is also offered by the building skin. Good exteriors are attractive, durable and require little maintenance. Exterior components are often the most neglected parts of a home.

► 1.0 GUTTERS AND DOWNSPOUTS

Function

Gutters and downspouts have two major functions. Firstly, they protect the walls of a building from water which would ordinarily run off the roof. This water can damage the wall surfaces and cause localized erosion at ground level.

The most important function of gutters and downspouts, however, is their contribution towards ensuring a dry basement. Regardless of the type of foundation wall, there is always the possibility for water penetration. Therefore, the less water there is in the soil near the foundation wall, the less likelihood of water penetration into the basement. Gutters should collect all water run-off, and downspouts should discharge the water into proper drains or onto the ground a good distance away from the foundation walls.

Size

On most houses, the gutters are attached to the fascia board at the edge of the eaves. In some houses, gutters are integral to the design of the eaves. The two most common sizes of gutters are four inch and five inch widths. Four inch gutters are acceptable for controlling the run-off from relatively small roof areas; however, five inch gutters are preferred because of their additional capacity. Five inch gutters are also less likely to allow water to overshoot the gutters when the water is draining off a steeply pitched roof.

Leakage

The most common problem with gutters is leakage. Leakage will occur with galvanized gutters as they rust through. Eventually, holes can develop in copper gutters as well. All types of gutters are prone to leakage at the joints. Missing end caps are another common source of leakage. Leakage can cause considerable damage to fascias, soffits and walls below.

Loose

Gutters often become loose and require resecuring. This is normally due to improper fastening during original installation or damage caused by ice during winter months.

Damage

Gutters and downspouts suffer from mechanical damage due to ladders, tree limbs, and the like.

Gutters should slope properly towards downspouts so as not to hold water.

Debris

Gutters often clog with debris. Sometimes, screens are installed to prevent leaves and twigs from getting into the troughs. These do not work well. They become loose and often fall out. They also make proper cleaning very difficult.

Integral or Built-in Gutters

Malfunctioning integral gutters can be very serious. The water leaking out of the gutters usually ends up in the structure, causing rot and other damage.

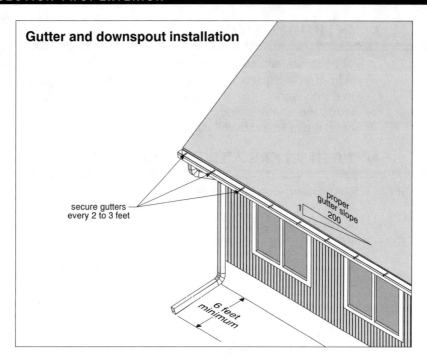

Gutter and downspout installation

secure gutters every 2 to 3 feet

proper gutter slope 1 200

6 feet minimum

Figure 1. Gutters and Downspouts

Downspouts   On many houses, the number of downspouts is inadequate. As a general rule, a downspout should be provided for every forty feet of gutters. Downspouts become disconnected from gutters, or get plugged with debris (particularly at elbows). Special screens are available for the top of downspouts to prevent the entry of debris. These screens must be cleaned regularly.

Downspouts are sometimes not well secured to the wall. They also tend to split open at the seams (from freezing). The seam is usually against the wall.

Downspouts along driveways or sidewalks are sometimes crimped. Galvanized steel downspouts often rust near grade level or where blockages have occurred.

1.1 Materials: Gutters can be made of several materials; however, the most common are aluminum, galvanized steel, plastic and copper. Integral gutters are usually framed in wood, and lined with metals such as lead or copper. There are advantages and disadvantages to the various materials used.

Aluminum   Aluminum gutters do not rust but they dent easily, particularly with tall, heavy ladders. Joints in aluminum gutters are usually riveted together and caulked. The caulking must be renewed every few years. Fortunately, the number of joints required in aluminum gutters is less than with other types of systems, as it is often fabricated on the job site from long rolls of aluminum stock. Aluminum gutter is also pre-finished and, therefore, is low maintenance. Life expectancy is estimated to be twenty to twenty-five years.

Galvanized
Steel

Some galvanized steel gutters are also pre-finished but most are not. Galvanized steel requires periodic painting. Joints in galvanized gutters are usually soldered together. This type of gutter has a twenty to twenty-five year life expectancy.

Plastic

Plastic gutters are generally designed for the do-it-yourselfer. Plastic comes in a limited color selection and some types tend to discolor with time. It is usually relatively small in size and some of the earlier systems are prone to cracking during cold weather. Its life expectancy is dependent upon the quality of the kit and the installation.

Copper

Copper gutters are considered to be the best; however, they are very expensive and not common. Copper can last fifty to one hundred years.

Wet
Basements

1.2 Downspout Discharge: Downspouts take the water from the gutters and discharge it into drains or onto the ground. Underground drains (usually made of clay tile, cast iron or plastic) have a habit of plugging or breaking from frost action. This cannot be determined from a visual inspection. If an underground drain malfunctions, localized water problems will likely develop in the basement in the area of the downspout. If this occurs, there are two options. Exterior digging and repairs can be undertaken; however, it is usually more advantageous to simply disconnect the downspout and redirect it to discharge away from the house.

All downspouts which discharge onto the ground should discharge a good distance away from the house (six feet or more, if possible). The slope of the ground in this area should be away from the house to direct water away from the basement.

On older homes, (pre 1950) downspout drains are often connected to floor drains in the basement. If there is a significant amount of debris in the discharge from the downspouts, it can plug the basement floor drains and cause backup. A more complete discussion of wet basement problems is included in 10.0 of the Interior section.

Onto Roof

Where downspouts discharge from an upper roof onto a lower roof, the section of the lower roof in the path of the water will deteriorate quickly. It is best to extend the downspout along the lower roof to discharge directly into the lower roof gutter.

► **2.0 LOT GRADING**

Proper lot grading is an important consideration when dealing with wet basements. No foundation wall system is completely impervious to water. Therefore, the likelihood of water penetration problems into basements and crawl spaces is partially dependent upon the grading of the lot adjacent to the foundation walls.

Wet
Basements

The theory is simple. If there is less water in the soil on the outside of the foundation wall, there is less chance of water getting to the interior. While there are exceptions to the rule, it can safely be said that the majority of wet basement problems can be eliminated, or at least reduced to a tolerable level, by improvements to exterior grading and proper performance of gutters and downspouts. The ground immediately adjacent to the foundation wall should slope away from the house at a rate of one inch per foot for at least the first six feet. This can usually be done by adding topsoil (not sand or gravel).

Where the general topography of the lot and surrounding lots is such that water is directed towards the house, further measures are sometimes required. A swale (a shallow ditch with gently sloped sides) may have to be constructed to divert water run off around the house to areas which are lower-lying.

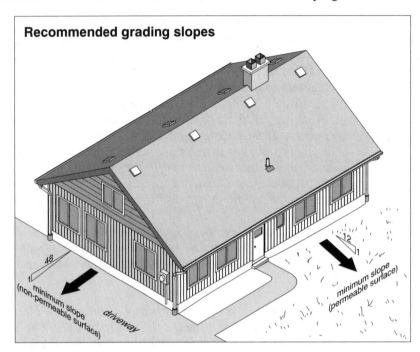

Recommended grading slopes

Figure 2. Lot Grading

If the general topography of the neighborhood is such that the house lies in the lowest area, grading improvements may improve the situation; however, further measures may be necessary. See 10.0 of the Interior section for more information on wet basement problems.

Ravine Lots

Ravine lots have potential erosion problems which can, in extreme cases, have catastrophic effects. Erosion can compromise the structural integrity of the house if the table land keeps disappearing.

From a one-time visit, it is not possible to determine the rate of erosion (if any); however, the presence of mature trees and heavy vegetation on the steeply sloped portions of the lot are a good sign in that they reduce erosion.

To prevent continuing problems, a soils engineer and/or landscape architect should be engaged to design retaining walls or other systems to hold back the earth, where erosion is noted.

2.1 Window Wells: When regrading, difficulties may be encountered with basement windows. Increased soil height adjacent to the house may partially bury basement windows. Under these circumstances, or with any basement window which is at or near ground level, a window well should be provided. It will prevent water penetration through the window, prevent rotting of window frames, break wood/soil contact and keep the window cleaner.

Window wells should be large enough to allow light in and should allow for easy cleaning of the window and well.

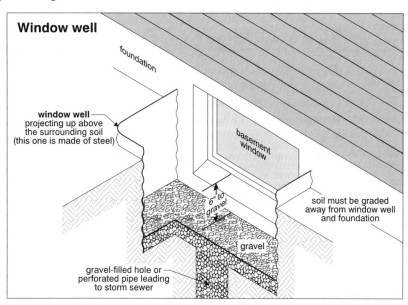

Figure 3. Window Well

Drainage and Covers   Ideally, the bottom of the window well should contain several inches of gravel to allow water to drain from the well. A drainage pipe, filled with gravel (to prevent it from collapsing, but still allowing water to pass) should extend down to the drainage tile around the perimeter of the footing (if one exists). As an alternative, a clear plastic dome cover can be installed over the window well to keep water and debris out.

Window wells are most often constructed of concrete or a corrugated steel shell. Chemically treated wood can sometimes be used; however, it should be avoided in termite prone areas.

▶ 3.0 DOOR, WINDOWS AND TRIM

The primary purposes of trim components on the exterior of a house are to protect the structural components from weather, prevent the entry of vermin, and to improve the appearance of the house. Trim is usually found around doors and windows, and at the eaves. The two most common components of the eaves are soffits and fascia. The soffit is installed horizontally, and covers the underside of the eaves. The fascia is a vertical component at the edge of the eaves. Normally, gutters are fastened to the fascia.

Aluminum   Trim components on houses are most commonly made of wood or aluminum. If aluminum components have been properly installed, they are relatively maintenance free. Occasionally, some sections require resecuring.

Wood Wooden trim components require regular painting, and maintenance. Trim components are often found to be rotted, missing, loose or damaged by vermin. Squirrels, birds and raccoons damage soffits and fascia to gain access to the attic space.

Painting and Caulking Exterior trim components including those around windows and doors, as well as soffits and fascia, are prone to weathering and to opening up at seams and joints. Improvements to paint and caulking should be considered regular maintenance items with some work typically required annually.

See also 4.16, Doors and Window Flashings in this section

► 4.0 WALL FINISHES

The primary function of wall finishes is to protect the building skeleton and interior from weather and mechanical damage. In some cases, the wall surfaces enhance the structural rigidity of the building (e.g. houses constructed of solid masonry, or log houses) where the exterior components are structural members.

Vines Vines and other vegetation are often found growing on wall surfaces. The disadvantages include increased levels of moisture held against the wall surfaces, and increased insect and vermin problems in the house. Depending on the type of plant, and the surface, considerable damage can be done. In the majority of cases, extensive damage does not occur. Each case should be examined individually, and if no damage is evident, should simply be monitored.

Vines should be kept away from wood trim around windows, doors and eaves for example, and should not obstruct water flow through gutters and downspouts.

Characteristics **4.1 Brick:** The two most common types of brick are clay and concrete. The characteristics of brick vary dramatically. Some brick surfaces are relatively soft, and erode with time. Other bricks are extremely hard. They can be easily damaged by mechanical action, or can crack due to water penetration and freeze-thaw action. Some bricks are extremely porous; others less so. Some bricks have a hard glazed outer surface; others are uniform throughout. Most bricks are not designed to be in contact with the soil, and should be kept six inches above grade.

Spalling Damage to brick surfaces, whether due to mechanical damage, freeze-thaw action or something else is known as **spalling.**

Sandblasting Brick is usually damaged by sandblasting. Brick which has a soft core and a harder crust is common on older houses (the same houses which tend to require brick cleaning). Sandblasting removes the outer crust and makes the brick more prone to deterioration. Once a house has been sandblasted, it is not possible from a single inspection to determine the rate of deterioration. This often requires monitoring over several years to determine if any remedial action is necessary.

Sealing Sealing the brick with a vapor permeable sealant or paint (to allow the brick to breathe) is sometimes successful. In extreme cases, brick requires replacement or covering with a material such as stucco.

Chemical Cleaning Chemical cleaning is an alternative to sandblasting which, although more costly, is less likely to damage the brick. The chemicals used are closely guarded secrets, but generally are based on muriatic acid. This is a very strong acid and use by the lay person is discouraged. Even left to the professional, the results are somewhat unpredictable. It is strongly recommended that a small test patch be done first, to ensure a satisfactory end product.

The chemicals are typically applied and allowed to soak for some time before washing off with a high pressure water spray. It is of course, more difficult to clean painted walls than walls which are just dirty. Care should be taken to minimize damage to vegetation at the base of the walls. It is common for some mortar damage to occur during cleaning, and repointing is usually necessary in at least localized areas.

Mortar

Mortar is a mixture of a binder (portland cement, lime, masonry cement), an aggregate (sand), and water. There are a great many types of mortars with a multitude of strengths, colors, and durability. Additives such as calcium chloride can enhance cold weather workability at the expense of strength and durability.

Mortar has several functions. It bonds individual masonry units together and prevents moisture penetration between units. It allows a tight joint between different masonry units despite size variations from one unit to the next. It provides a base for ties and reinforcing, used to secure the masonry wall to a back-up wall, or to enhance the strength of the entire wall. Mortar can form part of the architectural appeal of a masonry wall. Mortar used to secure bricks varies in strength and composition. Mortar deterioration is more common than brick deterioration. Ideally, the strength of mortar should be similar to, but not greater than, the strength of the brick. Sandblasting and high pressure liquid cleaning often damage mortar, and repointing is usually necessary.

A discussion of the many problems with mortars is beyond the scope of this book. Suffice to say that the majority of problems are the result of improper mixes, or careless workmanship.

Efflorescence

The white salty deposit which appears on many masonry walls is known as efflorescence. It is a result of water carrying dissolved salts to the surface of the unit and evaporating, leaving the crystalline salts on the surface. Efflorescence may be caused by low quality mortars or masonry units, or by excessive water penetration into or through the wall. In most cases it is not serious, and will disappear within a few months of new construction or chemical cleaning. Occasionally, efflorescence precedes mortar or masonry deterioration.

4.2 Stone: Many different types of stone surfaces are used in home construction. Some are constructed of extremely hard igneous rock such as granite, while most are constructed of softer sedimentary rock such as limestone, While stone surfaces are generally considered to be more durable than brick, they do suffer the same ills. Stone can crack or erode; however, the rate of deterioration is generally slower than that of brick. The quality and type of mortar used in stone construction varies, and mortar repairs are far more common than repairs to the stone itself.

4.3 Concrete Block: The use of concrete blocks as exterior wall coverings for residential construction is relatively rare; however, concrete blocks can function quite well as an exterior wall surface. Deterioration largely depends upon the configuration of the block (surface texture and shape) and the quality of the concrete. Concrete blocks are relatively porous and some can allow a significant amount of water penetration through the block. Painting the block can reduce water penetration significantly. As with all unit masonry construction, mortar deterioration is a common problem.

Conventional
Stucco

4.4 Stucco: Stucco is really the exterior equivalent of plaster, made of cement, lime, aggregate and water. Stucco can be thought of as a thin coat of concrete, with the cement and lime acting as binders, the aggregate providing the bulk and the strength, and the water initiating the chemical reaction. Much like plaster, it requires periodic maintenance as cracks develop. The amount of maintenance required depends largely upon the mix of the stucco, the lath used (if any), and the surface to which the stucco is applied.

Stucco over masonry walls tends to stand up significantly better than stucco over wood-frame construction. The rigidity of a masonry structure allows for virtually no flexing of the stucco, and consequently, less cracking and surface separation is likely to occur. Wood-frame walls expand and contract with changes in temperature and humidity, at a different rate than stucco. This leads to cracking which allows moisture deterioration, and separation of the stucco from the lath. Cracks and bulges often appear near floor levels because wood framing members shrink most in this area. See the discussion of Wood Shrinkage in 6.4 of the Structure section.

Repairs that match in color and texture are difficult to make. Stucco can be painted.

Synthetic
Stucco (EIFS)

Exterior Insulated Finish Systems look similar to stucco but are constructed of different materials. Rigid wall sheathing, such as plywood, is covered with foam insulation board. A thin base coat reinforced with fiber-glass mesh is then applied and covered by a thin acrylic finish coat.

Problems

Water gets behind the finish and insulation where it gets trapped. The water ultimately leads to rot of the sheathing and other structural components.

Water
Penetration

The water enters the wall system at locations where the stucco meets wall penetrations such as doors and windows. As there is seldom proper flashings at these locations it is imperative that the seams be well caulked. This is an ongoing maintenance issue.

Improved installation methods include the use of building paper between the insulation and sheathing and a drainage path for any water which does get into the wall. Unfortunately, neither trapped water or rot in the wall cavity are visible during a home inspection.

4.5 Wood Siding: There are many different types of wood siding. Problems associated with wood siding include rot and water penetration. Rot will occur wherever wood surfaces are subject to excessive moisture. Therefore, painting or staining is required on a regular basis. Even rot resistant woods such as cedar and redwood are helped by staining. Stain reduces warping, splitting, rot and discoloration. Water penetration and rot problems are most common at joints in the siding. Joints should be designed in such a way as to prevent water penetration. The horizontal joints on clap-board siding, for example, overlap one another; however, most vertical joints on this type of siding do not. Therefore, vertical joints should be caulked.

Ventilation   Wood siding holds paint better and lasts longer if the back of the siding has some air circulation. Old siding nails had round heads so that the overlapping piece of siding above would not sit tightly against the lower piece. This allowed some air circulation and broke the capillary joint between the two pieces of wood. This is a practice which has unfortunately disappeared. Where peeling paint is a problem, shims can be driven between the boards to promote drying.

Joints   With panel type wood siding, the majority of the problems occur at horizontal joints, as there is usually no overlap or batten strip. In well executed installations, a flashing is installed at horizontal joints to prevent water penetration.

Many wood siding systems require pieces of wood trim to be installed over the joints. The top surfaces of these pieces of trim are prone to rot. The rotted wood eventually allows water penetration at the joints. Horizontal surfaces should be kept well stained or painted, should be slightly sloped so water will drain off, and should be caulked where they meet vertical surfaces.

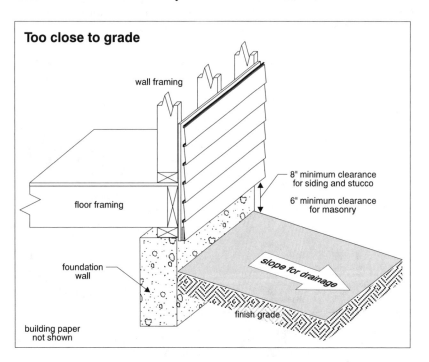

Figure 5. Siding Clearances

Splitting   Wood siding may split if improperly nailed. Too many nails may prevent natural expansion and contraction. Nailing too close to the edges will result in splitting.

Wood/Soil Contact   Wood/soil contact should also be avoided, as it promotes rot and provides an ideal environment for wood-boring insects. Wood siding should be at least eight inches above the soil.

Paint and Stain

With the exception of cedar, redwood, and pressure treated lumber, all wood used outside should be protected with paint or stain. Painting or staining is usually done every three to five years.

4.6 Metal Siding: A variety of metal sidings is available. Some are installed vertically, while others are installed horizontally. The most common materials are aluminum and steel. Of these, aluminum is used more frequently. Most problems associated with metal sidings are installation defects, rather than deficiencies with the materials themselves. A lack of adequate securing, and a lack of moldings and trim pieces where the siding butts other materials or changes direction are the most common problems. Metal sidings usually have a baked-on enamel finish and, generally speaking, the painted surfaces stand up well. However, some lower quality or older sidings tend to fade and chalk.

Ventilation

Metal sidings should be ventilated to allow air and moisture pressures to equalize on either side of the metal. Some early sidings did not breathe well and led to moisture problems in walls.

Insulated metal siding is available, although the amount of insulation is very small, typically.

Denting and Buckling

Metal sidings are prone to denting (particularly aluminum). Damaged sections can be replaced on an individual basis. Metal sidings expand and contract with changes in temperature. It is not uncommon to hear expansion noises when sunlight warms a wall of the house. Slots in the siding accommodate the nails. As the siding expands and contracts relative to the substrate, the siding can slide. If the nails are secured too tightly, the siding may buckle.

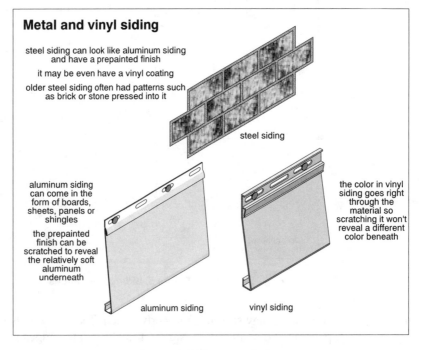

Metal and vinyl siding

steel siding can look like aluminum siding and have a prepainted finish

it may be even have a vinyl coating

older steel siding often had patterns such as brick or stone pressed into it

steel siding

aluminum siding can come in the form of boards, sheets, panels or shingles

the prepainted finish can be scratched to reveal the relatively soft aluminum underneath

the color in vinyl siding goes right through the material so scratching it won't reveal a different color beneath

aluminum siding

vinyl siding

Figure 6. Siding Installation

4.7 Vinyl Siding: Vinyl sidings are similar to metal sidings in that the majority of the problems are associated with installation, as opposed to the material itself. A lack of proper securing, and improper detail work at edges and corners are the most common deficiencies. Some vinyl sidings discolor with age. Most come in a limited color selection. Vinyl siding can become brittle during cold weather, and can be punctured or cracked. Individual pieces, however, can be replaced. Buckling vinyl siding may be the result of shrinking wood framing behind, or securing the siding too tightly to the substrate.

4.8 Wood Shingles: Wood shingles are normally cedar or redwood. Ideally, wood shingles should be stained on a regular basis for aesthetic reasons. Staining can be eliminated; however, the aging process on shingles used as siding is somewhat different than the aging process for wood shingles used as roofing material. Sections which are protected from sunlight and moisture will not age at the same rate. This results in sections which appear to be discolored. This is a cosmetic concern only. With age, wood shingles will lose their resins, and begin to warp and crack. As a general rule, when more than fifteen percent of the shingles require repair or replacement, total replacement is advisable.

Wood shingles can be painted; however paint sometimes peels from wood shingles as moisture escapes from the shingles. Staining is preferred.

4.9 Asphalt Shingles: Asphalt roofing shingles are sometimes used as siding. The biggest problem associated with using shingles in this orientation is that the shingles do not tend to lie flat. Modern shingles are of the self-sealing variety. A tar strip on the upper portion of one shingle is supposed to adhere to the lower portion of the shingle above, and should prevent the shingle from lifting or curling. Unfortunately, this process relies on gravity (the weight of the shingles) and sunlight (to heat up the shingles and soften the adhesive). This process works well on roofing systems; however, it does not work well when shingles are installed vertically. Therefore, shingles tend to lift, curl, and be prone to wind damage. (Shingles which have just begun to lift can be sealed in place.) They are easily patched, but matching colors is sometimes difficult.

4.10 Asbestos Cement (Mineral Fiber): Asbestos cement siding comes in shingle form. The material has a long life expectancy; however, it is brittle and subject to mechanical damage. Obtaining replacement components of any variety, much less the same color and texture, is difficult.

4.11 Clay Shingles: Clay shingles or tiles were often used on Victorian and turn of the century houses (usually in small areas, such as a gable). These shingles will easily last 100 years; however, they are brittle and subject to mechanical damage. Fasteners (nails) often fail, allowing individual shingles to fall. Replacements are not available. When painted, clay shingles look very similar to painted cedar shingles (which are sometimes used for repairs).

4.12 Slate Shingles: Slate shingles were often used on Victorian and turn of the century houses for siding on small areas, such as dormers and gables. The slates have an extremely long life expectancy; however, the nails which hold them in place tend to rust, causing the slates to slip out of position. Patching can be undertaken; however, it is difficult to match the color of aged slate. The general rule is that if more than ten to fifteen percent of the slates are damaged, an alternative siding material should be considered.

4.13 Insulbrick: Despite its name, insulbrick has very little insulating value. Various types of insulbrick were commonly used during the thirties, forties, and fifties. Insulbrick can be considered the forerunner to aluminum siding.

Insulbrick consists of a fiberboard sheathing coated with tar and sprinkled with granular material. The surface is embossed to look like brick, or sometimes stone. Obtaining replacement pieces is difficult, as the material is no longer made. Insulbrick siding will eventually wear out; however, the majority of the problems occur due to physical damage, and leaking joints. Caulking and resecuring are necessary from time to time.

NOTE: Insulbrick is frowned on by some insurance companies and lending institutions. This is thought to be due to its combustibility, and the fact that to some people, it connotes low-quality construction. Its bad reputation is unwarranted; however, the material can easily be covered with an alternative siding.

4.14 Artificial Stone: There are two common varieties of artificial stone. One is a brick substitute used on all or a portion of the exterior. The other is a thin veneer-type covering which is less than one inch thick. The former is installed like any other masonry unit. The latter is usually installed by providing wire mesh over the existing wall surfaces and setting the slices in a bed of mortar. The performance of this material is largely dependent upon the quality of the installation. Questions are often asked about how easily the thin slices can be removed. From a visual inspection, this is difficult to tell, as it depends how much damage was done to the original wall surface during the securing of the wire mesh. Also, there is often a considerable amount of mortar bonded to the original wall surface. Removal in this case is very difficult. The material is sometimes painted to change its appearance.

4.15 Hardboard And Plywood: There are a variety of hardboard and plywood sidings on the market. Some simulate wood siding, while others simulate stucco. Depending upon the type of material, the joints are sometimes intended to be covered with pieces of trim. Water penetration behind the trim tends to deteriorate the trim itself, and allow water penetration at the joints. Proper sealing and caulking of the horizontal surfaces of trim are required. Horizontal surfaces of panels which are not designed to be covered with trim should be installed with flashing, unless the joint in the material is specifically designed to prevent water penetration.

Buckling of hardboard siding is a problem caused by expansion of the hardboard when wet. This material expands more than wood when wet and, if it is securely nailed at each stud, it may buckle in or out. Securing the boards with clips or using smaller pieces are alternatives.

4.16 Door And Window Flashings: Some exterior doors and windows are arranged in such a way that the trim projects horizontally from the wall surface. In these cases, water tends to collect on the top of the wood trim, rotting the trim and leaking behind it. Ideally, metal flashings should be provided in these areas. The exposed edge of the metal flashing should be bent out to prevent water from dripping on the surfaces below. The flashing should tuck up under the siding or into a mortar joint in brick construction. (Most windows in masonry houses do not require flashings as the window frames are recessed.)

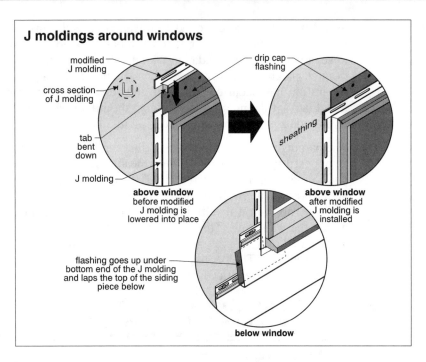

Figure 7. Window Flashing

Flashing is not required where the opening is protected by a roof overhang. As a general rule, if the distance from the window or door to the overhang is less than one-quarter of the overhang width, no flashing is needed.

Door and window sills should be sloped so that water drains away from, rather than toward the door or window. The sill should project far enough out so that water can drop off without wetting the area below. Good design incorporates a drip-stop (groove or projection on the underside of the sill), that prevents the water from being drawn back into the siding by capillary action.

4.17 Wood/Soil Contact: Wood/soil contact would be avoided to prevent rot and wood-boring insect infestations. Exterior wood siding material (and any wooden components) should be at least eight inches above the soil.

4.18 Exposed Foundation Walls: On virtually every house, the upper portion of the foundation wall (at least six inches) should be visible from the exterior. If it is not, there is risk of wood rot and/or infestation by wood-boring insects. Even houses with brick on the outside should have exposed foundation walls as there is risk of the sill plate and first floor joists rotting, and risk of deterioration to masonry designed for above grade use only.

Repointing   Foundation walls can be made of stone, brick, concrete block, cinder block, poured concrete, clay tile and wood. Mortar repair (repointing) is often necessary on the above grade portion of unit masonry foundations. Cracks in poured foundations should be patched.

Parging   Sometimes, the exposed foundation wall is parged. This is necessary on porous foundations such as brick or concrete block. It is not uncommon for the parging to separate from the foundation wall and break off. Localized patching of deteriorated parging is easily undertaken. If, however, large scale deterioration or separation has occurred, removal and reparging will be required. Expanded metal lath (of the non-rusting variety) should be secured to the foundation wall to provide a good base for the parging in areas where adhesion is questionable.

The parging should be lime based rather than Portland cement based (permeable as opposed to impermeable). Impermeable parging breaks off in large sections, due to moisture trapped behind it. The impermeable parging also causes dampness to rise up the wall to a level above the parging where evaporation can take place. Evaporation results in efflorescence forming on the wall surface and within the wall itself. This causes spalling brickwork and mortar deterioration. Lime based parging prevents this phenomenon from happening as moisture can pass through it. The parging itself is subject to efflorescence and spalling, but this is treated as sacrifice material.

► 5.0 PORCHES, DECKS, BALCONIES, ENTRANCES AND CARPORTS

5.1 Steps: Steps are commonly made of wood, concrete or masonry. If wood, the steps should be sturdy enough as not to flex with typical pedestrian traffic. One inch to 1-1/2 inches in thickness is normally sufficient. Stringers, the supports for treads, should be close enough together to provide adequate support for the steps.

Rise and Run   Regardless of the material used, all steps should be easy to negotiate. Steps should be at least 9-1/4 inches deep and no more than 8 inches high. They should be arranged in such a way so as not to collect water. Concrete steps should have an adequate footing to avoid settling and frost heaving.

Problems   The most common problems associated with wood steps are rot and attack by insects. Direct wood/soil contact should be avoided to minimize damage by rot, carpenter ants or termites. Carpeting should also be avoided on wooden steps as it retains moisture and promotes rot.

Concrete steps tend to crack or spall. Avoid using salt on these surfaces.

Some steps are constructed of brick. Certain types of brick should not be in contact with the soil as they absorb a considerable amount of moisture and suffer deterioration from freeze/thaw action.

Often, brick or wood steps are replaced with prefabricated concrete units which are relatively inexpensive and maintenance free. They have no frost footings and are allowed to "float".

Plywood should never be used for steps as the layers of glue tend to trap moisture, creating rot and delamination of the plywood.

5.2 Railings: Railings should be provided wherever there is a danger of falling (when the difference in height is greater than two feet). Railings should be sturdy enough to resist a person's weight and openings in the railing should be small (roughly four inches or less). Railings should be high enough to provide adequate protection; thirty-two to forty-two inches is common. On wide stairways, railings should be provided on both sides. Railings should not prevent drainage of water off porches, decks and balconies.

The most common problem with railings is their absence in areas where they are needed. Railings are also often loose, rotted or rusted.

5.3 Columns: Porch columns are designed to support a roof and/or a floor system. They can be constructed of wood, metal, poured concrete, or masonry. They must be strong enough to handle the imposed load and must have proper foundations and footings to prevent settling or frost heaving. Footings should be below the frost line, roughly four feet underground in many parts of North America.

The most common problems with porch columns are the result of simple deterioration. Brick columns tend to absorb a considerable amount of moisture, damaging the brick and mortar by frost action. Wood columns rot and are subjected to insect attack. Direct wood/soil contact should be avoided.

It is not uncommon for columns to shift out of plumb. They often require rebuilding from the footings up.

5.4 Beams: Beams should be strong enough to transport the roof or floor loads to a wall or column. They are typically wood, but can also be steel. Beams should be adequately supported and arranged to minimize rot and wood/soil contact.

Problems

The most common problems with porch beams is that they are undersized (overspanned), resulting in sagging. Additional columns can often be added to stiffen a beam. The beam can also be enlarged or replaced.

Porch beams are often poorly supported when columns have been removed or have shifted. The beam should rest on the column or wall support by at least three-and-one-half inches. Its full width should rest on the column. Many porch beams are concealed in a roof structure and are not visible, but years of roof leaks cause these beams to rot and the roof system to sag.

5.5 Joists: Porch or deck joists should be strong enough to carry the load of people, furniture, and snow. They are often overspanned, resulting in a springy floor system. Trapped moisture in a porch or deck structure often rots joists, weakening the structure and providing an ideal environment for termites and carpenter ants. Joists should be well secured to the building. A board, lag bolted to the structure, may support the joists from below. Joist hangers may also be used.

5.6 Floors: Porch floors should be sturdy enough to not flex between joists. If the floor system is constructed of wood, it should be arranged in such a way as to allow water to pass through it or drain off it. Carpeting should not be used as it tends to hold moisture, promoting rot. Plywood or waferboard should not be used for the same reasons.

If the porch floor is concrete, it should be sloped to drain water away from the building.

Some porch floors are covered with metal or canvas. In many cases, these materials have deteriorated and replacement is required. Some porches are covered with roll roofing or roofing felts and are not suitable for regular foot traffic.

5.7 Roof Structures: Porch roofs are often damaged by neglected roof coverings. Structural components should be carefully inspected when reroofing. Porch ceilings are of plaster, drywall, stucco, wood, concrete or metal. They are often damaged by roof leaks and vermin.

5.8 Skirting: Skirting is used around the perimeter of a porch to prevent vermin from getting under the structure. The skirting should allow for ventilation and direct wood/soil contact should be avoided.

► 6.0 WALKS, DRIVEWAYS AND LANDSCAPING

These components are addressed in a home inspection to the extent that they impact on the building.

Walks and driveways may be gravel, asphalt, concrete, stone, or pavers. Regardless of the material, they should be slightly sloped to drain water away from the house, rather than toward it. Improper slopes often cause wet basement problems, and in some cases, erosion and/or frost damage to building foundations. Where walks or driveways pull away from the building, water can accumulate along the foundation wall, again resulting in wet basement problems. In some cases a drain is required to carry surface water away. The drain should be sized to handle the maximum run-off from rains, and from melting snow where applicable. The drain should be arranged to prevent clogging with debris or frost damage to the drain assembly. The pipes leading from these drains cannot be examined during a home inspection.

Landscaping   Shrubs, trees, planters and so on can add to the value of a property, but can also adversely affect the building itself. The effect of vines on wall surfaces is addressed in 4.0 of this section. Shrubs too close to a building can hold water against walls, prevent wood components from drying out and provide pests with good access into the house.

Tree branches can cause mechanical damage to roof and wall surfaces, leaves can clog gutters and downspouts, and roots can clog drainage pipes and in severe cases, dislodge foundations. Raised flower gardens or planters can cause wet basement problems, especially as a result of heavy watering of flowers during the summer months. Where the original grade level has been raised by adding topsoil, there are three concerns. The building wall may be subject to damage if wood components are in contact with the soil. Water leakage into the building may be experienced if the soil is above the top of the foundation wall. The increased load exerted on the foundation wall can push the foundation wall inward, particularly in areas where frozen soil conditions may exist.

► 7.0 BASEMENT WALK-OUT

7.1 Frost Protection: Since the basement walk-out allows frost to go deeper, in northern climates additional protection must be provided. The foundations near the walk-out must be deeper, or insulation must be provided underneath and around the walk-out area to prevent frost penetration. Rigid plastic insulations are most common for this application.

Without proper frost protection, the walls of the house adjacent to the walk-out, can heave. Unfortunately, the components which provide the protection are buried and are not visible. The presence of frost damage to the house usually means that the existing walk-out has to be modified or removed. The options, then, are to abandon the walk-out, fill in the doorway and backfill the hole, or repair the structural damage and rebuild the walk-out. If rebuilding, provision of insulation for the new walk-out is the preferred repair approach as it is less expensive than underpinning the foundation walls.

7.2 Steps: Please refer to 5.1 in this section.

7.3 Railings: Please refer to 5.2 in this section.

NOTE: Railings should be provided on the perimeter of the opening as well as on the steps.

7.4 Drains: A drain at the bottom of a basement walk-out will prevent water accumulation which could eventually end up in the basement.

Drains are often absent or if present, are often plugged with debris. Drain covers should be provided which are designed to catch debris and allow water to flow away freely. A cover or a roof over the basement walk-out may preclude the need for a drain.

7.5 Door Threshold: In the event of a plugged drain, the door threshold should provide some protection against water entry into the basement. Thresholds are often absent, inadequate in height, or not waterproof. Concrete is the best material. They should be a minimum of four inches in height.

7.6 Walls: The side walls of an exterior basement stairwell are essentially retaining walls. Please refer to 9.0 in this section.

7.7 Cover or Roof: Please refer to 1.0 in the Roofing/Flashings/Chimneys section. While some basement walk-outs have legitimate roofs, others have covers, usually made of wood. Covers should be sloped to allow for water runoff and should be kept well painted to prevent rot. Horizontal ledges or other areas where water may collect should be avoided. Wood/soil contact should be avoided. Hinges and hardware should be adequate for the weight of the doors, and designed for outdoor use.

► **8.0 GARAGES**

8.1 Detached Garage: People's attitudes and expectations with respect to garages vary dramatically. Normally, the garage is lower quality than the house, and in poorer condition. Consequently, the necessity for repairs is far more subjective.

Garages are similar to houses in many ways. Problems with the garage framing, roofing and siding for example, are addressed the same way as house problems. Detached wood-frame garages, however, commonly have a somewhat unique problem — the absence of foundations and footings. These garages often have wood frame walls sitting directly on or very close to the soil. The garage itself may heave with frost action, but more importantly, the bottoms of the wood walls usually rot and the garage begins to lean. In the early stages this leads to misalignment of the overhead door, and over the long term, to structural failure.

Corrective action includes straightening the structure and replacing the bottoms of the wood wall system, with masonry typically. Depending on the overall condition of the garage, it may be more cost effective to remove and rebuild it.

8.2 Fire or Gas-Proofing: The walls and ceilings of attached garages which abut interior space, must form a fire separation from the house in some jurisdictions. In other areas the walls must only be gas-proofed to prevent toxic automobile exhaust fumes from entering the house. If the walls are constructed of wood studs, they should be covered on both sides with drywall with finished joints to ensure no leakage of fumes. Concrete block walls are considered adequate protection without drywall on the garage side, provided there is an effective vapor barrier on the house side.

8.3 Man-Door: Any door between the house and the garage should have an automatic door closer, should be tight fitting and weatherstripped for fire safety and to reduce the chance of gasoline or exhaust fumes entering the home.

8.4 Combustible Insulation: Additional insulation is often provided in garages. Combustible plastic insulation is very common. It should be removed or covered with a non-combustible surface such as drywall since it presents a fire hazard.

8.5 Floors: Minor cracks in garage floor slabs are common. Serious cracks and/or settling may indicate structural problems, but more commonly indicate an improper base below the concrete. Concrete floors should be a minimum of three inches thick.

Suspended Floors

Some garages are designed with a room below the area where the car is parked. These garages are sometimes of heavy timber construction or the floor slab is of steel and concrete. It is impossible from a visual inspection to determine whether these types of floor systems are properly designed. If they are of concrete and steel construction, salt penetration during the winter months can rust the structural steel and spall the concrete. The problems are similar to those of large multi-story parking garages. A specialist is required to investigate these. Generally, the surfaces of these floors should be treated to prevent moisture penetration into the concrete.

Wood floors (even heavy timber) can rot or decay from wood-boring insects. Mechanical damage and fire damage can also weaken these systems. In any garage with a suspended floor system, a structural engineer should be engaged to determine its safety.

8.6 Floor Drainage: Garage floors should be sloped to drain water out of the garage. If this is not possible, a drain should be provided. Often, drains in garages are neglected and are plugged, broken, or undersized. Settlement of garage floor slabs may affect the drainage so that water will not flow out.

8.7 Vehicle Doors: Garage doors are typically constructed of wood, hardboard, aluminum or steel.

There are a variety of ways in which garage doors can open; however, overhead sectional doors are preferred.

The most common problems with garage doors relate to hardware. Hinges, tracks, springs, and counterweight systems often require adjustment. Garages which have settled, resulting in a door frame which is out of square, contribute to the problem.

The bottom edges of wood garage doors tend to rot while the bottom edges of steel doors rust. The decision to repair or replace is somewhat subjective.

Door Openers

Garage door openers sometimes fail due to misalignment of the garage door or track. Some jurisdictions require that the opener be plugged into an electrical outlet not more than six feet from the opener.

Automatic Reverse – A Safety Issue

All garage door opening devices should have a safety feature which automatically reverses the door if it strikes something while closing. This feature reduces the risk of injury. Garage door openers equipped with this feature have a sensitivity adjustment. It is often set incorrectly.

▶ 9.0 RETAINING WALLS

Analyzing retaining walls is a tricky business. With most retaining walls, the important components are not visible. Also, determining the rate of movement of a retaining wall is impossible, from a one-time visit. Monitoring is normally required. In some cases, the angle of the wall gives a clue to the performance. Most walls are built with a slight lean to the higher side. If the wall is leaning away from the high side, it has probably moved. Once retaining walls begin to move, they rarely stop, although the movement may be slow and seasonal.

Retaining walls can be constructed of concrete, masonry, stone, wood or steel. There are several different designs.

Gravity Walls

Gravity walls are not very common. They rely on a huge mass (normally concrete) to hold back soil by the sheer weight of the retaining wall. Needless to say, walls of this type are not very economical because of their size.

Cantilevered Walls

Poured concrete retaining walls are more often a cantilever design. Looking at a cross section through the wall, the wall would look like an inverted "T". The inverted portion of the "T" is buried beneath the soil. The portion of the "T" which extends under the high side of the retaining wall makes use of the weight of the soil sitting on it to resist movement of the wall. The portion of the "T" protruding under the soil on the low side of the retaining wall stabilizes the wall and prevents it from tilting forward. The poured concrete is reinforced with steel to prevent the inverted "T" from breaking at the joint. Cantilevered retaining walls must have their footing below the frost line to prevent heaving.

Pile Walls

Pile walls consist of vertical members which are driven down into the soil to a depth that is sufficient to resist rotational movement caused by the soil on the high side of the retaining wall. Pile walls constructed of steel are often used as a temporary measure; however, small wooden pile walls in sandy soil or gravel can be effective.

Wood Walls

The most common type of residential retaining wall in frost areas is constructed of horizontal wooden members which are tied back into the soil with anchors (tie-backs). The anchors normally consist of a horizontal wood member installed at right angles to the retaining wall, heading back into the soil. Tie-backs are staggered through the entire wall system to provide resistance to movement. In some cases, "dead-men" are attached to the ends of the anchors to help secure the anchors. These horizontal members run parallel to the retaining wall itself. These walls do not extend below the frost line.

Prefab Walls   New wall systems consisting of interlocking sections of precast concrete have become available in recent years. These systems also use tie-backs and dead men.

Gabions   Gabions are also used as retaining wall systems. A gabion is a rectangular wire mesh basket filled with rock. They are not only used as retaining wall systems; they are commonly seen along river banks to prevent erosion.

Problems   The single biggest enemy of retaining walls is water. Saturated soil puts significantly higher pressure on retaining walls. If saturated soil is allowed to freeze, expansion can be significant, which puts even greater pressure on the retaining system. Needless to say, water also promotes rot of wooden retaining wall systems.

Well constructed retaining wall systems have a vertical layer of gravel behind the wall and drainage holes at the bottom of the wall. The gravel allows water to percolate through it quickly and the drainage holes give the water somewhere to go. Open wall systems, such as wood timbers, have enough natural openings that drainage holes, per se, are not needed.

Minor repairs to retaining walls can be undertaken by the homeowner. Patching cracked concrete retaining walls, for example, is valuable in that it allows for monitoring of future movement. Major retaining wall repairs or modifications should, however, be left to an expert. Retaining walls are often poorly built and can be very expensive to repair or replace.

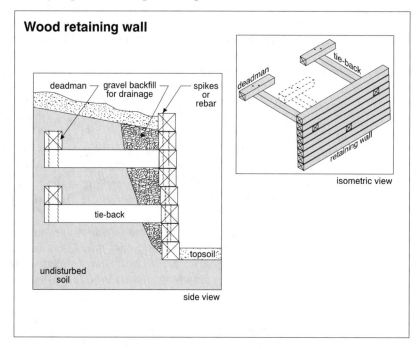

Figure 8. Wood Retaining Wall

3 STRUCTURE

► TABLE OF CONTENTS   Page

► INTRODUCTION

The structure of a home is the skeleton, which includes the foundations and footings as well as the floors, walls, and roof. Structures are judged by how well they are able to stand still. Successful structures do not move; less successful ones do, sometimes dramatically.

► 1.0 THE BASICS OF STRUCTURES

Gravity

What causes structures to move? In a word, gravity. Gravity is constantly working to get things closer to the ground, as a matter of fact, right to the centre of the earth. Structures are intended to create spaces, and some parts of the structure have to be further away from the ground than gravity would like. Strong structures resist gravity.

Structure Failures

There are generally three ways a structure may give in to gravity. a) If it is sitting on something that is not strong enough, the ground below it will fail. Better to build on bedrock than quicksand. b) If the skeleton of the structure is weak, it will not support itself. (The weight of the structure is the "dead" load.) A house of cards can be toppled by one weak link. c) If the "live" load on the structure is greater than expected, it will collapse. If we did not plan for the several tons of snow that accumulate on our roofs in the winter, houses would not last very long.

Wind

Wind is a force which acts intermittently on structures. While gravity is constant, wind forces vary from nothing up to hurricane proportions. Wind forces can push, pull or lift buildings. Buildings must be strong enough to resist the lateral and uplift forces of wind as well as the downward force of gravity.

Compression and Tension

What forces are individual structural components subjected to? The two basic forces are compression and tension. A material is under compression when it is being pushed from both ends. Tension is applied if it is pulled on. Components in simple compression tend to get shorter. Components under tension tend to get longer. Many building components feel a combination of compression and tension.

Some building materials and components are very good in compression. Others work well in tension. Some perform well in both. A pile of bricks is very good in compression; you can stand on it. However, it is very poor in tension. A child can pull the pile apart. A chain, on the other hand, is very good in tension. You can pull quite hard on both ends and nothing will give, but the moment you try to push on it, the chain collapses. It is not much good in compression.

Shearing and Bending

Different materials fail in different ways. Shearing and bending are common modes of failure. Shear occurs when adjacent faces of a material move in opposite directions. When a beam splits, or a brick cracks, it is because of shear. Bending is movement of a structural component out of its original position without shearing. (Actually there are some longitudinal shear forces.) A plank spanned between two chairs will bend if someone stands on it, particularly if they stand near the middle. The upper half of the plank is pushed together under compression; the bottom half gets slightly longer because it is in tension.

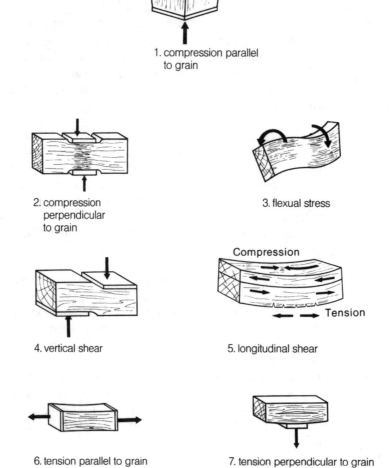

1. compression parallel
to grain

2. compression
perpendicular
to grain

3. flexual stress

4. vertical shear

5. longitudinal shear

6. tension parallel to grain

7. tension perpendicular to grain

Figure 1. Types of Stress

Building components which fail by bending are said to sag or buckle. Some materials can bend a significant amount without losing their strength. Brittle materials, however, do not bend much before they break. Ductile materials do. Ceramic tile is brittle, rope is ductile. Some ductile materials are elastic. This means they will go back to their original shape after being bent. A rubber ball is elastic; a nail is not.

Deflection   Deflection is a mild form of bending. If structures deflect just a little, people do not mind. Greater deflections or failure are not acceptable. Building codes stipulate how much deflection is acceptable. A typical floor joist, for example, is allowed to deflect 1/360th of its span, under its design load.

Material Selection   What makes a good building material? It should be good at resisting the forces of tension and compression. It should be cheap, easy to work with, light, long lasting, water resistant, and stable under different temperature and humidity levels. This is a tall order and no one material does it all. That is why houses are made up of many materials. Wood is one of the better materials at fulfilling a large number of these functions for small buildings. It is relatively good in both tension and compression. Concrete and brick are great in compression, but very poor in tension. Steel is good in both tension and compression.

Building materials are chosen with a strong view to cost-effectiveness. The goal is to assemble a structure that will perform as required for as small a cost as possible. This has led to some very small margins of safety and, of course, some failures. As new materials are developed, they are tried; in some cases, with great success; in other cases, with very poor results.

1.1 Structural Inspection: The structure is by far the most important part of the house. The safety and usability of the entire home depends on its structural integrity. The structural inspection is performed on both the interior and exterior. Since many of the structural components are buried below grade or behind finishes, much of the structural inspection is necessarily performed by looking for resultant movement. Where no movement has occurred, structural imperfections may well go undetected. New interior or exterior finishes and patching work may conceal imperfections over the short term. In these cases, identification of problems is often impossible.

Repairs   Structural repairs can be very costly, and in some cases the problem is so severe that repairs are not warranted. In many cases, a structural engineer should be consulted before making repairs. An incomplete understanding of a problem may lead to incorrect solutions and a possible life threatening situation.

► 2.0 FOOTINGS

Function: To transmit the weight of the house to the soil, without allowing the house to sink. (In any home, some settlement is typical within the first few years after construction.) Footings are located below the foundation walls and posts. The horizontal surface area of the footing is larger than the foundation, so that the load of the house can be spread out over a wide area. Footings are typically sixteen to twenty-four inches wide and six inches to sixteen inches thick. Footings carry the house loads below the frost line in climates where the soil freezes. The heavier the building and the weaker the soil, the larger the footing should be.

Typical Materials: Concrete, brick, stone. In modern construction, almost all footings are poured concrete.

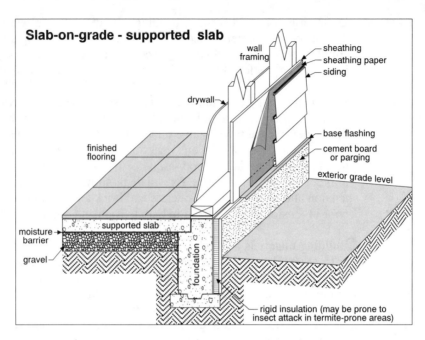

Figure 2. Footings

Problems

When the footings fail, the entire house moves. This is often a very serious problem. It is almost always expensive, and sometimes impossible, to correct. Since the footings are located below the soil and the basement floor, they cannot be seen. It is often difficult to know why they have failed.

Sometimes they will fail in one area only, and in most cases the failure is not uniform, (i.e. the building does not sink straight down but leans to one side or another). Often, one part of the house will pull away from the rest. This leads to cracking of interior and exterior wall surfaces.

Causes

Weak soils: Soils which are prone to compaction or movement do not support footings well. This includes recently disturbed soil. For example, if a basement is dug too deep, then backfilled to the correct depth, the disturbed soil under the footing is likely to compact over the first few years, resulting in building settlement.

Mud Sills

Absence of footings: This is not common on professionally built houses, but may occur in cottage construction as well as on porches and amateurish additions. Some homes were built on "mud sills". These are simply beams laid on the ground with walls built on top of the beams. These mud sills have to be replaced with a proper foundation and footing system as the sills rot, heave or settle.

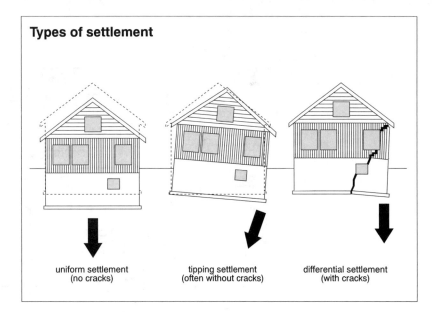

Types of settlement

uniform settlement
(no cracks)

tipping settlement
(often without cracks)

differential settlement
(with cracks)

Figure 3. Types of Settlement

Expansive soils: Some clay soils which expand and contract significantly with different moisture contents may also result in failure. These expansive soils can heave floors and foundations when they get wet. When they dry, they shrink and allow the building to drop. This is one of the most significant causes of house structure problems.

Tree roots can affect the moisture content of soils noticeably. Most soils have strengths which change with different moisture contents. Some change dramatically. These are poor building soils. Silts are also poor building soils, in many cases much weaker than clay.

Underground streams: These may erode or weaken soil below the footings, causing severe building settlement. It is, of course, very difficult to locate and trace underground streams. They often flow only at certain times of the year.

Undersized footings: This may be the result of poor design, or an additional load that has been added. For example, when a second floor is added to a bungalow, the weight may cause the footings to sink. The additional weight of a chimney can also cause localized footing failure.

Footing deterioration: The footing must be strong enough not to break apart under a load, and must be able to stand up to continuous exposure to damp soil.

Undermined or cut footings: If the basement floor is lowered, there is the risk that the footings will be broken off on the inside or will lose their support. Even if excavation is not done below the footings but down to the bottom of them, the lateral support for the footing may be lost, and the footing and foundation wall may move inward.

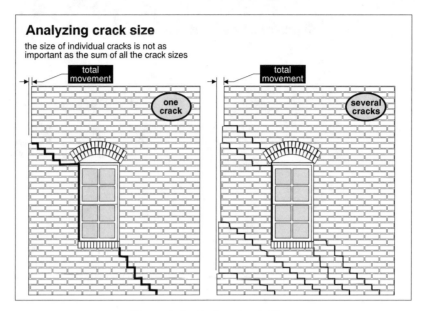

Figure 4. Analyzing Crack Sizes

Lowering Basement Floors

When a basement floor is lowered, the footings should be underpinned (lowered and, in some cases, enlarged). Alternatively, only the central section of the basement should be lowered, to avoid disturbing any of the soil near the footings. Depending upon how much the basement floor is to be lowered, the required clearance from the footings varies. A soils engineer is often consulted and a concrete curb (or Dutch wall) may be needed around the inside edge of the footings to ensure they are not compromised. One of the dangers in lowering basement floors is a greater risk of basement leakage. Notice in Figure 5 how the drainage tile outside is no longer in the correct location once the floor is lowered. It is too high to be effective.

When excavation is done on the exterior, (e.g. for an addition or swimming pool) the footings can be damaged or undermined in a similar fashion.

Slope influence: Houses built on or close to slopes may be subject to failures as a result of soil moving down the slope. This may be a slow steady process or a sudden event triggered by heavy rains for example. This can be extremely costly to correct.

Cut and fill lots: Houses built on sloping lots may be more prone to footing and foundation failures. The chances of building on disturbed soil are increased on lots such as these. Efforts made to level and terrace the lot may result in soil being cut out of the hill to form a level terrace under the back half of the house. This soil is then used as fill in the adjacent area where the front half of the house is to stand.

On sloping lots, large lateral earth thrust and hydrostatic pressure can be built up on the high side, as there is a tall column of soil against the upper basement wall. Water running down the slope tends to be blocked by the building and accumulate here.

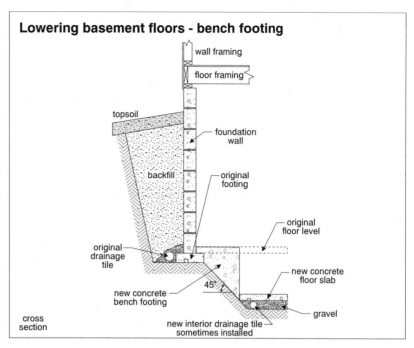

Lowering basement floors - bench footing

wall framing

floor framing

topsoil

foundation wall

backfill

original footing

original floor level

original drainage tile

new concrete floor slab

45°

new concrete bench footing

gravel

new interior drainage tile sometimes installed

cross section

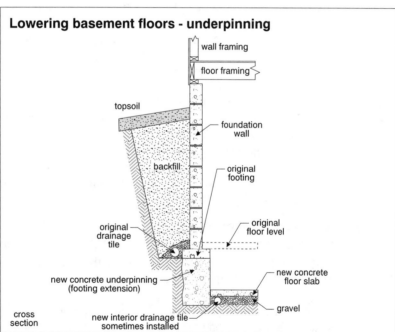

Lowering basement floors - underpinning

wall framing

floor framing

topsoil

foundation wall

backfill

original footing

original drainage tile

original floor level

new concrete underpinning (footing extension)

new concrete floor slab

gravel

new interior drainage tile sometimes installed

cross section

Figure 5. Lowering Basement Floors

On the downhill side, the footings may not be deep enough in cold climates. Frost heave can result where the footings are less than four feet below grade. The side of the house with the lower grade often has a walk-out basement, and chances of a footing being too shallow are greatest here.

The other danger is that the downhill half of the house is built on fill which may not be well compacted or may not be able to stay in place and support the house.

Adding an outside basement stairwell: This may compromise the footings. In order to be effective, the footings in cold climates must be below the frost level. When an exterior basement stairwell is added, the stairwell opening effectively lowers the exterior grade level, and also lowers the depth to which frost can penetrate. After the stairwell is in place, the frost can theoretically go down as much as four feet below the bottom of the stairwell opening. This can lead to localized frost heaving of the footings and the foundations.

A properly added exterior stairwell will include deepened foundations, or a completely insulated approach, to prevent frost penetration below the building footings.

Repairs: During an inspection, the results of footing failure can usually be seen. It is, however, difficult to know whether the building is still moving, and if so, at what rate. It is often necessary to monitor the building over a period of months or even years, to know whether the problem will warrant repair. A great many footing failures are not severe enough to warrant repairs.

Underpinning The usual corrective action is to underpin the footings. This means digging under the existing footing, usually from inside the house, and adding a new footing wider and/or deeper than the original. This has to be done in small sections since one cannot excavate under the entire house at one time. Usually two to four foot sections are done at a time. This is, of course, very expensive work.

Piles In some cases, where the soils are moving or are likely to move, underpinning is not appropriate. Piles driven deep into the ground are an alternative, but often so costly as to not warrant this type of repair to an existing building.

Bridging Where the problem is localized, the footings can sometimes be bridged across a weak area. For example, where there is a spring, the footing can be deleted above the spring, and a beam can be used above the weak area. This is an unusual and expensive approach.

In some cases, it is necessary to demolish the house. Depending on the soil conditions, it may or may not be cost-effective to rebuild on that lot.

► 3.0 FOUNDATIONS

Functions: To transmit the weight of the house from the above-grade walls and floors down to the footings.

To resist the lateral pressure of the soil on the outside of the basement or crawl space. The foundation acts as a retaining wall in this sense.

To carry the weight of the house below the frost line to prevent frost heaving in cold climates.

Typical Materials: Stone, brick, poured concrete, concrete block, cinder block, clay tile, wood. Most of these materials behave in a similar fashion. Wood foundations are the exception. These are addressed in Section 3.1.

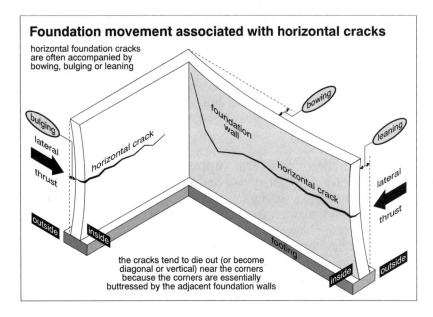

Figure 6a. Horizontal Cracks

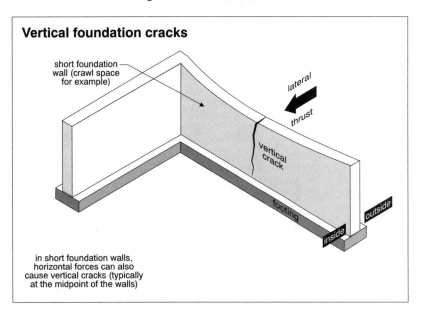

Figure 6b. Vertical Cracks

Cracks
Bowing
Spalling

Foundation walls may crack, bow, spall or shift. Cracks may be due to shrinkage, settlement or lateral forces. Some cracks are serious while others are insignificant. Bowing is usually the result of lateral forces. Spalling indicates poor quality materials. A professional home inspector will analyse these conditions, and where necessary, recommend further investigation. Some of the causes of foundation defects are outlined below.

Problems

Inadequate lateral support:

If the foundations do not provide enough lateral support, they will deflect inwards. This may be the result of mechanical forces exerted during back-filling; back-filling with frozen soil (cold climates only); unusual frost development in the soil immediately outside the building (cold climates only); foundation walls that are too thin or do not have adequate reinforcement; or the house floor system does not provide adequate bracing for the top of the foundation wall. This last problem is common on the high side wall on a sloping lot. Both unit masonry walls and poured concrete walls can fail if not properly built.

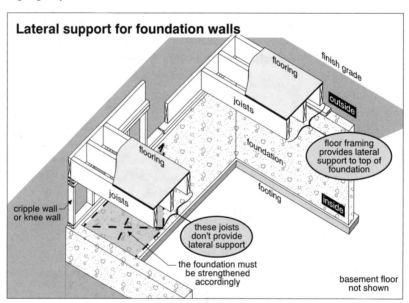

Figure 7. Lateral Support

Inward
Bowing

Foundation walls which move inward can be repaired by tying them back from the outside, using ties and anchors common in conventional retaining wall construction. Alternatively, buttresses can be provided on the interior. These often are comprised of concrete or concrete block structures built against the basement walls. A third choice is to build a new foundation wall inside the old. In some cases, it is necessary to replace the foundation.

Mechanical
Damage

Mechanical damage caused during backfilling operations, for example, can generally be repaired on a localized basis, although re-excavation is often necessary.

Height of
Backfill

The height of soil outside a foundation may exert enough force to cause the foundation to fail. Figure 8 provides a rough guide for the maximum height of fill for several foundation wall systems.

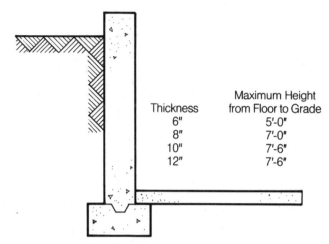

Thickness	Maximum Height from Floor to Grade
6"	5'-0"
8"	7'-0"
10"	7'-6"
12"	7'-6"

Poured Concrete (2000 psi)

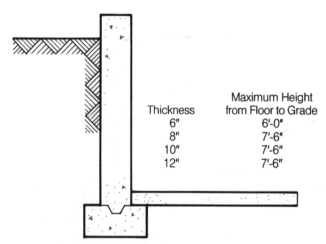

Thickness	Maximum Height from Floor to Grade
6"	6'-0"
8"	7'-6"
10"	7'-6"
12"	7'-6"

Poured Concrete (3000 psi)

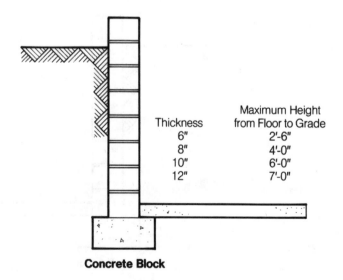

Thickness	Maximum Height from Floor to Grade
6"	2'-6"
8"	4'-0"
10"	6'-0"
12"	7'-0"

Concrete Block

Figure 8a. Thickness of Foundations (Laterally Supported)

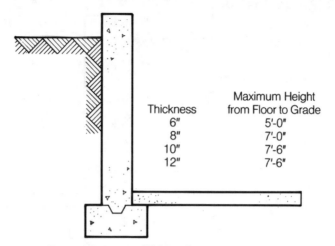

Thickness	Maximum Height from Floor to Grade
6"	5'-0"
8"	7'-0"
10"	7'-6"
12"	7'-6"

Poured Concrete (2000 psi)

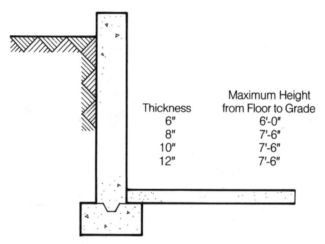

Thickness	Maximum Height from Floor to Grade
6"	6'-0"
8"	7'-6"
10"	7'-6"
12"	7'-6"

Poured Concrete (3000 psi)

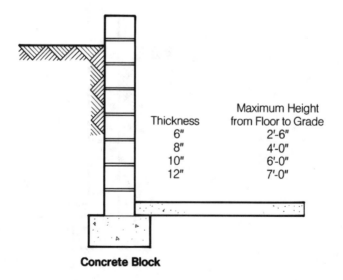

Thickness	Maximum Height from Floor to Grade
6"	2'-6"
8"	4'-0"
10"	6'-0"
12"	7'-0"

Concrete Block

Figure 8b. Thickness of Foundations (Laterally Unsupported)

Foundations too shallow: In cold climates, if the foundations are too shallow, frost may heave even the best built footings and foundations. On sloped lots, the possibility of shallow foundations is greatest on the low side. Properties with basement walk-outs should be watched for frost heave. See 7.1 in the Exterior Section.

Unheated Houses in Cold Climates

Conventional construction contemplates a house which is heated. An unheated house may have frost penetrating through the basement floor below the footings, leading to heaving. There is a risk involved in leaving a house unheated. Cottages built on piers, on bedrock, or on excellent draining sandy soils, are usually not damaged if left unheated.

Foundations and footings which are too shallow must be extended downward, or must be insulated to prevent frost penetration of the soil below the footings.

Another Cold Climate

Problem

Adfreezing: Adfreezing is a phenomenon whereby damp soil on the outside of the building will actually freeze to the building and as the soil heaves, it will pick up the top part of the foundation wall. Horizontal cracks in foundation walls just below grade typify this phenomenon.

Water Penetration: Water penetration can deteriorate the mortar in masonry foundations, reducing its strength and ultimately allowing shifting to occur. This is usually a slow, long term process.

Surface Water

Water related problems such as adfreezing and wall deterioration due to moisture penetration, can be minimized or eliminated with control of surface water on the exterior, in many cases. Good exterior grading with ground sloping down away from the building is important. Proper performance of gutters and downspouts is equally important. All roof run-off must be directed into a drainage system, or onto the ground at least six feet away from the building.

Ground Water

Where ground water is the problem (an underground stream or high water table), this may not prove adequate. In cases such as these, major repairs, sometimes including drainage tiles and/or a sump and pump, are called for. Consultants specializing in situations such as these should be engaged. See Section 10.0 in Interior.

Tree roots: The force exerted by large tree roots on the foundation wall can lead to deflection of the foundations. Some soil types shrink considerably as they dry out. If a large tree draws water from such soils below a footing, the footing may drop as the soil compacts. In this case, the tree damages the house without actually touching it.

In the short term, tree root damage can be arrested by cutting down the tree and leaving the roots in place. Over the long term, the roots may be expected to rot, leading to soil settlement, resultant water leakage and, in some cases, building settlement. The roots, in these cases, also have to be removed.

Poor concrete: Low quality concrete when subjected to damp soils may deteriorate, losing its strength. This is common in poured concrete foundations, built from the turn-of-the-century up to the 1920's. The interior or exterior face of the concrete may crumble (spall). Reducing moisture penetration will retard this action, but if the damage has progressed to a point where the structural integrity is compromised, sections of the concrete foundations may have to be completely replaced. This is an expensive undertaking.

Poor masonry: Some bricks are designed for use below grade. Many are not. The use of inappropriate brick will result in a shortened foundation life. Ultimately, the bricks have to be replaced.

Foundations not tall enough: Foundations should extend at least six inches above grade. Shorter foundations may allow water to damage sills, wall framing systems or even masonry. Most brickwork used in residential exterior walls is not designed to be in contact with the soil. The continuous exposure to moisture will damage these masonry units.

3.1 Wood Foundations: Preserved wood foundations were introduced in the early 1960's. Through the 1970's and 1980's, several thousand units have been installed. Life expectancies of the below grade wood are estimated in the fifty to one hundred year range, considerably less than many traditional building foundation materials. Some manufacturers offer sixty year limited warranties.

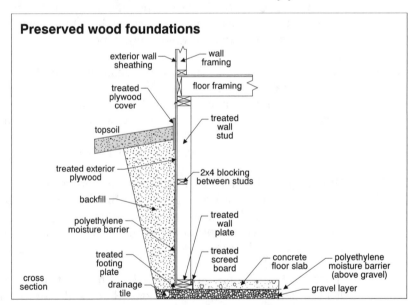

Figure 9. Wood Foundations

The wood is chemically treated to retard rot. Chemical treatment for wood used in foundations is more intensive than that typically used in wood for decks, fencing, etc. The wood foundations may rest on concrete or wood footings.

With wood foundations, special care must be taken to ensure that the foundation is able to perform its retaining wall function (adequately resisting lateral forces).

It is not known whether rot and termites will become a major problem on wood foundations. (See Sections 9.0 - 11.0) It is suspected that if this were to occur, masonry or poured concrete foundations could be retrofitted. Wood foundations should not be used in areas known to have termites.

3.2 Floating Foundations: Where the soil strength is poor, and there is uncertainty about how successful a conventional foundation and footing system will be, one alternative is to use a floating foundation. This could be a raft or a mat foundation. The characteristics of both include a reinforced concrete foundation which forms a continuous pad under the entire building.

Raft

A raft foundation has side walls (forming a basement or crawl space) of concrete, with steel reinforcing integral to the pad, forming a raft or boat. The goal in this type of construction is to end up with the soil below the building carrying the same weight as it did before the building was there. This is done by excavating the amount of soil that weighs roughly the same as the finished building.

Mat

A mat foundation is a thick floor slab which extends under the full area of the building. It is slightly thicker at the edges (and sometimes at intermediate points), and it floats on top of the soil distributing the building weight evenly over a large area. This is a stronger version of the slab-on-grade configuration described in Section 4.3.

Once a building is up, not much can be seen of floating foundation details. Like other footing and foundation systems, time is the best measurement device, and evidence of building shifting or settlement are the only clues for the home inspector. These special foundations usually have special design work done by engineers. It is desirable to know who designed and built the structure in case of questions or problems in the future.

3.3 Pile Foundations: Piles are steel, wood or concrete columns driven down into the soil. They are used in weak soils and may extend down through the poor soil, to reach a soil with good bearing strength. Piles may depend on friction between the sides of the pile and the soil for their support. They may also be point bearing at the bottom. The building itself rests on beams or walls which straddle the piles. Piles are expensive and once the building is up, there is often no way to know if piles have been used and where. Again, the presence or absence of building settlement is the only way to determine how successful the approach has been.

Piles and Grade Beams

In some areas, garages are typically constructed on piles. The piles support poured concrete grade beams for example, which in turn, support the wall systems. The garage floor is then poured on the undisturbed soil.

3.4 Piers

Function: Where continuous foundations are not provided, individual columns or "piers" may be used to support a building. The piers should rest on a footing below the frost line in cold climates and typically the pier supports a beam. The beam, in turn, supports the floor, wall and roof loads.

Piers are commonly found in houses where there is no basement or a partial basement. A crawl space often has a pier system supporting the structure above. Porches are also commonly supported by piers.

Typical Materials: Stone, brick, concrete block, cinder block, wood. Most of these materials behave in a similar fashion. Wood, of course, is the most vulnerable to moisture and insect damage. As a rule, wood/soil contact is best avoided.

Problems

Footings
Pier problems are often the result of inadequate footings. This will result in settlement of the pier and, of course, of the building above. If the pier base is not below the frost line in northern climates, frost heaving can be a problem. In both these cases, the piers usually have to be rebuilt. Similar problems can result in areas with expansive soils.

Overspanned
If the piers have too great a span between them, the beams may sag or the concentrated loads may cause the piers to sink. Adding piers is the obvious solution here.

Too Slender
Or Out
Of Plumb
If the piers are too slender or are out of plumb, they may not be capable of carrying their intended loads. Diagonal wood braces are used in some areas to help hold piers in place. Piers which are deteriorated as a result of moisture or mechanical damage should be repaired or replaced as necessary.

Wood piers can rot, be attacked by termites or other wood-boring insects, or be damaged mechanically or by fire. (See Section 9.0 - 12.0)

Skirting
Preserved wood performs better than most species of untreated wood. Where piers are used in lieu of a continuous foundation, the space between the piers usually has to be filled in to prevent soil from falling into the basement or crawl space. In above-grade situations, skirting keeps out animals and, to some extent, rain, snow and cold. Skirting may be wood, masonry or poured concrete, for example. Since it is not structural, per se, repairs to deteriorated skirting are rarely a priority. Wood skirting often deteriorates where it contacts the soil.

► 4.0 CONFIGURATION

Homes may have a basement, a crawl space, or neither. Many houses have partial basements and/or partial crawl spaces. The configuration has no bearing on the structure and is really determined by cost, or restrictions imposed by the building site.

4.1 Basements: Where conventional four foot deep frost footings are required a trench is needed around the house perimeter to install the footing and foundation system. Since this excavation has to be made in any case, it is not much more expensive to dig a big hole and create a basement. In warm climates where frost footings are not required, basements are rare.

The below grade space is inexpensive to build and can be used for anything from rough storage to living space. Basements commonly house the mechanical and electrical systems as well as the work room and laundry (although the laundry is placed upstairs in many new homes). Game rooms and family rooms are often located in basements, and complete apartments can also be built below grade.

Disadvantages of basements include the susceptibility to water leakage and lack of natural light. Windows in basements are usually small and high on the wall, since most of the wall is underground. Basement ceilings are often low, and even if there is no water leakage, they can be cool and damp.

4.2 Crawl Space: Where a trench is dug for the foundations, and the earth under the house floor is not removed, a crawl space is created. It may have an earth floor, although a concrete slab is more desirable for storage and moisture control. Many codes call for crawl spaces to be thirty-six inches high where access must be gained, although many are less. Some are entirely inaccessible. Areas which do not have mechanical services require only a twelve inch clearance in many codes. This makes access for structural inspection and repair quite difficult.

Venting

Since they are hard to get into, and usually poorly lit, crawl spaces can be uninspected for long periods. Where moisture levels are high over the long term, structural damage, due to rot and termite activity, can go unnoticed for some time. Crawl spaces should have one square foot of venting for every 500 square feet of area. This is rarely provided.

Heated crawl spaces in freezing climates should be vented in the summer only. The vents should be blocked off in the winter. Unheated crawl spaces should be vented year round. Crawl spaces with earth floors generally need venting more than those with concrete floors. It is acceptable to vent a heated crawl space by opening it into a basement. In this case, the crawl space can be vented year round.

4.3 Slab-on-grade Construction

Description: In this type of construction, a poured concrete floor rests directly on the ground. There is no basement or crawl space below the floor. The concrete slab, typically six inches thick, may or may not be reinforced with steel bars. Immediately below the slab, a moisture barrier is typically laid over about six inches of gravel. In modern construction, insulation is often provided below the slab.

There are three types of slab-on-grade construction; a) monolithic slab, b) supported slab, and c) floating slab. A monolithic slab is a concrete floor and foundation all poured as one. This can be thought of as a floor slab which is thicker around the edges. Steel reinforcing bar is typically used to strengthen the concrete between the floor slab and foundation.

A supported slab is independent of the foundation, in that it is not poured together with the foundation. It does however, rest on the foundation. The foot-

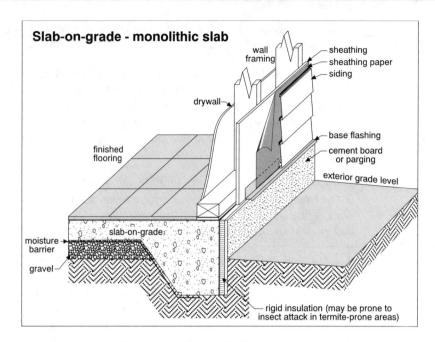

Figure 10a. Monolithic Slab-on-Grade

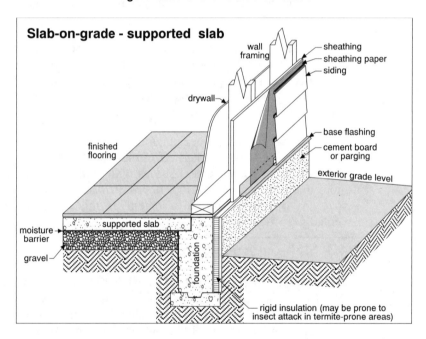

Figure 10b. Supported Slab-on-Grade

ings and foundation wall are installed first, with a four inch ledge at the top of the foundation which supports the slab where it is poured. Insulation or an expansion joint is used between the slab and the foundation. Basement floor slabs can be supported slabs.

The floating slab is entirely independent of the foundation. The foundation is poured or built first. The slab is not connected to the foundation, often separated from it by an expansion joint. This type of slab is common in garages of conventional houses.

Problems

From an inspection and maintenance standpoint, slab-on-grade is more restrictive than conventional construction using basements or crawl spaces. With slab-on-grade, none of the foundation is accessible, and early signs of problems cannot be picked up.

Systems Concealed

In conventional construction, basement or crawl space floors are often left as exposed concrete. Problems with water or termite infestation, for example, can be picked up early. With slab-on-grade, the concrete slab is normally covered by subflooring and finish flooring. Problems such as termites can go undetected for some time.

Where the slab is poor quality concrete, too thin, or missing reinforcing bar, the floor is prone to cracking and shifting. Subsurface erosion can also result in slab failure, as can areas excavated for plumbing or heating pipes. This leads to uneven floor surfaces, and the more openings there are in the floor slab, the more points of entry for water and insects. Substantial shifting or cracking can damage the plumbing, heating and electric services buried within the slab.

Cold

Older slabs are often uninsulated and the floors may be cold during severe weather conditions. Adding insulation is very difficult.

Water Leakage

The gravel base is intended to allow water to drain away quickly. If the gravel bed is too thin or incomplete, water in the soil below the slab may be drawn up into the floor through cracks, pipe openings, etc.

Slab Below Grade

Although good practice dictates that the top of the foundation (and the top of the floor slab) be at least eight inches above grade, this is often not the case. Poor original construction, building settlement and changes to exterior grade, can all result in the floor slab (and the bottom of the walls) being below grade. This means there will be a constant source of moisture from the soil, attacking the wall structure, and the wall and floor finishes.

Heating Pipes

Many floor slabs have hot water heating pipes (radiant heating pipes) embedded in the slab. These pipes are usually two or three inches below the top of the slab and may be laid eight to twelve inches apart through the slab. Leakage from the heating system may go undetected for some time. Apart from the adverse effect on the heating system, this can lead to sub-slab erosion, and ultimately, slab settlement. Flooding of the floor itself, while unpleasant, is preferable to undetected sub-slab erosion. Inspection and repair of radiant heating pipes in slabs is, of course, very difficult. Leaking plumbing pipes can have similar consequences.

*Heating
Ducts*
Slab-on-grade houses with forced-air heat often have heating ducts embedded in the concrete foundations and slab. Sometimes the ducts are partially collapsed during the concrete pouring process. Moisture in and around the slab can flood the ducts and rust the metal duct walls. The water standing in the ducts can become a health hazard. Rusted duct walls can come loose and collapse. Any of these will restrict at least some air flow through the system. Ductwork in poured slabs and foundations is, of course, difficult to inspect and repair.

► 5.0 FLOOR SYSTEMS

5.1 Sills

Function: To provide a level, continuous pad between the foundation top and the bottom of the framing system.

*Anchored
to Foundation*
Typically, the floor joists rest directly on and are secured to the sill. These sills should be anchored to the foundation. In modern construction this is accomplished using bolts anchored into the top of the foundation wall, passing through the sill and secured with a washer and nut.

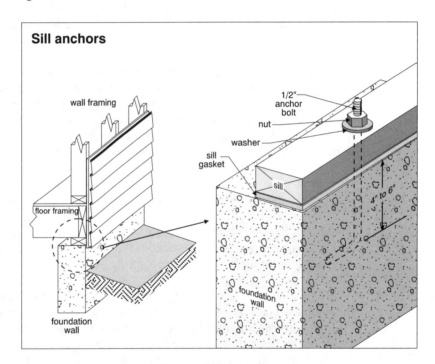

Figure 11. Sill Anchors

Typical Material: Wood. In new construction, the sill is typically a 2 x 4 laid flat. In older construction it may be a substantial wood beam (e.g. eight inches by eight inches). It should be appreciated that wood sills support wood framing members but not masonry, (i.e. a brick veneer wall sits directly on the foundation, not on a wood sill).

Problems

Rot and Termites

Wood sills very close to grade level are subject to rot and termite attack. (See Section 9.0 - 11.0) In some older houses, the sills are actually below grade level and may be in constant contact with the soil. This will undoubtedly lead to rot, and the sills may be expected to crush under the weight of the framing system as the rot advances.

Point Loads

Sills may be crushed as a result of concentrated loads. Steel posts built into walls will sometimes cause this.

Anchoring

Where the sills are not secured to the foundations, there is danger of the building shifting during high winds, when significant upwards and lateral forces can be generated.

End Bearing

If the joists are too short, and only the very end rests on the sill (less than one inch, for example), then the tremendous concentrated loads may lead to crushing of the sill or joist.

Ladder Sills

This system uses 2x4's or 2x6's on edge with short cross blocks every four feet along the top of the foundation. Concrete is poured, leaving the top faces of the ladder exposed. Floor joists are attached to the sill by toe nailing or metal straps. If the sill is within 6 inches of grade level, rot may be a problem. Anchoring is often weak in this system.

Any wood component in a house is, of course, vulnerable to fire and mechanical damage. (See Section 12.0)

Repairs: Damaged wood sills can usually be replaced readily. Where at or below grade, a material such as concrete would be more suitable. Poorly anchored sills can be secured, using bolts.

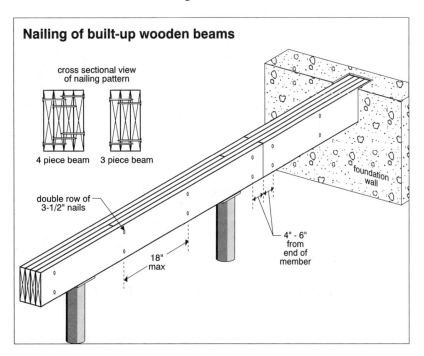

Nailing of built-up wooden beams

cross sectional view
of nailing pattern

4 piece beam   3 piece beam

double row of
3-1/2" nails

18"
max

4" - 6"
from
end of
member

foundation
wall

Figure 12. Built-Up Beam

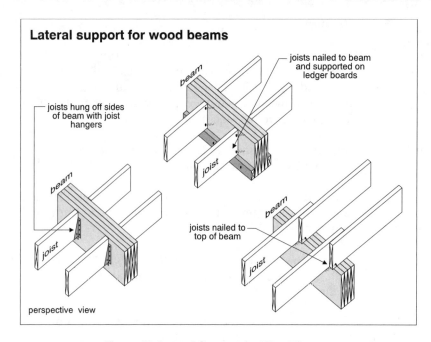

Figure 13. Lateral Support for Wood Beams

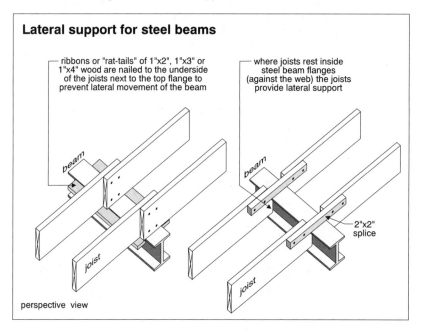

Figure 14. Lateral Support for Steel Beams

5.2 Beams

Function: To carry floor and wall loads horizontally to the foundations, walls, or posts.

Typical Materials: Wood (solid or built-up), plywood or steel.

Problems

Rot and Termites Wood building components are vulnerable to rot or termite attack, particularly where wood/soil contact may be present (see Sections 9.0 - 11.0). Beams below grade should have 1/2 inch clearance along the sides and at the end to allow for air circulation. Alternatively, they should be pressure treated.

Overspanned Beams which are undersized or overspanned (a common occurrence) may be expected to sag or crack. This may lead to ultimate failure of the entire framing system. Fortunately, this rarely happens, and almost never suddenly. Overspanned wood beams can usually be identified readily, and improvements can be made in a number of ways. Posts can be added or the beam can be enlarged. In some cases, the load can be reduced. In some areas, home inspectors will not comment on overspanning, but will recommend investigation by a specialist.

End Bearing Where the end bearing is inadequate, the beam can crush itself or its support. There is also potential for the beam to slip off its support. Typically, 3-5/8 inches is considered a minimum end bearing for beams.

Damage Mechanical damage can be done accidentally or intentionally. Beams which are notched, cut or drilled are necessarily weakened. Whether this is done at the top, middle, or bottom; and depending on how large the violation is; and how far it is from the supports, will determine whether or not corrective action is necessary.

Rotation Rotation of wood beams due to warping or poor end support is relatively uncommon but can lead to damage and ultimate failure.

Nailing and Butt Joints Built-up wood beams may not be adequately nailed. Normally, nails should be provided in double rows every eighteen inches along the beam. Where butt joints occur in wood beams, they should be located over the supports or as follows: the butt joints should be within six inches of the quarter point of the span. For example, if the span is twelve feet, the joint should be within six inches of the three-foot mark or the nine-foot mark of the span; (i.e. the joints should be 2-1/2 to 3-1/2 feet from the end supports).

Rust and Lateral Support Steel beams are susceptible to rust, particularly if the basement is damp. Steel should be painted to prevent rust. Lateral support for steel beams is typically provided by wood strapping secured to the joists. See Figure 13.

Securing to Posts Another common problem with steel beams is inadequate securing of the beam to posts. Wind uplift may generate enough force to cause the beam to lift off the post or impact may shift it so that support is no longer offered. The beam and post should be bolted, welded or clipped together.

Strength A visual inspection of a steel beam cannot determine its strength because it depends on more than size. The shape of the beam, the length and thickness of both the flanges and web, and the weight per linear foot, all influence beam strength. The carbon content of steel also affects its performance.

Fire Fire is an obvious concern with both wood and steel beams. Interestingly enough, a steel beam will lose its strength much earlier than will a wood beam, although a wood beam will actually burn and a steel beam will not. Steel is a material that loses its strength after being exposed to temperatures of 1000° F. for about four minutes. Examination of many fire sites shows steel beams that have sagged like spaghetti during a fire.

Steel beams can be much stronger than wood beams and are more resistant to rot, termite and mechanical damage, but are more expensive, heavier, and more difficult to work with. Relatively new plywood beams can be stronger than solid wood, yet are light, easy to work with and less expensive than steel. Steel beams should rest on steel posts or masonry. Wood beams can rest on wood members.

5.3 Posts/Columns

Function: To carry the load of the beam vertically down to the footings. In some cases, a post is introduced to carry a concentrated load (a large piano, for example) straight down to the footings without benefit of a beam.

Typical Materials: Brick, concrete block, poured concrete, wood, or steel.

Note: Every post or column should have a footing, typically concrete.

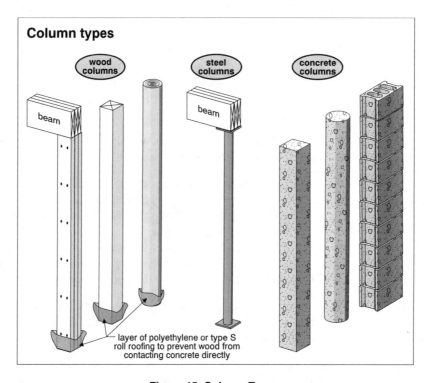

Figure 15. Column Types

Problems

Moisture

Masonry posts may be deteriorated as a result of moisture or poor mortar. Rising damp is a common problem with brick columns. This is characterized by deteriorated mortar and efflorescence (white salty deposits) on the bottom of the post. In some cases, the brick itself deteriorates (spalls).

Out of Plumb   Posts which are built or have been pushed out of plumb lose a good deal of their strength. Generally speaking, if the amount by which the column or post is out of plumb approaches one third of the thickness of the column, there may be concern about its integrity.

Rust   Rust on steel posts can be a concern. This is often a serious problem in a chronically flooding basement. Rust will quickly reduce the load carrying capacity of a steel post.

Rot and Termites   Wood posts are particularly vulnerable to rot and termite attack. This is especially true where the post penetrates the basement floor slab (as most old ones do). Corrective action often includes simply cutting off the bottom of the post and placing it on a concrete pad. (See Section 9.0 - 11.0)

Footing   A sinking post is usually the result of an absent or inadequately sized footing. Obviously, suitable footings should be provided.

Undersized   Column collapse is somewhat unusual but is normally the result of an undersized column or one which has suffered mechanical damage. A brick column should be at least twelve inches by twelve inches or ten inches by fifteen inches. Rectangular concrete columns should be at least eight inches by eight inches. Circular concrete columns should be no less than nine inches in diameter. Steel posts are three inches in diameter under normal circumstances. A top and bottom plate at least four inches square are required where the beam is wood. With a steel beam, the four inch plate is not needed, as long as the post is secured to the beam.

Secured to Beam   A post which is not well secured to the beam above can allow the house to shift during wind uplift forces. The beam should also be supported laterally to prevent it from moving sideways.

Fire   Fire will damage wood and steel posts, both. A steel post will fail much earlier than a solid wood post, although it will not bum, per se. Plastic deformation of steel occurs after approximately four minutes exposure to 1000' F. Temperatures in a fire can exceed this significantly.

5.4 Joists

Function: To carry loads from the floor boards to the foundations, beams or bearing walls. These are horizontal members typically wood 2 x 8, 2 x 10, or 2 x 12, twelve to twenty-four inches apart. They are laid on edge so that the sub-flooring is nailed to the two inch side. Floor joists should extend at least 1- 1/2 inches onto the foundation or beam at either end.

Joist Strength   It is interesting to note that the strength of a joist comes largely from its depth. Doubling a joist by putting another of the same size beside it will double its resistance to bending. Doubling the depth of a joist increases its deflection resistance eight times. For example, the equivalent strength (considering deflection only) of two 2 x 10's compared to four 2 x 8's can be compared by multiplying the base times the height cubed. It is interesting to note that two 2 x 10's are more resistant to deflection than four 2 x 8's for conventional house framing purposes (using the actual size rather than nominal size of the lumber, in the calculations).

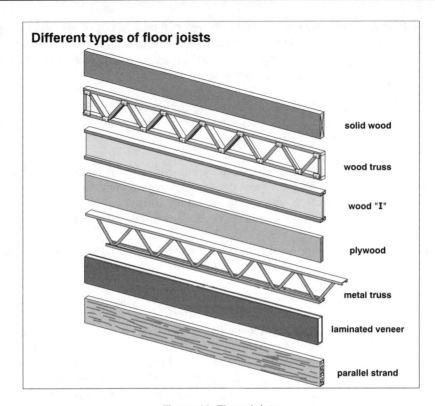

Different types of floor joists

solid wood

wood truss

wood "I"

plywood

metal truss

laminated veneer

parallel strand

Figure 16. Floor Joists

Typical Materials: Traditionally, wood. Recently, metal, plywood, and waferboard joists or wood trusses have been used. While the strength of conventional solid wood joists can be calculated readily from tables, special engineering considerations or individual manufacturer's calculations must be consulted to determine the strength of specialized floor joists or trusses.

Allowable Deflection: The deflection of a floor and joist system in modern construction may be quite surprising. Many codes allow a floor to deflect 1/360th of its length under normal live loading, if there is a finished ceiling below. For example, the following situation is acceptable by many codes: 2 x 10 floor joists spaced 16 inches on center span 15 feet. When the room is empty, there should be no perceptible deflection. When the room is occupied with furniture and people, the center part of the floor can be 1/2 inch lower than the floor edges. A 1/2 inch drop in the floor over a distance of 7-1/2 feet is certainly noticeable. While this is permitted by many modern codes, it may not be satisfactory to some home owners. It should be understood that codes are intended to be a minimum standard.

A very brittle floor finishing material, such as ceramic tile, would not tolerate a flex like this. More rigid floor structures are required where the finish flooring is brittle. Further, the load imposed by concrete over a wood floor (which may be done to receive ceramic tile), creates an additional load on the joists which must be considered.

Problems

Overspanned   Floor joists which are overspanned (undersized) are prone to excessive sagging. The acceptable span of a joist is determined by the load it will carry, the species and grade of lumber used, the depth of the joist, and the spacing between joists. In most cases, overspanned can be readily corrected by adding joists, or adding a beam below the joists. In some areas, home inspectors will not comment on overspanning, but will recommend further investigation by a specialist.

Rot and Termites   Rot and/or termites can affect joists, particularly where wood/soil contact exists. (See Section 9.0 - 11.0)

Damage   Mechanical damage to joists is common. Joists are notched, drilled and even cut through to accommodate heating, plumbing and electrical systems. In some cases, joists are cut around stairwells to improve headroom. Joists are sometimes notched at the end to rest on a beam or foundation wall. This can weaken the joist considerably. The joist usually cracks horizontally from the top of the notch towards the mid-point of the span. (See Section 12.0 for a description of permissible notches and holes.)

End Bearing   Where less than one-and-one-half inch end bearing is provided, the joists may be prone to crushing at the ends and/or slipping off the beam or foundation.

Joist Hangers   Metal hangers called "joist hangers" are used where joists cannot rest on a support. Here, the joists sit in the hangers which cradle the joist and are secured to the side of a beam or header.

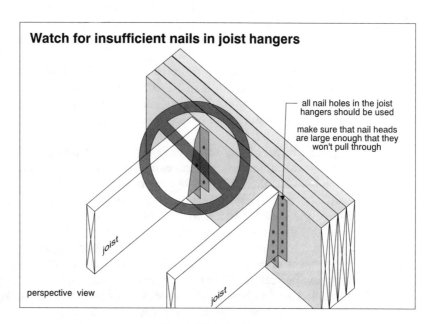

Figure 17. Joist Hanger

Fire   Fire damage can, of course, weaken joists. Generally speaking, char less than 1/4 inch deep will not seriously weaken joists. (See Section 12.0)

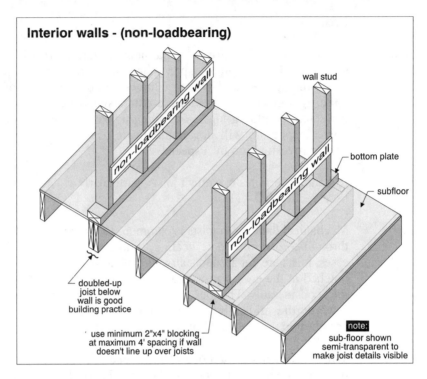

Figure 18. Doubling and Doubling Joists Below Partitions

Joists Below Partitions

Joists which are subject to concentrated loads are more prone to sagging. A joist below a parallel non-bearing partition should be doubled. If the joist is not doubled, 2 x 4 solid bridging with the 2 x 4s spaced no more than four feet apart is considered acceptable by many codes. Joists should not be used below load-bearing partitions. Beams or walls should be used here.

Concentrated Loads

Most floors are designed to carry loads of 30 to 40 pounds per square foot (psf). Larger loads can lead to excessive deflection and ultimately, failure. Special consideration may be needed for pianos, waterbeds, aquariums, and floor to ceiling storage of books or records, for example.

Offset Beating Walls

One of the problems often unfairly blamed on joists is that of the offset bearing wall. In houses with a beam and post configuration or a bearing wall in the basement, there is usually a wood-frame bearing wall above. Ideally, the wall above is directly over the beam or basement wall. In practice, this is rarely the case. If the wall is offset enough (sometimes twelve inches is enough), the floor joists under the first floor wall will be deflected. This will lead to a low spot here and a hump on the floor immediately above the basement beam or bearing wall. This sort of movement rarely creates an unsafe situation but can result in noticeable floor unevenness. This can be arrested by running a second beam and post system or bearing wall in the basement under the offset wall above, although this would reduce usable basement area. A typical code allowance is a three foot offset if not supporting a floor above, and a two foot offset if supporting one or more floors.

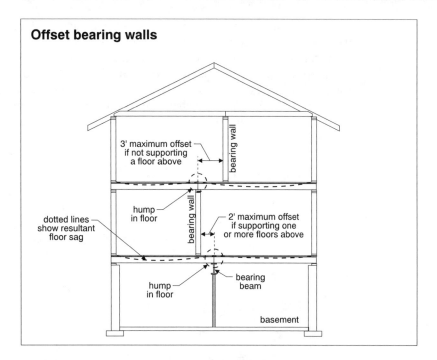

Offset bearing walls

Figure 19. Offset Bearing Walls

Jacking up a House

Damage to interior finishes must be anticipated when trying to push things which have settled over a period of time, back into place. Plaster which has moved slowly over many years will almost certainly crack if the framing is straightened quickly. Windows and doors which have been trimmed as their openings have moved out of square, will often show large gaps and may bind when a house is jacked up.

When using steel telescoping posts to straighten a house, it is recommended that the house be raised slowly. Many experts recommend raising the post a quarter of a turn per week over several weeks, to minimize the damage to finishes above. From a functional standpoint, as long as the movement is stopped, there is no need to level the house.

5.5 Stairwell Opening

Function: To create an opening in the floor joist pattern to allow a stairwell to pass through. Similar openings are provided to accommodate chimneys where they pass through floor framing systems. Also, basement windows often prevent floor joists from resting on the foundation walls. In these cases as well, openings must be created in the framing pattern. Staircases themselves are discussed in 5.0 of the Interior Section.

Headers and Trimmers

Normally, the joists which cannot get over to the wall are secured to a header. A header is made of the same size lumber as the joists (e.g. 2 x 8's). The header, which runs perpendicular to the joists, carries the load from the short joists (tail joists) over to trimmer joists. Trimmer joists are the joists on either side of the opening, which can run their full length.

As the openings get larger, it becomes necessary to double the headers and trimmers. When the headers and trimmers become long enough, they must be engineered. For example, when the opening is wider than thirty-two inches, the trimmers on either side should be doubled. When the opening is larger than forty-eight inches, the header itself should be doubled. When the opening is wider than six foot, eight inches, the trimmer should be engineered, and when the opening is larger than ten foot, eight inches, the header should also be engineered.

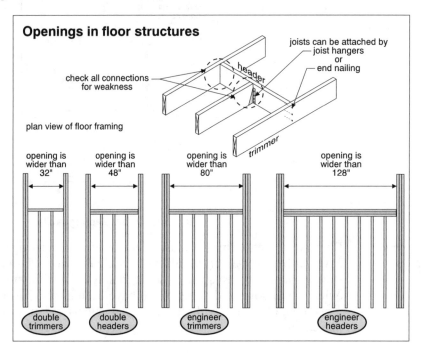

Figure 20. Framing Around Openings

Posts   Alternatively, posts can be provided at the comers of the opening to carr load from the header directly down to the floor. In this case, the trimmers could remain single. The header can also be supported with posts, or a bearing wall running under the header.

Materials: The same materials used for the joists are used for the headers and trimmers; typically wood.

Problems

Undersized and Notched   It is very common to have the trimmers and/or header undersized. It is also common to have the trimmer notched at the bottom of the stairwell to improve head room. This, of course, weakens the whole framing arrangement.

*Poor
Connection*

The shortened joists which are secured to the header are often poorly anchored. These joists (called tail joists) can often be seen pulling away from the header. Joist hangers (metal brackets) can easily resecure these tail joists. In other cases, the header is inadequately secured to the trimmers, and the header will be pulling away. Again, joist hangers can be used.

*Fire, Rot
and Termites*

Fire damage, rot and termites can all weaken the stairwell opening framing. (See Section 9.0 - 12.0)

5.6 Bridging/Bracing

Function: Bridging/bracing acts to restrain the joists from twisting and also helps to transmit loads from one joist to the next, reducing the springiness of the floor.

There is some question as to how well diagonal bridging performs the second function, and some recent building codes have changed dramatically, although inconsistently in their requirements.

Generally speaking, the diagonal bridging uses two inch by two inch pieces of wood. An alternative is solid blocking, using wood of the same dimensions as the joists. Either of these is considered adequate to restrain the joists from twisting. To be effective, the bridging or blocking should be in a straight line and should extend the full length of the floor. Also considered adequate is the sub-flooring secured to the top of the joists, in combination with a finished ceiling below. Wood strapping or metal ribbons along the bottom of the joists (sometimes called rat-tails) are also appropriate. Traditionally, one set of diagonal bridging or solid blocking has been provided for each joist span. Depending on configuration, more or less bridging or blocking may be required using today's standards

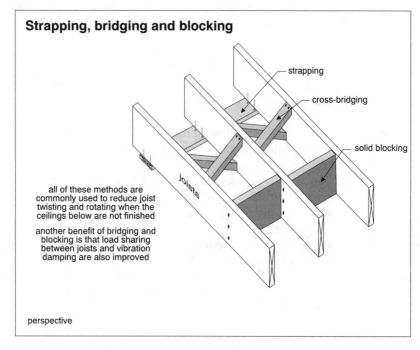

Figure 21. Types of Joist Restraint

Springy Floors

In practice, if the house is more than about two years old, the joists are not likely to twist if they have not already done so. If the floors are noted to be springy, adding solid blocking should help slightly to reduce springiness, if it is tightly fit and closely spaced.

Squeaking Floors

It should be noted that bridging and bracing does not reduce the squeaking of the floors.

5.7 Sub-Flooring

Function: To transmit the live loads of the people and furnishings to the floor joists. Sub-flooring may be covered with a finish flooring or may serve as a finish flooring itself.

Typical Materials: Historically, one inch thick wood boards were used as sub-flooring. More recently, plywood and waferboard has been used. Many current standards call for plywood or waferboard to be at least 5/8 inch thick when the floor joists are sixteen inches apart.

Problems

Springy Floors

Subflooring which is too thin will be springy and may fail under concentrated loads (e.g. a piano). This should be overlaid to provide a stiffer subfloor.

Squeaky Floors

Subflooring not adequately secured to the floor joists is likely to be squeaky, and may be springy. Most floor squeaks are the result Of Poor contact between the subflooring and joists. The weight of someone walking on a floor will temporarily push the subfloor down onto the joist. When the foot is removed, the subfloor will lift off slightly again. The noise is the nails squeaking as they slide in and out, or pieces of wood rubbing against each other. Solutions include renailing, screwing and gluing the subfloor to the joists. Shims can also be used between the subfloor and joists.

Water Daniage

Waferboard subflooring can be damaged by relatively small amounts of water. The board tends to swell, resulting in floor unevenness. The swelling also pulls the nails out of the joists or through the waferboard. Ultimately, of course, the board can lose its strength,

Edge Support

Diagonal plank subflooring must be supported where it meets the wall. The ends of some of the planks may be several inches from a floor joist and, if adequate blocking is not provided here, the floor will be weak in this area. Where plywood or waferboard subflooring sheets meet, the joint should be supported by joists, blocking or tongue and groove connections between the sheets. Failure to do one of these will result in weak areas.

Damage

Any subflooring can be mechanically damaged and, unless repairs are made, this can lead to an unsafe situation. A common problem is a hole cut for a heating register which was never installed. If carpet is laid, this may not be noticed until a furniture leg is put on the weak spot. Repairs are, of course, simple and inexpensive.

Uneven   Uneven subflooring can be irritating, although it is rarely a structural problem. Uneven joist installation is a common cause, as is debris on the top of the joists when the subfloor is laid. Swelled waferboard or delaminating plywood can also result in unevenness. Careless joining of tongue and groove sheets can lead to surface irregularity.

Fire, Rot   Subflooring is susceptible to rot, termite, mechanical and fire damage. (See
and Termites Section 9.0 - 12.0)

5.8 Cantilevers

Description: Floor joists may be cantilevered (extended) out through the building wall to form a deck or balcony. This is often done on an upper floor, where posts supporting the deck would be expensive and unsightly. The principle is that since wood is relatively stiff, if part of a joist is well secured at one end and part way along its length, the other end can be unsupported. The tricky part is to know how much of a joist can be unsupported. Many authorities are now saying that only one-sixth of the length of a wood joist can be cantilevered unless special engineering is performed. Where the joists are carrying roof loads, the amount allowed may be even less. Historically, no restrictions on cantilevering were placed, and many cantilevered structures are very springy.

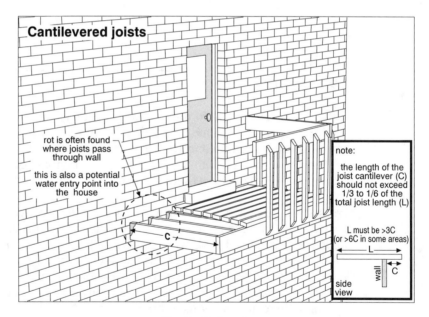

Figure 22. Cantilevers

Materials: Residentially, wood is used almost exclusively, although concrete and steel members can be cantilevered successfully.

Problems

Overspanned Where the joists are cantilevered too far, the deck or balcony will be weak. This is usually detectable by the springiness of the structure when walking on it. In severe cases, where heavy objects are stored on the deck, and there is an unusually heavy snow and ice load, failure is possible. Corrective action normally consists of adding posts or braces below the deck. In some areas, home inspectors will not comment on overspanning, but will recommend further investigation by a specialist.

Water Problems Since the joists penetrate the building wall, there is the possibility of leakage into the walls or directly into the home at the connection points. The joints between the joists and the wall must be kept well sealed.

Rot Any wood joist used outdoors will deteriorate before indoor wood. Cantilevered deck joists are particularly vulnerable, since water tends to be trapped at several places in wood deck structures. Even if the deck boards are properly spaced to allow good flow through drainage and air drying, the life of the outdoor wood may only be fifteen years. This depends on the type of wood, quality of the maintenance, and the paint or stain used. Where design is not good, the wood can deteriorate after only five years. Improvements usually mean abandoning the cantilever and providing a conventional post and/or brace system to support the deck. (See Section 11.0)

Fire and Termites Cantilevered wood structures are susceptible to termite, mechanical or fire damage. (See Section 9.0 - 12.0)

5.9 Floor Trusses

Function: Trusses perform the same function as joists (i.e. to carry the load from the subflooring to the foundation, beam or bearing walls). Trusses have not historically been used in residential construction, although the technology has been available for many years. The top and bottom horizontal members are called "chords". The shorter interior pieces are referred to as "webs".

Trusses can be designed for much longer spans than conventional wood joists. This means that in many residential applications, beams and posts or bearing walls could be abandoned, with the use of floor trusses. These systems also allow heating, plumbing and electrical systems to run through the truss. This leaves more clear headroom under the bottom of the trusses. Another truss advantage is that they do not warp, the way conventional floor joists can. They do not normally require bridging or bracing.

Trusses are deeper than joists and can restrict headroom in some cases. As a general guide, the truss is 1/12 to 1/20 the depth of its span. Most trusses are ten inches to eighteen inches deep.

Trusses can be cantilevered over greater distances than conventional joists, if so designed. Trusses are slightly more expensive than conventional joists, although that may change as they become more popular.

Typical Materials: Wood, steel, plywood. Most floor trusses are either Pratt or Warren type. (See Figure 41 in this section)

Problems

Upside Down   Some trusses are designed so that either the top or bottom chord can rest on the wall. Others must rest on the chord designed to carry the load. Careless field installation may result in a much weaker system than was intended if the truss is placed upside down on a wall. Unless the truss manufacturer's literature is available, this cannot usually be detected during a visual inspection.

Cut   Trusses cannot be cut around openings, the way joists can. Conventional joists can be field cut to appropriate lengths. A truss cannot be cut. All odd length trusses must be engineered. Site conditions which are not foreseen or last minute plan changes, can lead to wasted money and delays, when working with floor trusses. If one new truss has to be made up to fit a special situation, an entire construction crew can be put on hold.

Fire, Rot and Termites   Floor trusses are vulnerable to mechanical abuse, fire, rot and termites. (See Section 9.0 - 12.0)

5.10 Concrete Floors: Concrete floors in residential construction are usually not structural. Basement and garage floor slabs rest on the ground and are usually poured after the house is built. Modem building practices use three inch thick slabs, although old ones may be as thin as 1/2 inch. These may be shifted or broken. Replacement is not a priority, structurally, but is often done to make a basement or garage more usable. Many slabs do not slope to drains. Resloping is rarely done because it is expensive and the problem of water on a floor is rarely serious.

Suspended   Concrete floors which span throughout the house across supports are not common. In very few houses is it possible to look up from a basement or crawl space and see a concrete floor. The exception is concrete front porch slabs above cold cellars in the basement.

Supported concrete floors above grade are common in high-rise and commercial buildings, and employ steel reinforcing. They are usually supported on steel beams or joists. Many systems are largely prefabricated. They are heavier and more expensive than conventional wood floors, but are also stronger and more fire resistant. It is not possible to evaluate a suspended concrete floor system during a home inspection.

► **6.0 WALL SYSTEMS**

6.1 Walls - Masonry

Typical Materials: Brick, stone, concrete block, cinder block, clay tile, glass block. Masonry walls are typically comprised of two wythes (layers) of masonry, usually four inches thick each. A typical brick wall is approximately eight inches thick before application of the interior plaster or drywall. The inner wythe (layer) is most often brick, concrete block or cinder block. The outer wythe, exposed to the weather, is usually weather resistant brick or stone. A masonry wall is a load bearing component of the building that transfers the weight of the roof and floors down to the foundations. The foundation must be at least as wide as the wall to carry the weight of the wall system.

Identification: In most cases, a solid masonry wall can be identified by the header courses (rows where the brick is turned end-wise to tie the inner and outer wythes of the wall together). This is done every five to seven courses (rows) up the wall. Sometimes every brick in the course is turned end-wise. Often, only every other brick is turned, and sometimes the pattern is quite random. In most cases, however, there are at least some of the units which are turned in every fifth, sixth or seventh course.

It is also possible to use metal ties or specially sized bricks to join the inner and outer wythes. If this is done, the wall will show no header courses, and it will not be apparent that it is a solid masonry wall.

Masonry walls have not been used on single family homes since the early 1970's, with few exceptions.

Mortar used to bind masonry units together is a combination of cement, sand, and water. For more information on mortar, refer to 4.1 in the Exterior Section.

Problems

Lean or Bow Where the inner and outer wythes are not adequately secured together, the outer wythes can lean outwards or bow outwards. The entire brick wall may lean or bow due to foundation settlement or the wall being too thin to carry its load. If a wall leans, the ultimate danger is that it may fall. The more immediate danger, however, is that the rafters and joists resting on the wall may slip off as the wall moves out away from the building. Since the ends of joists may only rest on the wall by an inch or two, a relatively small lean can create an unsafe situation. If floor or roof joists slip off their supports, the framing system will collapse.

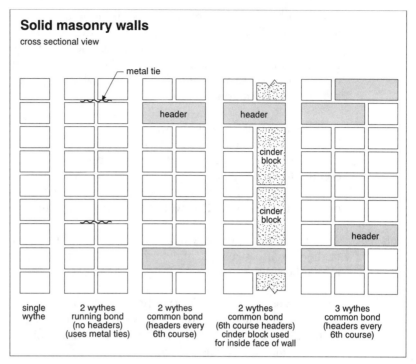

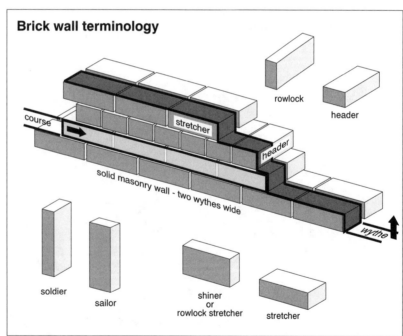

Figure 23. Solid Masonry Walls

Rafter Spread   Spreading rafters on the roof may push the top of the walls out, resulting in an unstable situation.

Out of Plumb   The wall may be built out of plumb, or may be pushed out of plumb by mechanical forces (such as a wall being struck by an automobile), or failure of another component of the building.

Wavy   Brick walls are sometimes wavy. As you look up the wall, the brick surface is not smooth. The waves often have crests every five to seven courses. Some say this is a result of building too quickly. The theory has it that bricks are laid on top of bricks where the mortar has not had time to set and strengthen. This makes more sense with old lime mortars which took longer to set, than with modem cement mortars.

Another theory to explain the waviness is that a full bed of mortar was not laid between each course of brick. If the mason was skimping, only the front edge of the brick would get mortar. This could lead to the back part of the bricks coming together and creating a bulge at the front. It is suggested where ties or headers were used every five to seven courses, a full mortar bed would be used on these courses only. This would explain the repetitive pattern of the waves.

Deteriorated   The structure of the wall can be compromised if the masonry units themselves or the mortar between them deteriorates. It is important that the strength of the mortar be similar to but not stronger than the brick.

Corbelling   Brick can be corbelled (offset) only about one inch beyond the brick below (i.e. one brick does not have to be set exactly on top of another). However, the tot corbelling must not exceed one-third of the wall thickness. Corbelling beyond this limit may lead to instability.

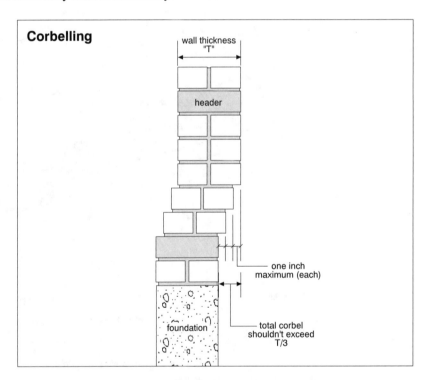

Figure 24. Corbelling of Solid Masonry Walls

On Side   Hollow bricks or concrete blocks are weak if laid on their sides. They should not be expected to carry loads when on their sides.

Cracks Cracks in brickwork may appear for several reasons. Some are quite serious while others are not. Cracks should be used as clues, and their size, location, direction and rate of growth are all indicators of what is happening. Generally speaking, cracks through mortar joints are less serious than cracks through the brick or block, but there are exceptions.

When needed Corrective Action: If a masonry wall is bowed out of plumb by approximately one sixth of its thickness (typically measured half way up the wall), it may be unsound. Joists may pull out of their pockets in the wall before the wall gets to the point of falling. This causes collapse of the framing system in the house. A wall which is leaning out of plumb by one-third of its thickness (measured from top to bottom) may be unsound.

Anchoring In some cases, the brick walls can be tied back into the building using anchors and steel rods or cables. However, if the movement is the result of foundation difficulties, it may be necessary to completely rebuild the wall after underpinning the foundations.

Establishing the appropriate corrective action may require a structural engineer, and repairs should only be undertaken after the cause of the movement is fully understood.

6.2 Walls - Wood Frame

Function: Wood frame walls are load bearing walls which carry the weight of the roof and floors down to the foundations. They may be interior or exterior walls.

Studs also provide space for insulation and surfaces to secure interior and exterior finishes. Some studs are load bearing, others are not. Bearing stud walls should have a double top plate. Non-bearing stud walls may have only a single top plate. A single bottom or sole plate is provided in either case. Incidentally, no matter how skillful a building expert is, he cannot determine whether a wood wall is bearing by tapping on it.

Typical Materials: Historically, two-by-four studs have been used, spaced sixteen inches on center, although more recently, two-by-six exterior studs have become common in energy efficient homes as they provide additional space for insulation between the studs. Metal studs are not used much on single family homes although they are common in commercial construction. Metal studs are usually non-load bearing.

Problems

Rot, termite, mechanical damage, fire damage (see Section 9.0 - 12.0), poor quality lumber, and overspacing can all be problems. Replacing weakened wood members or adding wood studs are the correct solutions.

Nailing and Openings Inadequate nailing can lead to difficulties. Openings in walls may not be adequately framed. Wall sections above large openings for picture windows, for example, often sag if the openings are not bridged with appropriate lintels.

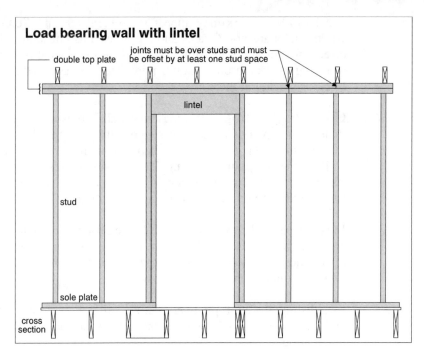

Figure 25. Load Bearing Wall with Lintel

Buckling   Some wood stud walls are susceptible to buckling under loads. This is particularly true if the walls are not braced with girts (solid blocking near the mid point introduced horizontally between adjacent studs), or if interior or exterior finishes are not provided. If finish is provided on one side of the wall, girts are not required. An unfinished basement bearing wall with no girts may be susceptible.

Longer studs are also more susceptible to buckling. An easy way to understand this is to hold both ends of a yardstick and try and push the ends toward each other. The yardstick buckles very easily in the middle. This is more difficult to accomplish with a six inch ruler of the same material.

Where an upward extension of the building is planned, special engineering consideration should be given, It may be that a conventional two-by-four wood-frame wall with studs sixteen inches on center cannot safely carry a load imposed by a third floor addition. In lower quality construction, stud spacing may be twenty or twenty-four inches. This greatly restricts the ability to extend the building upwards, without stiffening the walls.

Condensation Condensation damage to studs in exterior walls is becoming a concern, especially where insulation is being upgraded in older houses, and good interior air/vapor barriers on the warm side of the insulation are not provided. Since the process is largely concealed, it is difficult to spot during a visual inspection and may act for a long time before the damage is noticed. In some cases, peeling exterior paint will be one indication that wall condensation is a problem.

It should be understood that this is typically a seasonal problem, with the condensation occurring during the winter months only. Warm moist air enters the wall from the house. As it passes through, the air cools. Cool air cannot hold as much water as warm air. Condensation forms inside the wall as the air cools and gives off its water.

Low Quality Lumber Poor quality studs or studs which warp and bow shortly after construction can lead to unsightly wall surfaces in new construction. There is no easy answer to this problem. The bowed or twisted studs have to be removed and replaced.

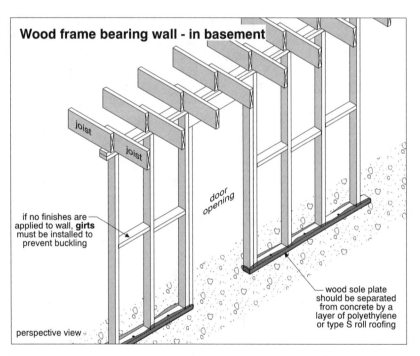

Figure 26. Wood Frame Bearing Wall

Green Lumber   Building with lumber which is too wet or "green" can result in problems such as shrinking, warping, or bowing. A moisture content of more than nineteen percent is considered too high for wood used in residential construction.

6.2.1 Balloon Framing: Balloon framing was common in the late 19th and early 20th centuries. This wood-frame construction technique employed conventional wood studs and floor joists, the same wood as used now. The principal difference, was that the wall studs were erected before the floor systems, and the wall studs were continuous from the foundation up to the roof line. The construction process involves setting up the wall studs, and then essentially hanging the floor systems from them. When completed, this resulted in a rigid structure, although unless adequate fire stops were provided, this type of construction could allow a fire to move very quickly through the stud spaces and engulf the house in flames in a short time.

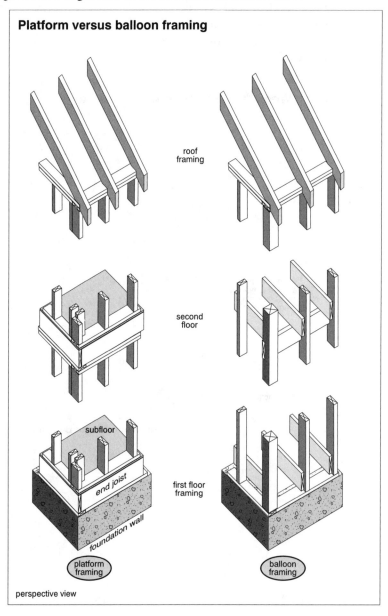

Figure 27. Platform Versus Balloon Framing

44

6.2.2 Platform Construction: Platform or Western framing, as it is sometimes known, employs a slightly different approach. On top of the foundations, a wood floor joist and subfloor system is provided. On top of this system, studs which are one story high are erected. If the house is two stories, a second floor platform is assembled on top of the studs, and then a second set of studs is put on top of this platform. This can be extended up to form a three story house as well. There are no great advantages to platform construction over balloon framing other than the ease of installation and some savings in terms of material costs. The performance of the two systems is roughly equivalent, and neither type of framing should be a strong consideration when purchasing a home.

6.3 Walls - Wood Frame Brick Veneer

Function: To transmit the loads of the roof and floors down to the foundation.

Typical Materials: A brick veneer wall employs a structural wood frame inner wall, and a four inch thick masonry outer section (veneer) which does not have any load bearing responsibility. Typically, metal ties are used to secure the brickwork to the exterior sheathing and, consequently, no header courses are typically employed in the brickwork. This usually enables one to visually differentiate between a masonry wall and a brick veneer wall. (see Section 6.1)

Brick veneer walls have been built essentially as long as we have been building with brick and in fact, are the only type of brick walls commonly built in single family homes after about 1970.

Rain Screen Principle Since roughly 1970, brick veneer walls have had weep holes provided at the bottom. A brick veneer wall built today employs a rain screen principle. This principle acknowledges that a wind driven rain will pass through a brick wall, and as a result, a one inch air space is left behind the brick, between the inner face of the brick and the sheathing on the wood studs. Water is allowed to pass through the wall and run down the inner face of the brick, or the outer surface of the sheathing.

At the bottom row of bricks, every fourth vertical mortar joint (typically) is left out. A flashing is used that allows water at the bottom of the wall cavity to drain out through the weep holes. The flashing prevents the water from entering the foundation. It is also common to find weep holes above door and window openings in the brick walls. Where steel lintels are used above openings, the joint between the steel and the brick above should not be caulked. Water may be trapped behind the caulking and rust the steel.

The other function of the weep holes is to allow a balancing of the pressures on either side of the brick. If air is allowed to enter the cavity behind the brick, as wind is blowing on the brick, the pressure differential, and hence the tendency for water to be driven through, is reduced.

A variation on weep holes is rope wicks in every fourth mortar joint in the bottom row of brick. Where weep holes or wicks are noted, the wall is brick veneer.

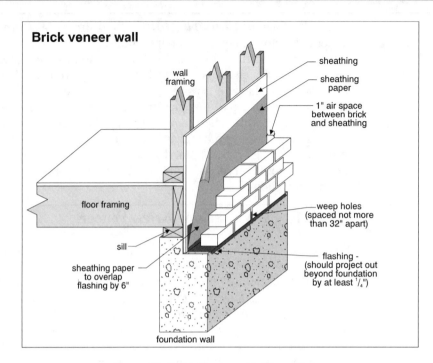

Brick veneer wall

wall framing

sheathing

sheathing paper

1" air space between brick and sheathing

floor framing

weep holes (spaced not more than 32" apart)

sill

flashing - (should project out beyond foundation by at least $1/4$")

sheathing paper to overlap flashing by 6"

foundation wall

Figure 28. Brick Veneer with Weep Holes

Problems

Foundations

Bow

Although the brick veneer has no load bearing responsibilities, it must sit on a foundation built to sustain the weight of the brick. If the foundation is not substantial, the brick veneer wall may crack and/or settle away from the wood-frame wall. If the brick veneer is inadequately tied to the wood-frame wall, again the brick may bulge or pull away.

Deteriorated

Brick or mortar which is defective or deteriorated can lead to serious problems. In the worst cases, the brick veneer wall has to be rebuilt. Most brick is not designed to be in contact with the soil, and should be kept six inches above grade.

Weep Holes

If weep holes are filled or omitted, water penetration through the brick can collect in the wall cavity, leading to brick deterioration, and ultimately the deterioration of the sheathing and studs as well.

Flashing

Similar results occur if the flashing is inappropriate or the space between the brick and sheathing is filled. The flashing cannot normally be seen during an inspection.

Corbelling

Excessive corbelling can also be a problem (see Section 6.1.)

The wood-frame wall itself is subject to the problems described in Section 6.2.

Metal Angles

In some cases, the brick veneer is supported on angles bolted to the foundation. If there is any movement at all, the brick may crack, bulge, or pull away from the wall behind.

6.4 Walls - Logs

Function: The same as other exterior wall systems. The logs carry the roof and floor loads and support the interior and exterior finishes, if any. Historically, the logs were often the exterior and interior finish as well. Connection of one log to the next is important. Each log should be attached to the log below in at least three places. Fasteners should be no further than six feet apart. This connection system is, of course, not visible during a building inspection. Modern work utilizes precisely cut logs, keyed together, with gaskets between logs.

Other Sidings

It is interesting to note that many older log homes were covered with wood sheathing such as clap board on the exterior as soon as the homeowners could afford it. Stucco was also used on the exterior in some cases and plaster was often applied on the interior. Some old log homes look quite different than they did when they were built. The foundations were typically stone, and wood shingles or shakes were most often the roofing material.

Chinking

Chinking was traditionally used to fill the gaps between the logs. This was typically a mortar made of clay, sand and other binders, such as animal hair. Where gaps were large, stones would often be fitted in before the chinking was applied. Due to the expansion and contraction of logs across the grain, chinking usually had to be redone every year, at least in part.

Problems

Wood Shrinkage

Traditional log construction today is unpopular in some areas for a number of reasons. It is a relatively expensive way to build and wasteful of wood products. Further, wood tends to shrink and expand with changes in moisture content to a much greater degree across the grain that it does along the grain. That is to say, a log wall is likely to grow shorter as the wood dries out and taller when the wood is wet. A wood stud wall will, with the same changes in moisture content, shrink and expand much less because the wood grain is vertical rather than horizontal.

If wood changes its moisture content from nineteen percent to five percent (typical in a house), its length may change by zero point one percent (0.1%) along the grain, but its width may shrink by two point five percent (2.5%) across the grain. This means an eight foot long stud may only shrink one-tenth-of-an-inch, while a stack of logs eight foot high may shrink by 2-1/2-inches. This can be a significant problem with windows, doors and other building components attached to a log wall.

Chinking

Regular maintenance is required in chinking the gaps between the logs in traditional log homes. The modern materials now available perform much better.

Rot

It is common to find that the logs at the bottom of the wall (where they may have been in contact with earth) are rotted. They can be removed and replaced, by jacking the rest of the house up temporarily. This is obviously an expensive undertaking. This is not likely to be a problem with modern log houses built on conventional modern foundations.

Concealed Damage

Where the logs have been covered with siding, a good deal of concealed water damage can be done and a visual investigation will rarely reveal the true condition of all of the structural log components.

6.5 Post and Beam Construction: This type of construction which utilizes wood members much larger than conventional wood-frame construction, is not common residentially, although it can be found on older country properties and was commonly utilized for barns, mills, churches and other large buildings. There are some prefabricated kits now available and some builders who employ this building technique. Other names for this type of construction include timber, heavy timber or semi-mill construction.

The structural skeleton of this building style is a relatively small number of large wood beams and posts. This is very different from conventional framing which uses a large number of smaller wood studs and joists to carry the loads down to the foundations. The floor and roof planks were typically two inches thick, and spanned framing members which were usually several feet apart. Old floor boards can be very wide, with twelve to fourteen inch planks not uncommon. In newer construction, the width is often limited to about eight inches by local codes, for fear of warping problems.

Traditionally, the heavy posts and beams were solid wood. In reproduction homes built today, built up or glue-laminated beams and posts are also used. In the original versions, the heavy wood posts were often flared out at the top to increase strength. A feature of these homes was the way the wood sections were connected. Very sophisticated mortise and tenon connections were utilized, as were dovetail joints. Many of the homes were assembled without nails, wood dowels often being used in their place.

The walls were often heavy plank and in some cases were load bearing, although for the most part they simply provided a weathertight skin. The planks could be installed horizontally or vertically, and typically were at least two inches thick.

These houses were expensive to build both in terms of construction materials and labor. Large pieces of good quality lumber have become harder and harder to obtain. Because the wood components were very heavy, and sophisticated joint connections were used, construction was labor intensive.

Problems

Lack of Rigidity

Since the skeleton consisted of a few large components and relatively few connections, rigidity could be a problem, particularly where the sheathing did not perform a stabilizing function. Because of the intricacy of some of the connections, there was a good deal of room for error, and a poor understanding of load transmissions could lead to connection failures.

Expansion and Contraction

Checking

The very large timbers undergo significant dimensional changes with changes in moisture content. These buildings are not static, and tend to expand and contract with changes in season and humidity. As timbers dried out, checking often developed. Checks are longitudinal cracks, parallel to the grain, which widen as they get further from the heartwood. In many cases, this is not a structural concern, although a large check running horizontally through a beam does reduce its load carrying capacity. Where continuous checking in a post could lead to buckling, steel clamps can be provided around checked posts.

Foundations   Because of the skeletal nature of the framing, large concentrated loads were carried to the ground. Foundation systems were often too weak in areas of concentrated loads, and much stronger than they had to be in other areas.

Specialized   Since this type of construction is specialized, and not seen frequently, local
Inspection   authorities and professional home inspectors alike will not be intimately familiar with it. In some cases, a specialist is required to comment on components of the structure.

Repair   Repair or replacement of components of post and beam construction is often difficult without compromising the aesthetic or architectural appeal of the home. In repairs as in new post and beam construction, the strength of structural components must be demonstrated using engineering calculations, rather than rules of thumb or tables.

6.6 Arches

Function: To redirect the load above an opening in a masonry wall to the solid wall sections on either side. An arch performs the same function as a lintel.

Arch Loads   The area that the arch supports can safely be thought of as a triangle above the arch. The height of the triangle is roughly half the width of the opening. This means that a window with twenty stories of brick above requires the same arch as a window with six feet of brick above.

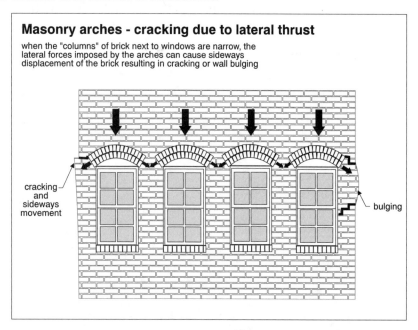

Figure 29. Masonry Arches

Typical Types: There are several different types of arches, although the function is essentially the same. Stone, brick and concrete are the most common materials used. Segmental arches are the most common, made up of several pieces. The arch must have a rise of at least I inch for each foot of its span.

Jack arches are arches where the top and bottom of the arch are horizontal. Failure of these arches is common where steel lintels are not provided in addition to the arch work. This is not a common type of arch.

Some arches have a larger masonry unit at the top. This is called a keystone, and is often the architectural focus of an arch and window system.

Problems

Too Flat or
Too Narrow

Lateral
Thrust

Failure in arches is common where the rise is an absolute minimum, or the arch is not quite wide enough to clearly span the opening. Another common problem of arches is slight movement of the walls on either side. This is particularly common where a window or door opening is very close to the end of a wall. On one side of the arch, there is often not enough mass to resist the lateral thrust of the arch transferring its load to the wall beside. As the thin section of wall pushes outward, the arch drops.

Deterioration

Mortar or masonry deterioration can, of course, lead to failure. Differential foundation movement may allow the arch to open up and drop. Another problem is forward movement of the arch out away from the building. This is usually caused by foundation movement or mortar and masonry deterioration.

Corrective actions include rebuilding the arch or adding a lintel.

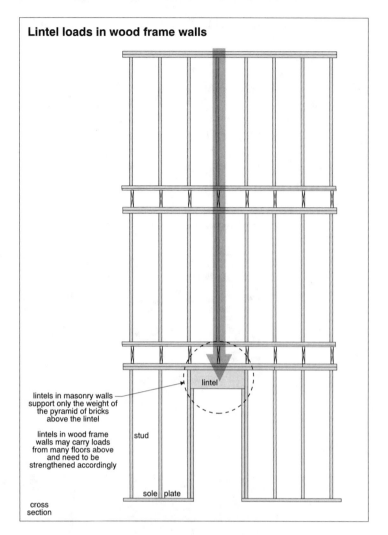

Figure 30. Lintels Loads

6.7 Lintels

Function: The function of a lintel is to transfer the load above an opening to the solid wall sections on either side. A lintel performs exactly the same function as an arch. Lintels are typically flat, and use the inherent strength of the material to transmit the load, rather than the arch principle.

Lintel Loads   The area that the lintel supports can safely be thought of as a triangle above the lintel. The height of the triangle is roughly half the width of the opening. This means that a window with twenty stories of brick above requires the same lintel as a window with six feet of brick above.

Typical Materials: Steel, wood, stone and concrete.

Problems

Undersized and End Bearing

The lintels may be undersized for the load. Inadequate end bearing of the lintels may lead to failure. Steel lintels on masonry walls should be at least six inches wider than the opening on either side. This cannot usually be seen. Steel lintels are subject to rust. The rusting steel expands and typically causes horizontal cracks in the mortar joints at the window corners. Wood lintels are susceptible to rot, termite attack, fire and mechanical damage. Concrete and stone lintels are subject to cracking or spalling.

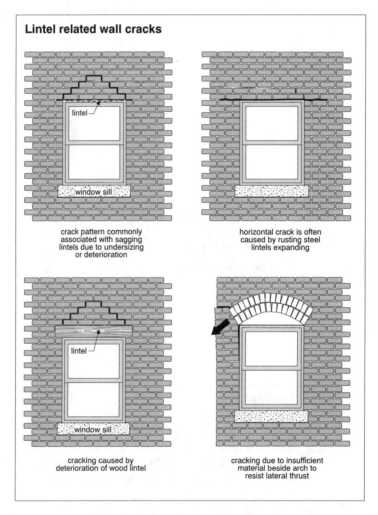

Figure 31. Lintel Related Wall Cracks

Missing

In amateurish construction projects, windows may be added to masonry walls or brick veneer walls with no arch or lintel provided. This will often work in the short term, but problems usually develop over time. Missing or inadequate lintels should be replaced.

Caulking

Steel lintels supporting brick veneer should have no caulking between the steel and the brick above. Caulking may trap water and rust the steel.

► 7.0 ROOFS

7.1 Rafters

Function: To support the roof sheathing and transmit the roof loads to bearing walls or beams below. The term "rafter" is associated with sloped roofs. When these members are found on a flat roof, they are called "roof joists", although they do exactly the same job.

Rafters can usually be seen overhead, when standing in the attic. Some rafters support finished ceilings, for example, where there is a cathedral ceiling. In this case, insulation is often fit between the rafters.

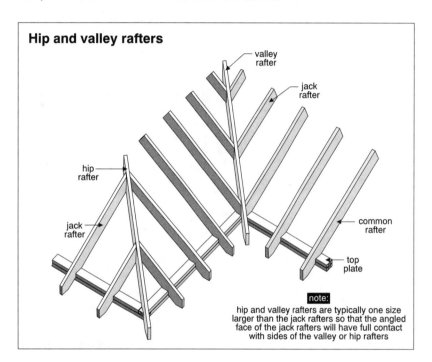

Hip and valley rafters

valley rafter

jack rafter

hip rafter

jack rafter

common rafter

top plate

note:
hip and valley rafters are typically one size larger than the jack rafters so that the angled face of the jack rafters will have full contact with sides of the valley or hip rafters

Figure 32. Hip and Valley Rafters

Typical Materials: Wood two-by-fours, two-by-sixes or two-by-eights, spaced sixteen to twenty-four inches on center. Note: Conventional rafters are being replaced by prefabricated wood trusses in some modern construction. The engineered trusses can span greater distances less expensively than conventional rafters.

When calculating the span of a rafter system, the horizontal projection rather than the actual length of the rafter is used. Knee walls or collar ties are considered to provide intermediate support, effectively reducing the rafter span.

Problems

Overspanned   Wood rafters are susceptible to rot, termite and fire damage. (See Section 9.0 - 12.0). If they are overspanned or spaced too far apart, the roof will sag. In some areas, home inspectors will not comment on overspanning, but will recommend further investigation by a specialist.

Rafter Spread   If rafters are not adequately secured to the walls at the bottom edge, the rafters may spread. This is a fairly common problem on older houses, particularly with gable roofs. It is often noted at the soffits, because the soffits pull away from the house wall as the rafters spread. In other cases, the spreading rafters may push the top of the wall outward. This can be very serious.

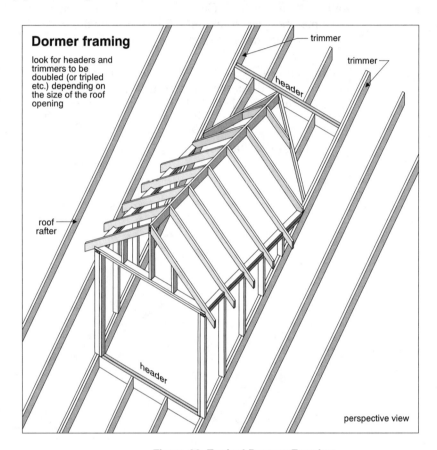

Figure 33. Typical Dormer Framing

Condensation   Attics which have good insulation but poor ventilation may be susceptible to condensation problems. Condensation will attack the roof sheathing and the rafters. Left unchecked, this can lead to roof structure failure. Corrective action includes improved ventilation and replacing damaged wood.

Damage   Occasionally, mechanical damage is a problem in rafters, although for the most part, there is very little activity in or near the rafters after the house has been built. Pests such as raccoons are capable of chewing through rafters, if so inclined.

Concentrated Loads   In some cases, a roof rafter configuration which is ordinarily acceptable, fails because of a concentrated roof snow load. Split level houses are susceptible to this problem, for example. When a house has two levels, depending upon wind direction and snow accumulation in the winter, it is not unusual for snow drifts to form on the lower roof, near the wall of the higher section. This can lead to excessive loads on the rafters in these areas. The rafters may crack, sag or spread at the bottom. The roof can be strengthened in this section to carry the greate loads.

7.2 Collar Ties

Function: To prevent rafters from sagging inward. They do the same job as knee walls.

Typical Materials: These are typically wood members (two-by-fours or two-by-sixes) installed horizontally half way up the attic space. They are connected at either end to opposing rafters and act as stiffeners to prevent the rafters from sagging in the middle. There should be one collar tie for each pair of opposing rafters. If they are more than eight feet long, there should be a rat-tail or other sort of bracing attached to the mid point of the collar ties to prevent them from buckling in the middle.

Problems

Buckling

Collar ties are susceptible to buckling, and it is not uncommon to find that an inappropriate lumber size has been used. For example, a two-by-four makes a fairly good collar tie, but a one-by-eight does not. Because of the very thin dimension of one inch, if you push on either end of a one-by-eight (which is exactly what rafters do), it is fairly easy to bend it in the middle. It is much more difficult to bend a two-by-four by pushing from either end.

Missing

Another common problem with collar ties is that they are not provided on each rafter. It was very common on older houses to provide collar ties only on every third rafter. In some cases this has worked, although in many cases, particularly with the added weight of multiple layers of roof shingles, this is not adequate. Collar ties can be added readily.

Bracing

If lateral bracing has been omitted, collar ties more than eight feet long may buckle. Bracing can be easily installed.

Wrong Location

Often collar ties are too high up or too low down. Ideally, they should be near the mid-point of the rafter span.

Nailing

If not nailed securely to the rafter, the collar tie may slip under load.

Low Slope Roof

Collar ties are only effective where the roof slope is four in twelve or greater. Larger rafters, or knee walls are typically used on lower slopes on a retrofit basis to strengthen a roof.

Like any other wood member in a house, collar ties are susceptible to rot, termite and fire damage and mechanical damage. (See 9.0 - 12.0)

Failed collar ties may only be noted when there is a heavy roof snow load. Under light loading, the roof may spring back into place.

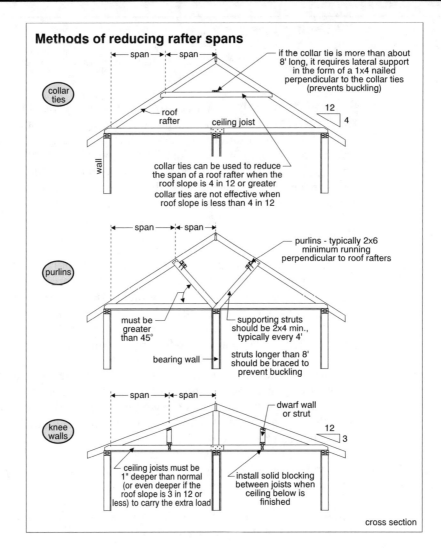

Figure 34. Reducing Rafter Spans

7.3 Knee Walls

Function: To prevent rafter sag, the same as collar ties.

Typical Materials: These are small walls, typically built with wood two-by-four studs, located in the attic. They run from the attic floor up to the underside of the rafters near their mid-point. In 1- 1/2 or 2-1/2 storey houses, these knee walls sometimes form the walls of a room on the upper floor. These rooms often have a partly sloped ceiling as a result.

Problems

Poorly Secured and Weak Floor   Like any wood component, they are subject to rot, termite, mechanical damage and fire damage. (See Section 9.0 - 12.0) If the knee walls are not adequately secured to the rafters or to the joist below, they will move. If the floor joist system below is not strong enough, or there is no partition below, this can lead to deflection in the ceiling below, with resultant ceiling finish damage.

Location   If the knee wall is not near the mid span of the rafters, it may not be effective in preventing rafter sag. In many cases, where the roof line is fairly long, a knee wall is used on the lower end of the rafter to provide immediate support and a collar tie is used higher up. Where there is both a collar tie and a knee wall, they should be placed to provide equally sized rafter spans.

7.4 Roof Trusses

Function: Roof trusses perform the same function as rafters, collar ties, knee walls, and ceiling joists. The roof truss holds up the roof sheathing and shingles, transferring the roof loads to the outside or bearing walls. The bottom of the truss also supports the ceiling finish, upon which the insulation rests.

Typical Materials: Most trusses used in residential construction are made up of wood components. The top and bottom members of the truss are referred to as "chords". The interior members of a truss are referred to as "webs". Individual wood members of the trusses are secured together with "gusset plates". These may be made of plywood or steel.

Different configurations of trusses have different strengths, and engineers can use the shape and component size that best suits them. Trusses are typically preengineered systems. Trusses are normally spaced twenty-four inches apart, but this can vary, again depending on the spans and depth of truss desired.

There are two common truss types used residentially. The Fink or "W" has web members that form a "W". The Howe truss can be identified by vertical web members, including a vertical web running up to the peak. The Howe trusses are somewhat stronger, although as long as spans are within the capabilities of the truss, either will perform well. There are many variations of these found in residential construction.

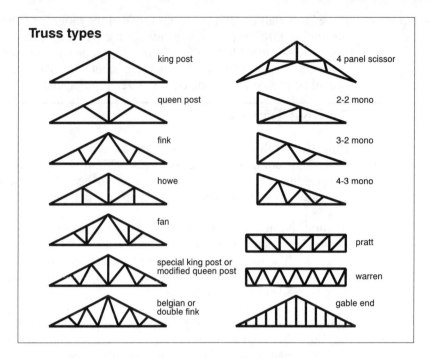

Figure 35. Roof Trusses

In either truss type, the webs should be at least two by fours, unless special engineering consideration has been given. Where the compression webs are longer than six feet, they are susceptible to buckling under heavy loads. Braces, such as I x 4's should be fastened to the midpoints of these webs.

Where the bottom chord has a long span between support points, it may not be strong enough to carry the ceiling load. If the span is more than ten feet between support points, the bottom chord should be at least a 2 x 5. If the span is more than twelve feet, the bottom chord should be a 2 x 6. Again, special engineering consideration can result in deviations from these rules of thumb.

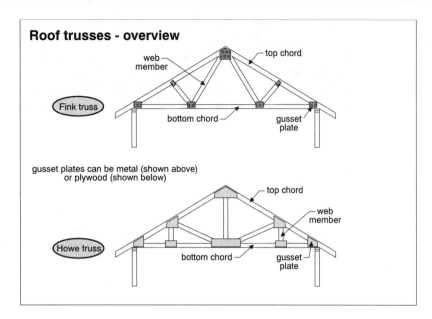

Figure 36. Roof Trusses

Problems

Like any wooden member, trusses are subject to rot, tennite damage, mechanical damage and fire. (See Section 9.0 - 12.0)

Cut

Individual chords or webs which are cut or damaged can be a serious problem. Cutting a truss in one spot may seriously compromise the entire truss structure. Where trusses have to be cut to accommodate chimneys or other interruptions in the roof line, special engineering consideration should be given.

Fastening

Trusses must, of course, be well secured to ensure their performance.

Overspanning

Overspanning of trusses can lead to deflection under load and, in worst cases, roof collapse. Reasons for overspanning, other than a simple error made on original construction, would include re-roofing with a heavier roof covering, or greater snow loads than expected, due to unusual conditions or drifting. Overspanning cannot typically be identified during a home inspection, but evidence of deflection or failure would be noted.

Repairs

Reinforcing trusses which are overspanned is more difficult than strengthening a rafter roof system. An engineer specializing in this area should be consulted to determine the most cost-effective approach.

Trusses with compression web members longer than six feet may be subject to buckling. Braces should be added to the midpoints of the webs. One brace attached to each web with two nails should connect several webs in adjacent trusses. The braces should be at least 1 x 4's.

Ceiling Support

Undersized bottom chords should be stiffened to prevent ceiling sag and cracking of ceiling finishes. Adding a second member to the bottom chord would normally be satisfactory.

Truss
Uplift

A phenomenon known as "truss uplift" is relatively common in new houses. This is not well understood, but does involve the bottom member (chord) of the truss deflecting upward during winter weather. It is argued that the temperature and humidity changes in the attic during the winter months affect the sections of the truss above the insulation level, differently than the bottom chord buried in the insulation. This results in an upward bowing of the bottom chord.

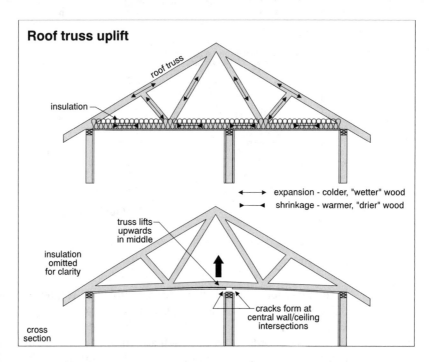

Figure 37. Truss Uplift

The result of truss uplift is that the center section of the bottom chord moves upward, and gaps as large as 1-1/2 inches appear at the top of the interior walls, where they join the ceiling. The ceiling is picked up by the truss. It is less common but also possible, that the entire wall below will be lifted up, and separation will occur between the bottom of the wall and the floor.

At present, a good solution is not known for this problem, although common corrective action is to secure a molding to the ceiling (but not to the wall). As the ceiling moves up and down, the molding will slide up and down the wall although no gap will appear. Another solution is to disconnect the ceiling drywall from the truss. Alternate ceiling support is generally necessary.

Research is being conducted into control of this phenomenon. Truss uplift is not a serious structural problem.

7.5 Roof Sheathing

Function: To support the roof covering and transmit the load of this material as well as the live loads due to snow, ice and wind to the rafters, trusses or roof joists.

Typical Materials: Wood plank, plywood or waferboard. For the first half of this century, virtually all roof sheathing was wood plank. Plywood roof sheathing in four foot by eight foot panels became popular in the 1960's and waferboard panels arrived in the 1970's.

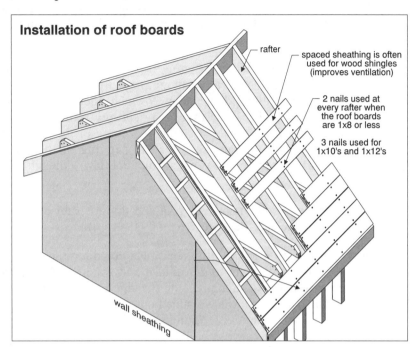

Figure 38. Roof Boards

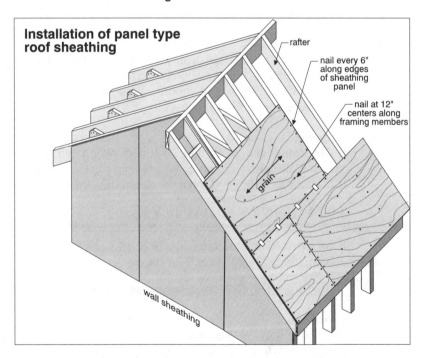

Figure 39. Panel-Type Roof Sheathing

Plywood should be laid with the surface grain perpendicular to the rafters, trusses or joists. The eight foot length should be across the rafters with the ends resting on a rafter. Their other edges should also be supported, typically by metal "H" clips located between rafters. The panel type sheathing is typically separated from adjacent panels by at least 1/16 inch to allow for swelling of the wood members during periods of high humidity. The "H" clips also serve to accomplish this.

The thickness of the sheathing is determined by the spacing of the rafters. Modern construction typically employs trusses or rafters on twenty-four inch centers and plywood sheathing 3/8 inch thick (or waferboard sheathing 7/16 inch thick). This leads to a fairly springy roof surface when walked upon. Unusually heavy loads or slight weakening of the plywood due to high moisture levels in the attic can lead to sagging of the sheathing between the supports. Normally this is not a structural flaw, although it is unsightly.

Problems
Like any wood component, roof sheathing is subject to rot, termite, mechanical damage and fire. (See Section 9.0 - 12.0)

Condensation Condensation in an attic can cause considerable problems. Plywood roof sheathing will begin to delaminate and waferboard sheathing will swell. This can cause loss of strength in the sheathing and render the nailing of the sheathing ineffective as nails are pulled out of the rafters, or through the sheathing. In severe cases, the roof covering has to be removed, and the sheathing replaced.

Too Thin Sheathing which is too thin for the application will deflect under load and result in sagging of the roof line. Aesthetically, this is generally considered unacceptable, although sagging to the point of failure would be unusual.

Edge Support Unsupported edges of roof sheathing may lead to differential movement between two panels. This can lead to horizontal ridges appearing in the roofing. Incidentally, seams parallel to rafters in panel roof sheathing should occur only over the rafters and should be staggered. If the sheathing is unusually thick, edge support is not necessary.

FRT Plywood Fire-retardant treated plywood was recognized as a problem in the late 1980's. Delamination and weakening of this plywood can lead to a loss of roof shingles and ultimately collapse. Where it has begun to fail, it should be replaced. If it seems to be in good repair, it should be closely monitored.

► 8.0 MASONRY CHIMNEYS

Function: The structural function of a chimney is to carry its own weight down to the foundations and footings.

Typical Materials: Brick, stone, and concrete block.

Problems
Corbelling Chimneys with excessive corbelling (one row of bricks projecting out and overhanging hanging the row below) or undersized foundations are prone to movement.

Foundation Localized foundation settlement in a house around the chimney is fairly common, typically because the foundations were not large enough to carry the additional weight of the masonry. This is true both in original construction work, and where a masonry chimney has been added. The chimney may eventually fall over, but the problem can become very serious well before this point. A chimney which begins to lean or pull away may develop cracks or gaps which allow smoke and heat to get near combustible materials. A fire hazard may exist with every misaligned chimney.

Three Sided   Occasionally, chimneys are added to the outside of existing houses. Many of these are only three sided, using the house wall as the fourth side. This is acceptable only under some circumstances. It may be permitted where a brick veneer wall is made of solid masonry units and is spaced out at least 1/2 inch from combustible sheathing. On solid masonry walls, twelve inches of solid masonry must separate the flue from any wood joists or beams. A visual inspection will not determine whether the installation is safe.

Wood Contacting Chimneys   Wood building members should not contact masonry chimneys. Generally speaking, interior wood should be at least 2 inches from the chimney. On exterior wood, this can be reduced to 1/2 inch. Where it is necessary to frame into the chimney, there should be 12 inches of solid masonry between the wood and the flue.

▶ 9.0 TERMITES

NOTE: In some jurisdictions, inspection for termites and other wood-boring insects is strictly controlled by government bodies. In these areas, a discussion of termites is beyond the scope of a home inspection.

9.1 Subterranean Termites:

Description of Termites: Termites are by far the most serious insect which can attack the home, since they are the only insects which actually consume the wood. Subterranean termites are found throughout the U.S. and in the southern parts of some Canadian provinces.

Colonies   Subterranean termites have been known to exist in North America for over sixty years. The termites live in a sophisticated social colony in the soil, not in the wood. In colder climates, their colonies are usually located below the level of frost penetration, and are typically close to some moisture source. When termites travel, they do so by moving through wood, soil or shelter tubes which they construct. Termites will not expose themselves to the open air, as their bodies can dry out very quickly. Subterranean termites do not swarm in some areas.

Shelter Tubes   Shelter tubes are very small tunnels which the termites build across any open surface they want to traverse. The shelter tubes are made of earth, debris, and a material they excrete which acts as a binder to hold the tubes together. These tubes are typically sandy in color and can readily be broken open by hand. An initial tube may be less than one 1/4 inch in width, although several tubes can be built together over time, and the entire grouping may be one or two inches wide.

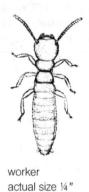

worker
actual size ¼"

soldier
actual size ⁵⁄₁₆"

queen
actual size ½"

Figure 40. Termites

Colony Members   A colony is usually made up of the larvae nymphs, reproductives, soldiers, and workers. The eggs that are laid, hatch and develop into workers, soldiers, or reproductives. As their names suggest, the soldiers' function is to protect the colony. The workers build the shelter tubes, tunnel through the earth, and collect the food. It is these workers which do damage to houses.

Workers   The workers are whitish and usually about 1/8 to 1/4 inch long. They resemble very small ants, although this is of academic interest only, since one will never see a termite roaming about a house. The workers enter the wood and consume it, in very small quantities, of course. The wood is partially digested, taken back to the colony and regurgitated to feed the other members.

Since the termites do not like to be exposed to the air, they will typically eat through the inside of a piece of wood, often following the grain. They tend to eat in parallel galleries, and leave a smooth honey-combed appearance on the inside of the wood. Termites will eat any kind of wood, although damp or rotted wood is slightly easier for them to break down. Termites need a regular supply of moisture, and workers return to the colony every twenty-four to forty-eight hours.

Frass   A small amount of frass is usually found inside the damaged wood. These are small gray flecks, and are different than the powdery wood (sawdust) generated by carpenter ants. Carpenter ants will tend to push the wood debris out of the tunnels, while termites, of course, consume this material.

New Colonies   New colonies can be started by less than fifty insects, and termites are typically moved by the relocation of infested wood or soil. Moving firewood or relocating a shrub or tree can carry a termite infestation to a new area. The natural movement of a colony is very slow, although splinter colonies can break off from the main colony and establish themselves anew.

Since the chemical treatments used at present are designed to protect only the house, very few insects are usually killed during a chemical treatment. The colony simply finds a new source of food and may remain where it is or relocate slightly.

Signs   When watching for signs of infestation, the shelter tubes are usually a first indication. The second indication is usually damaged wood, although often the wood has to be probed to identify the damage, since it tends to be on the interior rather than at the surface. An infestation can develop unnoticed behind finished basement floors or walls, for example, where shelter tubes would not be visible, and wood damage may remain concealed for some time.

Risk Reduction

Minimizing the risk of termites includes breaking wood/soil contact and avoiding accumulation of wood scraps around the outside of the house. The dryer the soil is, the less likely a termite colony will become established. Wet areas should be dried out to prevent this from happening. Crawl spaces and areas under porches can be kept dry with good ventilation. While it is not an absolute defense, any small gaps and cracks in the below grade foundations should be kept sealed.

9.1.1 Termite Treatment:

Function: To eliminate or prevent subterranean termites attacking a building.

Description: Performed by licensed pest control specialists, the chemical treatment employs products such as chlorpyrifos. These chemicals are believed to be effective over a twenty to thirty year period. The chemical is injected into the soil around the building, through the basement floor and foundations, as well as through any posts or other penetrations in the basement floor. The idea is to create a chemical envelope around the house.

It should be understood that termites live in a colony in the soil and that chemical treatment does not kill the colony, but simply prevents the colony from sending its workers into the building to collect wood to feed the colony.

Attached Homes

Incidentally, it is also necessary to treat all attached buildings to ensure effectiveness of the treatment. An envelope created around one half of a building will not prevent infestation to the other half and entry of the termites into the treated half through the upper levels.

Warranty

Most termite treatment contractors will offer a warranty at a fairly modest cost based on an annual re-inspection. Any re-infestation is typically corrected by the contractor.

Cost

The cost of the treatment varies, but is typically $1,200 plus the cost of any wood/soil breakage. Government grants may reduce the cost. It should be recognized that repairs to damaged wood are not covered by most government grants.

Identification: Evidence of chemical treatment can be looked for in sidewalks or driveways around the house, in the form of plugged holes roughly the size of a quarter, spaced anywhere from twelve to twenty-four inches apart. Similar holes may also be found on the exterior foundation walls above grade, on the interior foundations walls, on the basement floor just inside the exterior walls, and on interior floors around the base of columns and interior walls, etc. In some cases, the treatment is also injected directly into the columns.

Another sign that chemical treatment may have been undertaken is the obvious breakage of wood/soil contact. A wood post with a relatively new concrete base, a concrete pad at the bottom of an old wood basement staircase, etc., are signs that wood/soil contact has been broken.

Break Wood/Soil Contact: It is important to remove any wood/soil contact in termite prone areas, even if chemical treatment is undertaken. There should be at least six inches between any wood and soil, both inside the building and out.

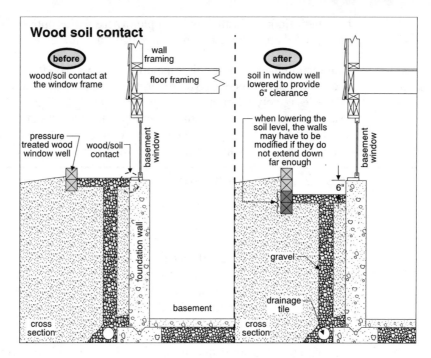

Figure 41. Wood/Soil Contact

Areas of typical wood/soil contact include crawl spaces, porches, stoops, decks, steps, basement windows, window wells, posts, walls, and basement staircases.

Concealed Wood Damage: Wherever termite activity or termite treatment is in evidence, it raises the question of whether any structural damage has been done. If none is visible, it may be difficult to know whether damage is concealed or has been repaired. Without disassembling the house, this is impossible to verify; however, the building should be monitored for sagging structural components, floor springiness or other signs of structural weakness. It is not unusual for termites to attack a house, passing through the floor and wall systems up into the attic. Wood damage may occur a considerable distance from the point of attack in the basement. It is not usually possible to identify the extent of termite damage, since termites move through the center of wood members, trying not to go through the outer edges.

9.2 Drywood Termites: Drywood termites inhabit the southern United States and the coastal areas of California. Drywood termites are occasionally introduced into other areas via wooden furniture or other wooden objects from their southern distribution in the U.S., Caribbean and even Asia, Africa and Australia. These termites infest utility poles, fence posts, trees, and structures (primarily around perimeter areas and where wood joins other wood).

Characteristics Unlike subterranean termites, drywood termites;

a) Do not require soil to build their nests, and do not bring soil into the chambers.
b) Do not construct shelter tubes out of soil (although some species will cement fecal pellets together to bridge a gap in the wood).
c) Cut across the grain of undecayed, dry wood to excavate large chambers.

Detection Fecal matter and other debris (called frass) is stored in unused chambers or kicked out of small kick holes. These holes are often protected by the soldier caste or blocked off by hardened debris. The fecal pellets are hard, six-sided and concave. Piles of these pellets may be found on window sills or beneath other infested surfaces. Other detection methods include;

a) Sounding the wood for cavities.
b) Looking for evidence of shed wings.
c) Looking for blistered wood on surfaces where galleries are close to the top.
d) Probing wood to discover live termites.
e) Using a stethoscope to hear activity within the galleries.

NOTE: Parts d). and e). would typically be done only by a pest control specialist.

Damage is often not as extensive as subterranean termites due to smaller colony sizes.

Control Control is achieved by removal of the damaged wood, and the addition of heat, electrical current, or insecticide injected into the nest and galleries. Tenting and fumigation is used where the infestation is large or the nest is difficult to isolate.

9.3 Dampwood Termites: Most dampwood termites are found tropically worldwide, however, some inhabit deserts. In the United States, they are primarily west of the Rocky Mountains, extending down into California. One species is found in British Columbia.

Characteristics Dampwood termites prefer nesting in decayed wood or wood with a high moisture content and will sometimes infest tree roots. They do not require soil in which to live. The galleries are not kept clean, containing numerous six-sided, concave fecal pellets. A few pellets are discarded from openings in the wood. Some species will infest structures, primarily in areas that are poorly maintained as a result of water exposure or wood/soil contact. Moisture control is the primary key to preventing and eliminating dampwood termite infestations.

► 10.0 OTHER WOOD-BORING INSECTS

Carpenter ants, round head borers, powder post beetles and furniture beetles are also insects which can infest houses and cottages.

Carpenter ants, probably the best known of these insects, are typically 1/4 to 1/2 inch long, often black or dark brown. Carpenter ants and the other insects mentioned do not actually consume the wood, but make their nests in it.

The amount of structural damage these pests do is very limited, although elimination can be tricky.

Conventional pesticides are used and, with carpenter ants, the nest has to be treated. In cases where the nest cannot be located, the entire building is treated. Carpenter ants like kitchen areas, because of the food. They also are frequently found in damp areas. Rotting wood or wood below leaky windows, roofs, or plumbing fixtures are favored nesting spots. The nest may be in floors, cupboards, doors or frames, window sills, porches, etc., out of sight. Since carpenter ants are usually most active during May, June and July, they may not be noted on a one-time inspection. Seeing one or two ants does not necessarily mean an infestation, but this should be watched.

► 11.0 ROT

Fungus

Rot is a form of deterioration that occurs in wood under certain conditions of temperature, moisture and the presence of oxygen. The decay is caused by fungus which attacks the wood cells, causing the cells (and the wood as a whole) to collapse. The fungus that causes rot requires a temperature of roughly 40° F. to 115° F. to be active. Above that temperature, the fungus can be killed and, below that temperature, the fungus becomes dormant, but can be reactivated once the temperature increases.

Moisture Needed

Sufficient moisture has to be available for rot to occur. When the moisture content of the wood exceeds approximately twenty percent, fungus spores which are naturally present in the atmosphere can be sustained and grow within the wood. Once the rot forming fungus is established, it will continue to grow and decay the wood while the wood remains wet. If the lumber is dried to below twenty percent moisture content, the rot will spread no further and will become dormant.

As the rot progresses, the wood cell walls collapse, leading to a loss of strength and the formation of cracks perpendicular to and parallel to the grain. The wood can be broken off in small cubes.

Oxygen Needed

Oxygen must be present for rot to develop. This explains why wood submerged in water will not rot. Under normal circumstances in houses, of course, there is adequate oxygen to support rot fungi growth.

Recommended Practices and Solutions

Avoid Trapped Water

Wood structures must be properly designed to resist rot. Wherever possible, the design should prevent cyclical wetting and entrapment of moisture. All joints should be free draining. Ledges, valleys and troughs where water can collect should be avoided. End grains of wood should be well protected, as they are capable of soaking up large amounts of water through capillary action.

Resistant Wood

Some woods, including cedar and cypress, for example, are naturally resistant to decay fungi. Various wood treatments (such as pressure treating), can enhance the rot resistance of wood. In the case of pressure treating, copper arsenate salts (typically) are forced into the wood cells under pressure. It is these salts that give the wood a greenish tint.

Wood/Soil
Contact

Avoiding the direct contact of wood with soil will inhibit rot by helping to keep it dry. Good ventilation of porches and crawl spaces, for example, is also important in eliminating rot.

Leaks

Appropriate flashing details at joints to promote good drainage, and a well maintained protective coat of paint or stain, will also help to fight rot. Leaking roofs and gutters, if uncorrected, can create an ideal environment for the establishment of rot fungi. Similarly, wood in the area of kitchens and bathrooms can be susceptible to rot if there are leaking pipes or fixtures.

► 12.0 MECHANICAL DAMAGE AND FIRE DAMAGE

Mechanical damage to wood structural members can take several forms. It may be split, broken or crushed during handling or while the building is under construction. It is unusual for all the wood in a home to be free of at least minor mechanical damage. The extent and location of the damage determine whether replacement or repair is needed. The entire system must also be considered. If the wall, roof, or floor system is vastly over-designed, one damaged member may not be critical.

Notches
and Holes

Similar consideration is given to mechanical damage caused by cutting, notching or drilling holes in wood members. Again, there are several criteria which help determine whether corrective action is warranted. Some simple rules are set out in Figure 42.

Structural members which have been weakened can usually be resupported easily.

Fire

Fire damage to a building can be severe or cosmetic. As a very general rule of thumb, major structural members with less than 1/4 inch of char do not require resupporting. This, of course, depends on the size, orientation and function of the member. Where there is doubt, specialists in this field can be consulted.

Another type of fire damage should be considered. Where wood structural components are too close to fireplaces, furnaces, etc., the wood around them may begin to char as it overheats. This can occur at temperatures as low as 250° F. This will allow the wood to ignite easily if exposed to higher temperatures even briefly. Charred wood around heat generating appliances is a danger sign which should not be ignored.

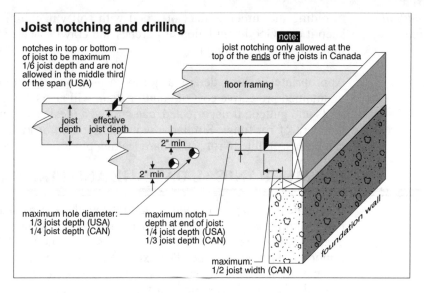

Figure 42. Notches and Holes

4 ELECTRICAL

TABLE OF CONTENTS

▶ INTRODUCTION

The electrical system is very important from both a safety and convenience standpoint. Generally speaking, electrical systems are expanded and upgraded over the life of a house, rather than taken out and replaced on a regular basis.

▶ 1.0 THE BASICS

1.1 Definitions: It is useful to understand some of the basics of alternating current. Incidentally, all typical house wiring is alternating (rather than direct) current. Two very simple formulas will be helpful.

1. V = IR. Here V is the voltage in volts, I is the current in amps, and R is the resistance in ohms.

2. P = VI. Here P is the power in watts, V is the voltage in volts, I is the current in amps.

TABLE 1.
ALTERNATING CURRENT (AC) BASICS

V = Voltage   P = Power   I = Current   R = Resistance
(volts)   (watts   (amps)   (ohms)
           or kilowatts)

Formulas: 1. $V = IR$
                 2. $P = VI$

1000 watts = 1 kilowatt

1 kilowatt = 3,412 BTU/hr (for heating purposes).

1.2 Voltage: Voltage is the potential energy of the electrical system. A large electrical voltage means that a large potential electric force is available. Most houses are equipped with a 120/240-volt system which can provide 240-volts or 120- volts.

Ohms   **1.3 Resistance:** The resistance of any given material to the movement of electricity through it is measured in ohms. When there is effectively no resistance, the current flow is very large. This is referred to as a short circuit. This unsafe situation will blow a fuse or trip a breaker after some time.

Conductors   Good electrical conductors have relatively low resistance. Copper wiring, for example, is a good conductor. Silver is even better, but considerably more expensive. Aluminum is not quite as good a conductor as copper, but it is less expensive. A larger sized aluminum wire is needed to carry the same current as a smaller copper wire.

Insulators   Materials which are very poor conductors have a high resistance and are referred to as insulators. Materials such as wood, rubber, ceramic and most plastics are good insulators. Air is a very good insulator.

Water   Tap water is usually a very good conductor, and that is why water and electricity are dangerous together. Where water comes into contact with live electrical equipment, it can carry the electricity readily to areas it was not intended to go.

Light Bulb   Every electric appliance (for example, a light bulb) has some resistance. When the small wire (filament) inside a light bulb breaks, the light goes out because the circuit has been opened. The air between the pieces of wire which have broken presents a very large resistance. There is no electrical flow and therefore, no light.

Amps   **1.4 Current:**   The current, measured in amps, is the flow of electricity that results when a voltage is applied across a given resistance. Rearranging Formula 1. from Table 1 we can determine the current by dividing the voltage by the resistance (I = V/R).

Electrical Flow   When an appliance is turned on, electricity will flow. The flow of electricity generates heat. The more amps flowing through a circuit, the hotter a given size of wire will get. Since the voltage is fixed at roughly 120 volts, the amount of current that flows will be the result of the resistance in the circuit. If an appliance malfunctions or too many appliances are plugged in, the current flowing through the wire will be more than the wire can safely handle, and the wire will begin to overheat. The fuse or circuit breaker shuts off the electricity at the point when it may overheat the wire.

The Danger   It is the current flowing that electrocutes people. Generally speaking, a current of less than 1 amp is considered capable of killing someone. A 60 watt light bulb normally draws about 1/2 amp. Remember though, the amount of current depends on resistance. Putting a wet finger into a light socket may be enough to kill someone.

Watts   **1.5 Power:**   Power is measured in watts, and is calculated by multiplying the voltage times the current. For example, a 1200 watt hair dryer when subjected to a potential of 120 volts, will allow (I=P/V) 10 amps to flow through it. A house with a 240 volt power supply and 100 amp main fuses may be said to have a capability of (P = VI) 24,000 watts. This is commonly referred to as 24 kilowatts (1 kilowatt is 1000 watts).

Kilowatt-Hours (kWh):   This is a measure of electricity consumption. If 1000 watts are used continuously for one hour, then 1 kilowatt-hour has been consumed. This is how electricity is purchased from the utility. The electric meter records kilowatt hours used in the house. If each kWh costs ten cents and one uses 1000 kWh in a month, the electrical bill for that month would be $100.

1.6 Wire Size (Gauge): The amount of current a wire can carry (in amps) is determined largely by its diameter. A larger wire can carry more current. Normal household circuits are designed to carry 15 amps, and #14-gauge copper wire will do this safely. Table 2 shows common wire sizes and how much current they can safely carry. Notice that aluminum is not as good a conductor of electricity, and a larger wire has to be used to carry the same amount of electricity.

TABLE 2.A
MAXIMUM AMPERAGE FOR COMMON WIRE SIZES
PER NATIONAL ELECTRIC CODE (NEC) - U.S.A.

	Copper			Wire Size	Aluminum or Copper Clad Aluminum		
Temperature Rating	60°C	75°C	90°C		60°C	75°C	90°C
	15	15	15	14			
	20	20	20	12	15	15	15
	30	30	30	10	25	25	25
	40	50	55	8	30	40	45
	55	65	75	6	40	50	60
	70	85	95	4	55	65	75
	85	100	110	3	65	75	85
	95	115	130	2	75	90	100
	110	130	150	1	85	100	115
	125	150	170	1/0	100	120	135
	145	175	195	2/0	115	135	150
	165	200	225	3/0	130	155	175
	195	230	260	4/0	150	180	205
				250 MCM	170	205	230

TABLE 2.B
MAXIMUM AMPERAGE FOR COMMON WIRE SIZES
PER CANADIAN ELECTRICAL CODE (CEC) - CANADA

	Copper			Wire Size	Aluminum or Copper Clad Aluminum		
Temperature Rating	60°C	75°C	90°C		60°C	75°C	85-90°C
	15	15	15	14			
	20	20	20	12	15	15	15
	30	30	30	10	25	25	25
	40	45	45	8	30	30	30
	55*	65	65	6	40	50	55*
	70	85	85	4	55	65	65
	80	100	105	3	65	75	75
	100	115	120	2	75	90	95#
	110	130	140	1	85	100	105
	125	150	155	1/0	100	120	120
	145	175	185	2/0	115	135	145
	165	200	210	3/0	130	155	165
	195	230	235	4/0	155	180	185
				250 MCM	170	205	215

Note:
1. *60 amps permitted for house services and subservices.
2. # 100 amps permitted for house services and subservices.
3. Tables based on 30°c (86°F) ambient temperatures, maximum.
4. Tables based on not more than 3 conductors in cables.
5. Several variations and exceptions exist for these general rules.
6. All wire gauges are AWG (American Wire Gauge) except 250 MCM.
7. Wires up to #10 gauge are solid (single strand). Larger wires are multi-strand.

1.7 Voltage Supplied to Homes (220 - 240): Most homes today are provided with a nominal 240 volt service. (Within the house it is broken down for most appliances to 120 volts.) This is the target voltage set by the utility. Their goal is to have 240 volts available to all houses at all times. At high demand times (around 5:00 pm to 6:00 pm daily, for example), the voltage may drop. In severe cases, a "brown-out" occurs. This is a situation where the utility cannot provide anywhere near 240 volts. In most cases, however, the "slight dips" in voltage are not noticed by the homeowner.

In the 1950's, houses were intended to receive 110/220 volts. This was improved to 115/230-volts in the early 1970's. The target voltages have increased over the years to improve the electrical service available to homeowners.

1.8 Cycles: Alternating current changes direction (or alternates) several times per second. In some areas, until the late 1940's, household electricity was 25 or 50 cycle. This means the current flow reversed its direction 50 or 100 times per second. Since the early 1950's, the system has been exclusively 60 cycles per second. This is an improvement to service, as 25 cycles resulted in lights that flickered more than with the 60 cycle power.

1.9 Household Circuits: A typical household circuit has 120-volts available. A typical wire size (gauge) of #14 is used, and a fuse or circuit breaker rated at 15 amps, controls the circuit. This means the circuit is capable of supplying 1800 watts. If a 1200 watt hair dryer is connected to this circuit, everything would be fine. A current of (I = P/V) 10 amps would flow.

1.10 Circuit Overload: If a second 1200 watt hair dryer is connected to the circuit already drawing 10 amps, what would happen? Roughly 20 amps would be drawn, the wire would heat up, but the 15 amp fuse would eventually blow. This safety device keeps the wire from overheating and causing a fire. If someone had accidentally put in a 30-amp fuse, it would allow the wire to overheat, possibly causing a fire.

It is unfortunate that electricity is not smart enough to know what size wire it is running through, and shut itself off if things start to get too hot. Since it does not do that, we need properly sized fuses or circuit breakers to protect the circuit.

Overcurrent Protection Devices

1.11 Fuses and Breakers: Fuses and breakers are both overcurrent protection devices. They shut off the power when more current is flowing through a circuit than should be. Both fuses and breakers perform the function equally well. The advantage of a circuit breaker is that it can be turned back on after the overload situation is corrected. A fuse has to be replaced.

Time Delay: Many fuses today are type "D". These are time delay devices which do not blow immediately. They will, for a short time, allow more than the rated current to flow through the circuit. (Although regular fuses allow some excess current, type D fuses allow even more.) Since overheating develops with time, this is acceptable in the very short term.

Some electric motors starting up will, for a fraction of a second, draw a great deal of current. With an ordinary fuse, this causes nuisance blowing. This may lead people, out of frustration, to put in an oversized fuse. The time delay feature allows these electrical loads to occur briefly without causing nuisance blowing.

Type "P" Fuses: These fuses have an added safety feature. The low melting temperature of this fuse makes it very sensitive to heat build-up around the fuse, which is not the result of too much current flowing. For example, if the fuse is loose, there may be a poor connection between the fuse itself and the fuse holder. With a current of less than 1-amp, this can lead to overheating and eventually, a fire. A type "P" fuse would blow much sooner than an ordinary fuse.

Type
S and C
Fuses

These special screw-in (plug) fuses are non-interchangeable. This means that the wrong size fuse will not fit into the fuse holder. This provides improved safety over the older fuses which could be interchanged. Modern panelboards incorporate this feature. Type S fuses are not used in Canada.

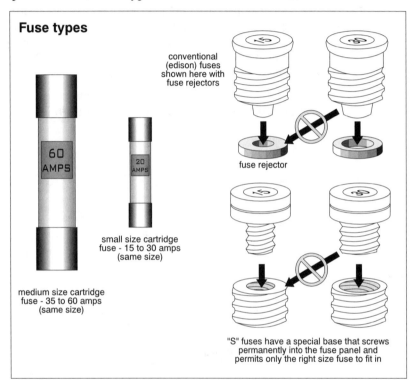

Fuse types

conventional (edison) fuses shown here with fuse rejectors

fuse rejector

small size cartridge fuse - 15 to 30 amps (same size)

medium size cartridge fuse - 35 to 60 amps (same size)

"S" fuses have a special base that screws permanently into the fuse panel and permits only the right size fuse to fit in

Figure 1. Fuses and Breakers

1.12 Damaged Wire: If a wire is nicked or is poorly connected, the wire effectively is smaller and likely to overheat in that area. In this case, a fuse or breaker would not protect the wire against overheating. A normal 10-amp load from a hair dryer could result in overheating and possibly a fire. It is easy to see why damaged wire is a safety hazard.

▶ **2.0 SERVICE ENTRANCE**

2.1. Service Entrance Cable: A typical house has 240-volts, brought in through overhead or underground wires from the street supply. A normal system is composed of three wires. The black and red wires are live, and the white wire is neutral. The potential between the black and white wire is 120-volts, between the red and white is 120-volts, and between the black and red is 240-volts. (Incidentally, the "red" wire often has black sheathing, just to make things confusing). The size of the service entrance cable determines how much electricity is available to the house. Either copper or aluminum cable may be used. Aluminum connections should be coated with an anti-oxidant (grease-like material) to prevent corrosion.

Damaged

Clearance

2.2 Overhead Wires (Service Drop): If the overhead wires appear damaged or frayed, notify your utility. They will often repair or replace these lines without expense to the homeowner. If these wires are less than fifteen feet above ground, or are within three feet (beside or below) of a window or door opening, the utility or an electrician should be consulted. Tree branches should be kept trimmed away from wires.

2.3 Conduit or Cable: The electrical conduit or cable coming down the outside of the house from an overhead service should be well secured to the house and should be arranged so that water cannot enter the conduit or cable. The wires should be kept away from window and door openings and the conduit or cable should be arranged so that the overhead wires are high enough to be out of the way of people and vehicles.

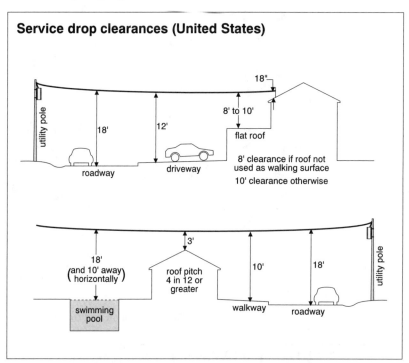

Figure 2a. Service Entrance Equipment

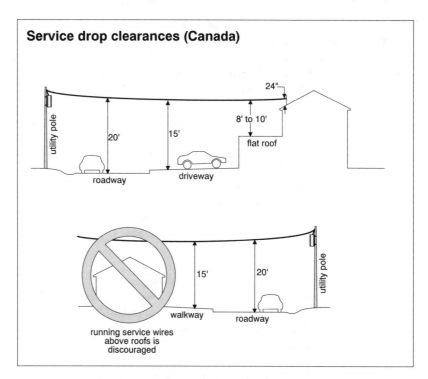

Figure 2b. Service Entrance Equipment

Clearance   Generally speaking, the top of the service mast and the wire itself, should be at least fifteen feet above the ground. A thirty-six inch clearance from windows is generally required. Where the conduit protrudes through a roof covering, it should be flashed to prevent leakage into the roof system, and should go at least eighteen inches above the roof. (Thirty-six inches are required in Canada).

Drip Loop   A drip loop prevents water entering the service conduit. The service wires form a loop below the service head which allows water to drip off the wire, rather than run along it, into the conduit.

Size   The size of the conduit is not a reliable indicator of the electrical service size in the house.

Outside Building   The conduit may be run along the outside of the building for a considerable distance if protected from mechanical damage. Worn or frayed cable which allows water into the service box or panel can cause rust or corrosion. An exposed neutral conductor may be a shock hazard if the service grounding system is defective. Once inside the building, the conduit or cable must be kept as short as possible. Ideally, the service box should be located immediately

Inside Building   at the point where the conduit or cable goes into the house. This avoids exposing the conduit or cable to mechanical damage.

Underground   An underground cable should be at least twenty-four inches deep under normal landscaped areas and at least thirty-six inches deep under driveways or parking areas.

Seal Hole
Through Wall
The conduit should be sealed where it passes through the wall to prevent water and air penetration. It is not unusual for condensation to develop inside service boxes as a result of poor sealing of the electrical conduit where it passes through the wall. This can cause corrosion inside the service box, resulting in an unsafe situation.

2.4 Service Size: As the power enters the house, it goes into a service box which has two fuses or two circuit breakers (sometimes connected together to look like one big breaker). One fuse is for the black wire and one fuse is for the red. No fuse is necessary (or permitted) for the neutral wire. The fuses are rated at the amperage that the wire can safely carry (60-amps, 100-amps, etc.). Where there are two 100-amp fuses in the service box, the house has a 100-amp service. Please note that one cannot add the two fuse ratings together to get the house service. See Table 3 for ratings of various service entrance wires.

While it is best to verify the cable size to determine the service size, this is often not possible. In most cases, the ratings on the main fuses or circuit breakers are taken to reflect the service size accurately. With very few exceptions, this is reliable. The nameplate data on the panelboard or hydro meter is not a reliable service size indicator.

In the U.S., the minimum service size on new work is 100-amps. In Canada, 60-amp services are permitted for houses or residential units up to 800 square feet in floor area. On larger homes, 100-amp service is the minimum.

TABLE 3.

TYPICAL SERVICE ENTRANCE SIZES

Minimum Wire Size U.S.A.		Service Size (amps)	Minimum Wire size Canada	
Copper	Aluminum		Copper	Aluminum
10*	8*	30	10*	8*
6*	6*	60	6	6
6*	4*	70	4*	N/A
4	2	100	3	2
2	1/0	125	2	2/0(1/0)
1/0	2/0	150	1/0	3/0
2/0	4/0	200	3/0	250MCM

Note: 1. *-not found on new work.
2. All wire gauges are AWG except 250 MCM.
3. Several variations are possible, depending on such things as the type of wire, the temperature rating, etc.

Not a Safety Concern

2.5 Larger Service: A house with an electrical service which is too small is not a safety concern, but it is an inconvenience. An electrical service which is marginally sized or undersized may lead to blowing of the main fuses (not the branch circuit fuses in the service panel) or the main breakers. The fuses can be replaced within a few hours by the utility or the breakers can simply be reset by the homeowner. However, this is inconvenient in that the entire house (or at least half of it) will be shut down.

Changing Wires

Increasing the service size may mean replacing the wires coming from the street to the house, installing new conduit, a new meter base and probably providing a new service box. If the wires run overhead, this is not a big problem. If the wires are underground, a problem may present itself. This could mean excavation and replacement.

Meter Location

On old houses, it is often necessary to relocate the service entrance to the side of the house facing the utility lines, so that the meter can easily be accessed by the meter reader. Generally speaking, meters now have to be on an outside wall within three feet of the front wall of the house. Most utilities require the meter to be relocated when upgrading the service.

New Panel

In some cases, enlarging the size of the electrical service will also necessitate replacing the service panel. If the rating of the panel is smaller than the upgraded incoming service, the panel may become overheated under heavy load. It is common to find old houses with 100-amp service boxes with 100-amp fuses, but wire rated for only 70-amps, and a service panel only rated for 70-amps (or 66-amps).

60-amp Service

It should be understood that maximum load occurs only intermittently. There are many houses with 60-amp capacity which provide good service. Normal household lighting and small appliances will not normally draw 60-amps. It is the heavy appliances such as an electric stove, clothes dryer or central air conditioning system that draw 20 or 30-amps each. It is easy to see if three such appliances were in use and other normal house appliances were activated, a 60-amp service would be overloaded. In a small household, it is not difficult to avoid the simultaneous use of an electric stove and an electric clothes dryer. This is more likely to occur with larger families, of course.

Additions and Electric Heat

The amperage drawn by different appliances is outlined in Table 4. A larger service may be necessary where an electrically heated addition is to be built. The same would apply for electrically heated finished attic spaces or finished basements. Depending on how much additional capacity is available, a larger service may be needed.

TABLE 4.

TYPICAL POWER AND CURRENT FOR HOUSEHOLD APPLIANCES

	Typical Watts	Amps
Stove and oven (all burners and oven on)	9,600	40
Clothes dryer	5,000	20
Central air conditioner	5,000	20
Electric water heater	3,000	12.5
Kettle	1,500	12.5
Toaster	1,200	10
Microwave oven	1,500	12.5
Electric frying pan	1,200	10
Coffee maker	1,200	10
Dishwasher	1,200	10
Iron	1,000	8.5
Portable electric heater	1,500	12.5
Room air conditioner	1,200	10
Central vacuum system	1,500	12.5
Hair dryer	1,200	10
Portable vacuum cleaner	800	7
Clothes washer	500	4
Furnace fan	250	2
Trash compactor	500	4
Blender	360	3
Refrigerator/freezer	500	4
Food waste disposal	500	4
Waterbed heater	400	3.5
Color T.V.	360	3
Video cassette recorder	120	1
Stereo	120	1
Electric blanket	180	1.5
60 watt lightbulb	60	0.5
1/4 horsepower motor	700	6
1/2 horsepower motor	1000	8

Note: Watts and amps vary with appliance size and manufacturer.

30-amp Service/120 Volt Service

30-amp services are not considered adequate for modern lifestyles and should be replaced. Similarly, 120-volt services are generally inadequate and again, should be upgraded.

2.6 Service Box: The service box includes a circuit breaker which can be used to shut off all the power in the house, or a switch with a handle located on the outside, and the service fuses inside. The cover on the service box is often sealed by the utility.

The service box may stand alone, although in modern homes, the service breaker is often incorporated into the service panel. In either case, it is important that the rating on the box itself, is at least as large as the service entrance cables and fuses or breakers inside. For example, if a house has service entrance wire and fuses rated for 100-amps, a box rated for only 60-amps is not acceptable. More than 60- amps flowing through this box may lead to overheating.

Every home should have a disconnect means so the system can be shut off. Working on a live electrical system is very dangerous. In the U.S. (and in some Canadian situations), it is permitted on existing installations to have up to six switches to disconnect all the house power.

In the 1950's, a 50/70-amp service box was used in some areas. This is a circuit breaker type disconnect which may be considered equivalent to a 60-amp disconnect. If equal amounts of current are flowing through the black and red wire, the breaker will trip at 50-amps. This situation is referred to as a "balanced load". If there is more current flowing through one of the main wires than the other (an unbalanced load), the breaker will trip when one wire is carrying roughly 70-amps.

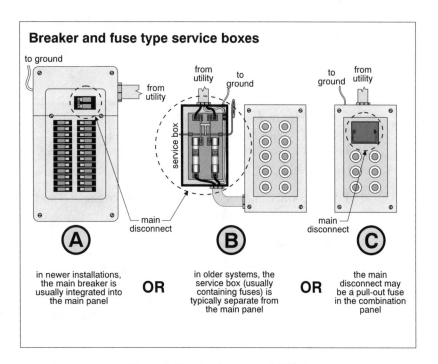

Figure 3. Service Boxes and Panels

In a conventional 60-amp service with circuit breakers, the breakers will trip when the current in either leg reaches 60-amps. Where fuses are used in the main service box, each fuse works independently. If more than 60-amps flows through one fuse it will blow. This leaves roughly half the house without power, including part of the electric stove, for example. If more than 60-amps flows through the other fuse, it too will blow, leaving the entire house without power. See Table 4 for the watts and amps used in household appliances.

Damaged or
Undersized

2.6.1 Main Switch or Circuit Breaker: If the main switch is inoperative, or if the box is corroded or damaged, it should be replaced. A service box which is rated at a smaller amperage than the main fuses or breakers should also be replaced. This is very rare.

Sealed by
the Utility

Most modern systems have the main breaker incorporated into the service panel. Separate service boxes may be sealed by the utility. These cannot be opened by the homeowner or home inspector. The seals are provided for two reasons. The first reason is safety. There is live electrical power inside this box, even if the main switch or breaker is shut off. Under no circumstances, should the homeowner attempt to work inside this box or change the main fuses or breakers.

The second reason for the seal is that the service box is often located upstream of the meter. The seal discourages people from trying to steal electricity by taking power from the service box without having it go through the meter. If there is a seal on the service box which appears to be very old, it may be wise to contact your local utility and ask them to ensure that the switch is in good operating order.

House Power
Left on

The main switch or breaker is not normally shut off during a home inspection, since it would shut down the entire house. This can disrupt clocks, timers and computers, for example, and can result in damage to some motors and compressors. However, once a homeowner takes possession, he or she should ensure that it does operate properly.

Size

2.6.2 Main Fuses/Breakers: If improperly sized, the main fuses or breakers would have to be replaced. Similarly, if one or both of the fuses are blown, replacement of the fuses is necessary. Fuses cannot be tested without destroying them.

Poor
Connections

Poorly connected fuses should be better connected and in some cases it is necessary to replace the service box itself.

TABLE 5.

**WIRE SIZES AND FUSE OR BREAKER SIZES
FOR ELECTRIC HEATING**

Heater Rating	Voltage	Minimum Wire Size		Maximum Fuse Size
		COPPER	ALUMINUM	
500 watts	120	14	12	15
1000 watts	120	14	12	15
2000 watts	240	14	12	15
5000 watts	240	10	8	30

Fuses should be Type P or D.

Both Fuses Same Size

The two main fuses should be the same size. Where they are different sizes, an electrician should be engaged and the correct size provided. The main breakers should be linked together or provided with a single handle so that both must be shut off together.

2.7 System Grounding: Grounding has always been required on all residential electrical systems. Up until approximately 1960 it was required only on the service panel. Subsequent to 1960, it has been used on all branch circuits, including lights and electrical outlets. A ground wire is a wire that connects an electrical system to ground. Ground is a safe place to dispose of unwanted electricity.

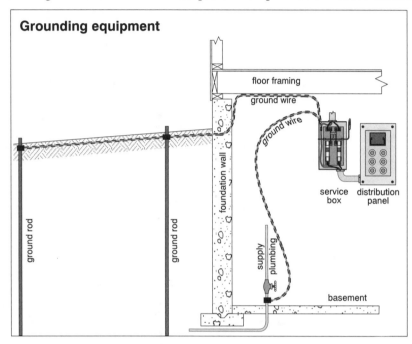

Grounding equipment

floor framing

ground wire

ground wire

foundation wall

service box   distribution panel

ground rod

ground rod

supply plumbing

basement

Figure 4. Grounding to Water Supply Piping

Generally speaking, the grounding wires are connected (via bonding wires) to those metallic parts of an electrical system that are not supposed to carry electricity. These metal components, however, are close to things where electricity is present, and it is recognized that if something goes wrong, the outside of a metal cabinet could become live. Bonding the ground wire to this metal cabinet ensures that if something does go wrong and someone touches the cabinet, he or she will not get a shock. Checking the quality of the grounding system is beyond the scope of a home inspection. The ground wire, the service box, and neutral wire are all electrically bonded together, at the box.

In most houses the electrical system is grounded to the water supply piping. In the U.S. since 1987, a driven ground rod is required in addition. Ideally, the ground wire should be connected to the supply piping near its point of entry into the house. If connected downstream of the water meter, a jumper wire should be provided across the meter.

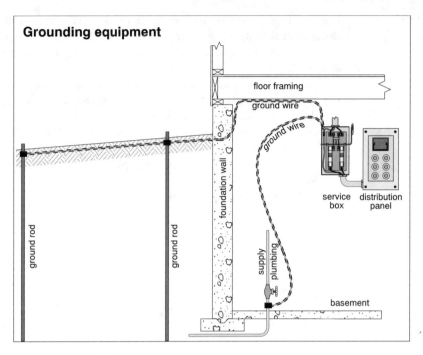

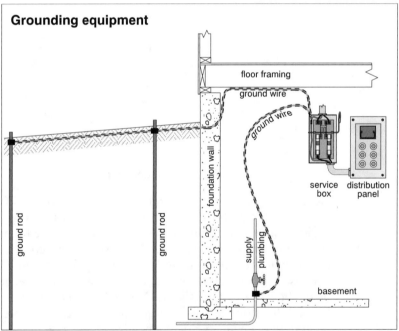

Figure 5. Grounding Equipment

Ground Rods In some cases, grounding to the water system is not effective. Where plastic supply piping is used, for example, alternative grounding system must be arranged. In Canada, this is accomplished with two metal rods, driven into the ground. In the U.S. a single ground rod is used.

Ufer Ground   Although uncommon, other grounding configurations may be found where typical methods are not possible. Ufer grounds (concrete encased electrodes) use a long copper wire or bar encased in the concrete footing. Plate and ring electrodes consist of a metal plate or ring of wire buried in the ground. None of these is visible and they are not evaluated during a home inspection.

Ground Wire Sizes   In Canada, #8 gauge wire is used for electrical services up to 100-amps, #6 gauge for 101 to 125-amps, #4 gauge for 125 to 165-amps, and #3 gauge for up to 200-amps. In the U.S., a #8 gauge wire is used for services up to 125-amps, and #6 gauge for up to 175-amps and #4 gauge for 200-amps. Where grounding is to a rod, #6 gauge copper is the largest required. Bare aluminum is not considered acceptable as a ground wire since it is subject to severe corrosion when exposed to moisture. Aluminum ground wire must be one size larger. In Canada, aluminum is not allowed as a system grounding conductor.

Missing

2.7.1 Grounding Problems:

    The system ground is missing in some cases. It may have been omitted from the original installation, or removed during amateurish electrical or plumbing rearrangement; or the original ground may have been left behind when the service panel was relocated. Adding a new ground wire is not difficult or expensive. Checking the quality of the grounding system is beyond the scope of a home inspection.

Lack of Bonding   The ground wire, the service box, and the neutral wire are often not electrically bonded at the service box. This situation should be corrected promptly.

Ineffective Grounding   The system ground may be ineffective. If the connections are poor, the quality of ground is suspect. If there is a splice in the ground wire, a potentially weak connection exists. Ground wires are sometimes ineffective because they are secured to pipes which are no longer in service. This is common on galvanized steel supply pipes which are abandoned. If the plumber does not move the ground wire over to the new piping, the grounding system will be defeated.

Ground Rods   Where the plumbing system is partially plastic piping (often at its point of entry into the house), grounding to the plumbing system is not acceptable. Grounding to buried rods is the correct solution. In Canada two rods, each ten feet long are buried in the ground, about ten feet apart. They are bonded by copper wire and the ground wire is connected to one of the rods. These rods may be below the basement floor. In the U.S., a single eight foot ground rod of copper or stainless steel is used. The top of the rods and the connection points of the wire to the rods, should be one foot below grade.

Jumper Around Meter   If there is a water meter on the plumbing system, the grounding may not be effective if the ground wire is connected to the plumbing downstream of the water meter. This can be corrected by relocating the ground wire upstream of the meter, or providing a jumper wire around the meter .

Di-electric Connections   Some piping connections are a special di-electric type, intended to prevent oxidization where two different metals are joined. These special connectors remove the metal-to-metal contact, and interrupt the continuity of any ground wire connected downstream. The ground wire should be relocated upstream of any di-electric connector.

► 3.0 SERVICE PANEL

3.1 Panel Description: Electricity is carried from the service box to the service panel. The black and red wires are each connected to a live busbar (a current carrying metal bar with several connection points) and the white wire is connected to the neutral busbar. Each branch circuit fuse (or breaker) is directly connected to either the red or black busbar.

Location

Panelboards are not allowed in clothes closets or areas where there are flammable liquids (U.S.A.). In Canada, panels are not allowed in clothes closets, bathrooms, stairways, or kitchen cabinets.

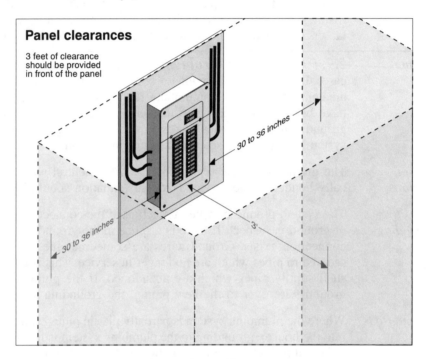

Panel clearances

3 feet of clearance should be provided in front of the panel

30 to 36 inches

30 to 36 inches

3'

Figure 6. Panel Clearances

Typical Household Circuit

The black or red branch circuit wire for an individual circuit is connected to its own small fuse (or breaker). The current flows from the black or red (usually the "red" wire is also black) service entrance wire, through the service box, to the panel, through the busbar, through the fuse or breaker, and into the black or red wire for the circuit. The current goes out, completes its circuit, running through whatever fixtures or appliances are in use on the circuit, and comes back through the white wire. The white circuit wire is connected to the neutral bar, which is attached to the service entrance white wire. It doesn't matter whether power is taken from the black or the red busbar. The result is the same; a 120-volt distribution circuit has been established. The fuse (or breaker) for this circuit is typically 15-amps and the wire is typically #14-gauge copper.

Number of Circuits

The service panel has several 120-volt circuits (at least sixteen are required for most homes) and one or more 240-volt circuits for large electric appliances. Many codes now require a panel with room for twenty-four or more 120-volt circuits.

Damaged or Loose

3.1.1 Damaged/Loose Panel:
Where the panel is damaged mechanically or by water, it should be replaced. Poorly secured panels should be resecured to the wall. Old ceramic fuseholders, which may or may not be in a metal cabinet, are considered obsolete and unsafe. These should be replaced. These panels, which may be found on walls or ceilings, have exposed terminal connections, and it is very easy to accidentally touch a live wire while changing a fuse.

3.1.2 Panel Overcurrent Protection (Undersized Panel):
Typically, the panel rating is the same as or larger than the service size and the rating of the main fuses or circuit breakers. Where the panel rating is smaller, the panel must be replaced with a larger one suitable for the incoming service size. Alternatively, the main fuses or breakers could be downsized.

3.1.3 Room for More Circuits in Panel:
It is desirable to have room to add more circuits in any panel. If there is no room, an auxiliary panel can be added in most cases. Recognizing the need for growing electrical demands, new homes are required to have room for at least two extra circuits in their panel. When upgrading to a 100-amp service, many jurisdictions require a panel which can accommodate twenty-four or more circuits.

3.2 Auxiliary Panel (Sub-panel):
In many homes, when the service panel was filled, an auxiliary panel was added. This does not bring more power into the house; it simply allows for more branch circuits to carry electricity to more areas of the house. Over the years, it is not unusual to find more than one auxiliary panel added.

3.2.1 Auxiliary Panel Problems:

Feed Wire

Where an auxiliary panel is used, the wire running from the service panel to the auxiliary should be protected by overcurrent devices in the service panel. For example, a 60-amp auxiliary panel should be provided with #6-gauge copper wire. This wire running from the service panel to the auxiliary should have 60-amp fuses or a double pole breaker located at the service panel. It is slightly less desirable, although acceptable, to provide 60-amp fuses at the auxiliary panel end of this wire, as long as the wire does not exceed five feet in length and is in a metal conduit. On very small auxiliary panels, no overcurrent protection device may be needed at the service panel.

Doubled-up Circuits (Double-taps, Double-lugs)

In some cases, circuits in the panel are doubled by adding another wire to the terminal screw. This is not permitted unless a special connector, designed to hold two wires, is provided. Securing three wires under one terminal screw is never acceptable.

In many cases, an auxiliary panel may be adequate as a corrective measure. It is wise to install an auxiliary panel slightly larger than what is needed immediately, in anticipation of future electrical demands.

Where the service panel has fuses, and circuit breakers are considered desirable, or where the service panel is in suspect condition, it may be best (although more expensive) to replace the service panel with a larger circuit breaker panel. Again, there should be enough room in the new panel to add more circuits. A twenty-four circuit panel is typical.

Bonding

The ground wire and neutral wire should not be bonded in an auxiliary panel.

3.3 Fuses and Breakers: Fuses and breakers perform the same function. The advantage of a circuit breaker is that it can be turned back on after the overload situation is corrected. A fuse has to be replaced. When a new fuse is put in or the circuit breaker is reset, if the overload situation has not been corrected, the circuit will trip again. While it is a nuisance to have to reset a breaker, it is more of a nuisance to have to replace a fuse, particularly if a spare is not available.

Dangerous Practices

Practices such as wrapping a blown fuse with foil or putting a penny in a fuse block, are foolish and may result in a major fire.

Overfusing

One other disadvantage of fuses is that it is possible to put in a wrong size. It is unfortunate that 15, 20, 25 and 30-amp fuses all fit into the same fuse block. Circuit breakers are typically not changed by the homeowner and are less likely to be incorrectly sized.

Which Circuit Is Off?

Most circuit breakers trip by moving the switch to the middle position, others simply switch to the off position. It is usually very easy to see which circuit breaker has tripped. The circuit is re-activated by simply "switching" the breaker off and on again. With fuses, it is not always easy to see which one has blown. On the glass type fuses, you can usually see if you look closely through the glass, but on a cartridge type fuse it is often very difficult to know.

Testing

Some electricians prefer fuses because a circuit breaker is a mechanical device which can fail. While this is true, circuit breakers can be tested; that is, switched to the off position, or subjected to current flow beyond their rating. A fuse can be manufactured incorrectly, with a fusible link which is not the correct size. A fuse cannot be tested without destroying it.

Fuse Rejectors

One of the safety devices available for fuses is a fuse rejector washer. This is a small plastic ring which is retrofitted into the fuse block. Depending on its size, this fuse rejector can prevent the wrong sized fuse from being screwed into the fuse block. Modern panelboards have a fuse rejection feature that prevents inserting a larger size fuse than intended.

Overfusing

3.3.1 Fuse/Breaker Problems: The most common electrical flaw found residentially is fuses which are the wrong size for the circuit wire. This is an unsafe condition and should be corrected promptly. Table 2 indicates the appropriate size of fuse for the given wire sizes. As a very coarse rule of thumb, stoves have 40-amp fuses, dryers and air conditioners have 30-amp fuses, and general household circuits have 15-amps. There are a multitude of exceptions to these rules.

Damaged or Loose Components

A broken or damaged fuse holder or circuit breaker should be replaced. Poorly secured fuse holders or circuit breakers should be resecured or replaced as necessary.

3.4 240-Volt Circuits: Heavy duty appliances, such as electric ranges and stoves, clothes dryers, air conditioners and water heaters, use 240-volts. Here, the black wire and red wire are both used in the circuit. For some of these appliances, a white neutral wire is also used. Three wires run to the appliance instead of two. Two fuses (or breakers) are needed; one for the black wire, and one for the red wire. These two fuses (or breakers) should be the same size, and should be linked so that if one is pulled out, the other must be pulled out with it. This is a safety feature in the event that people forget that these appliances have two fuses. If only one fuse were removed, there would still be power to the appliance. It would not be safe to work on the system. (With breakers, a handle tie is used, so that if one breaker is off, the other must be off too. Alternatively, a single throw double pole breaker can be used).

3.5 Linking Circuits: Linking is used to ensure two fuses or breakers are disconnected at the same time. The overcurrent protection devices (fuses or breakers) for any circuit with more than one powered connection must cut power to both legs simultaneously. This includes 240-volt appliances, such as an electric stove, clothes dryer, water heater, or large air conditioner. This also includes cable used for some electric heaters, split kitchen receptacles, (top and bottom halves of outlet are on different circuits), et cetera.

Pull-Out Fuse Holders

It should not be possible to pull out one fuse without pulling out the other one of the pair. Similarly, it should not be possible to switch off one circuit breaker without switching off the other. With breakers, this can be accomplished with a tie handle which mechanically joins two breaker handles, or preferably, a double pole breaker with a single throw handle. This is important where three wire cable is used, because shutting off one fuse or breaker will leave power to an appliance through the second live wire, although the person intending to work on it thinks all the power is shut off.

Damaged

3.6 Panel Wires: Damaged wires inside the box should be replaced or repaired promptly. Wires can be damaged by pinching them with the cover plate, damaging them as they are pulled through the cable holes coming into the box, or through careless work in the box.

Overheated

Overheated cables or evidence of arcing should be investigated by an electrician; not only should the cable be repaired or replaced, but the source of the overheating should be identified. Looking at a cable, it is difficult to tell whether overheating was a one-time situation or whether it is an ongoing intermittent problem. **This requires immediate attention by an electrician.**

Loose

Wires should be secured in place where they pass through the walls of the box. If the wire outside the box is pulled, the connection itself inside the box will not be pulled loose. Where the wire has not been secured, it should be done.

Missing Damaged or Loose

3.7 Panel Cover Plate: Missing or damaged cover plates should be replaced. Cover plates poorly secured should be resecured. Great care should be taken in removing and replacing cover plates and, ideally, the power should be disconnected prior to removing the cover plate.

3.8 Unprotected Panel Openings: Where the panel does have room for more circuits, or where a fuse block has no fuse, there may be a situation where a person could inadvertently touch a live electrical component. Wherever this situation exists, the opening should be covered or fitted with a fuse. Installing a blown fuse on a spare circuit to fill an opening in the panel is acceptable.

3.9 Abandoned Wire in Panel: It is not considered good electrical practice to abandon wires and leave them loose inside the panel.

Abandoned wires should be removed or appropriately terminated so that there is no chance of them contacting a live electrical component.

3.10 Access to Panel: The panel should be accessible with the center of the panel roughly five-and-one-half feet above the floor. Some panels may be mounted upside down. The three foot area in front of the panel should be kept clear.

3.11 Connections: Loose connections may lead to overheating, arcing, or short circuits. It is often difficult to notice a loose connection during a visual inspection, but where noted, it should be addressed promptly.

► **4.0 BRANCH CIRCUIT WIRING**

4.1 Branch Circuit Wire: The wire used to carry electricity from the panels to the fixtures and appliances is typically copper. Each piece of cable is made up of two conductors and one ground wire. The copper conductors are wrapped with insulation, usually rubber or plastic. The ground wire is not insulated. This group of three wires is wrapped in a sheathing which may be paper, cloth, rubber, plastic or metal.

Black and White Wire　One conductor has black insulation and is usually the live or hot wire. The other conductor has white insulation and is referred to as the neutral. Neither wire should be touched when there is power to the circuit. When electricity flows under normal circumstances, the black and white wires carry the current. The voltage available is 120-volts, and the current flow is less than 15-amps.

Ground Wire　The ground wire is normally idle. If there is a problem, the ground acts as an escape route for the electricity, inducing the current to flow through this wire to the ground, rather than into a person, causing an electrical shock. Grounded distribution wiring was introduced to residential electric systems in the late 1950's.

Three Conductor Cable　Some special circuit wiring has an additional live or hot wire. It is color coded red and is included where more power is needed. For example, 240-volt appliances such as stoves and electric clothes dryers use three-conductor plus ground cable. Split kitchen receptacles also use three-conductor plus ground cable, to effectively create two 120-volt circuits.

Wire Gauge　The normal wire size is #14-gauge. This is capable of carrying 15-amps safely. A fuse or circuit breaker rated at 15-amps should always be provided on a #14-gauge copper circuit to shut off the power if more than 15-amps flows. In some regions, 20-amp circuits may serve kitchen or other outlets. The wire size for these circuits should be #12-gauge. If no fuse or breaker were present, the wire would try to carry more current, but would overheat, eventually starting a fire. See Table 2 and Section 3.3.

Damaged

4.1.1 Wire Problems: Wire which is damaged mechanically or as a result of overheating should be replaced. Wire which is nicked, for example, is effectively smaller in diameter at that spot. The smaller the wire diameter, the more difficult it is for electricity to move through. (The resistance is higher.) This can lead to localized overheating, and eventually a fire.

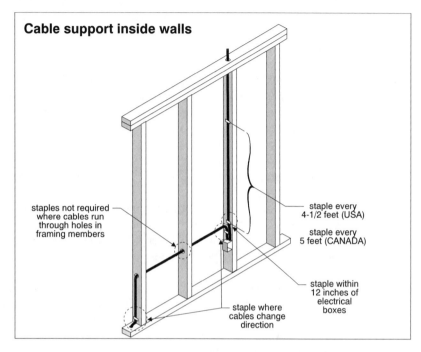

Cable support inside walls

staples not required where cables run through holes in framing members

staple every 4-1/2 feet (USA)

staple every 5 feet (CANADA)

staple within 12 inches of electrical boxes

staple where cables change direction

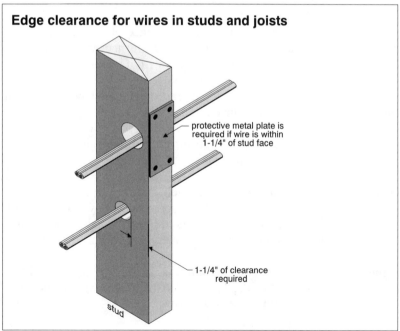

Edge clearance for wires in studs and joists

protective metal plate is required if wire is within 1-1/4" of stud face

1-1/4" of clearance required

stud

Figure 7. Cable Support and Protection

Bushings Wire should be protected from the metal edges of panels and boxes. This is usually done with bushings, grommets or cable clamps.

Loose Wiring which is poorly secured should be resecured as necessary. The wire should be secured where it enters a panel, junction box or fixture. The wire is again secured within twelve inches of the box, and every four and-a-half (USA) or five feet (Canada) thereafter. If cable staples are used, only one wire should be secured under each staple. Staples should be the appropriate size for the wire.

Exposed to Damage Wires should not be exposed to mechanical damage. Wire should be run through joists in unfinished basements, rather than secured to the underside. Care must be taken when drilling wood structural members to avoid weakening them. Where wires are run through studs or other framing members into which nails may be driven, the wire should be set well back from any nailing surface, to avoid a nail being driven into the wire. Alternatively, steel plates should be used to protect the wire from nails or screws. See Figure 7.

Exposed in Attic Ideally, the joists should be drilled and the cables should be run through them. Although very common, it is considered poor practice to secure the cable to the top of the joists or to the lower side of the rafters if the joist-to-rafter clearance is more than thirty-six inches.

Damaged Insulation The insulation on wiring is often gnawed on by rodents. Mice and squirrels in the attic, for example, can damage wiring insulation and create a very real fire hazard. This is often difficult to detect without pulling back the attic thermal insulation. Where pests are known to have been in a home, it is wise to call in an electrician to inspect the wiring.

Surface Wiring Where wiring is run on the surface of walls, baseboards or other interior finishes, it should be protected from mechanical damage with a rigid covering. Alternatively, flexible metal or rigid metal cables can be used.

Ducts and Piping Wiring should be kept at least one inch away from heating ducts and hot water piping. Thermal insulation can be used to separate these materials.

Undersized Wire which is too small for the appliance it serves or for the rest of the circuit wiring should, of course, be replaced.

Junction Box Connections made in branch circuit wiring should be inside junction boxes. Where these boxes are not provided, they should be added, and where cover plates are missing, they should be provided. The only exception to this is the original knob-and-tube connections, which may be acceptable if undisturbed.

Extension Cords Extension cords should not be used as permanent wiring, and should never be stapled to walls, floors or trim. Cords should not run under carpets or go through doorways or windows.

Abandoned Wiring Wires which are not in use should be removed or the wire ends should be terminated in junction boxes.

Exterior Wiring

Exterior wiring should be of a type suitable for outdoor use (typically NMW cable). Exterior wiring should be protected from mechanical damage and special exterior junction boxes are required. Note: Solid conductors (#10 gauge and smaller) cannot be run overhead for fear of fatiguing the metal.

4.2 Overloaded Circuits: While it is difficult to tell from a typical visual inspection, the number of lights and outlets on any given branch circuit should be such that the circuit will not draw more than 15-amps under normal circumstances. At a maximum, twelve outlets may be connected to each circuit. The practical limitation, however, is if one of the outlets is used for a hair dryer which may draw 10-amps, it is probably wise to connect the circuit only to other outlets which will be used for very low drawing appliances such as clocks, radios or lights. Generally speaking, a circuit should have a combination of electrical outlets and lights.

4.3 Dedicated Circuits: Some appliances require a dedicated circuit. That is a circuit where only one appliance is to be connected. This includes the furnace or boiler, dishwasher, food waste disposal, compactor, central vacuum system, refrigerator, freezer, washing machine, whirlpool, and electric heaters. Split receptacles (outlets where the top and bottom halves are on separate circuits) are also usually on dedicated circuits.

A home inspection will not normally reveal which circuits are dedicated. These are determined when the electrical circuits are labelled.

Not a Safety Concern

Dedicated circuits are rare in older houses and it is very difficult to verify during a visual inspection. It is not a major expense to rearrange this, and the danger is not one of life safety, simply of convenience. Without dedicated circuits for each of these appliances, there is the possibility of nuisance fuse blowing or circuit breaker tripping with several appliances in use simultaneously.

Fridge and Freezer

The reason a refrigerator or freezer gets a dedicated circuit is to prevent food spoilage. If it is on a circuit with other appliances, the fuse may be blown as a result of a problem with another appliance. The fuse may not be replaced immediately, if the home owner doesn't know that the refrigerator or freezer is also on this circuit. As a result, food may be spoiled.

Furnace or Boiler

It is for a similar reason that a furnace should be on a dedicated circuit. If the circuit has an overload due to another appliance, the house will be without heat. This can result in freezing if the home is unoccupied for some time.

Heavy Current Draw

The other dedicated circuits are so arranged because the heavy electrical draw from the appliances uses most of the 15-amps available to that circuit. Putting additional outlets and lights on the circuit may lead to regular shut-downs.

4.4 Knob-and-Tube: Knob-and-tube wiring was used residentially until approximately 1950. While different than the wiring that is used now, it is not necessarily an inferior wire. This wire gets its name from the ceramic knobs by which it is secured and the ceramic tubes which are used where the wires pass through wood-framing members, such as joists.

*Separate
Black and
White*

The main difference between this system and modern cable, is that the black wire and the white wire run separately, independent of each other. In modern cables, the black wire, white wire (and ground wire) are all wrapped up in a single cable. With knob-and-tube wiring, it took roughly twice as long to wire a house, since every light fixture and outlet had to have a black wire and a white wire run to it. Today, running a single cable provides a black and a white (and a ground wire). It was felt originally, that having the black wire and white wire separate was safer, since there was very little chance of the black and white wires ever touching, creating a short circuit. This has not proved to be a big problem with modern cables.

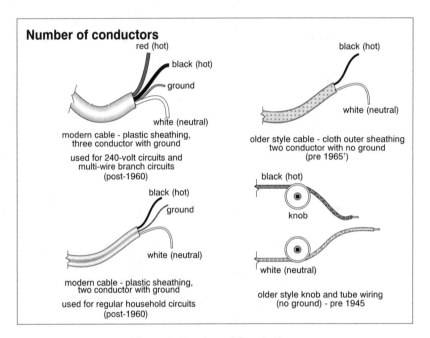

Figure 8. Number of Conductors

*No Junction
Boxes*

Another difference between knob-and-tube wiring and modern cable is that with knob-and-tube wiring, electrical junction boxes were not used wherever wires were joined together. In modern construction, any time two wires are joined, the connection must be made inside a closed metal box. Knob-and-tube connections were made by twisting the wiring together, soldering the wires, and wrapping the connection in rubber, then in electrical tape. While no longer a common practice, if properly done, these connections will serve indefinitely. Most modern attempts at these connections are woefully inadequate. They are, of course, more susceptible to mechanical damage than modern connections inside boxes.

*Wire
Insulation*

Another distinction between knob-and-tube wiring and some modern cables is in the insulation. The knob-and-tube wiring used rubber and cloth insulation around the wiring. In modern cables, each wire has plastic insulation typically, and the entire cable is wrapped with another layer of plastic. Over the years, these sheathing materials have included cloth, paper, rubber, metal and plastic.

*Brittle
Insulation*

Breakdown of the insulation on knob-and-tube wiring is most often the reason it has to be replaced. This is frequently the result of overheating or mechanical abuse.

No Ground Wire

One last difference between knob-and-tube wiring and some modern cable is the absence of a ground wire. As mentioned earlier, knob-and-tube wiring was used up until 1950. From the 1950's to 1960, two conductor cable was popular although no ground wire was included. In approximately 1960, ground wires began to be incorporated into the two conductor cable, and electrical receptacles included a third hole (U-ground) thereafter.

Replacement

While knob-and-tube wiring must be recognized as old, it is not necessary to replace it as a matter of course. It should be inspected and evaluated on an individual basis.

Poor Connections

4.4.1 Knob-and-Tube Wire Problems: Problems with knob-and-tube wire almost always result from amateurish connections made after original installation. Since original connections were made without junction boxes, many home owners feel that they can make connections to knob-and-tube wiring without junction boxes, as well. This is an unsafe practice, particularly since the chance of making a splice as good as the original connection is very remote. In any case, this violates modern electrical codes.

Since knob-and-tube wiring is invariably old, it has been subjected to more home handymen, mechanical abuse (such as skis, lumber, etc. stored on top of the wire in the basement), and is more likely to have suffered wear and tear. Pinched wiring and damaged insulation is a problem, particularly in unfinished basements, where the wiring is exposed.

Brittle

Another problem with knob-and-tube wiring is, if the wire has overheated in the past as a result of overfusing, a poor connection or damaged cable, the insulation may become brittle. Flexing the knob-and-tube wire will give some indication as to whether it has become brittle, although this can be a dangerous practice. It is not recommended that this be done by a lay person. Often the wire becomes brittle in areas where heat builds up, such as in panelboards. In exposed areas, where inspection is easy, there is usually good air circulation, and little heat build-up. The wires are least likely to be brittle in these areas.

Circuits Extended

Since older electrical systems had few circuits by today's standards, the chances of a knob-and-tube circuit having been extended over the years are very good. The additional loads and the possibilities of poor connections do create an argument for replacing older knob-and-tube wiring.

Replacement

While it is typically not necessary to pull out all old knob-and-tube wiring and replace it, it is common to remove the sections exposed when renovations are undertaken. For example, when basements are finished, the readily accessible knob-and-tube wiring at the basement ceiling level could be replaced prior to adding a ceiling finish. The wiring running up through the walls to the first and second floors, however, is usually not changed. This is considered acceptable, as long as the wire is in good repair.

Insurance Difficulties

In 1996, many insurance companies began to get nervous about knob-and-tube wiring. We think unduly so. Some companies will only grant insurance after an inspection and approval by the local authorities. Many companies will not offer insurance on houses with knob-and-tube wiring.

Two Fuse Circuits (Fused Neutrals)

Another problem specific to knob-and-tube wiring is the presence of two fuses on a single circuit. Both the black and white wires have fuses on some very old panels. If the fuse on the neutral wire blows, the circuit will be open, and fixtures and appliances on this circuit will not be operative. It is not safe, however, to work on the circuit! Power is still available through the circuit, right up to the blown fuse. A person touching the circuit may well be grounded and could provide a path for electricity to flow. The person would get a shock in this case. In all modern systems, there is only one fuse for each circuit leg. The fuse must be located at the source of the circuit, where the live (black) wire is connected to the panel.

4.5 Aluminum Wire: Aluminum wiring was commonly used from the late 1960's until about 1978. It was introduced because it was less expensive than copper. It was recognized from the beginning that aluminum wiring is not quite as good a conductor of electricity as is copper. Therefore, for a conventional 15-amp household circuit, for example, #12-gauge aluminum was used in place of #14-gauge copper. Other wire sizes were also suitably increased.

Thermal Expansion

Some other properties of aluminum, however, were not recognized and did cause some difficulties. Firstly, aluminum has a higher co-efficient of thermal expansion than copper. This means that when the wire heats up (as all wire does when electricity passes through) the aluminum tends to expand more than copper. This leads to the wire trying to move out from under the terminal screws. This phenomenon is called "creep" and can lead to poor connections and subsequent overheating.

Soft

Secondly, aluminum is softer than copper, and electricians used to working with copper would often nick aluminum wiring inadvertently. Nicking the wire, of course, reduces its diameter, and its ability to carry electricity safely. Localized hot spots can develop where the wire has been nicked. Further, if the wire is bent after it has been nicked, it will often break.

Insulating Oxide

Lastly, the oxide of aluminum that forms on the wire is a very poor electrical conductor. All metals rust or oxidize to some degree. The greenish copper oxide that forms on copper wiring does not result in a problem. The oxide that forms as aluminum corrodes, can lead to higher resistance and higher temperatures.

Cu-Al CO/ALR and COPALUM

As a result of these difficulties, special components, designated Cu-Al, were produced. These included wire connectors (wire nuts), electrical receptacles, circuit breakers, stove blocks, etc. In most cases, these improvements were found to be satisfactory. However, electrical receptacles continued to be a problem. The subsequently designed receptacles, and those that are now required, were designated CO/ALR. See Figure 9.

COPALUM connectors, used in the U.S.A., are specially designed to join aluminum wire to copper. The copper wire is then attached to a standard receptacle, switch, etc.

Acceptable

As long as proper connectors are used, and the connections are made without damaging the wire, aluminum wiring is considered safe. It is permitted for use by many electrical codes, although it is not commonly used in homes due to the adverse publicity it received during its early problem years. It is still used commonly by utilities in street wiring and for service entrance cables.

Connectors

4.5.1 Aluminum Wire Problems: Where aluminum wire exists, and special connectors have not been provided, they should be added. In some cases it is difficult to know whether the connectors are appropriate. The safest thing is to replace them with those known to be appropriate. For example, the small solderless type connectors (e.g. wire nuts) are so small that they are not marked Cu-Al. They are now color coded, but on older ones it is difficult to know whether or not they are appropriate. Since they only cost a few cents each, it makes sense to replace them with those known to be the correct type.

Cu-Al and CO/ALR

Electrical outlets should be replaced with those designated CO/ALR. Service panels and their components, and other connectors designated by the utility should be replaced with components designated Cu-Al.

Pig-tails

One alternative to using special connectors is to join the aluminum wires to short "pig-tails" of copper wire just before they connect to outlets, distribution panel terminals, et cetera. The connection between the aluminum and copper wire is made with a connector known to be appropriate. This is not recommended for two reasons. First, every connection added to an electrical system is one more potential problem area. Second, in some cases, the addition of one more connection in a junction box can lead to an overcrowding situation. However, the COPALUM system is an acceptable way to enhance the safety of aluminum wires.

COPALUM

Summary

In summary, the provision of the special connectors is not an expensive undertaking (usually a few hundred dollars if done by an electrician) and is well worthwhile. In many areas, the utility will inspect a house with aluminum wiring. Where there is evidence of a problem, they will insist that any dangerous flaws be corrected. However, this can hardly be considered a disadvantage, since a safe electrical system should be a priority for any homeowner. Where there is only a small amount of aluminum wire, it is often easier to replace it with copper wire than to replace all the connectors, especially if the service panel would have to be replaced.

► 5.0 LIGHTS, OUTLETS, SWITCHES AND JUNCTION BOXES

Damaged, Poorly Secured, Overheating

5.1 Lights: Damaged light fixtures should be replaced. Light fixtures should be well secured to junction boxes. They should never be supported by the wiring. Light fixtures should be arranged so that they are not susceptible to overheating. Some fixtures require clearance from combustibles, and some can only be installed in certain orientations.

Pot Lights

Recessed light fixtures (unless specially designed) should not be installed in areas where insulation will blanket the fixture, impeding normal heat dissipation. This can be a problem on the upper floor of the house, and although there are ways of overcoming it, it is often difficult to verify whether the installation has been made safely. (For example, in a cathedral ceiling, one would have to disconnect the power and remove the fixture.) Where pot lights are used in a thermally insulated area, an electrician should be engaged to verify the safety of the system. Relocation of the insulation, or replacement of the fixture are the corrective actions.

Damp Areas

Lights used in areas where dampness may occur, should be of a special type. This includes lights in shower stalls, saunas and outdoor light fixtures.

Stair Lighting   Adequate lighting must be provided for all service areas of the house, including the furnace room. Light for stairwells which have more than four steps should be switched both at the top and bottom. This eliminates the need to walk up or down poorly lit stairs. (The basement stairs are generally excluded from this requirement.)

Heat Lamps   Heat lamps at ceiling level should be located beyond the swing of any doors. If a door is left partially open, and it happens to be directly below a heat lamp, a towel or article of clothing flung over the top of the door can be ignited, causing a fire.

Grounding   Lighting fixtures, outlets, switches and junction boxes should be grounded as required by the manufacturer.

Obsolete   Very old style porcelain light fixtures, used without electrical boxes, are not safe and should be replaced. Live electrical connections are exposed on these fixtures.

Light fixtures in closets are a convenient feature, but the lights must be kept clear of areas where they may be damaged, or where storage may accumulate directly against the light bulb. Lights should not be installed above or beside shelving units in closets. Lights above the doorway are usually safe.

Won't Work   Inoperative lights may be the result of:

1. A burned out bulb.
2. A faulty light fixture.
3. A poor connection in the box.
4. A flaw in the wiring leading to the box.
5. A problem with the switch controlling the light.
6. A problem with the wire between the panel and the switch.
7. A blown fuse or tripped breaker.
8. A poor connection within the panel.

If the problem is not simply a burned out bulb or a blown fuse, it is normally necessary to contact an electrician to resolve the difficulty.

Polarized   **5.2 Outlets (Receptacles):** An outlet is a point where an electric appliance can be plugged in. Until 1950 most electrical outlets were ungrounded. They had only two slots in them, one connected to a black wire and one connected to a white. A small percentage of these had the two slots a different size, (polarized receptacles) so that a polarized appliance could only be installed in the proper orientation. The convention is that the smaller slot is supplied by the terminal connected to the black wire and the larger slot is connected to the white.

Light Socket Polarity   With the exception of a few appliances, polarity was not considered too important for a long time. Even today, some appliance plugs are polarized and some are not. A floor lamp is a good example of an appliance that now has a polarized plug. The reason for this is that when changing a light bulb, there are two electrical components of the light socket which may be live electrically. The threaded collar around the socket is one half of the connection, and the brass button at the bottom of the socket is the other connection. A person is much more likely to touch the threaded collar which comes up to the top of the socket when replacing a light bulb, so it is considered safer to make that the white (neutral) connection. The black (live) connection at the bottom of the socket is less likely to be touched.

*Black
to Brass*

Modern outlets have a brass colored screw on one side to which the live (usually black) wire is connected. The white or neutral wire is connected to the silver colored screw on the opposite side, and the ground wire is connected to the ground screw (usually green) near the end of the outlet.

*Push-in,
Bayonet
or Dagger*

Some modern outlets do not have screws on the sides, but have holes in the back, into which the wires are fitted. These are called "bayonet" ,"dagger", or "push-in" type connectors, because of the way the wire is inserted. These outlets were particularly troublesome when used with aluminum wire.

*CO/ALR
and
COPALUM*

Special outlets used with aluminum wire are designated CO/ALR and use larger screw heads and special screw plates to hold the aluminum securely in place. The letters CO/ALR are stamped into the metal tab at the top or bottom of the outlet. They can only be seen by removing the cover plate. See Figure 9. COPALUM connectors are also acceptable in the USA.

*Grounded
Outlets*

The grounding of electrical outlets which became popular after 1960, and is now mandatory, affords additional protection. The ground wire is a third wire which normally conducts no electricity. It is there as a safety escape route, in case something goes wrong with the appliance or receptacle. When an appliance malfunctions, a cord is damaged, or a receptacle is faulty, it is possible that live electricity may be brought to a point where it could be touched by a person, leading to an electric shock. The purpose of the ground wire is to provide a path which the electricity will follow, rather than flowing through a person touching the system. Electricity will take the path of least resistance.

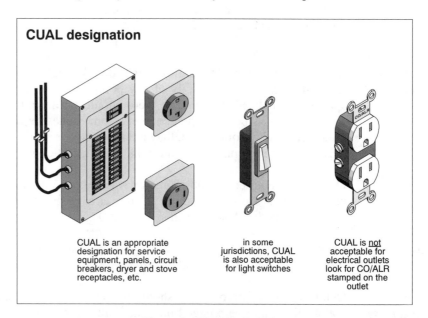

CUAL designation

CUAL is an appropriate designation for service equipment, panels, circuit breakers, dryer and stove receptacles, etc.

in some jurisdictions, CUAL is also acceptable for light switches

CUAL is not acceptable for electrical outlets look for CO/ALR stamped on the outlet

Figure 9. CUAL Designation

It should be understood that grounded receptacles are only of value where appliances with grounded plugs are used. There are very few home appliances with grounded plugs. These include refrigerators, washing machines, microwaves, waterbed heaters, computers, and some power tools, for example. Grounded plugs incidentally, also provide polarizing, since plugs can only be put into outlets one way.

Filling the Ground Slot (Some Areas Only) — In some cases, it appears that an electrical system is grounded but it is not. Since the early 1960's, the only type of electrical outlet that could be purchased, in some regions, is one with the third grounding hole. When replacing old two-prong outlets, three-prong outlets must be used. However, unless this grounding hole is wired back through the house to ground, it is of no benefit. Some electrical authorities require that the third pin be filled, when the outlet is not grounded, to prevent plugging in a three-pronged appliance to an upgraded but ungrounded plug.

GFI's as an Alternative — When using a grounded appliance in a home built before 1960, one should ensure that the receptacle is grounded. Use of three-to-two adaptors is not considered safe and has been disallowed by electrical authorities. Similarly, connecting the ground pin to the neutral is not acceptable. Installing a ground fault circuit interrupter on an ungrounded circuit with ground type receptacles will improve the safety of the system. Many electrical authorities will now accept ground fault circuit interrupters as an alternative to grounding.

Where two-prong appliances are used, it does not matter whether the outlet is grounded or not.

For an explanation of split receptacles, see Section 5.2.3.

Location on Walls and Floors — **5.2.1 Outlet Problems:** Outlets are generally installed on walls about twelve inches above the floor. In older houses, they were installed in baseboards, within two or three inches of the floor. However, electrical outlets located directly in the floor should be removed or should be a special type suitable for this application. Water spilled onto the floor can create an electrical hazard. Other hazards include metal objects such as hairpins and paper clips.

Number of Outlets — In new construction, electrical outlets should be located so that there is an outlet within six feet horizontally of any point along the wall (in finished living spaces). Translated, this means there should be an outlet every twelve feet along the wall. Above kitchen counters, some codes require outlets every four or six feet, and in some areas, they are required to be split receptacles (receptacles where the top half and bottom half of the outlet are on separate circuits).

Bathrooms — Outlets are required in bathrooms or washrooms, although the outlets should be as far away from the bathtub or shower as is practical (at least three feet). Outlets should be close to basins.

Loose or Damaged — Electrical outlets which are loose or damaged should be repaired or replaced. Similarly, cover plates should be replaced when damaged.

Octopus Connectors — Octopus connectors to outlets should be avoided. These connectors allow several appliances to be plugged into one duplex receptacle. These situations can lead to overheating and fires.

Weathertight Outlets — Special weathertight outlets are required outdoors or where water may contact the outlet.

20-amp Circuits — Where local authorities allow or require 20-amp circuits, outlets should be rated for 20-amps.

Worn   Worn outlets may not retain plugs securely. This creates a dangerous situation.

Won't Work   If an outlet is inoperative, it is possible that:

1. The outlet itself is defective.
2. The wires inside the box at the outlet are not properly connected. (Intermittent problems usually mean a loose connection.)
3. There is a problem in the wire between the panel and the outlet (perhaps at another box upstream).
4. There is a blown fuse or tripped breaker in the panel.
5. There is a poor connection or damaged wire in the panel.
6. The power has been turned off.

5.2.2 Ungrounded Outlets:
In houses built before 1960, almost all outlets are ungrounded. Where only two-prong appliances are to be introduced, this does not pose a hazard. However, where three-prong plugs (grounded appliances) are used, the electrical outlet must be grounded.

Difficult to Know   It is sometimes impossible to determine visually whether an outlet is grounded. In any house built in the 1960's or later, all outlets should be grounded. The grounded outlets are the three slot type. On an old house, two slot outlets were used. These are definitely not grounded. However, when these outlets are replaced, three slot outlets are often used, because in some areas the two slot type are no longer available. These outlets will not be grounded, since there is no ground wire in the box to connect to. Without testing, one cannot tell whether three slot outlets are grounded.

Adaptors   In many areas, three-to-two adaptors are available. These allow a grounded appliance to be used with an ungrounded plug. The idea is that a grounding connection on the adaptor is extended to a suitable ground. In practice, this rarely occurs and as a result, a potentially unsafe situation may be created. Consequently, these adaptors are no longer approved, or available, in some areas.

Filled Ground Slot   When three slot outlets are installed, but no grounding wire is in place, the third slot should be filled with an epoxy or a pin designed for that use (only where permitted). This will prevent a grounded appliance inadvertently being connected to this outlet.

Broken Ground Pin   In some cases, people have broken off the ground pin on a grounded appliance so that it will fit into an older two slot outlet. This is unsafe and should not be done.

Grounded Appliances   A grounded outlet is required wherever a grounded appliance is used. This may include an automatic clothes washer, portable dishwasher, microwave oven, some refrigerators, vacuum cleaners, kettles, many power tools, electric lawn mowers, personal computers, and waterbed heaters, just to name a few.

Adding Ground Wire   Ideally, the wires supplying an ungrounded outlet should be replaced with a grounded cable, or a solid ground wire (#12-gauge) can be added and connected to a suitable ground (such as a supply water pipe, in most cases). A new grounded outlet can then be installed. This is often a difficult job and may be expensive depending on the location of the outlet and accessibility of a grounding source. Since many people do not understand the importance, it is something that is not done as often as it should be.

*Adding
a GFI*

It can be argued that adding a ground fault circuit interrupter on a circuit with an ungrounded outlet will provide adequate protection. Many electrical codes accept the ground fault circuit interrupter as an alternative to grounding, under some circumstances, and this will certainly improve the situation. It is not, however, as safe as a grounded GFI outlet.

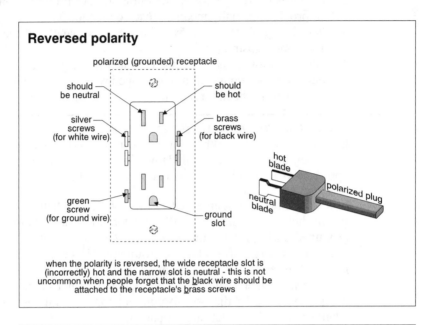

Reversed polarity

polarized (grounded) receptacle

should be neutral

silver screws (for white wire)

green screw (for ground wire)

should be hot

brass screws (for black wire)

ground slot

hot blade

neutral blade

polarized plug

when the polarity is reversed, the wide receptacle slot is (incorrectly) hot and the narrow slot is neutral - this is not uncommon when people forget that the black wire should be attached to the receptacle's brass screws

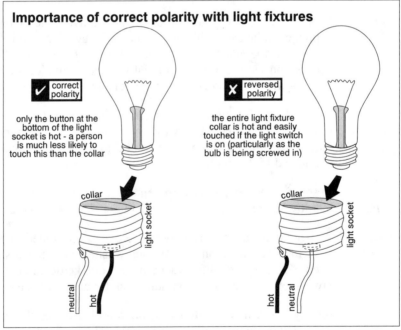

Importance of correct polarity with light fixtures

✔ correct polarity

only the button at the bottom of the light socket is hot - a person is much less likely to touch this than the collar

collar

light socket

neutral hot

✖ reversed polarity

the entire light fixture collar is hot and easily touched if the light switch is on (particularly as the bulb is being screwed in)

collar

light socket

hot neutral

Figure 10. Reversed Polarity

5.2.3 Split Receptacles:

Split receptacles which are always the grounded type, are commonly used in the kitchen. These are special outlets in which the upper and lower halves of a duplex receptacle are on two different fuses or poles of a breaker. This means that a kettle can be plugged into the upper half of the outlet and a toaster into the lower half, without danger of overheating or blowing a fuse. Introduced as a requirement by many electrical authorities in the late 1960's, this has become standard practice. Typically, all outlets above counters in new kitchens are now split. The fuses or breakers protecting a split receptacle should be mechanically linked. See Section 3.5.

Converting to split receptacles requires running new cable from the panel to the outlet and a second fuse or circuit breaker. The two halves of a split receptacle must be fed from opposite poles of the service (i.e. one side from red the other side from black). Failing to do this creates a potentially dangerous situation. Split receptacles are susceptible to the same problems as conventional outlets.

5.2.4 Reversed Polarity Outlets:

When the black wire is connected to the silver terminal screw on an outlet, and the white wire is connected to the brass screw, this is referred to as reversed polarity.

A reversed polarity outlet can compromise the safety of an electric appliance, depending on how it is wired. A grounded appliance may have its grounding made ineffective by reversed polarity.

With reversed polarity outlets, it is possible for some appliances to have their housing become live in the event of a malfunction. It is also possible for some electrical equipment to operate improperly with reversed polarity. This may include a home computer, a stereo system, etc.

Corrective action simply involves disconnecting the circuit and re-connecting the wires, so that black joins brass and white joins silver.

5.3 Arc/Ground Fault Protection:

Modern electrical systems make use of special electrical devices to reduce the risk of shock and fire hazards. While most codes require the installation of these devices during electrical installation, most do not call for these devices to be installed on older wiring, although the extra protection afforded by these devices is desirable.

5.3.1 Ground Fault Circuit Interrupters:

These special electrical devices shut the power off to a circuit when as little as .005 amp is leaking. Under normal circumstances, the current flowing through a circuit is the same at any point. That is to say, if there are 5 amps flowing through the black wire going out, there should be 5 amps flowing through the white wire coming back.

Miswired

In addition to the normal problems that may be the result of miswired electrical receptacles, a miswired GFI receptacles may not turn off even if the internal mechanism works properly.

In some jurisdictions, GFI protection is considered an appropriate upgrade where grounded (three-prong) equipment is to be used on ungrounded circuits. Even though GFIs do not add a ground wire to a circuit, they can detect a shock and shut the circuit off before the shock becomes fatal.

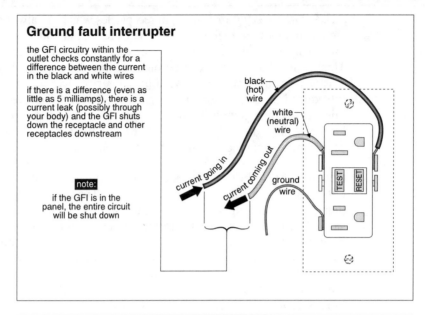

Ground fault interrupter

the GFI circuitry within the outlet checks constantly for a difference between the current in the black and white wires

if there is a difference (even as little as 5 milliamps), there is a current leak (possibly through your body) and the GFI shuts down the receptacle and other receptacles downstream

note:

if the GFI is in the panel, the entire circuit will be shut down

black (hot) wire
white (neutral) wire
current going in
current coming out
ground wire
TEST RESET

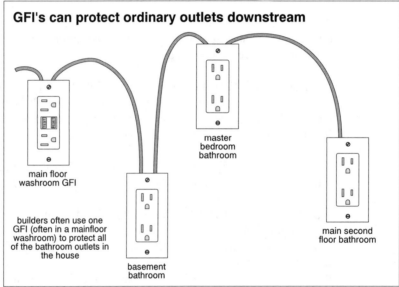

GFI's can protect ordinary outlets downstream

main floor washroom GFI

builders often use one GFI (often in a mainfloor washroom) to protect all of the bathroom outlets in the house

basement bathroom

master bedroom bathroom

main second floor bathroom

Figure 11. Ground Fault Interrupter

Missing   GFIs may not be provided in new homes as required by local jurisdictions. Replacing conventional breakers with GFI breakers is not difficult, although GFI breakers are more expensive than conventional breakers.

5.3.2 Arc Fault Circuit Interrupters: Arc fault circuit interrupters (AFCIs) are devices that help protect against fires by detecting arc faults. An arc fault is an electrical problem that occurs when electricity moves from one conductor across an insulator to another conductor. Light and heat are generated as the current passes through the insulator, which may be air or a solid insulating material. Arc faults are common where electrical cords are damaged, or where outlets are not properly installed.

Arc faults are dangerous because the heat generated may ignite nearby combustible material, starting a fire. Arc fault currents are often too small to trip a breaker or blow a fuse. A GFI will not detect many arc faults.

AFCI breakers are like a Ground Fault Circuit Interrupters (GFIs) in that one device protects the entire circuit. While AFCI breakers look like GFI breakers, and have test button, they are different. GFIs are designed to prevent electrical shock. AFCIs are designed to prevent fires. GFIs look for electricity that is not where it's supposed to be by detecting electrical current running through ground wires. AFCIs look for overheating by monitoring the waveform of the circuit voltage. There are some devices that provide both AFCI and GFI protection.

AFCI protection may be provided by a breaker in the electrical panel, or through special AFCI receptacles. Either may protect a number of outlets.

Where Needed   In houses built after 2001, AFCIs have been required on circuits serving bedrooms. In some areas, only receptacles need to be protected. In other areas, all electrical fixtures require protection.

Missing   AFCIs may not be provided in new homes as required by local jurisdictions. Replacing conventional breakers with AFCI breakers is not difficult, although AFCI breakers are more expensive than conventional breakers.

Damaged Loose or Obsolete   **5.4 Switches:**   Damaged or loose switches or cover plates should be repaired or replaced as necessary. The old push button switches (with two circular buttons which push into the switch and pop out) are generally considered unsafe and should be replaced. Reproduction switches of this type are now approved and available in North America, for the architectural purist.

Improper Operation   Any switch that works only intermittently, or that causes the lights to flicker, should be replaced promptly.

Location   Generally speaking, switches should be located about forty-eight inches above the floor, and stairwell lighting should be switched both top and bottom. Switches in bathrooms should be as far as possible from bathtubs and showers, ideally five feet or more. Some electricians prefer the light switches outside the bathroom door.

3-Way Switches   Three way switches are required in order to control lighting from both the top and bottom of most stairways.

Won't Work   An inoperative switch may be:

1. A problem within the switch mechanism.
2. A problem with the connections of the wire in the box at the switch.
3. A flaw in the wire between the panel and the switch (including boxes upstream of the switch).
4. A problem downstream in the circuit from the switch which makes it seem like the switch is faulty.

5. A blown fuse or tripped breaker in the panel.
6. A damaged or poorly connected wire at the panel.
7. A burned out light bulb.

An electrician should be contacted to locate and correct the problem.

Missing   **5.5 Junction Boxes:**   Where electrical connections are made with no junction boxes, the danger of electrical shock and fire is increased. With the exception of the early knob-and-tube wiring, all connections should be made in certified metal or plastic junction boxes. Junction boxes not only protect the connection itself, but secure the wires coming into the box and hold them in place. Connections made without junction boxes, made with junction boxes not properly secured to framing members, or made without the wires secured.

Special   Special junction boxes are required on building exteriors. This applies to other
Outdoor Boxes damp locations as well.

Accessible   All electrical junction boxes should be accessible for servicing. This means they cannot be covered by plaster, drywall or pancling, for example.

5.6 Cover Plates: Missing or damaged cover plates may allow the unintentional touching of live electrical connections, and may also allow dirt, dust and water into electrical connections, causing unsafe conditions.

Light fixtures, outlets, switches and junction boxes should all be provided with cover plates as necessary, to ensure safety.

5.7 Low Voltage Lighting Control: In a small percentage of houses, a special wiring system was installed to control light fixtures. This system, used primarily in the 1950's and 1960's, employed 12 or 24-volt wiring (instead of the more common 120-volt wiring) to control light fixtures. The wires used for the switches are typically much smaller than the #14-gauge wire commonly used. This system can usually be recognized in a house by the presence of the unusually shaped rectangular or oval switches for the lights.

Convenience   The system was employed in order to provide additional safety and convenience. In most of the systems, the light in a room could be turned on by the wall switch near the door, but could also be controlled from a remote central panel, often located in the master bedroom. Many of these systems were set up so that any light in the house could be controlled from the central panel. When going to bed, for example, one could turn off all the lights in the house.

Safety   Because of the low voltage supplied to the light switches, (remember voltage is a measure of the potential electric force available) there was very little danger of electrocution at a light switch. This system is somewhat complex and uses a low voltage transformer and a number of relays. It did not become popular, although it may still be found in some houses.

5 HEATING

► **TABLE OF CONTENTS** Page

▶ INTRODUCTION

The purpose of a heating system in the North American climate is obvious. How well a heating system performs is not so obvious. A well designed heating system is large enough to provide adequate heat on the coldest day, is reliable, is inexpensive to install and to operate (efficient), is quick to respond to its controls, is able to heat all parts of the home equally or differentially, as the occupants desire, and is safe. There is no one heating system which performs all these functions to perfection. Every heating system is a compromise in one way or another, with low initial cost often being the predominant criteria for selection.

▶ 1.0 HEATING OBJECTIVES

Simply put, the goal is to generate bundles of heat, and to distribute them to the various parts of the building. Several fuels can be used to generate the heat. Some bum oil or gas, commonly referred to as fossil fuels, and others use the heat released by electricity flowing through coils. There are newer systems where existing heat is simply captured, stored and released in the home. This includes heat pumps and solar heating, for example. Decisions as to which fuel is the best are based on the fuel cost, how much of the heat generated can be used (the efficiency of the system), and the cost and durability of the equipment used to provide the heat.

The heat is often generated centrally, in a furnace or boiler, and is distributed throughout the house via air in ductwork or water in pipes. If the heat developed by the gas, oil, or electricity is transferred to air, the system is called a furnace. Where water is the heat transfer medium, this is a boiler. Any fuel can be used with either distribution system.

It is possible to generate some heat in each room and not bother with a distribution system. Old English castles with fireplaces in each room are examples of this approach, Another example is a house warmed with electric baseboard heaters. There are advantages and disadvantages to each approach, and these are discussed in this section.

▶ 2.0 UNITARY ELECTRIC HEATERS

Some houses are heated entirely by electric heaters while others employ electric heat as a supplement to the main heating source.

With the exception of electric furnaces and boilers (which are dealt with later in this section), electric heating systems are unitary rather than central. In other words, the heat is generated within the room or space which is to be heated, as opposed to a central system where the heat is generated in one location and then distributed through the house.

The most common type of electric room heater is the baseboard heater. The second most common type is the forced-air wall unit which contains a heating element and a fan.

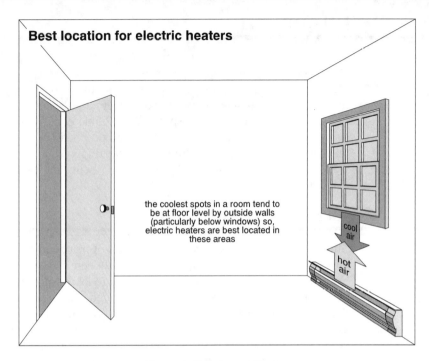

Best location for electric heaters

the coolest spots in a room tend to be at floor level by outside walls (particularly below windows) so, electric heaters are best located in these areas

cool air

hot air

Figure 1. Baseboard Heater

Thermostat   In either case, the controls can be directly on the units or wall mounted. These controls are simply thermostats. They control an individual unit or a particular area of the house which contains more than one heater. Wall mounted thermostats tend to be the preferred (and more expensive) method as they are easier to reach and, according to some, more accurate.

Floor Mounted   Some electric heaters are floor inserts. They are similar to baseboard heaters; however, they are installed directly in the floor. They are designed for locations such as in front of patio doors and floor length windows. These units may include a fan. Obviously, the controls for these systems are wall mounted.

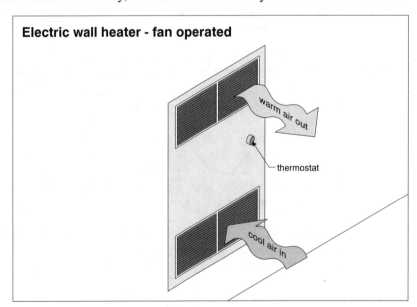

Electric wall heater - fan operated

warm air out

thermostat

cool air in

Figure 2. Unitary Electric Heaters

Floor mounted heaters may be found covered with rugs or mats, particularly during the summer. Blocking the air flow may lead to overheating. It is common to find boots, mitts, et cetera, drying on floor mounted heaters. This is poor practice since the heater will rust.

Clearances   With electric heaters it is important to follow the manufacturer's recommendations for clearance from combustible materials. Draperies, for example, should be kept eight inches above the heaters. Alternatively, the drapes can be three inches in front of the heaters as long as they are at least one inch above the floor.

Radiant   There is one more type of unitary electric heating system - that being electric
Heating   radiant heat. Electric radiant systems rely on large surface areas to heat up to the point where they radiate heat to a room. Electric radiant systems are almost always found in ceilings. They consist of wires which are embedded in the ceiling and spaced two to eight inches apart. Some systems employ pre-wired panels which fasten together. When operating, the ceiling will be warm, but not hot, to the touch.

If the distribution wire itself malfunctions (breaks), it is often difficult to locate the problem in the wiring. Some utilities have special equipment which can be used to locate the problem. In most cases, these systems are abandoned when they fail, and are replaced with electric baseboard heaters.

With any radiant heating system, care must be taken not to damage the system when drilling holes or mounting things such as light fixtures.

Special patching materials are available for treating cracks and other flaws in heated ceilings.

One common complaint about radiant heating systems is the shadow effect. Since radiant heat works the same way as sunlight, some people's legs feel cool if, for example, they are sitting at a dining room table for several hours. The table shades their legs from the direct radiant heat.

Advantages   There are several advantages and a few disadvantages to unitary electric heating. The advantages are:

1. Temperature can be controlled room by room or at least zone by zone.

2. The equipment is relatively inexpensive to purchase and install when compared to other forms of heating.

3. By the very nature of unitary heating, all of one's eggs are not in one basket.

4. Electric heating is quick to respond.

5. Electric heat is clean.

6. It can be used to supplement the primary source of heat within a house.

7. Electric heat takes up little room space and virtually no distribution space when compared to ductwork or hot water piping.

8. It requires no chimney and no combustion air.

5

Disadvantages   The disadvantages are:

1. In some areas, electricity is more expensive than other heating fuels.

2. The addition of several heaters to supplement an existing heating system may necessitate upgrading the electrical service. (It will require a large electrical service if the house is to be totally heated electrically.)

3. Unitary electric heating has no ability to filter, humidify or cool the air.

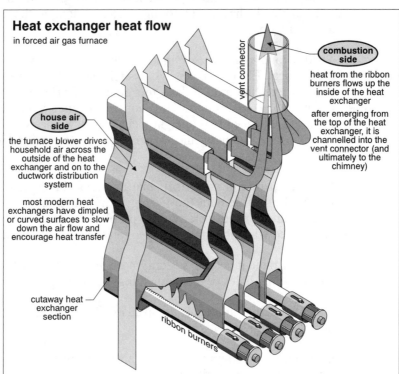

Heat exchanger heat flow
in forced air gas furnace

vent connector

combustion side
heat from the ribbon burners flows up the inside of the heat exchanger

after emerging from the top of the heat exchanger, it is channelled into the vent connector (and ultimately to the chimney)

house air side
the furnace blower drives household air across the outside of the heat exchanger and on to the ductwork distribution system

most modern heat exchangers have dimpled or curved surfaces to slow down the air flow and encourage heat transfer

cutaway heat exchanger section

ribbon burners

Figure 3. Heat Exchangers

▶ 3.0 FURNACES (Forced-Air Systems)

Furnaces are central heating systems in that the heat is generated in one location and then distributed through the house.

With the exception of electric furnaces, all furnaces have three major components: a heat exchanger, a burner, and a blower.

Heat Exchanger   The heat exchanger is the most critical component of a furnace. It separates the air which is being heated from the burning fuel. While the configuration of heat exchangers varies, a heat exchanger can be thought of as a metal box inside another metal box. The interior box has fuel burning in it. The heat from the burning fuel warms the interior box. Air is then passed through the outer box where it picks up heat from the hot walls of the inner box. In this way, the burning fuel never comes in direct contact with the house air. This is called an indirect fired heating system.

Burner   A burner is used to generate heat in the heat exchanger. The most common furnace fuels are natural gas and oil. (Wood, coal and propane can also be used.) Oil burners and gas burners are very different in appearance; however, their function is the same.

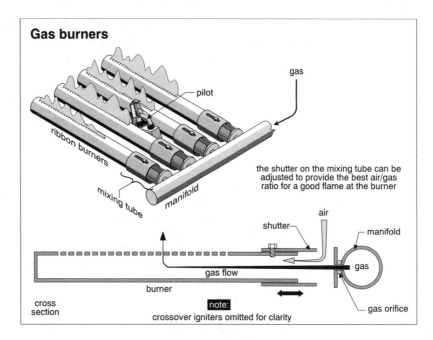

Figure 4. Gas Burners

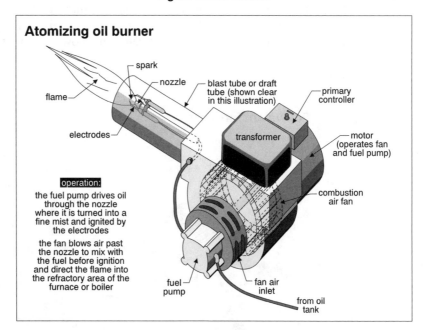

Figure 5. Oil Burner

7

A gas burner is fed from a valve which allows gas to enter the burner where it is mixed with air and ignited. Gas burners can be of several shapes; however, the most common type is the ribbon burner which is not unlike the burner found on a gas barbecue.

An oil burner is somewhat different since it is dealing with a liquid fuel rather than a gas. A pump is used to force the liquid fuel through a nozzle, causing it to atomize (break up into small droplets). A fan blows air through the burner to mix with the atomized oil. The mixture is ignited by a spark, creating combustion.

Blower

Once heat has been created on one side of the heat exchanger, household air is blown across the other side of the heat exchanger to pick up the heat and distribute it through the house. All modem furnaces have a blower to draw air back to the furnace through the return air ductwork, blow the air through the furnace, and out the supply air ductwork. Older furnaces worked on gravity. They relied on the warm air generated in the heat exchanger to rise by natural convection through the ductwork in the house. Cooler, heavier air fell down the return ductwork by gravity.

Electric Furnaces

While all fuel burning furnaces are basically the same, electric furnaces are slightly different. They are very similar in operation to a hand held hair dryer. Since there is no actual combustion within the furnace, there is no need for a heat exchanger or a burner. These components are replaced by electric heating elements sitting directly in the air stream. The blower simply forces air across the heating elements, and the warmed air heads back to the rooms in the house via ductwork.

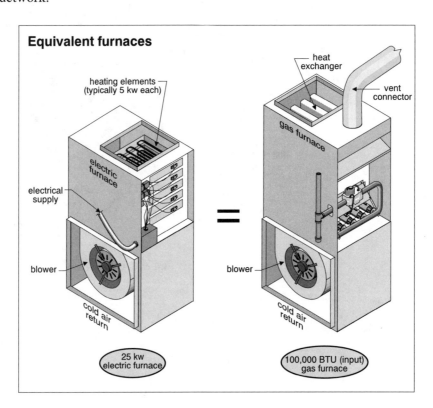

Figure 6. Electric and Gas Furnaces

Fan/Limit Switch

In addition to the major components there are safety controls and minor components. Forced-air furnaces have a fan/limit switch. This switch has several functions. It tells the blower to come on when the furnace is up to temperature. The blower does not start automatically when the burner begins to fire because the air which would come out through the registers would be coot (and feel drafty). It waits until the temperature is high enough within the furnace to provide warm air at the registers. At this point, it comes on. The fan/limit switch does not shut off the fan when the burner is shut off. Since there is some residual heat in the heat exchanger, the fan keeps blowing until the temperature within the furnace drops to the point where the air coming out of the registers would feel cool. The last, and probably most important, function of the fan/limit switch is to shut off the burner if the temperature within the furnace gets too high.

Proving Ignition

Depending upon the type of furnace, there is also a safety device to verify ignition. Obviously, it would be unsafe to pour unburned gas into a furnace, without burning it. A potentially explosive condition would exist. Most gas furnaces have a pilot which ensures that the gas is ignited. A thermocouple (heat sensor) verifies that the pilot is running. If, for any reason, the pilot goes out, the thermocouple sends a message to the gas valve telling the gas valve not to open under any circumstances.

Some gas furnaces do not have a continuous pilot. Instead, the pilot is ignited by a spark. Again, there is a sensor to ensure that the spark successfully ignited the pilot. If it does not, the gas valve will not open. A new system called "hot surface ignition" is doing away with pilots on some furnaces. A silicon-graphite ignitor spins like a grinding wheel until it is white hot. It ignites the main burner. A sensor ensures that combustion occurs or it shuts the gas valve.

Some oil burners have a similar sensing device which ensures that ignition has occurred. Other oil furnaces have a device on the exhaust pipe (called the primary control) which measures the temperature of the exhaust gases. If the oil burner is pumping oil into the combustion chamber and the primary control senses that the exhaust pipe is still cold, it shuts off the oil burner because it realizes that the combustion chamber is being filled with unburned oil.

Exhaust Flue

There are other minor components found on most furnaces. With the exception of electric furnaces, all furnaces have an exhaust pipe to discharge the products of combustion. The exhaust pipe (exhaust flue or breeching) carries the exhaust gases from the furnace to the chimney.

Filters

Furnaces also have a filter to clean the air before it enters the furnace. This prevents the inner components of the furnace from becoming clogged with debris. The filter system also improves the quality of the air throughout the house.

Most furnaces have a conventional filter; however, electronic filtering devices are available. Electronic air filters have three stages. The first stage is a mechanical filter similar to a conventional filter. The second stage gives the particles which pass through the mechanical filter a magnetic charge. The third stage consists of collector plates of opposite polarity. The charged particles are attracted to these plates.

Humidifiers Many furnaces also have a humidifier. The humidifier simply adds moisture to the air, as the air within a house during the winter time tends to be drier than people would like. Some humidifiers are sophisticated while others are extremely simple. See 12.4 in this Section.

Ductwork In addition to the furnace itself, there must be a means of distributing the heat. Furnaces employ two sets of ductwork: ducts to supply the air to the various rooms in the house, and a return air system. Every room in the house should have at least one supply air register. Ideally, each room would have a return air register; however, most houses have fewer return air registers (which collect air from several rooms). Houses which were built with central air conditioning often have dual return air registers located near floor level and near ceiling level. The high level return air registers are designed to collect warm air during the air conditioning season while the low level registers collect cool air during the heating season.

▶ 4.0 BOILERS (Hot Water Systems)

Boilers are central heating systems in that the heat is generated in one location in the house and distributed via piping to the various rooms.

The word boiler is somewhat confusing in that hot water systems do not actually boil the water. They heat it to about 160 degrees F, typically. Some hot water systems have been converted from steam.

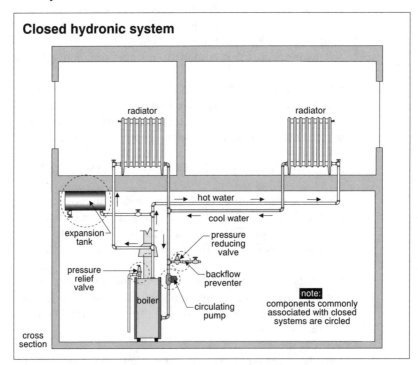

Figure 7. Closed Hot Water Systems

Closed Systems

Modern boilers are "closed" systems. The water in the boiler, in the piping, and in the heat source within each room, is under pressure. The pressure within the system is normally a few pounds higher than what is required to force water up to the highest level within the house. In a typical house, this pressure would be twelve to fifteen pounds per square inch.

As the system heats up, the water expands and the pressure builds. An expansion tank, or cushion tank, normally located near the boiler, has air trapped in it. As the water expands, it begins to fill the expansion tank, compressing the air. This prevents excessive pressure build-up in the system, as the water gets hotter.

Closed systems normally have a circulating pump to force the water through the system.

Open Systems

Before closed or pressurized systems, boilers were "open". The water within an open system is not under pressure. There is an expansion tank; however, it is not a pressure vessel. The expansion tank (or gravity tank) on open systems is located above the highest radiator within the house. It is normally found in a closet on the top floor. When the system is cold, the expansion tank has very

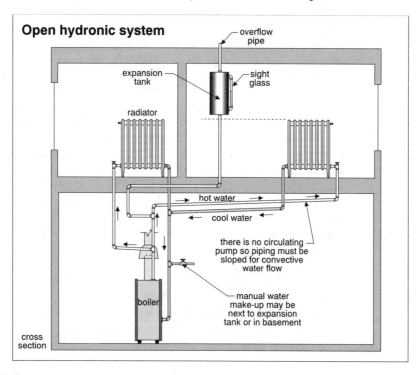

Figure 8. Open Hot Water System

little water in it. As the system heats up, the water expands and begins to fill the tank. The tank is designed to easily handle all of the extra volume that is created by expansion. Expansion tanks on open systems usually have a sight glass on their exterior. This allows one to determine the level of the water within the system. If the system is low on water, it is simply added until the tank begins to fill, when the system is cold. If the tank is overfilled when the system is cold it will overflow as the system heats up. An overflow pipe emerges from the top of the expansion tank. It typically passes through the attic and discharges onto the roof, or down into a floor drain.

Open systems do not have circulating pumps. The water is moved through the system by gravity.

Heat Exchanger

With the exception of electric boilers, all boilers have two major components: a heat exchanger and a burner. The heat exchanger contains the burning fuel on one side and the water to be heated on the other. The flame heats up the metal and the metal in turn heats the water. Heat exchangers are made of cast iron, steel or copper.

Burners

To burn fuel within the heat exchanger, a burner is required. The most common fuels are natural gas and oil. The burners on hot water systems are very similar to those on warm-air furnaces discussed in the previous section (3.0 Furnaces).

Automatic Water Tank

In addition to the major components, closed systems often have automatic water make-up devices to add water to the system as needed. On an open system, water is added manually by opening a valve on the pipe between the plumbing and heating system, until water is visible in the bottom of the expansion tank. On a closed system, a cold water plumbing pipe is connected to the boiler, with a special valve between. It is not a direct connection because the plumbing water pressure fluctuates and is too high for the heating system. Therefore, a pressure reducing valve is installed so that the pressure within the heating system does not exceed the right amount. If the plumbing system were ever drained, there would

Back-Flow Preventers

be the possibility of impure water from the heating system draining back into the plumbing system. Consequently, in recent years, automatic water make-up systems have contained a back-flow preventer.

Safety Devices

There are also safety features built into a boiler. The first safety device ensures that ignition has taken place. Without proper ignition, the oil burner or gas valve, is shut down. (See Proving Ignition in Section 3.0.) The second safety device is a high temperature limit. Should the water within the system exceed a safe temperature (about 200 degrees F.), the system will shut down.

On closed systems, a pressure relief valve is provided. Should the pressure in the system exceed thirty pounds per square inch, the pressure relief valve will discharge water. Open systems do not require a pressure relief valve as they are not pressurized, and excess water simply overflows from the top of the expansion tank.

Low Cut Off

Some larger boilers have low water level safety devices to shut down the system if there is insufficient water in the boiler.

Radiators

Once the water in the boiler is heated, it is distributed through the house. Radiators are the most common form of hot water heating distribution. Radiators are constructed of cast iron. Most radiators have a control valve at one end. This valve allows the water to the radiator to be shut off and, theoretically, it allows the amount of water flowing through the radiator to be adjusted so that the radiator gives off more or less heat. Seldom are radiator valves throttled down. They are normally wide open, and commonly leak if turned.

A small bleed valve is located near the top of the radiator. This allows air which is trapped within the radiator to be removed. This is normally done annually. It is not unusual to find this valve obstructed with paint.

Convectors   Hot water convectors are an alternative to radiators. Convectors are either cast iron or are tubing (usually copper) fitted with aluminum fins. Convectors take up less space because they are usually less than twelve inches high. Radiators are typically twenty-four to thirty-six inches high. However, convectors have to be longer than radiators to produce the same heat, and because they heat up and cool down more quickly than radiators, can result in uneven heating.

Radiant   Some hot water heating systems employ piping buried in floors or ceilings. The
Heating   piping heats the floor or the ceiling which in turn radiates the heat to the room. The pipes have traditionally been galvanized steel, black steel, or copper, although recently, flexible plastic tubing has been used. The pipes are usually buried about three inches below the surface and are eight to sixteen inches apart.

► 5.0 CONVERSION FROM HOT WATER TO FORCED-AIR

There are several reasons to consider conversion from hot water to forced-air heating. Among the more common are the ability to add central air conditioning, humidification and air cleaning, and the desire to get rid of the bulky radiators. To help make the decision easier, outlined below are some of the considerations.

Advantages of Hot Water Heat

a) Provide more even heat than forced-air systems.

b) No uncomfortable drafts from the distribution system.

c) Usually quieter than forced-air systems.

d) Does not circulate cooking odors through building (more important in two family homes).

e) A new boiler is smaller than a new furnace.

f) Piping requires less room in walls, floors and ceilings than ductwork.

Advantages of Forced Air Heat

a) Easy to add air conditioning, humidifying and air cleaning equipment.

b) Furnaces are less expensive to purchase than boilers.

c) There is a greater range of furnaces to choose from at each level of efficiency (conventional, mid, and high).

d) Heating registers do not occupy as much space in a room as radiators.

e) A leak in an air distribution system does not lead to water damage, as does a leak in heating pipes.

f) Ductwork is less expensive to install or relocate than piping.

Factors which make conversion appealing.

a) The boiler is old and may have to be replaced in the near future.

b) The house is a bungalow with an unfinished basement, or has a configuration which makes it very straightforward to install ductwork.

c) Central air conditioning is to be provided in any case (either independent or conventional).

d) There are plans to renovate extensively, so that opening up walls and ceilings is not a large additional expense.

Sample Situation

Assume that some or all of the factors listed above apply. Consider the following costs.

a) Replacement boiler (conventional)	$2,500 to $4,000
b) Replacement boiler (high efficiency)	$5,000 to $9,000
c) Add independent air conditioning	$8,000 to $15,000
d) New forced air-furnace (conventional)	$1,500 to $2,500
e) New forced-air furnace (high-efficiency)	$2,500 to $3,500
f) Conventional central air-conditioning	$2,000 to $3,000
g) Remove radiators and piping, and install ductwork and registers	$9,000 to $17,000

Based on the writers' preferences, the choices would be either b) plus c), or e) plus f) plus g). Using the median costs in both scenarios, the cost would be roughly $18,500 in either case. One would financially be indifferent between the two choices in this example.

Conclusion

In any given situation, one or more costs may vary dramatically from the set of figures above. As can be seen, several factors should be considered in making the decision to convert from hot water to forced air. The weight given each factor will vary from household to household, and the decision becomes subjective rather than right or wrong.

► 6.0 CONVERSION FROM OIL TO GAS

If one is planning to convert from an oil-fired heating system to a gas-fired system, a chimney liner may be necessary. (Please refer to 7.0 Chimney Liners and 14.17 Chimney/Chimney Liner).

If the present oil system is older, but still functioning, plans for conversion may be deferred. It may be prudent, however, to have a gas line installed in the near future. (The installation typically takes several weeks from the request date.) If the existing system fails during the heating season, a new gas system can then be connected quickly. In some locations, gas can be brought into the house at little or no cost if a gas appliance is connected (e.g. a rental water heater). Where this is not available, the cost may run $500. - $1,000. This discussion assumes, of course, that natural gas is available in the street. If the local gas company will rent a gas conversion burner, this may be the best option in the short term.

Mid or High Efficiency   One of the incentives for changing to gas is the much wider selection of furnace types. There are more mid and high efficiency gas furnaces than oil.

No Chimney   High efficiency and some mid efficiency furnaces do not need a chimney. They can discharge exhaust gases straight outside through the house wall. This can be an influence in the decision to convert, if the chimney for the oil furnace is in poor condition, or if a liner would be required on conversion to a conventional gas system.

► 7.0 CHIMNEY LINERS

Masonry chimneys may be lined or unlined. An unlined chimney simply has brickwork exposed on the interior. The brickwork on a lined chimney is protected. The liner may be a metal pipe, clay tiles, or asbestos cement pipe. Some experts feel clay tile liners are not ideal for gas heating systems.

As a general rule, oil-fired furnaces do not require a lined chimney because the products of combustion are not as corrosive to the chimney as the products of combustion from a gas-fired system. Since gas burns at a much lower temperature than oil, the exhaust gases are significantly cooler. As the exhaust gases travel up the chimney, they cool even more. Condensation can form on the inside of the chimney flue. When the furnace shuts off, the chimney cools and the condensation which has been absorbed into the brick and mortar freezes. This freeze/thaw action deteriorates the brick and mortar. This will eventually result in major chimney work being necessary.

If the debris falling to the bottom of the chimney is not cleared, it can eventually plug the furnace exhaust pipe causing the products of combustion to back up into the house. This is a very unsafe situation. Therefore, as a general rule, conventional and some mid-efficiency gas furnaces require a lined chimney flue. Most oil furnaces do not.

Metal Chimneys   Metal chimneys do not require liners. In some cases the top sections corrode, and require replacement. The design of caps for metal chimneys has changed over the last fifteen years. New materials are also being introduced on metal chimneys to extend their life.

Electric furnaces, some mid-efficiency furnaces, and high efficiency furnaces are normally not connected to a conventional chimney and, therefore, a liner is not required for these units.

► 8.0 EFFICIENCIES

8.1 Conventional Systems: Both furnaces and boilers are classified by their efficiency. Until the mid 1970's, all systems were of similar design and efficiency. Almost all had an operating (steady state) efficiency of approximately eighty percent. In other words, when the furnace or boiler was operating, eighty percent of the heat that was produced from burning the fuel went into the house. The other twenty percent went up the chimney.

Since a boiler or a furnace has to be capable of providing enough heat during the coldest day of the year, it is capable of providing more than enough heat every other day of the year. Consequently, systems do not run perpetually during the winter. They simply come on when heat is called for by the thermostat and shut off when the house is at the desired temperature. In fact, most heating systems are oversized and do not even run continuously on the coldest day of the year.

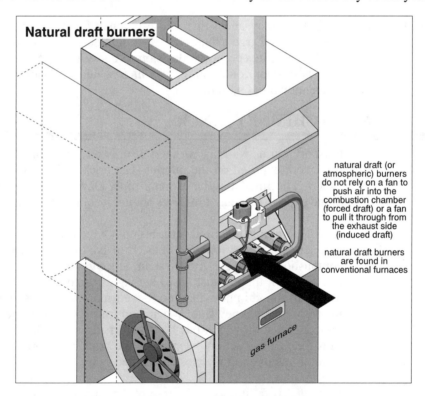

Figure 9. Natural Draft Burners

Losses   When a boiler or furnace is not operating, warm house air is escaping up the chimney. Even when the system is operating, a good deal of warm house air is lost up the chimney, just maintaining adequate draft for the exhaust gases. On gas-fired systems, some fuel is wasted keeping the pilot on. Also, when a boiler or furnace is starting up or cooling down, it is not operating at full efficiency. If you combine the off cycle losses with the start-up and cool-down losses, and add in the twenty percent losses during normal operation, the average seasonal efficiency of a conventional boiler or furnace is about fifty-five to sixty-five percent. With the advent of more efficient furnaces and boilers, the standard system became known as a conventional system.

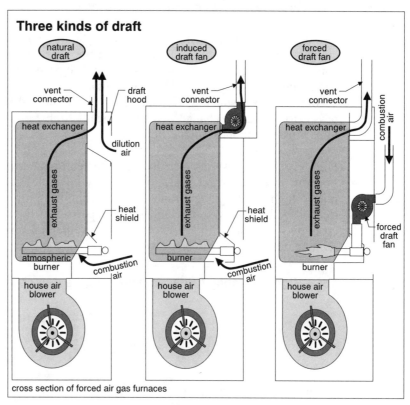

Figure 10. Types of Draft

8.2 Mid-Efficiency Systems: Most mid-efficiency boilers and furnaces are essentially conventional units (although a few have a secondary heat exchanger) with some modifications to reduce off cycle losses. A motorized vent damper may be used in the exhaust pipe to prevent heat from escaping up the chimney when the system is shut down. Alternatively, the system includes an induced draft fan in the exhaust pipe which only operates when the system is on. Continuous pilots are replaced with spark ignited pilots. Their seasonal efficiency is not much lower than their operating efficiency. Therefore, most have a seasonal efficiency in the eighty percent range. These systems require annual maintenance, like any other.

8.3 High Efficiency Systems: High efficiency furnaces and boilers go a step further, The main reason conventional systems are limited to eighty percent operating efficiency is condensation. If you bum gas, for example, and steal too much heat in the process. the exhaust gases will be so cool that condensation will form. (In the winter time, water often drips from the exhaust pipes of cars due to condensation in the exhaust system. Automobile exhaust is visible in the winter because the water vapor condenses when it hits the cold air.)

Condensing Systems

High efficiency furnaces and boilers are also known as condensing units. Their interior components are designed to withstand the corrosive condensate which forms (similar to the corrosion which rusts out your car muffler). High efficiency furnaces and boilers have a drainage system to get rid of condensate.

While a conventional furnace or boiler has a single heat exchanger, high efficiency units have more than one heat exchanger - some having three.

Pulse Systems

Some manufacturers of high efficiency systems employ an unconventional combustion system. This system relies on pressure waves to force products of combustion out of the combustion chamber. The pressure wave is reflected back and ignites the next gas/air mixture to continue the process. The "pulse" process becomes self perpetuating. The hot gases forced out of the combustion chamber pass across a heat exchanger where the heat is transferred. These systems tend to be noisier than most high efficiency systems.

High efficiency systems also incorporate features similar to mid-efficiency systems, to limit the off-cycle losses. They have a seasonal efficiency in the mid to high ninety percent range. Some reliability problems have been experienced with these systems, and some experts feel their higher maintenance costs over the life of the furnace may offset the efficiency advantages. Long term durability has yet to be proven.

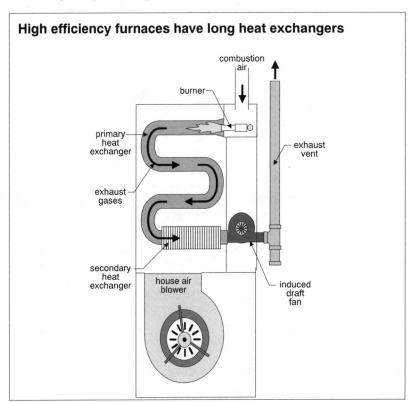

Figure 11. High Efficiency Gas System

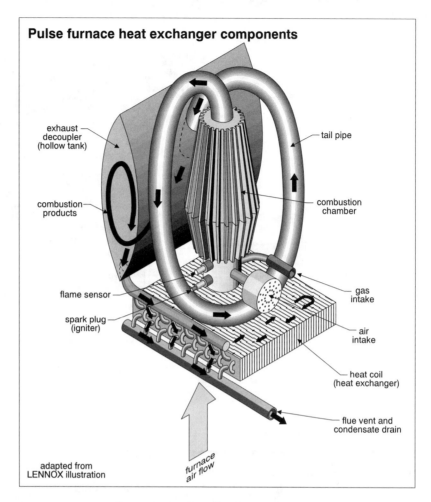

Pulse furnace heat exchanger components

exhaust decoupler (hollow tank)

combustion products

flame sensor

spark plug (igniter)

tail pipe

combustion chamber

gas intake

air intake

heat coil (heat exchanger)

flue vent and condensate drain

furnace air flow

adapted from LENNOX illustration

Figure 12. High Efficiency Pulse System

Since there are more components in a high efficiency system, there is more to go wrong and, consequently, regular maintenance should be somewhat higher than a conventional furnace. At least annual servicing is required.

Electric Heating

Electric boilers, furnaces and room heaters do not have the same problems as fossil fuel burning systems. Since there are no products of combustion there are no exhaust gases to deal with and consequently, no condensation. No heat is lost outside through a chimney, because no chimney is needed. At first glance, one would assume that electric heating systems are one hundred percent efficient. This is almost true. Electric heating systems do have some minor losses. When an electrical heating element is hot enough to glow, for example, some of the energy is lost as light. Electric heating works out to be about ninety-eight percent efficient.

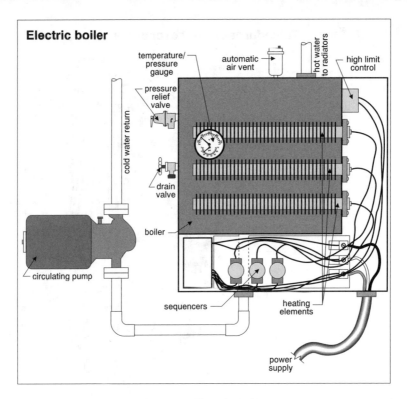

Figure 13. Electric Boiler

► 9.0 CAPACITY

Ratings Capacity refers to the amount of heat the system can generate. Heating systems which burn fossil fuels have an input and an output rating. The output rating is a percentage of the input rating. The percentage will depend on whether the system is a conventional, mid-efficiency or high efficiency system. The ratings are given as B.T.U.'s per hour. A B.T.U. is a British Thermal Unit and it represents the amount of heat required to raise the temperature of one pound of water by one Fahrenheit degree.

Electric heaters are rated in kilowatts. One kilowatt is equal to 3412 BTU/hr.

Heat Loss Heating systems are sized by calculating the heat loss from the house. The heat loss is dependent upon the size and configuration of the house, the construction, the amount of insulation, the type, size and orientation of the windows, as well as several other variables. Without doing full heat loss calculations, it is not possible to accurately determine the required heating system size. Most houses, however, should have systems with output ratings of 30 to 60 B.T.U.'s per hour per square foot of house. Many older house heating systems are higher. In energy efficient new homes and in attached housing (where there are fewer exterior wall surfaces), the figures may be lower.

Smaller Sizes Current philosophy dictates that systems should be sized so that they run for longer periods of time to keep the house warm. The longer a furnace or boiler is running, the more efficient it is. A unit which comes on for a very short period of time and shuts off suffers considerable start-up and cool-down losses. There are also losses with conventional systems, when they are not operating, from such things as heat escaping up the chimney.

If the system appears to be undersized, it is best to take a "wait and see" attitude. Remember that heating systems are sized for the coldest day of the year. It is better to supplement the heating than replace the furnace or boiler. A cold section of a house may be the result of poor distribution, rather than a furnace or boiler that is too small.

▶ 10.0 FAILURE PROBABILITY

Every boiler or furnace contains several components which, if they fail, will cause the boiler or furnace to stop operating. For example, if a ten dollar thermocouple fails on a gas-fired furnace, the pilot will shut off. With the pilot shut off, the furnace will not operate. The intent of providing a failure probability is not to guess when one of several minor components might break down.

Heat Exchanger

The failure probability is intended to give an indication of how likely the furnace or boiler is to fail in a way in which it must be replaced. For most systems, failure by this definition, means a crack or a hole in the heat exchanger. Since most of the heat exchanger is not visible, the actual condition of the heat exchanger cannot usually be determined during a home inspection. Because a home inspection is not technically exhaustive, the likelihood of failure is based on probability rather than testing or furnace tear down. A conventional gas-fired furnace, for example, contains a heat exchanger which has an average life expectancy of twenty to twenty-five years. A twelve year old furnace of this type would have a low failure probability. Furnaces between twelve and seventeen years would have a medium failure probability while furnaces above seventeen years of age, would have a high failure probability.

There are, however, manufacturers of conventional gas-fired, forced-air furnaces whose heat exchangers have a reputation for failing in ten to fifteen years. Therefore, the failure probability might be considered high on one of these manufacturers' eight year old units.

Retrofit

Most high efficiency furnaces require more air flow across the heat exchangers than conventional furnaces. Older, smaller ductwork and/or an air conditioning coil can restrict air flow which increases the temperature rise within the furnace. This can result in premature failure of the heat exchangers and void the warranty. This condition may not be identified in a home inspection.

Most copper and steel boilers have a life expectancy of twenty to twenty-five years, although some are notorious for their ten to fifteen year lives. Older style cast iron boilers last much longer than conventional furnaces and a thirty year old unit may only have a medium failure probability. The condition of the unit may also affect the estimate. A unit which shows considerable corrosion, for example, may have a shorter than average life expectancy. See 13.1 in this section.

Electric Systems

Electric furnaces do not have a heat exchanger. Instead, they contain electric heating elements and controls for the elements. Every single component can be replaced. With age, however, electric systems can get to a stage where replacement of the entire unit makes sense, due to lost reliability and a lack of available replacement parts. Electric boilers have a water jacket which will eventually rust. Although there are not great statistics on these units, a life expectancy of twenty to twenty five years may be reasonable.

With unitary electric heating (an independent heater in each room), failure probability is meaningless as all of one's eggs are not in one basket. Electric heating elements are like automobile headlights. Their life expectancy is not well defined.

► **11.0 GAS PIPING**

Gas piping in a house is commonly black steel or copper. Leaks can create an explosion hazard and should be treated as emergencies. The house should be vacated immediately without operating anything which may cause a spark including switches, telephones or doorbells. More information on gas piping can be found in Plumbing, Section 4.0.

► **12.0 WARM AIR HEATING SYSTEMS**

12.1 Furnace (Heat Exchanger): The condition of a furnace hinges on the condition of its most critical component, the heat exchanger. (Some furnaces have more than one heat exchanger.) It separates the flame and exhaust gases from the air in the house. The hot gas on one side of the heat exchanger never comes in direct contact with the air which is being circulated over the other side of the heat exchanger. A heat exchanger fails in one of two ways - it rusts through or it cracks. With either condition, the products of combustion escape through the hole in the heat exchanger and into the air supply to the house. When this happens, a new heat exchanger is necessary. A crack or hole in a heat exchanger is usually not visible, and typically will not be identified during a home inspection.

Life Expectancy   Heat exchangers have an average life expectancy of twenty to twenty-five years. If the furnace is nearing this age, other components are also beginning to wear and consequently very few heat exchangers are replaced. Pulling a furnace apart and replacing the heat exchanger costs almost as much as replacing the whole furnace. In most cases, the entire furnace is replaced.

Humidifiers   Defective humidifiers, leaking condensate trays from air conditioning systems or extremely damp basements can cause heat exchangers to rust prematurely.

Corrosive Environments   There are some environments where chemicals in the air are also corrosive to a heat exchanger. Swimming pool chemicals, paint strippers and the chemicals commonly found in hair dressing shops, for example, will rust out a heat exchanger very quickly. In a corrosive environment, a furnace with a specially protected heat exchanger is recommended.

Manufacturing Defect   Some manufacturers have a reputation for heat exchangers with short life expectancies. With some of these units, the manufacturer will replace the heat exchanger; however, in many cases, the furnace has to be replaced at the owner's expense.

Improper Fuel Conversion   When conversion from oil to gas became popular, there were some oil furnaces which should not have been converted but were. These are oil furnaces with a secondary heat exchanger. These systems worked well on oil, as the secondary heat exchanger, located above the blower, preheated the return air from the house before it went into the main portion of the furnace.

Unfortunately, since gas burns at a lower temperature than oil, this arrangement tended to cause condensation inside the heat exchanger above the blower. This section would rust out, allowing exhaust gases to be drawn into the air supply for the house. These furnaces should be replaced with furnaces designed for gas. Other furnaces are not suitable for conversion to gas for other reasons. Where there is any doubt, a qualified service representative should be consulted.

12.2 Gravity Warm Air Furnace: Gravity furnaces are often known as "octopus" furnaces because of the large round ductwork that emanates from the body of the furnace.

The mode of operation of an octopus furnace is similar to a conventional furnace except there is no fan to draw house air to the furnace, blow it through the furnace, and push it out of the air registers in the house. Instead, the system works on gravity (convection) relying on warm air to rise through the supply ducts and cool air to settle back through the return duct to the furnace.

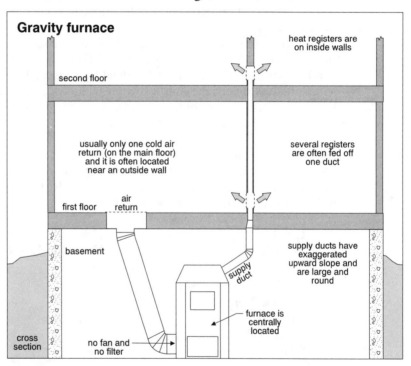

Gravity furnace

heat registers are on inside walls

second floor

usually only one cold air return (on the main floor) and it is often located near an outside wall

several registers are often fed off one duct

air
first floor return

basement

supply ducts have exaggerated upward slope and are large and round

supply duct

furnace is centrally located

cross section

no fan and no filter

Figure 14. Octopus Gravity Warm Air System

Almost all gravity warm air furnaces are obsolete and even if the heat exchanger has not failed (which would require immediate replacement of the furnace) a good argument can be made for replacing the unit because of the inefficiency of the system. Reduced heating costs would pay for a new furnace in a few years.

Ductwork Modifications
Octopus furnaces are usually located in the middle of the basement. The large round ducts have to slope up from the furnace to the supply registers, allowing the warm air to rise by convection. Ductwork is modified when an octopus is replaced because the old round ductwork which takes up a lot of space is not necessary with modern furnaces. New furnaces are more compact and can be located along a wall, usually close to the chimney. Since a fan forces air through the ducts, the ducts can be smaller, rectangular and run along the ceiling horizontally, opening up the basement space.

12.3 Blower/Blower Motor: The air movement section of a furnace consists of a blower and motor. This section of the furnace is responsible for drawing return air back from the house to the furnace, pushing the air past the heating section of the furnace and back out the supply air registers within the rooms. The most common problems with these components are burned out motors and worn bearings.

On some newer systems, the motor is mounted within the blower and drives it directly. On older systems, however, the motor is external to the blower and drives it via a pair of pulleys and a belt. Belts and pulleys are often in need of adjustment.

If furnace filters have been missing for some time, blowers get extremely dirty. A dirty blower moves less air, making the furnace work harder and the house less comfortable. Dirt build-up can also cause the blower to get out of balance. This will cause excessive noise and vibration. Sometimes, vibration causes the entire blower unit to become loose. In other cases, the blower bearings may fail.

12.4 Humidifier: Most central humidifiers are relatively inexpensive pieces of equipment added to forced-air furnaces. Their purpose is to raise the humidity levels within the house during the heating season. If too much humidity is added, however, condensation forms on windows and on other relatively cool house surfaces. Condensation can also form inside wall and ceiling cavities, causing rot and deterioration.

Humidity Levels

Unfortunately, the ideal humidity level for the house is not the same as the ideal humidity level for people. People tend to appreciate higher levels than are desirable from the house's perspective. To prevent condensation and mildew, the following should be observed:

Outside Temperature	House Humidity Level
-20 degrees F.	15%
-20 to -10 degrees F.	20%
-10 to 0 degrees F.	25%
0 to +10 degrees F.	35%
+10 and above degrees F.	40%
Summer months	Off

Humidifier Types

There are several different types of humidifiers. The most inexpensive type consists of a tray with evaporative pads. Some of these units are designed so that the tray sits inside the plenum, immediately over the heat exchanger, while others are designed so that the tray sits outside the plenum beside the furnace. These are generally low quality humidifiers that allow for no control over humidity. When the furnace is on they are humidifying; when the furnace is off, they are not. The units that sit inside the plenum are particularly troublesome, in that they tend to leak and drip onto the heat exchanger. This can cause premature rusting of the heat exchanger and failure of the furnace.

Location

Drum type humidifiers are perhaps the most common type. They should be mounted on the return air ductwork with a bypass duct to the supply plenum. These units have controls and the previously recommended humidity levels should be followed.

Adjustment

Drum type humidifiers have several common problems. The water level often requires adjustment. Without proper adjustment, the tray overflows which can cause damage to the furnace. The tray sometimes overflows because mineral deposits foul the automatic water supply valve, causing it to stay open, even when the tray is full. The drum pad itself tends to clog up with mineral

Leaks

deposits seizing the drum, which in turn burns out the motor. Replacement parts for these humidifiers are readily available. The water supply connection to the supply plumbing pipe is a common leakage point.

Duct Damper

Where central air conditioning is found, a humidifier duct damper should be present. This damper should be kept closed during the cooling season to prevent air conditioner coil ice-up.

Trickle Atomizing And Steam Humidifiers

Trickle (cascade) type humidifiers that allow water to fall over a special pad are usually high quality units. The water that is not evaporated is collected and flows to a drain. Atomizing humidifiers and steam generating units are also high quality and are rarely seen residentially. These higher priced units tend to work well; however, they are expensive to install. Due to their design, the inner workings cannot be inspected during a visual examination.

12.5 Conventional Air Filters: There are several different types of conventional air filters; however, they all perform the same function - to filter the air before it travels into the furnace and out through the registers. Conventional air filters sit in the return air plenum, just upstream of the blower. Some are cleanable while others are disposable. Regardless of the type, they should be checked monthly.

Conventional air filters are inexpensive. It is a wise practice to replace or clean them regularly. Clean filters improve the comfort of the home and help to reduce heating costs.

Non-combustible filters should be used in furnaces where the exhaust pipe passes through the return air portion of the furnace.

12.6 Electronic Air Filter: Electronic air filters clean the air to a much greater extent than conventional mechanical filters. Because they help to remove pollen and cigarette smoke particles, these are good units for people who suffer allergies. The units have a preliminary mechanical filter to remove larger airborne debris. The smaller particles which get through the filter are electrically charged and then collected on plates of opposite polarity. When one hears an intermittent sparking or crackling noise, the unit is functioning properly.

Cleaning

Because electronic air filters are extremely efficient, they get dirty quickly. They should be checked or cleaned once a month. The manufacturer's cleaning directions should be followed carefully. (Some can be placed in the dishwasher.) Care should be taken when removing the components from the ductwork as there is potential for an electric shock due to the electrical charge which is built up within these units. The power to the unit should be turned off about thirty seconds before opening the filter compartment. The furnace fan should also be turned off before servicing the filter.

When the removable components are put back in the ductwork, care must be taken to ensure that they are installed in the right orientation. An arrow indicating air flow should point toward the blower. Approximately ten percent of the filters noted during inspections have been installed backwards.

Activated charcoal filters to help absorb odors are sometimes added to electronic air filters. These arc usually in a metal frame, just downstream of the electronic filter collector plates.

From a visual inspection it is not possible, in all cases, to determine whether a unit is malfunctioning or simply in need of cleaning. In some cases, the power supply has been interrupted and simply needs to be reactivated.

Settings

12.7 Fan/Limit Switch: The fan/limit switch is essentially a temperature sensor. It measures the temperature of the air within the furnace above the heat exchanger. For normal operation, it is designed to turn the blower on and off at pre-set temperatures. When the furnace is operating in the autornatic" mode, it will not blow cold air through the registers because the fan/limit switch won't turn on the blower until the air in the furnace is up to temperature (130 - 150 degrees F.). It will also continue to blow after the burner has shut off as long as the temperature in the furnace is relatively high (90 - I 10 degrees F.). In this way, residual heat in the furnace is distributed through the house. (Some modern furnaces use a simpler control for the fan, which times it to come on two or three minutes after the burner, and shut down two or three minutes after the burner.)

Override

Most fan/limit switches have a manual override button which allows for continuous fan operation. In houses with central air conditioning or a heat pump, this manual override function is often abandoned as this can be accomplished by a switch on the thermostat.

High Limit

The most important function of the fan/limit switch is to shut down the furnace if the temperature of the air gets too high (170 - 200 degrees F.). This may be due to an inoperative fan or crack in the heat exchanger, for example. In this sense, it is a safety device. Some units have a separate high limit switch.

Problems

Sometimes, fanAimit switches are out of adjustment, causing the furnace or the blower to short cycle (turn on and off at short intervals). If this is the case, the unit should be adjusted. Other causes of short-cycling include thermostat and heat exchanger problems.

If the limit setting is too high, or the switch is defective, the furnace can overheat. In some cases, this can cause a fire by igniting dust inside the ductwork or combustible materials nearby. This system should always be checked during regular furnace servicing.

12.8 Electric Plenum Heater: Some forced-air fuel burning furnaces are equipped with an auxiliary electric plenum heater. Electric plenum heaters are not designed to work in conjunction with the furnace. Normally, they are arranged so that the electric plenum heater will first try to satisfy the heating demands of the house. If it cannot keep up, the plenum heater will switch off and the furnace will come on. Electric plenum heaters are most commonly found on oil-fired furnaces. Much like electric furnaces, heating elements can bum out. These can be replaced.

In houses with small (60-amp) electrical services, electric plenum heaters (typically 9 kilowatts and 37.5 amps) may be controlled by a device which will shut them down if there is a high demand for electricity in other portions of the house.

An inoperative plenum heater may be due to a burned out element, malfunctioning controls, or may simply be shut down by the device which senses the use of too much electricity in other parts of the house (in which case it is not malfunctioning). If the furnace is operating, the heater cannot be tested.

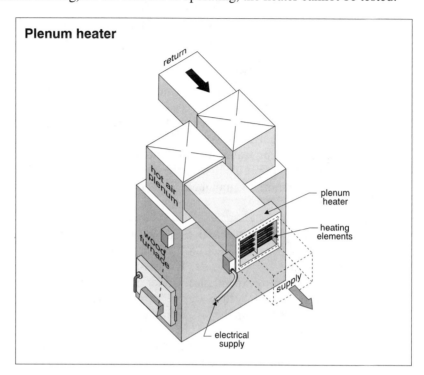

Plenum heater

Figure 15. Electric Plenum Heater Over Furnace

► 13.0 HOT WATER HEATING SYSTEMS

13.1 Boiler (Heat Exchanger): It should be noted that while hot water heating systems are called boilers, they do not actually boil the water, they only heat it to about 160°F., typically (steam heating systems, discussed in 17.0 of this section, do actually boil the water). Some hot water boilers have been converted from steam. This may not be determined during a home inspection. A boiler consists of a burner and a beat exchanger. The burner simply generates heat within a combustion chamber. The heat exchanger allows the heat from the flame to pass through it and heat the water on the other side of the heat exchanger. The heat exchanger is the most critical component of the boiler. When a heat exchanger fails, it rusts through or cracks and allows leakage into the combustion chamber or leakage through the exterior casing of the boiler.

Heat Exchangers

Heat exchangers in boilers can be made of a variety of materials. Some are cast iron, while others are copper or steel. Heat exchangers in old heavy cast iron boilers have a life expectancy of thirty-five to fifty years, although there are exceptions which last up to eighty years. It is not possible from a visual inspection to determine how many years of life remain in these boilers. They do not fail like clockwork.

Most newer, lighter boilers, regardless of the material used in the heat exchanger, have an average life expectancy of twenty to twenty-five years. There are exceptions to this rule and some steel boilers have life expectancies of only ten to fifteen years.

In some cases, a rusted heat exchanger which is leaking can be repaired; however, in most instances this is not the case, and a new boiler is needed.

13.2 High Temperature Limit: The high temperature limit is a safety device which is intended to shut off the boiler if the water within the system reaches a temperature of approximately 200 degrees F. The word boiler is actually a misnomer as boilers do not raise water temperature to the boiling point (unless it is a steam system). The high temperature limit prevents the boiler from boiling. Boiling water builds up pressure which may rupture the boiler or piping. One common problem with these units is leakage at the point where the high temperature limit is mounted. Secondly, the unit itself can require recalibration or repair.

Closed Systems

13.3 Expansion Tank: (For an explanation of open and closed systems, refer to 4.0 in this section.) When heat is applied to the water in a heating system, the water expands. The expansion tank or cushion tank provides space for the water to expand into. Under normal circumstances, the expansion tank is partially filled with water. The remainder of the tank contains trapped, compressed air. As the water in the system beats up and expands, it consumes some of the space occupied by the air, by simply compressing the air further. Air is easily compressed, water is not. The expansion tank is normally mounted in the basement, above the boiler.

Tank Waterlogged

If the expansion tank has no air in it, (in other words, the tank is waterlogged) it has no capacity to accept more water. When the boiler comes on and the water in the system is heated up, the pressure in the system rises to the point that the pressure relief valve operates. Therefore, a leaking or dripping pressure relief valve may mean a waterlogged expansion tank.

Since the air in an expansion tank eventually gets absorbed into the water, expansion tanks have to be drained periodically to prevent them from becoming waterlogged.

Some modem expansion tanks have a diaphragm in them, which prevents the water from coming in direct contact with the air. Therefore, the air is never absorbed into the water and unless the diaphragm fails, the tank will theoretically never become waterlogged.

Open Systems

On some older heating systems, the expansion tank is located on the top floor of the house, above the level of the highest radiator. In these systems, the expansion tank is commonly found in a closet. These systems are called "open" systems and are not pressurized. The top of the expansion tank has a pipe which should discharge to the building exterior or floor drain. If the system overflows, the expansion tank simply discharges water out of the pipe (often onto the roof).

On some of these open systems, the pipe from the expansion tank to the building exterior has been disconnected. They often terminate in the attic. If the system should overflow, a considerable amount of water damage can occur in the house.

With the exception of periodic draining, expansion tanks are maintenance free. Some expansion tanks, however, do require replacement when they rust through and leak.

13.4 Pressure Relief Valve:
The pressure relief valve is a safety device which prevents the pressure within the system from exceeding a pre-set limit (usually thirty pounds per square inch). Because the water which could discharge from a pressure relief valve in an emergency situation would be extremely hot and under relatively high pressure, the discharge from the pressure relief valve should be piped down to a distance of approximately six inches above the floor. This reduces the risk of scalding anyone nearby.

Pressure relief valves often leak. Sometimes this is due to a defective valve seat or debris caught on the valve seat. These problems are easily rectified. Often, a leaking pressure relief valve is reflective of nothing more than a waterlogged expansion tank. (See Expansion Tank above).

Sometimes, pressure relief valves which leak chronically are blocked off. This should never be done, as the relief valve is an essential safety device.

Pressure relief valves are not found on "open" hot water systems.

13.5 Pressure Reducing Valve:
on older systems, water has to be added manually from time to time to compensate for leakage, evaporation, and air absorbed from the expansion tank. On modem systems, water is automatically added through a pressure reducing valve. The pressure reducing valve allows water to fill the system on an as-needed basis. It connects the boiler to the plumbing system. It is typically set at approximately fifteen pounds per square inch (higher in some three storey houses). If the pressure within the heating system drops below fifteen pounds, the pressure reducing valve simply adds water from the plumbing system.

The most common problems with pressure reducing valves are leakage and improper adjustment.

Most boilers have pressure gages on them. If the boiler is cold, the pressure gage on the boiler should indicate roughly the same pressure as the pressure reducing valve (12 - 15 psi). If the two numbers are not the same, it could indicate a pressure reducing valve which is out of adjustment or a defective pressure gage. There may also be a closed valve between the valve and gage. If no water discharges after opening a radiator bleed valve on the top floor, this indicates a similar problem.

13.6 Back-Flow Preventer: A back-flow preventer works in conjunction with a pressure reducing valve as part of the automatic water make-up system. The back-flow preventer stops water in the heating system from backing up into the plumbing system. For example, if the water in the plumbing system was drained to repair a faucet, it is conceivable that pressurized water in the heating system could back up into the plumbing system. This would present a health hazard. The back-flow preventer only allows water to flow into the heating system. It allows no water to flow out.

These are not found on all systems, although many municipalities now require them on new or replacement installations. The most common problem with back-flow preventers is leakage.

13.7 Low Water Cut-Out: The low water cut-out is a safety device which shuts off the boiler if the amount of water within the boiler is insufficient. Unfortunately, this device cannot be functionally tested without draining the heating system.

Like most safety controls, the most common problem is leakage. Only the largest residential systems have low water cut-outs.

13.8 Isolating Valves: Isolating valves are simply valves for the water leaving the boiler which, if turned off, shut off water to a portion of the house. These valves are not very different than valves in a plumbing system. Most are manually operated, although sophisticated multi-zoned houses with more than one thermostat may have electrically operated valves.

The most common problems are leakage and seizing. Since the valves are not used often, they tend to seize. These valves are not functionally tested during an inspection as the first time a valve has been turned, after sitting for any length of time, it is prone to leakage.

13.9 Circulating Pump: The circulating pump on a hot water heating system is the equivalent of the blower on a forced-air system. Its responsibility is to move the heated water through the house. On older systems, this is done by gravity (convection); however, on newer or updated systems, a circulating pump moves the water more efficiently. "Open" systems do not employ circulating pumps. (Open and closed systems are discussed in 4.0 of this section.)

Depending upon the type of boiler, the circulating pump is designed to run continuously, or intermittently when the water in the boiler is above a certain temperature. Others operate only when the boiler is operating. This last arrangement is the least desirable.

The most common problems associated with circulating pumps are leakage, worn pump bearings, burned out pump motors and defective temperature sensors which control the pump.

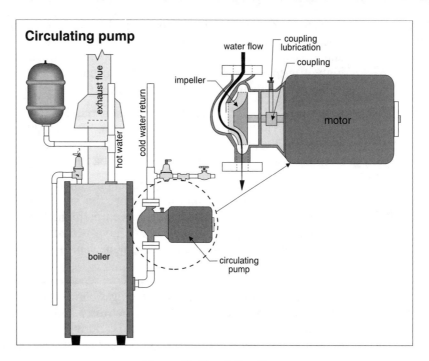

Figure 16. Circulating Pump

Many modern boilers (e.g. copper tube boilers) have a safety interlock that prevents the boiler from operating unless the pump is running. These boilers would quickly overheat if water was not flowing through them.

► 14.0 GENERAL

Physical Condition

14.1 Exhaust Flue: The exhaust flue on any heating system is designed to carry the exhaust gases to the chimney from the furnace. They are typically a single wall galvanized steel pipe, six inches to ten inches in diameter. They should not be aluminum. Sections should be screwed together. Problems include poor connections, corroded metal, and improper slope. Flues should not extend into the chimney far enough to obstruct the flow of gases out of the flue and up the chimney.

Length

Depending upon the location of the heating system relative to the chimney, some exhaust flues are too long. Exhaust flues from oil furnaces should be no more than ten feet in length.

Slope

Because exhaust gases are warm, it is important that the exhaust pipe has a proper slope to promote the flow of exhaust gases toward the chimney (minimum of one-quarter inch per foot).

Draft Air

Exhaust Gases

Most furnaces need air to maintain draft up the chimney, in excess of the air needed for combustion. Where this is not available, exhaust gases may not go up the chimney. Exhaust gases spilling from the exhaust flue, draft hood or burner area, may present a life threatening situation. This problem requires immediate action.

Clearance to Combustibles

Exhaust flues become extremely hot. Exhaust gases can be 300-700 degrees F. They are often too close to combustible surfaces. A minimum of nine inches clearance should be provided for oil furnaces and special collars should be used where the exhaust flue passes through a combustible material. Gas furnace flues should be at least six inches from combustibles.

High
Efficiency
Systems

Exhaust from high efficiency boilers and furnaces is handled quite differently. The exhaust gases have a much lower temperature (roughly 140 degrees F.) and are usually discharged through a plastic pipe to the building exterior. Most high efficiency heating systems have induced draft which means there is a fan drawing the exhaust gases out of the furnace.

Mid-
Efficiency
Systems

Some mid-efficiency furnaces also discharge exhaust gases out through the house wall. These gases are relatively hot, and combustible clearances (six inches) must be maintained on stainless steel exhaust flues. These flues can run as much as forty feet inside a house, depending on manufacturer's recommendations.

High
Temperature
Plastic Venting

Some mid-efficiency furnaces and boilers use high temperature plastic venting. In some jurisdictions, Ontario for one, the sale of these materials namely Plexvent, Ultravent and Sel-Vent has been prohibited due to cracking and separation of joints. Some home owners have been forced to replace the entire furnace because no approved replacement vent pipe was available. Approved replacement systems are anticipated.

14.2 Gas Burner: The most common gas burners are point source burners, ring burners and ribbon burners. Burners get dirty and the small orifices (particularly on ribbon burners) plug with debris. Burners also become misaligned and the flame does not point in the right direction. Burners can also rust.

Dirty
Misaligned
Rusted

Incomplete
Combustion

The air supply can be restricted if the burners are in a small closed room or if the burners are dirty or incorrectly adjusted. This results in incomplete combustion, higher heating costs, and, in some cases, condensation problems. In severe cases, carbon monoxide poisoning may occur. See Section 14.5. This is a life threatening situation.

Flashback

On some heating systems (particularly with ribbon burners) "flashback" is a common phenomenon when the system first starts up. While this is not a problem with the burners themselves, the resultant damage is caused by the burners. In a flashback situation, some of the ignited gas spills out of the front of the heating system. Heat shields, provided on most systems, prevent any serious damage under these conditions; however, in extreme cases, control wiring and other components of the heating system have been badly burned. If there is any evidence of scorching or burning outside the combustion chamber, a specialist should be contacted.

14.3 Oil Burner: Oil burners consist of a fan to force air into the combustion chamber, a pump to force oil into the combustion chamber, a nozzle to convert the oil to a fine mist, and an ignition system to ignite it. During a visual examination of a heating system, very little of the oil burner can be inspected, due to its design. Problems can occur with any of these components and a specialist should be contacted.

Even burners which are working may be burning very inefficiently, and heating costs will rise. Oil burners should be serviced annually. Old systems should have an annual efficiency test. Efficiency cannot be tested during a home inspection. Burners starved for air will be costly to operate and may generate dangerous carbon monoxide gas.

14.4 Primary Control: The primary control is found on most oil-fired heating systems. It is a device which is mounted on the exhaust flue in most cases. The primary control is a safety device which senses the temperature in the exhaust flue. Its purpose is to verify combustion. If the oil burner is pumping oil into the furnace and the primary control senses no heat in the exhaust pipe, it concludes that the oil being pumped into the furnace is not being ignited and it shuts off the pump. Most primary controls have a reset button on them. It should

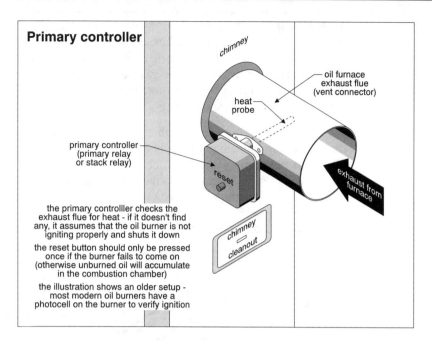

Figure 17. Primary Control

be pressed only once if the furnace fails to ignite. Pushing the reset button several times could allow an unsafe accumulation of oil in the combustion chamber. Some newer oil burners use a cadmium sulfide "eye", or photocell, on the oil burner that verifies ignition.

Combustion and Draft Air

14.5 Combustion Air: All fuel burning systems need air to mix with the fuel. Therefore, if the furnace or boiler is in an enclosed room, ventilation should be provided. Draft air is also needed to ensure the exhaust gases will be carried up the chimney. As a rough rule, fifteen cubic feet of combustion air and fifteen cubic feet of draft air are required to safely burn one cubic foot of natural gas. This is normally accomplished by providing grilles in the furnace room door. Two square inches of ventilation should be provided for every 1,000 B.T.U.'s (input capacity). Ideally, half the ventilation is near the floor, and half is near the ceiling.

Outside Air

Some heating systems use combustion air brought in from the exterior. This is done so that the air burned during the combustion process is cold outside air, rather than air which has already been heated. Using air which has been heated is wasteful, since it costs money to warm the air, and cool air actually burns better. Houses which are tightly sealed to improve energy efficiency may require outside combustion air, to prevent starving the burner for air.

With most of these arrangements, the furnace room becomes cold during the winter and freezing pipe problems can occur if there is any plumbing in the furnace room. Freezing heating pipes can also be a problem, if the heating system should happen to malfunction.

Furnace rooms which bring in outside air should be well insulated to keep the rest of the basement comfortable.

High Efficiency Furnaces

Some high efficiency furnaces bring outside air directly into the burner through a closed pipe. This avoids the cold furnace room problem. An adequate supply of air is verified by the pressure sensors in the furnace, before the burner is allowed to fire.

14.6 Pilot/Thermocouple: Most gas-fired heating systems have a continuous pilot. The pilot lights the burner when the gas valve opens. In conjunction with the pilot is a thermocouple which simply proves ignition. If the thermocouple is not satisfied, the gas supply to the pilot is shut off, and the main gas valve will not open. Thermocouples are prone to failure, but are easily replaced by a heating specialist.

There is great debate over whether a continuous pilot should be left operating during the summer time. One school of thought suggests that the heat from the pilot provides some warmth for the system and prevents condensation in damp basements, thereby extending furnace life. The other school of thought is that a pilot running all summer long is a waste of energy. The debate continues.

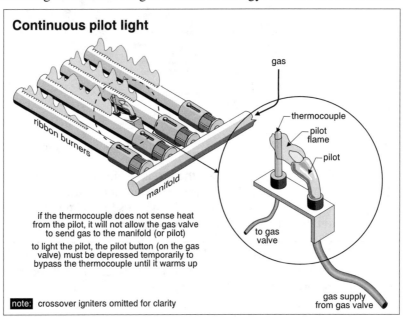

Continuous pilot light

gas

thermocouple

pilot flame

pilot

ribbon burners

manifold

if the thermocouple does not sense heat from the pilot, it will not allow the gas valve to send gas to the manifold (or pilot)

to light the pilot, the pilot button (on the gas valve) must be depressed temporarily to bypass the thermocouple until it warms up

to gas valve

note: crossover igniters omitted for clarity

gas supply from gas valve

Figure 18. Pilot/Thermocouple

Some newer heating systems have an intermittent pilot which is ignited by a spark plug. Pilot ignition is then verified by a thermocouple. See Figure 18. On some systems, if the pilot does not light after a few attempts, the whole system shuts down. This can create problems if the house is vacant as freezing pipe problems can ensue. Adjustment of the pilot or thermocouple will usually rectify this problem.

14.7 Pilotless Ignition: Oil-fired systems and some mid and high efficiency gas systems do not have a pilot. On these systems, a spark or hot surface ignition system (a spinning "grinding wheel" which glows white hot) is used to ignite the fuel when heat is called for. These systems contain a safety device which shuts down the entire heating system if ignition is not proved after a certain amount of time. Depending upon the arrangement of the system, some will try again after a certain period, while others will not. This can pose a problem in an unattended house as the heat can be off for long periods of time until the problem is discovered.

14.8 Motorized Vent Damper: Vent dampers are commonly found on mid efficiency gas-fired heating systems. The vent damper closes off the exhaust flue when the heating system is not in use, to prevent warm air from the house escaping up the chimney. This does not affect the steady state efficiency but

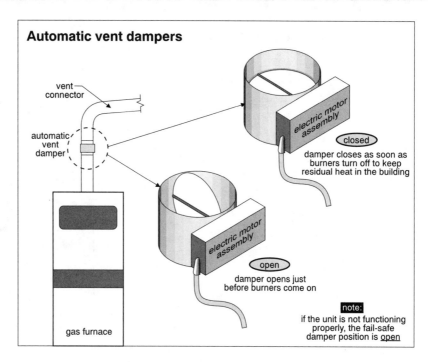

Automatic vent dampers

vent connector

automatic vent damper

electric motor assembly

closed

damper closes as soon as burners turn off to keep residual heat in the building

electric motor assembly

open

damper opens just before burners come on

note:
if the unit is not functioning properly, the fail-safe damper position is <u>open</u>

gas furnace

Figure 19. Motorized Vent Damper

improves the seasonal efficiency. These systems are designed to be fail-safe. In the event the vent damper does not open, the furnace or boiler will not come on (if it did come on, all of the exhaust gases would end up in the house).

Vent dampers spend their time in a corrosive environment and therefore are prone to failure. They should be checked annually. Some experts suspect that their life expectancy can be as short as three years. Vent dampers cannot legally be retrofitted onto existing heating systems. They are approved for gas furnaces only, in some areas.

14.9 Induced Draft Fan: Some mid-efficiency and most high efficiency systems employ an induced draft fan on the exhaust side of the furnace or boiler to pull products of combustion through the unit. This helps to ensure good draft, and reduces heat loss during off cycles, because the fan, at rest, restricts the flow of air to the outside. Again, because of their working environment, these fans have a high failure rate and should be serviced annually.

14.10 Barometric Damper: Barometric dampers are found on oil-fired systems and forced draft gas systems. The barometric damper allows for constant draft in the chimney when the system is on. Air from the basement is drawn into the exhaust flue, but exhaust gases are not allowed to escape out of the flue. The barometric damper is mounted on the exhaust flue and looks like a round swinging door. Barometric dampers are often corroded, out of adjustment, or simply inoperable. They are inexpensive items which are easily repaired; however, they should be maintained in good condition.

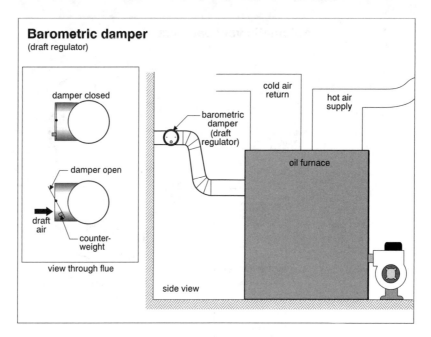

Figure 20. Barometric Damper

14.11 Clearance From Combustibles: The exhaust pipes on conventional oil heating systems should be a minimum of nine inches from combustible surfaces. A six inch clearance is required on gas furnaces. B-Vents (insulated flue pipes) require a one inch clearance. Three inches of air space should also be maintained between the plenum (supply ductwork section immediately above the furnace) and combustible surfaces. Clearances are also required from the sides and rear of the heating plant itself. These clearances vary from unit to unit. On modern systems, the information is given on a plate attached to the boiler or furnace.

14.12 Refractory (Fire Pot): Refractory is found in some boilers and furnaces. It may be a similar material to firebrick found in fireplaces and, in some cases, is firebrick. Its purpose is to protect the other components from direct contact with the flame. Refractory deteriorates with time and exposure to flame and requires repair or replacement from time to time. It is often not visible without dismantling the system or breaking a mortar seal.

14.13 Condensate Line: On high efficiency heating systems, the products of combustion are cooled to the point where condensation forms. This condensate (water) must be collected and must flow to a drain. Sometimes, the drain lines are plugged or poorly installed.

Some cities require the condensate to be neutralized before it goes into the drains. (It is somewhat acidic and some local authorities fear it may deteriorate some types of city drain piping.) Neutralizing kits are available through furnace manufacturers.

14.14 Condensate Pump: If a condensate line (Refer to 14.13 in this section) cannot flow by gravity to a drain, a condensate pump must be installed. The pumps are relatively inexpensive; however, they are a high maintenance item as they tend to fail with great regularity.

14.15 Gas Valve: On gas-fired heating systems, the main gas valve is one of the Most important components. It contains most of the brains of the heating system. Its operation is simple. It is designed to open and allow gas into the combustion chamber; however, it uses feedback from several safety devices to determine whether it is safe or appropriate to allow gas into the combustion chamber. The reliability of gas valves is high. Replacement is neither difficult nor terribly expensive.

White-Rodgers 36B
A particular White-Rodgers gas valve has been known to cause overheating problems as a result of an intermittent malfunction. The valve in question is a White-Rodgers 36B series. Valves which are date coded 7630 through to 7752 are the ones which are considered to be problematic. If any Model 36-B gas valve is present, a heating contractor, the furnace manufacturer, or the valve manufacturer should be contacted.

14.16 Heat Shield: A heat shield is found on some conventional forced-air furnaces. It is located at the point where the ribbon burners project into the heat exchanger. In many cases, the heat shield is loose, rusted, or missing. If this is the case, it should be repaired or replaced. The heat shield is not normally removed during a home inspection.

14.17 Chimney/Chimney Liner: Not all heating systems require a chimney. Electric heating systems do not as there are no products of combustion. High efficiency, and some mid-efficiency heating systems have an exhaust pipe which does not connect to a chimney.

Metal
The majority of heating systems are, however, connected to a chimney. The chimney can be metal or masonry. Modem houses often have metal furnace chimneys (which are actually Class B vents). With time, the corrosive exhaust gases can deteriorate a metal chimney. Metal chimneys more than ten years old should be inspected carefully. Other problems with metal chimneys include poor connection of sections, poor support for the chimney, missing rain caps, and inadequate clearance from combustibles (one inch is required for Class B vents). Rain caps for metal chimneys have changed over the last fifteen years. Newer designs are less susceptible to corrosion. The metal itself is also changing on newer systems.

Masonry
Masonry chimneys can be lined or unlined. An unlined masonry chimney simply has brick or concrete block on the interior. While this is suitable for most oil furnaces, it is not suitable for the vast majority of gas furnaces. Most gas furnaces require a chimney liner to protect the masonry from the exhaust gases. The liner can be metal, clay pipe, or asbestos cement pipe.

Shared Chimneys
In attached housing, it is common for two houses to have one chimney. Each home has one flue, typically. When repairs to the masonry are required, the cost is often shared. Where this situation exists, the neighbor should be consulted prior to starting chimney work.

Shared Flues
A furnace and a fireplace, for example, should not share a single flue in a chimney. For more information, see 8.9 in the Interior Section.

Safety

14.18 Chimney Clean-Out: Chimney flues without metal liners should have a clean-out door at the base of the chimney to remove debris. If debris is allowed to build in the bottom of the chimney, it could eventually block off the exhaust flue for the heating system, and cause exhaust gases to back up into the house. This is an unsafe situation. The frequency of cleaning will depend on the rate of accumulation of debris in the base of the chimney.

Liner

If a considerable amount of debris consisting of mortar, sand and small pieces of brick continue to accumulate in the base of the chimney, a liner should be considered to prevent further chimney deterioration. A specialist should be consulted.

14.19 Thermostat: The function of a thermostat is to turn on the heating system when the temperature near the thermostat is lower than the desired thermostat setting, and shut the system off when the desired temperature is reached.

Location

The location of a thermostat is critical. It should not be placed in areas where there are drafts, a heat source such as a fireplace, or a heating duct in the wall behind the thermostat. It should not be placed behind doors, on outside walls, or in areas where it is likely to receive a considerable amount of direct sunlight. All of these factors can fool the thermostat into thinking the house is warmer or cooler than it actually is. Relocating a thermostat is not a difficult job.

Set-Back Feature

Many modern thermostats have set-back functions which allow the temperature to be lowered during periods when the occupants are away or sleeping. As a general rule of thumb, the maximum set-back employed should be no more than nine Fahrenheit degrees as cooler temperatures create higher relative humidity levels which can result in condensation problems. Also, some heating systems (particularly hot water systems) are not capable of returning the house to its original temperature in a reasonable amount of time if the set-back is too large.

Blower Control

Some thermostats have a control for the blower on forced-air systems. They allow for the blower to work automatically (coming on only when the furnace is on) or continuously. Continuous operation is normally used when an electronic air filter has been provided, as it allows for a constant cleaning of the air within the house.

Problems

Thermostats can function improperly if they are dirty, not level, or improperly calibrated. They can also suffer mechanical damage. Most thermostats contain an anticipator which is a device which prevents overshoot. Overshoot occurs when the heating system heats the house to a higher temperature than the thermostat is calling for. The anticipator must be calibrated to the specific furnace or boiler. If it is not, overshoot or short cycling may occur.

Location

Leaks

Abandoned

14.20 Oil Tank: Oil tanks should be 10 feet from burners. Oil tanks are usually maintenance free; however, leaks can occur in the tank, filter and oil line leading to the burner. Leaking filters and lines can be easily repaired or replaced; however, repairing a leaking tank is seldom done. Most are replaced. Some tanks are located outdoors underground. Inspection of these is not possible during a home inspection.

Condensation

Leakage from tanks is usually the result of rusting which occurs due to water in the tank (from condensation). It settles to the bottom of the tank as it is heavier than oil. This is where most of the rusting occurs. It is best to keep the tank full during the summer months to keep condensation to a minimum.

14.21 Electric Elements/Wiring: Most electric furnaces and boilers have multiple heating elements. The average size for a single element is roughly five kilowatts. Heating elements in electric systems are much like car headlights. They burn out from time to time, however, it is impossible to predict when this will happen. Most electric furnaces and boilers are designed with a sequencer to turn on the heating elements one by one, so that they don't all come on at once and create a large electrical surge. Sometimes, sequencers or relays malfunction which may lead one to believe that an electrical element is burned out when in fact it is not. Therefore, this should be checked by a qualified technician.

The wires leading to heating elements and various controls sometimes overheat in electric furnaces. Any burned wires or components should be replaced.

14.22 Fuses/Breakers: Most electric furnaces and boilers have built-in fuses or breakers. Under normal circumstances, these should not trip or blow. If they do, a specialist should be consulted. The main fuses or breakers at the electrical panel may also cut off power to the furnace or boiler.

14.23 Electric Heaters: Some houses are heated entirely by electric heaters, while others employ electric heat as a supplement to the main heating source. Electric heaters are much like automobile headlights. It is impossible to tell when one is likely to burn out. Fortunately, most are easily replaced.

Electric heaters can be missing, undersized, damaged, rusted, dirty or wired incorrectly. The thermostat can also be defective. Heaters designed to operate at 240 volts can be incorrectly wired at 120 volts. They will not work as efficiently as they should. This will not normally be picked up on a home inspection.

Many basements with warm air furnaces have heating supply registers overhead. These areas often prove to be cool since warm air rises. The heat from these registers lingers near the ceiling level and escapes up to the main floor. One of the common cures is to add electric baseboard heaters to augment the supply. Similar improvements can be made in houses with hot water heating, where some rooms have no radiators, or rads on the ceilings. Relocating the main heat source down to near floor level is another approach.

14.24 Heat Recovery Ventilators: Heat recovery ventilators are also known as air-to-air heat exchangers. They are typically used in houses where increased ventilation is required and there is a desire to recover some of the heat from the air which is being discharged from the building.

UFFI

Heat recovery ventilators are often used in houses which have been insulated with urea formaldehyde foam insulation, in order to increase the number of air changes in the house. Sometimes, the house is kept under positive pressure to help expel formaldehyde gases.

In Energy Efficient Houses

They are also used in energy efficient houses where the number of natural air changes is so low that mechanical ventilation must be provided. Normal minimum requirements call for one third to one half air change per hour.

Indoor Pools

Heat recovery ventilators are commonly used with indoor swimming pool heating systems because many air changes are needed to reduce humidity.

Principle of Operation

One or more blowers move air across a heat exchanger transferring heat from the air being exhausted to the incoming air.

Connections

The fresh air duct should not be directly connected to the return air duct of the furnace unless recommended by the manufacturer. A gap between the fresh air duct and a grill on the return air duct should be maintained to avoid unbalancing the airflow and to allow for tempering of the cool air. This may not be needed if the fan is kept on at high speed.

Intake and Exhaust Hoods

The intake and exhaust hoods on the exterior should be at least six feet apart and three feet from the corner of the building. The intake hood should be at least eighteen inches above grade and at least three feet away from driveways, gas meters or any exhaust vents. The exhaust hood should be at least eight inches above grade.

Problems

Blowers and motors will wear out. Filters can be clogged or missing, resulting in clogging of the heat exchanger. Defrosting cycles can go awry, condensate trays and lines can plug or leak. In corrosive environments, damage can occur to the heat exchanger unless it was specifically designed for that environment.

► 15.0 DISTRIBUTION

Register Location

15.1 Supply Ducts/Registers: Every habitable room should have at least one supply register. Supply registers should be located near exterior walls, below windows. However, it is often not cost-effective to relocate existing registers.

Problems

Common problems with supply ducts and registers are air leaks, disconnected or obstructed ducts, dirty ducts, ducts sized adequately for heating but inadequate for air conditioning, ducts sized for conventional furnaces, but inadequately sized for high efficiency systems, and unbalanced ductwork (too much air coming through one register and not enough air coming through another). Rooms without return registers may be cool if the door is closed. Supply ductwork adds warm air until the room is pressurized. Then the flow stops. Cutting 3/4 inch off the door bottom allows the air to circulate.

Undercut Doors

Registers

Air registers are often missing, broken, or painted shut. They are easily replaced. Supply registers should not be located in garages, since automobile fumes may enter the house when the system is not operating. Many basements have supply registers at the ceiling level only. If the basement is to be finished, it is best to relocate the registers near floor level, since heat rises. If this is not done, the room can feel cool during the winter. An alternative is to provide auxiliary electric baseboard heat.

Gravity Furnace

Ductwork modifications are required when replacing a gravity warm-air furnace with a modern furnace.

Heating Ducts in Concrete

Slab-on-grade houses with forced-air heat often have heating ducts embedded in the concrete foundations and slab. Sometimes the ducts are partially collapsed during the concrete pouring process. Moisture in and around the slab can flood the ducts and rust the metal duct walls. The water standing in the ducts can become a health hazard. Rusted duct walls can come loose and collapse. Any of these will restrict at least some air flow through the system. Ductwork in poured slabs and foundations is, of course, difficult to inspect and repair.

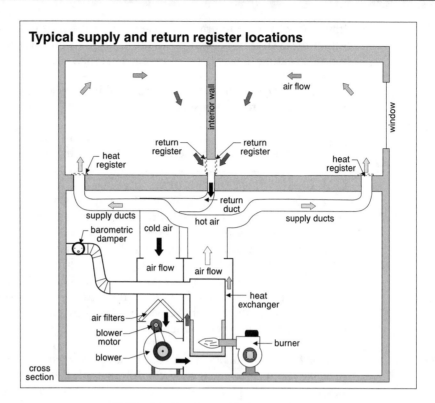

Figure 21. Supply and Return Air System

15.2 Return Air Registers: Ideally, every room which has a supply register should have a return air register; however, this is almost never the case. In many older homes there are one or two centrally located return air registers. Rooms which have supply air registers and no return air registers should have doors which are undercut somewhat, so that air can escape from the room back to the return air register, if the doors are closed. The total supply register area should be equalled by the total area of the return air registers. It is common in older homes to find inadequate return air.

High and Low Levels In sophisticated and high quality installations, there are often high level and low level return air registers, in some rooms. These systems are set up for air conditioning and heating. During the air conditioning season, return air is taken back to the air conditioning system from high registers, collecting warm air at ceiling height. During winter months when heating is required, floor level cooler air is drawn back for heating. A damper on the lower return air register dictate which register will be in use. Compromise systems in modem houses often have low level returns on the first floor and high level returns on the second.

Return air ductwork is often in need of cleaning as large floor mounted return air registers seem to be a collection place for debris. Older return grills in floors are often broken and may not be safe to walk on, or place furniture on.

Location Ideally, the supply registers should be located on an outside wall below a window, and the return register should be located on an opposite wall. In some houses, return air registers were provided near the supply air registers. Some of these systems short circuited themselves in that the warm supply air is simply drawn back into the return air register, with little heat going to the room itself. Sometimes, simply blocking off the poorly located return air register will improve heating in a specific room considerably.

Return air registers should not be provided in garages, since automobile fumes may be drawn into the house.

Supply and return registers will not perform if the air flow is obstructed. Carpeting and furniture should be kept clear of air flow paths.

15.3 Radiators/Convectors: At least one radiator or convector should be provided in each habitable room. Most radiators are of cast iron construction. They are heavy and take a considerable amount of time to heat up. By the same token, they take a long time to coot down and, consequently, tend to produce even heat. Convectors, on the other hand, are normally much lighter weight and are designed to transmit heat quickly to the surrounding air. Therefore, the heating within a room containing convectors is likely to be more cyclical than a room containing radiators. This does not pose a problem except in systems where only some radiators have been replaced by convectors. In this situation, uneven heating can be encountered.

Removal

In some houses, radiators or convectors have been removed to allow for changes (to make room for kitchen cabinets, for example). As a general rule of thumb, they are not cost-effective to re-install. It is much easier to install an electric baseboard heater than a radiator. The same is true if one is planning on relocating a radiator. It is probably best to simply remove it and replace it with electric heat.

Radiators and convectors respond more slowly if air movement around them is obstructed. Reflective materials (aluminum foil, for example) behind radiators help direct heat into the living area.

Problems

If air is trapped in a radiator, it will not heat properly. The air can be released through the bleed valve (see 15.5 in this section).

If the radiators on the top floor of a home are not filled with water because there is not enough in the system, the rads will be cold. Correction on an open system means opening the valve to the plumbing system to add more water. The same procedure is used on a closed system without an automatic make-up valve. Where a make-up valve is present, it may be clogged, or the pressure may be set too low.

Other problems include leaks, usually at the control valves (see 15.4 in this section), and cracking, if the water in the system freezes.

15.4 Radiator/Convector Valves: Most radiators or convectors have a valve controlling the water flow through the unit. These valves are used infrequently and, consequently, when they are used, they often leak. These valves are not operated during a home inspection.

Even valves which are left undisturbed are prone to leakage over time. While the valves are relatively inexpensive to replace, the damage from a leaking valve can be extensive. Consequently, they should be inspected on a regular basis. Ideally, repairs should be undertaken during the summer months, as the work requires draining the heating system.

15.5 Bleed Valves: Radiators and most convectors have a small valve at the top to "bleed" off air which gets trapped in the unit. Trapped air reduces the amount of water in the radiators or convectors, reducing its ability to generate heat.

Radiators or convectors should be bled at least annually. The valves are delicate and easily broken. The very small valve openings can be obstructed by dirt or paint. They are prone to seizing or leaking; however, they are easily replaced. This requires at least partial draining of the system.

If no water comes out of the bleed valve after the pressurized air is released, more water has to be added to the system. See 15.3 in this section.

15.6 Piping: The piping on most hot water heating systems is black steel (not galvanized); however, some modern systems have copper piping. Steel piping corrodes, however, the rate of deterioration tends to be slow as the water within the heating system is rarely replaced. Eventually, it becomes chemically inert and, consequently, the rusting process is stopped. Draining the water from a heating system every summer is not recommended, since the pipes will deteriorate more quickly. On occasion, corroded pipes and connections are discovered. They should be replaced on an as-needed basis.

15.7 Motorized Dampers: Some sophisticated warm-air heating systems are zoned. Thermostats in various areas of the house control dampers which open and close, directing air to the areas where heat is needed. As a general rule, motorized dampers in residential installations tend to be neglected and often break down. In many systems, they are abandoned or removed. It is not possible during an inspection to verify the proper operation of zoned systems.

15.8 Zone Valves: On some sophisticated hot water heating systems different areas of the house are controlled by different thermostats. These thermostats will operate motorized valves which open and close to direct hot water to the areas of the house that require heating. As a general rule, maintenance on these valves tends to be neglected and they are often abandoned. It is not possible during an inspection to verify the proper operation of zoned systems.

Another way to get zone control of a hot water system is with multiple circulating pumps. The thermostats control different pumps, directing water to specific zones, on demand.

15.9 Hot Water Radiant Heating: Radiant heating systems rely on large surface areas heating up to a point where they radiate heat to a room. Most radiant heating systems are found in ceilings; however, some radiant systems are installed in floors. Surface temperatures remain relatively low; however, they should be warm to the touch when the system is operating.

On hot water radiant systems there are several potential problems: one is pipe blockage which prevents the flow of water through the system, rendering it inoperative. While this type of problem is not found frequently, it is difficult to locate the blockage. A more common problem with hot water radiant systems is leakage. When a leak occurs, however, it is usually easily located due to the obvious water damage. (This is not true if the leakage is below the basement floor.)

Heating pipes can be buried too deep (more than three inches) in concrete floors, resulting in slow response to the thermostat and some heat loss. There may be unwanted fluctuations in temperature. Hot spots and cold spots may be noted if pipes are too far apart (more than eight to sixteen inches).

These systems are susceptible to building settlement, and especially with steel or copper, the pipes can be broken as the house moves.

With any radiant heating system, care must be taken not to damage the system when drilling holes or mounting things such as light fixtures. Special patching materials are available for treating cracks and other flaws in heated ceilings.

On systems where only a part of the house is heated radiantly, the lower temperature operation requires mixing valves and the long runs of small diameter pipe require separate pumps due to friction loss.

15.10 Electric Radiant Heat: A description of electric radiant heat can be found on Page 5 of this section. If the concealed wires break, it is often difficult to locate the problem. Some local utilities have special equipment that can locate the problem. In many cases, these systems are abandoned in favor of baseboard heaters. As with hot water radiant systems, care must be taken not to damage the system by drilling holes in the ceiling or by mounting light fixtures. Surface finish cracks are common with electric radiant systems. Special patching compounds are available for repairing cracks.

▶ 16.0 LIMITATIONS

16.1 System Shut Off/Inoperative: If the power supply to a system, or the pilot light for a system is off, the system cannot be tested.

16.2 Summer Test Procedure: During the portion of the year when the heating system is not normally operating, the heater, furnace or boiler is tested by turning up the thermostat. This will result in a partial test of the heating unit; however, the adequacy of the distribution system and amount of heat cannot be ascertained. Problems which may only show up during long term operation of the heating system may go undetected.

16.3 Air Conditioning/Heat Pump Operating: A furnace will not be tested if the central air conditioning or heat pump system is in operation. This would put unnecessary stress on the system.

▶ 17.0 STEAM BOILERS

Steam boilers are not installed residentially today except as replacements on older steam systems, but may be found in older homes. The boiler itself is similar to a hot water boiler, typically made of cast iron or steel. As with hot water boilers, the cast iron systems last longer than steel. Generally speaking, a hot water boiler may be expected to last slightly longer than a steam boiler made of the same material. The fuel can be coal, gas or oil, similar to a hot water boiler.

Identification   A steam boiler may be distinguished from a hot water boiler by the presence of a water level gage (sight glass or gage glass). This is a vertical glass tube which indicates how much water is in the boiler. The boiler is typically three quarters filled with water. If water cannot be seen in the glass tube, the boiler should not be operated. Similarly, the water level in the tube should not fluctuate wildly during operation.

Operating Pressures   Steam systems in houses operate at 1/2 to 5 psi steam pressure. This is lower than hot water systems (12 to 20 psi). Steam pressures which are too high can affect the boiler water level and steam delivery to the radiators.

The radiators, piping and top section of the boiler are filled with air when the boiler is at rest. When the boiler comes on and steam is generated, the steam moves through the system displacing the air. The air is released through air vents on the rads or on the piping system. As the steam hits the relatively cold surface of the radiators, it condenses giving up its heat to the rads. The heat is transferred from the rads into the room, similar to a hot water system. The condensed water flows back to the boiler to be reheated.

One-pipe Systems   A one-pipe steam system has a single pipe attached to each radiator. Steam moves through this pipe to the rad, and the condensate flows back to the boiler through the same pipe. The pipe is sloped (at roughly one inch every ten feet) so that the water can drain back. This type of system typically has an air vent at each rad. The one-pipe system cannot be converted to a hot water system without the addition of a second pipe.

Two-Pipe Systems   The two-pipe system has one pipe for carrying steam to the rad, and a smaller pipe for returning condensate water to the boiler. Radiators on a two-pipe system typically do not have air vents on the rads themselves. On the return line (condensate line) there is a steam trap which allows water and air to pass through, but closes when confronted with steam. This keeps the steam in the piping and radiator system where it can heat the building effectively.

Air is vented out of the system by a main air vent. The two-pipe system can be converted to hot water, which may yield more efficient heating, and better control of the heating. Conversion can be tricky, and problems can be encountered if the work is not done professionally. A specialist should be consulted.

Generally speaking, two-pipe systems are considered somewhat more economical to operate than one-pipe systems.

Radiators   The radiators are typically provided with a supply valve that can be opened or closed, and may have an air vent. The supply valves can be opened or closed part way on a two-pipe system, but should be either fully opened or fully closed on a one-pipe system. Sophisticated and relatively expensive supply valves are thermostatically controlled, to allow zone control of the heating.

Air vents may have an adjustable air opening. This is used for balancing the system, so that the air vents close to the boiler can be throttled down, causing air to be released more slowly. Ideally, all radiators become fully charged with steam at the same time. In practice this rarely occurs.

Wet Return or   Depending on whether the return line joins the boiler above or below the
Dry Return   boiler water level, the system is described as wet return or dry return. In a wet
                     return system, a "Hartford Loop" should be provided to prevent a leak in the
                     return piping from allowing water to leak out of the boiler. Since there is a
                     great deal of piping, the possibility for leakage is high. If the water leaks out of
                     the boiler, this will at best leave the house without heat, and at worst will crack
                     the boiler.

Controls   The steam boiler has three primary safety controls.

                     1) A high pressure limit will shut off the boiler if the pressure is too high. This
                     system is usually connected to the boiler with a pig tail piping configuration.
                     The pig tail is filled with water, so the steam won't corrode the control.

                     2) A low water cut-out is set to shut off the burner if the water level in the
                     boiler drops below a given level. Some of these are located inside the boiler,
                     but the majority arc mounted externally. An external low water cut-out has a
                     blow-off valve or bleed valve which should be operated weekly. When water
                     is released from this valve, the burner should shut off. It is not unusual for this
                     to be neglected.

                     3) A pressure relief valve is usually set at 15 psi to relieve pressure which may
                     build up in the boiler as a result of a malfunction.

                     Other controls include water level and pressure gages to monitor the operation
                     of the system. There is also a manual or automatic water make-up valve so that
                     water can be added to the system. Many service people recommend not relying
                     on an automatic water make-up valve to ensure adequate water supply.

Strengths of   Steam systems are simple with a gravity circulation system. No pumps or fans
Steam Systems   are required. If heat is lost in a building, there is no danger of freezing pipes or
                     radiators. (The boiler itself can freeze, of course.) In order to work on the sys-
                     tem, it is not necessary to drain water out of pipes and rads as is the case with
                     the hot water system..

Weaknesses of   They are slow to respond compared to hot water and are not generally as fuel
Steam Systems   efficient as hot water systems. Steam radiators can be very hot and this can be
                     somewhat dangerous if there are young children in the house. The boiler must
                     be at a lower elevation than the radiators to provide steam to each rad, unless
                     there is a pump on the return water (condensate pump). Poorly tuned steam
                     systems can be very noisy. Since they are not common, there are few qualified
                     people to work on them in most areas.

Operating   Since steam boilers are for the most part older, the availability of parts can be
Problems   a problem. Obstructed air vents will prevent the system from heating up. Air
                     vents stuck in the open position will be inefficient and can be dangerous as
                     steam is released directly into the room.

                     If the water level in the system drops, the boiler may crack as it overheats. If
                     the system floods with water, the piping and radiator systems may allow water
                     to leak out.

If the blow-off for the low water cut-out is not tested regularly, the cut-out may not operate properly and may fail to shut the boiler off in a low water situation.

If the pipe slope is incorrect due to poor installation or building settlement, this system can be very noisy and heat distribution can be very uneven.

If the steam trap fails in the open position, the system will be inefficient and the house will be uncomfortable. Similarly, if the steam trap is clogged, steam may be unable to move properly through the pipes and rads.

These are only the common problems associated with steam systems. The list is by no means exhaustive.

Summary   A steam boiler should be fully serviced by a specialist upon taking possession of the home. It is important that the homeowner know how to maintain the system and that the maintenance procedures be followed. If it is a two-pipe system, consideration can be given to conversion to hot water. Again, a specialist should be consulted.

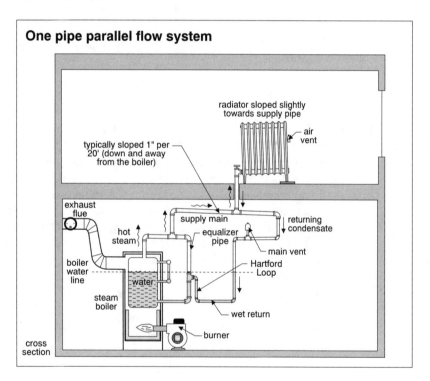

Figure 22. One-Pipe Steam System

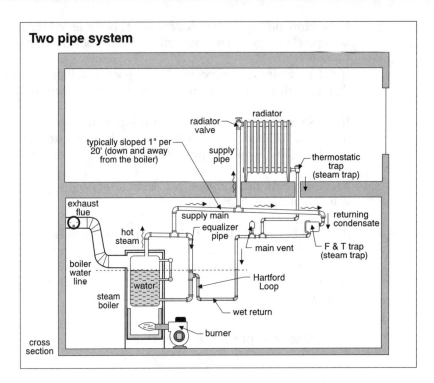

Figure 23. Two-Pipe Steam System

► **18.0 Combination Heating Systems**

Description   Combination heating systems provide domestic hot water as well as heating the house. In simple terms the heat source is a special water heater. It has conventional connections to be hooked up to the plumbing system. It also has an extra inlet and outlet connection intended for a fan coil unit. The water heated within the tank can flow to the plumbing system or it can flow to the fan coil unit. The fan blows air across the coil, picking up heat. The warm air is distributed throughout the house via ductwork.

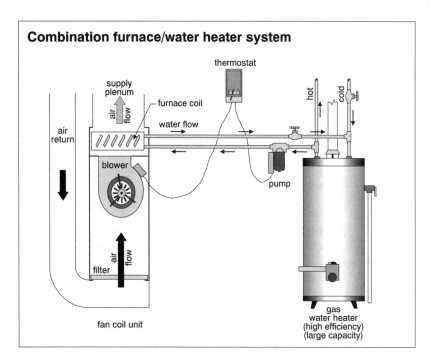

Figure 24. Combination System

The concept is not new. Years ago, many boilers had a loop coming from the boiler to heat domestic water. These older systems relied on a heat exchanger within the water tank so that the water used for heating never came in contact with the potable water.

These older systems used the boiler to heat the water in the house. New combination systems work the other way around. They use the water heater to heat the house. The principal difference is that the water flowing through the fan coil unit is potable water which is returned to the water tank and will eventually end up in the plumbing system. It is for this reason that new combination systems cannot be connected to older radiator systems. They can only be connected to brand new fan coil units, connected to the system with new piping.

Problems   Combination systems tend to have modest capacity. Generally speaking, the systems are not larger than 75,000 Btu's/hour. Early experience has indicated that some systems are undersized for heating. As a result, homeowners have turned up their domestic water temperature to as high as 160/170°F. This has resulted in scalding situations and pressure relief valves leaking. If the units
Mixing Valves   are to be operated at such high temperatures, mixing valves to cool the domestic hot water are required.

Some jurisdictions are insisting that the systems be designed so that the water temperature can be no more than 140°F and the design water temperature of the air handler is 130°F. This means that more airflow is needed to heat the house. The ductwork in many houses is not designed to handle higher volumes of air. Therefore, these systems would appear to be most practical in climates where the heating demand is relatively small compared to the domestic hot water demand.

New Technology

With respect to reliability and problems, the systems are too new to forecast. Some manufactures are using high quality stainless steel for the tank, combustion chamber and exhaust flue. These units are suspected to have a long life expectancy.

The fan coil units are not necessarily made by the same manufacturer. Consequently, quality and life expectancy can vary.

6

COOLING/HEAT PUMPS

THE

Home Reference

BOOK

TABLE OF CONTENTS

► INTRODUCTION

There are many types of air conditioning systems; however, they all work on the same principle. They move heat from a relatively cool space to a relatively warm space. The systems all take advantage of some basic scientific laws of liquids and gases. When liquids evaporate into gases, they absorb a considerable amount of heat. When gases are condensed back into a liquid state, they give off heat. In addition, if the pressure of a gas is increased, the temperature will also increase. Most systems use the refrigerant "Freon", a substance which changes state at temperatures and pressures which are well suited to this application.

► 1.0 AIR CONDITIONING

1.1 Air Cooled Air Conditioning: Air cooled air conditioning systems usually work in conjunction with a forced-air furnace. The systems have two main components: the evaporator unit located in the ductwork immediately above the furnace, and the condenser unit located outdoors. The refrigerant enters the evaporator as a cold liquid and absorbs heat from the household air to boil the liquid and turn it into a gas. The resulting reduction in air temperature also causes water in the house air to condense, reducing humidity levels within the house. This dehumidifying helps make the house more comfortable.

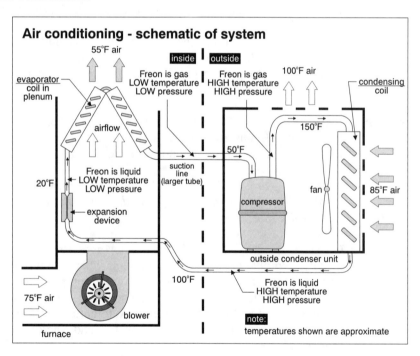

Figure 1. Air Cooled Air Conditioning

The refrigerant, which is now a gas, moves outdoors to the condenser unit. The compressor squeezes the gas into a smaller volume. All the heat which is contained in the gas is also squeezed into a smaller volume and consequently, the gas becomes hotter than the outside air. The hot gas then enters the condenser coil. A fan in the condenser unit blows outdoor air across the coil and cools the gas. As it cools, it condenses into a liquid. The liquid then passes through a pressure reducing device which causes the temperature of the liquid to drop below that of the household air. The liquid passing through the evaporator coil is evaporated into a gas again, stealing more heat and humidity from the house and the cycle continues.

Compressor   The compressor which moves the refrigerant through the lines and compresses the refrigerant is the heart of the system. It is usually located outdoors in the same cabinet as the condenser.

1.2 Water Cooled Air Conditioning: Water cooled air conditioning systems work essentially the same way as conventional systems which are air cooled. They have a section above the furnace which evaporates a liquid into a gas and steals heat from the house. The gas is then compressed to concentrate the heat (consequently raising the temperature). Then, instead of blowing outside air across the gas to cool it, water from the plumbing system in the house is used. Consequently, the condenser portion of the air conditioning system does not have to be outdoors. It is normally located in the basement near the furnace.

Once the water has cooled the gas back down to a liquid, the warmed water must be disposed of. It is no longer drinkable and, therefore, must go down the drain. As an alternative, some people use the warm waste water to fill a swimming pool or water the lawn.

Compressor   On these systems, the compressor is just as critical as it is on an air cooled system. It is the heart of the air conditioner. The compressor is located in the basement and, therefore, it is not subjected to the extremes of the outdoors.

NOTE: On water cooled air conditioning systems, water must flow through the system when it is operating or severe damage can occur to the unit. The supply water valve must be open.

On systems where the discharged water goes straight down a drain, there is usually no problem. However, on systems where the water can go down a drain or be used to water the lawn or fill a swimming pool, there are usually several valves which dictate where the water will go. It is imperative that at least one valve be open to allow water to flow. Automatic valves are available; however, like any mechanical device, they can fail and, therefore, should be checked regularly.

1.3 Independent Air Conditioning: in houses which are heated by some other means than a forced-air system, central air conditioning systems are independent of the heating. Since there is no distribution ductwork, special air conditioning ducts must be added. They are identical in operation to the air conditioning systems described above; however, the evaporator coil does not sit in the ductwork above the furnace. Instead, it sits in independent ductwork.

On an air conditioning system which shares ductwork with a heating system, the blower for the heating system is used for air conditioning. With an independent system, a separate blower must be provided.

Ductwork   Independent systems are normally located in attics; however, they are sometimes in the basement. Most independent systems are installed on a retrofit basis and, consequently, there are limitations as to the size and location of the ductwork. Limited space dictates that many of the systems must have very small ductwork. Most of these systems employ round, flexible, insulated ductwork which has a very small diameter. To compensate for the small ducts, the velocity of the air travelling through the ducts is increased dramatically. With these systems, discharge nozzles (diffusers) mounted in ceilings are used instead of conventional heating registers. A large return air grille is typically ceiling mounted on the top floor. Other than the size and location of ductwork, and the location of the major components, these systems are very similar to conventional air conditioners.

Disadvantages Because independent systems are normally installed on a retrofit basis, a few compromises have to be made. Attic mounted units are more difficult to service simply because of their location. Also, a system mounted in the attic tends to be noisier than a system mounted in the basement. Special care should be taken in attic installations to prevent leakage of condensate into the living space below. Please refer to 16.0, Attic Drip Pans, in this section.

Since independent systems are normally installed in houses which did not have ductwork, it is not uncommon to take advantage of the ductwork to perform other functions. Therefore, electronic air cleaners, humidifiers, and plenum heaters are sometimes found with independent systems. For more information on these components, please refer to the Heating Section.

NOTE: Systems employing humidifiers which are attic mounted are prone to winter freezing problems.

1.4 Gas Chillers: Gas chillers work on the same basic principle as conventional air conditioners in that they rely on changes of state of a refrigerant at different pressures. Rather than using a compressor to drive the system, heat is used. While this sounds contradictory, the systems do work. The process tends to be more complicated than for conventional air conditioning.

The system consists of a pressure vessel containing a strong solution of liquid ammonia (modem systems use lithium bromide). When heat is added, ammonia is boiled off, producing a high temperature, high pressure vapor. The refrigerant vapor is then cooled to a liquid state (at high pressure). The still relatively hot liquid ammonia is then pushed to the evaporator where it passes through a flow restrictor which drastically reduces its pressure and, consequently, its temperature. The evaporator is a tank in which water, warmed by the household air in a coil over the furnace, is cooled by the ammonia. (The chilled water, then returns to the coil over the furnace where it can cool the household air.) Heat from the water causes the ammonia to boil off again. This relatively cool ammonia (low pressure) gas is then mixed with a low pressure weak solution of hot liquid ammonia. This mixture is cooled until the vapor is absorbed into the solution making it a strong solution again. A high pressure pump sends this solution on its way back to the pressure vessel for the process to begin again.

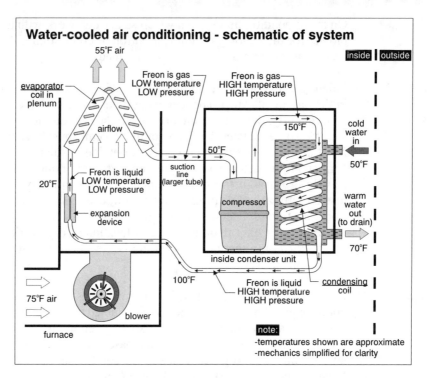

Figure 2. Water Cooled Air Conditioning

Very few gas chillers are still made for residential applications and replacement parts are not available for some systems. Consequently, when a gas chiller fails it is normally replaced by a conventional air conditioning system.

It is essential that a qualified serviceman work on gas chilling systems as the pressure within the system is extremely high.

► 2.0 HEAT PUMPS

A heat pump is simply an air conditioner which can work in reverse to help heat the house when cooling is not needed. During the cooling season, it collects heat from the interior of the house and discharges it to the exterior, like any other air conditioner. During the heating season, the opposite is true. This is accomplished by simply reversing the flow of the refrigerant. The condenser becomes the evaporator and the evaporator becomes the condenser.

Refrigerator Analogy

To further illustrate the idea, one might consider a refrigerator as a heat pump working in the heating mode to heat a kitchen. The temperature within the refrigerator is obviously cooler than the temperature within the kitchen, yet the refrigerator's cooling system is able to steal heat from the inside of the refrigerator and release the heat into the kitchen, via the coils on the back of the refrigerator.

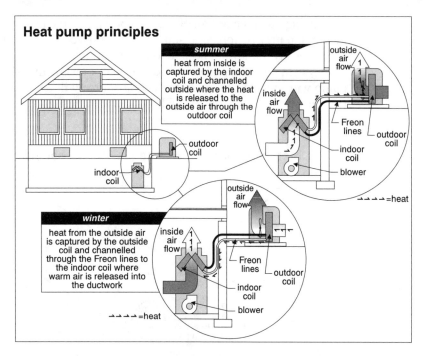

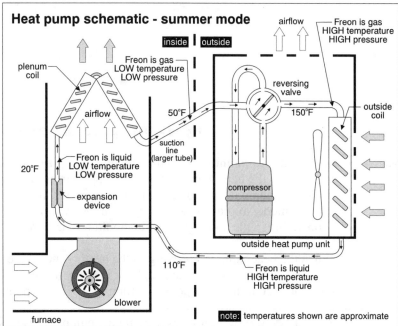

Figure 3. Air Source Heat Pump

As with conventional air conditioning, the compressor is the most critical component.

Economical Operation In northern climates, heat pumps are not capable of carrying the entire heating load of a house. They are only practical to operate when the outside air has enough heat that it can be collected economically. In other words, when it costs more than a dollar's worth of electricity to get the heat pump to generate a dollar's worth of heat, the system is no longer efficient and is shut down. At this stage, the central heating system takes over.

Depending upon the design of the heat pump and the insulation of the house, the heat pump may be forced to shut off earlier. Even if the heat pump is operating economically, it may not be able to generate enough heat to keep the house warm (the system has slipped below the balance point). If this should occur, the heat pump will shut off and the main heating source will take over. This assumes that the furnace is gas or oil. Electric furnaces and heat pumps can run simultaneously.

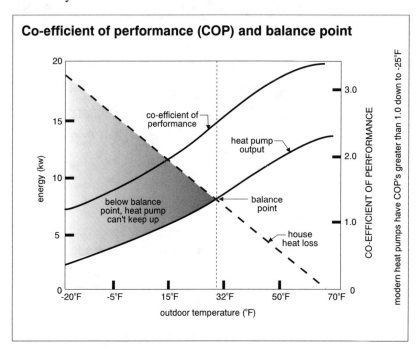

Figure 4. Heat Pump Balance Point

Limited Testing   A heat pump cannot be tested during exceptionally cold periods of the year, when the heat pump is not working. During other portions of the year, if the heat pump is operating in the heating mode, it should not be tested in the cooling mode, to prevent added stress on the system. Conversely, if the system is operating in the cooling mode, it should not be tested in the heating mode.

Drafty   When the heat pump is operating in the heating mode, the air coming out of the registers feels drafty to some people. It is not as warm as the air from the registers when the furnace is operating (roughly 90°F. as opposed to 120°F.).

2.1 Air Source: Most residential heat pumps are very similar in appearance to air cooled air conditioners. There is an outside box which is used to dissipate heat during the air conditioning season and collect heat during the heating season. These systems are called air source heat pumps.

Furnace

2.2 Auxiliary Heat: As mentioned earlier, heat pumps are not capable of carrying the entire heating load during the coldest parts of a northern winter. With most systems, the heat pump has to eventually shut down and let the furnace take over because there is not enough heat in the outside air to be collected economically.

Kool-Fire

Some systems are designed to fool the heat pump. They have a burner (usually natural gas) outdoors below the evaporator coil (the coil which is collecting the heat). Just when the system is about to shut down and pass over its responsibilities to the furnace, the outdoor burner comes on and the evaporator coil thinks that there has suddenly been a heat wave. All of a sudden there is enough heat in the outside air to keep going. These systems do not require a furnace to supplement the heat pump because the heat pump never experiences the coldest part of the winter – or at least it thinks it doesn't. It's being fooled by an outdoor auxiliary heater.

Advantages

These systems require no furnace and no chimney.

Disadvantages

These systems have a high initial cost. Long term durability and life expectancy are unknown, however oxidation has been noted on the burner and the coil as a result of condensation.

2.3 Ground Source And Water Source: Rather than using outside air to collect or dissipate heat, some systems use the ground or water. A ground source heat pump has piping running through the ground which is used to collect or dissipate the heat. The piping can be installed horizontally (shallow) or vertically (deep) below the ground surface.

Some systems use two wells instead of piping. Ground water is pumped from one well. Heat is extracted from the water and the water is pumped back into the other well.

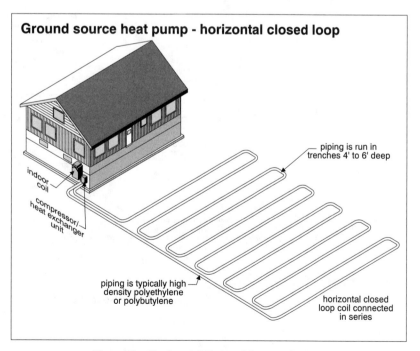

Ground source heat pump - horizontal closed loop

indoor coil

compressor/ heat exchanger unit

piping is typically high density polyethylene or polybutylene

piping is run in trenches 4' to 6' deep

horizontal closed loop coil connected in series

Figure 5a. Horizontal Ground Source System

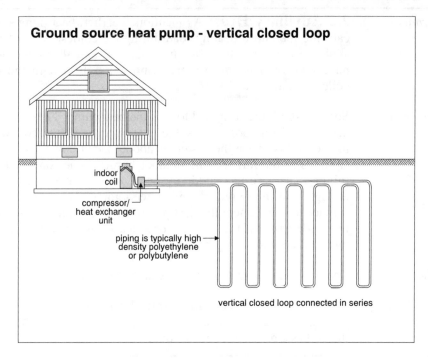

Figure 5b. Vertical Ground Source System

In houses located near a reasonably large body of water, the water can be used as a source for collecting and dissipating heat. These systems are called water source heat pumps.

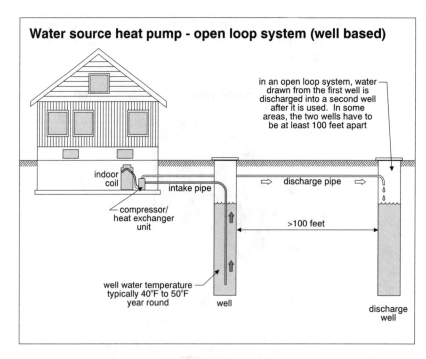

Figure 6. Water Source System

The advantages of ground source and water source heat pumps are that the medium, namely the ground below the frost line or the water below the ice in a pond or river, never freezes. Consequently, there is more heat available to be collected during winter months. In addition to high installation costs, the disadvantage of these systems is that the buried piping in the ground or the water can develop a leak which is difficult to locate and repair. On two well systems the discharge well can become blocked causing water to bubble to the surface

In some instances, environmental laws prohibit the use of ground or water source heat pumps.

2.4 Independent Heat Pumps: In houses which are heated by some other means than a forced-air system, heat pump systems are independent of the heating. Since there is no distribution ductwork, special ducts must be added. They are similar in operation to other heat pump systems described above; however, the indoor coil does not sit in the ductwork above the furnace. Instead, it sits in independent ductwork.

Blower

On a heat pump system which shares ductwork with a heating system, the blower for the heating system is used for the heat pump. With an independent system, a separate blower must be provided.

Ductwork

Independent systems are normally located in attics; however, they are sometimes in the basement. Most independent systems are installed on a retrofit basis and, consequently, there are limitations to the size and location of the ductwork. Limited space dictates that many of the systems must have very small ductwork. Most of these systems employ round, flexible, insulated ductwork which has a very small diameter. To compensate for the small ducts, the velocity of the air travelling through the ducts is increased dramatically. With these systems, discharge nozzles (diffusers) mounted in ceilings are used instead of conventional heating registers. A large return air grille is typically ceiling mounted on the top floor. Other than the size and location of ductwork, and the location of the major components, these systems are identical to conventional heat pumps.

Disadvantages

Because independent systems are normally installed on a retrofit basis, a few compromises have to be made. Attic mounted units are more difficult to service simply because of their location. Also, a system mounted in the attic tends to be noisier than a system mounted in the basement. Special care should be taken to avoid leakage of condensate into the living space below. Please refer to 16.0 Attic Drip Pans, in this section.

Independent systems are often limited in size (capacity). Therefore, they are not practical in some instances.

Since independent systems are normally installed in houses which did not have ductwork, it is not uncommon to take advantage of the ductwork to perform other functions. Therefore, electronic air cleaners, humidifiers, and plenum heaters are sometimes found with independent systems. For more information on these components, please refer to the Heating Section.

NOTE: Systems employing humidifiers which are attic mounted are prone to winter freezing problems.

► 3.0 COOLING CAPACITY

Both air conditioners and heat pumps have a rated cooling capacity. Heat pumps also have a rated heating capacity which varies, depending on outside temperature.

Ratings

The ratings are given in tons. A ton represents 12,000 B.T.U.'s per hour. A B.T.U. is a British Thermal Unit and it represents the amount of heat required to raise the temperature of a pound of water by one Fahrenheit degree (or in the case of cooling, the amount of heat which must be absorbed to lower the temperature of a pound of water one Fahrenheit degree).

Heat Gain

Cooling systems are sized by calculating the heat gain for the house. The heat gain is dependent upon the size and configuration of the house, the construction, the amount of insulation, the type, size and orientation of windows, as well as several other variables. Cooling systems are sized to keep the house roughly fifteen to twenty degrees cooler than outdoors during the hottest day of the year.

In northern climates, heat pumps are not designed to carry the entire heating load for a house. They are sized to meet the cooling demands of the house. The heat they provide varies with the outdoor temperature. The colder it gets, the less heat they can provide.

Without performing detailed heat gain calculations, it is not possible to determine the size of system which will be adequate for a house. In addition, some systems (both heat pumps and air conditioners) are installed without matching condenser and evaporator coils. One coil might be rated for two tons while the other is rated for two-and-one-half tons. It is not usually possible to determine this at the time of an inspection. Incidentally, the size of systems such as these is approximated by taking the outdoor coil rating and going 1,000 B.T.U. in the direction of the plenum coil rating. For example, if the outdoor coil is 36,000 B.T.U and the indoor coil is 30,000 B.T.U., the system capacity is roughly 35,000 B.T.U.

Most often, inadequate air conditioning or heat pump performance is due to an inadequate ductwork system as opposed to undersized equipment. As a general rule, however, most houses have systems sized at one ton cooling for every seven hundred to one thousand square feet of house in moderate climates, and four hundred and fifty to six hundred square feet of house in warmer climates. Modern, well insulated and designed homes may need considerably less. Older, energy inefficient homes may need more. From a durability standpoint, most installers say it is better to slightly undersize a cooling system. The equipment will probably last longer if this is done.

► 4.0 FAILURE PROBABILITY

Any piece of mechanical or electrical equipment can fail at anytime. It is impossible to determine which component of your car, for example, will fail next. It could be a door handle which would be inconvenient, or it could be the engine block which would be catastrophic. A ten dollar fan belt or a three dollar gasoline filter can render your car immobile.

The same is true of an air conditioning system or a heat pump. Since it is impossible to determine when a minor component will fail, we have concentrated on the major components and estimated failure probability by considering the age and condition of the equipment. The type of failure we have contemplated would involve replacement of one or more major components, or replacement of the entire system. The compressor is the major component of these systems.

► 5.0 COMPRESSOR

The compressor is the heart of every heat pump and air conditioning system (with the exception of gas chillers). It is responsible for moving the refrigerant through the system, and compressing the refrigerant to the point where it becomes a high pressure, high temperature gas. Once the gas is in this state, it is capable of giving off heat. A compressor can be thought of as simply a pump for gases.

Life Expectancy

The life expectancy of a compressor is typically ten to fifteen years, in moderate climates and eight to ten years in hot climates. It is not uncommon for a compressor to constitute thirty to fifty percent of the cost of an entire system. Unfortunately, from a visual inspection it is usually not possible to tell whether the compressor in the system is the original or a replacement. Residential compressors are hermetically sealed, and cannot be closely examined. Therefore, when looking at a twelve year old air conditioner, it is not possible without dismantling the system, to determine whether the compressor will need replacement in the near future or whether the compressor has recently been replaced.

Depending on the unit age, replacement of a failed compressor may not be cost effective. If the unit is so old that replacement parts are not readily available or if the system uses an older refrigerant which is now banned (a suspected ozone threat), it may be better to replace the entire condenser unit, rather than just the compressor.

Easily Damaged

Severe damage can occur to air conditioning compressors if they are turned on when the outside temperature is below 60° F. (15° C.). Some compressors contain a small heating element which must be on for twelve to twenty-four hours prior to the compressor starting up. If the heater has not been turned on, or if the outside temperature is low, the compressor should not be tested.

Cannot Test

The compressor for a heat pump must operate over a much larger temperature range than an air conditioner compressor; however, below a given temperature the heat pump is locked out and the only source of heat is the furnace, or back up plenum heaters. Under these conditions, the compressor cannot be tested.

The compressor (located outdoors in most systems) must be kept level (within roughly ten degrees). Failure to do so will damage the compressor.

► 6.0 PLENUM COIL

The plenum coil sits in the ductwork immediately downstream of oil or gas furnaces and upstream (usually) of electric furnaces. On an air conditioning system, the plenum coil (known as the evaporator coil) is used to transfer heat from the house air to the refrigerant within the coil. On a heat pump, the coil works the same way in the summer, and in reverse during the heating season when it transfers heat from the coil to the air being passed across it. In the winter, it is acting as a condenser.

Coils are normally made of copper or aluminum tubing to which very thin fins are attached to enhance the heat transfer. With age, coils can corrode. This can result in a blockage of the refrigerant line or leakage.

Temperature Drop

The temperature drop across the coil should be 14° to 22° F. If fins are not cleaned regularly, air flow across the coil can be blocked by dust and other foreign matter. Dirty fins are also a common problem where the furnace filter is dirty or missing. The fins are extremely delicate and can easily be damaged. Low air flow can lead to excess temperature drop across the coil, resulting in ice build-up problems. Too low a temperature drop also indicates the need for service. The problems may include fan size or coolant pressures.

The plenum coil is not visible or readily accessible.

► 7.0 OUTDOOR COIL

The function of the outdoor coil is to transfer heat from the refrigerant to the outside air when the system is in the cooling mode. On a heat pump, the system works in reverse during the heating mode, transferring heat from the outside air to the refrigerant.

The coils are constructed of copper or aluminum and have very fine fins attached to improve heat transfer. As with plenum coils, outdoor coils are subject to corrosion, blockage and leakage. Air flow across the coil can be inhibited by dirt or other foreign matter. Damaged fins will reduce efficiency.

Ice Up

Air flow can also be inhibited on a heat pump during the heating mode if the coils ice up. This happens because the outdoor air is being cooled to a point where it can no longer hold its water vapor. The moisture falls out of the air as liquid and quickly freezes on the coil. Heat pumps have a defrost cycle to prevent ice up problems. Some are timed defrost cycles while others operate on a demand defrost system.

► 8.0 WATER COOLED COIL

A water cooled coil performs the same function as the outdoor coil on an air cooled central air conditioning system. It is a condenser which cools the refrigerant to the extent that it returns to a liquid state.

Rather than using a finned coil with air passing across it, this coil is surrounded by a water jacket to take the heat away.

As with all coils, there is potential for a "Freon" leak. There is also the possibility of a water leak from the jacket. Corrosion from recycled pool water (which contains chlorine) is also a possibility and, consequently, reusing pool water as opposed to fresh water is not recommended.

► 9.0 OUTDOOR FAN

The function of the outdoor fan is to move air over the outdoor coil. This cools the refrigerant during the cooling mode or adds heat to the refrigerant in the heating mode.

Outdoor fans are subjected to the elements and blades can be damaged by foreign matter. Also, motors and bearings can wear out. The outdoor fan section can wear out prematurely if the intake air or the exhaust air is obstructed. This will also greatly reduce efficiency. Consequently, it is important to keep the area around the outdoor unit free of obstructions.

► 10.0 CONDENSATE TRAY/LINE/PUMP

When an air conditioning system or a heat pump is cooling, household air passing across the cold plenum coil causes condensation to form. This condensation is collected in a condensate tray. A condensate line carries the water from the tray to a floor drain or sink, arranged so that siphoning cannot occur. Condensate can also be discharged into the ground outside the house.

If the water cannot flow by gravity, a condensate pump is installed to pump the water to a suitable location. The condensate should not discharge directly into a plumbing vent or stack, nor onto a roof.

While the condensate tray is not visible, there is sometimes evidence of a malfunction.

Water stains can sometimes be detected on the top of the furnace indicating a cracked or broken condensate tray, a condensate tray which is not level, or a condensate tray which has a plugged outlet and is overflowing. It is essential that the condensate tray function properly or the excess water will drip onto the heat exchanger (the most critical component of the furnace). Water dripping on a heat exchanger can rust it prematurely, requiring furnace replacement.

The condensate line which takes the condensation from the tray to a drain can be leaking, missing, broken, or plugged. On systems requiring condensate pumps, it is important that the pump be inspected monthly. While the pumps are relatively inexpensive and are easily replaced, they are prone to failure.

► 11.0 REFRIGERANT LINES

Refrigerant lines which are normally copper, transfer refrigerant back and forth between the condenser and the evaporator. Refrigerant lines which contain cold vapor should be insulated to prevent condensation from forming. With conventional air conditioners and heat pumps, this is the larger tube between the plenum coil and the outdoor unit.

The most common problems with refrigerant lines are mechanical damage, leakage and corrosion. Refrigerant lines are frequently damaged where they pass through the house wall. It is preferable, although not critical, to keep the length of refrigerant lines to a minimum.

► 12.0 INDOOR FAN

The purpose of the indoor fan is to move air across the indoor coil picking up or giving off heat. The warmed or cooled air is distributed throughout the house. On conventional air conditioning systems and heat pumps, the indoor fan is actually the blower for the furnace (usually modified for increased air flow). On independent systems, a separate fan is provided.

Problems   Fan bearings and motors can wear out. On belt driven fans, the belt tension can be incorrect or the pulleys improperly set up. Missing filters allow the blower to get dirty. Fans which are out of balance can be extremely noisy, especially attic fans since the noise is transmitted through the rafters and ceilings.

Fan Size   If the fan is too small, air flow through the house will be weak. The air at the registers may be cool, but the velocity will be too low. An oversized fan will give very strong air flow, but the air will not be as cool as it should be. The system may also be noisy.

► 13.0 DUCTWORK

The ductwork distributes the heated or cooled air throughout the house. Ductwork can be disconnected, obstructed or dirty. Supply and return registers can be missing, damaged, inoperative or covered with furniture or carpets. Ductwork originally designed for heating only, may be undersized for cooling. When air conditioning or a heat pump is being added to an existing system, the size of the ductwork may limit the size of the air conditioning or heat pump . On poorly matched systems, the air flow at the registers will be weak. In most cases, major ductwork modifications are not cost-effective.

Humidifiers   Poor humidifier installations can cause air conditioning problems. The most common by-pass humidifiers are mounted on furnace ductwork near the air conditioner. A section of ductwork runs between the supply and return ductwork, with the humidifier in the duct. A damper should be provided to shut off the air flow through this duct during the cooling season. If there is no damper, or it is left open in summer, the air conditioner will suffer. At best, efficiency will be reduced. At worst, the evaporator coil will ice up.

Balancing   Where heating and cooling systems share the same ductwork, rebalancing of the distribution system is usually necessary when switching from heating to cooling and vice versa. The rooms requiring the most cooling are usually not the rooms which require the most heating. Rebalancing is best accomplished by moving dampers located in the ductwork. To a lesser extent, rebalancing can be accomplished by opening or closing the grilles on the registers.

Damaged   Ductwork may be crushed, separated or obstructed, either during original construction or subsequently.

Ducts in Concrete   Slab-on-grade houses often have ducts embedded in the concrete foundations and slab. Sometimes the ducts are partially collapsed during the concrete pouring process. Moisture in and around the slab can flood the ducts and rust the metal duct walls. The water standing in the ducts can become a health hazard. Rusted duct walls can come loose and collapse. Any of these will restrict at least some air flow through the system. Ductwork in poured slabs and foundations is, of course, difficult to inspect and repair.

► 14.0 ATTIC DUCTWORK INSULATION

On any system that has ductwork passing through the attic, it is important to provide proper insulation on the ductwork. Without insulation, extreme temperatures in the attic can reduce the effectiveness of the system significantly. Some ductwork is manufactured with integral insulation for this purpose. In some attic installations, insulation is missing, improperly installed, or of insufficient quantity (minimum of R-7).

► 15.0 SUPPLEMENTAL COOLING

In many houses, there are rooms which are not heated by the central heating system. In most cases, heating is supplemented by electric baseboard heaters. While these will do an adequate job of heating, they are of no value when cooling is required. In areas such as these, or areas supplied by insufficient duct-work, supplemental cooling may be required. It is often easier to install a window mounted air conditioner to provide or supplement the cooling in a given area, than it is to make major modifications to the ductwork.

► 16.0 ATTIC DRIP PAN

On independent heat pump or air conditioning systems which have indoor components located in attics, a drip pan should be provided as an extra safety precaution. Should the condensate tray overflow, the drip pan acts as a second line of defense. The drip pan should have its own drain line. A common drain line between the condensate tray and drip pan may cause a flood if it plugs. In this case, there is no second line of defense. Some drains discharge into the plumbing stack. This is not permitted in some areas and it is a better practice to discharge straight outside. While they are not always installed, drip pans are considered to be a wise investment as their omission can result in damaged ceilings.

► 17.0 WATER LINES

On water cooled air conditioning systems, water is provided from the plumbing system. The waste water must go down a drain or may be used for watering a lawn or filling a swimming pool. The water is non-potable (non-drinkable) and cannot be re-introduced to the drinking water.

On systems where water can be directed to one of several locations, it is imperative that the supply valve and at least one discharge valve (on some systems they are automatic) be open during operation so that there is water flow through the air conditioning system. A lack of water flow can seriously damage the unit.

On some installations, the waste water is not only used to fill the swimming pool but it is also recycled to cool the air conditioning system and heat the pool. A loop is created, flowing pool water through the air conditioner. This is not considered to be advisable as the chemicals in the pool water can cause corrosion to the air conditioning system. The warm pool water also reduces the efficiency of the system.

► 18.0 THERMOSTAT

The purpose of a thermostat is to ensure that the temperature within the house is maintained at the temperature setting which is called for by the homeowner. For this reason, the location of the thermostat is critical. It should not be exposed to drafts, direct sunlight, heating sources or cooling sources.

Most houses which have central air conditioning or a beat pump have a single thermostat which controls the furnace and the air conditioner or heat pump.

Switching Modes

Most thermostats that are designed for heating and cooling require the operator to choose the mode of operation. Once the mode of operation is chosen, the thermostat attempts to maintain the desired temperature. One should Dever switch back and forth between heating and cooling modes on the thermostat. As a rule, at least fifteen minutes should elapse between operation of the heating system and operation of the cooling system, and vice versa. Most thermostats for air conditioning also have a fan switch. This switch allows for continuous or intermittent operation of the blower.

Multiple Thermostats

Houses which have multiple heating and cooling systems or zoned heating and cooling have more than one thermostat. Ibis is as it should be. However, some houses with a single furnace and an air conditioner or heat pump have more than one thermostat. This is often the case with independent air conditioners or heat pumps, or systems installed on a retrofit basis. In this case, the thermostats should be interlocked to prevent simultaneous heating and cooling. If they are not, care should be exercised.

Heat Pumps

Thermostats for heat pumps are somewhat different. They are normally arranged in such a way as to allow the heat pump to attempt to maintain the desired temperature first. Should the heat pump fail to keep up, it is shut off and the furnace is activated. Most heat pump systems have a switch on the thermostat marked "emergency heat". This switch enables the operator to bypass the heat pump and rely solely on heat from the furnace.

Heat pumps should not be run in the cooling mode when outside temperatures are below 65°F Above 65°F, heat pumps should not be run in the heating mode.

► 19.0 HOUSE FAN

Some houses have exhaust fans (usually located in the hallway on the top floor) which are used to cool the house during summer months. Most of these fans have no ductwork associated with them; they simply discharge into the attic. The attic must bc well vented to take full advantage of these fans. They can be extremely powerful and draw a significant amount of air out of the house.

Avoid Winter Use

Problems arise when they are used during winter months (to clear the house of cigarette smoke during a party, for example). Since they draw so much air out of the house, the house is under negative pressure and outside air tries to get back into the house any way it can. One way air gets back into the house is by coming down the chimney. This can cause fireplaces to smoke and heating systems to backdraft. In addition, it causes a significant amount of warm moist air to be discharged into the attic where it can cause condensation problems.

Therefore, house fans should ideally be scaled off during the winter to prevent their use and prevent warm moist house air from sneaking by the fan into the attic.

► 20.0 EVAPORATIVE COOLER

Principles of Operation

Evaporative cooling systems are used in warm, dry climates such as those found in southwestern United States. Evaporative coolers use a high volume, low speed blower to draw outside air into the house, typically through a moist cooling pad. As the air passes over the moisture, the water absorbs heat from the air. This evaporates some of the water and lowers the temperature of the air delivered into the house. A pump draws water out of a tray to keep the pads wet. Variations include a drip type cooler which allows water to drip down through the air flow. No pads are used with this system. The rotary type cooler has a drum made up of fine metal screening which rotates through a tank of water. The air passes over the upper part of the rotor, again evaporating some of the moisture.

Water Supply and Blower

The water level in the tank or tray is maintained by a connection to the supply plumbing in the house. A float valve allows water to be added as needed. An electric motor drives the blower.

Problems

Evaporative coolers do not work well when the air outside is humid. Also, since the indoor air ends up being relatively humid, a drop in temperature can lead to condensation in the house and ultimately, mildew and bacteria problems. Also, water sitting in the tray or tank may become stagnant during idle periods. The unit should be drained seasonally. Difficulties with electric motors and blower bearings for example, are common failure points. Spray type units may have the spray nozzles clogged and water pads may become dirty, restricting air flow. Rust and leakage of the enclosures are other common problems.

Independent of Heating Ductwork

Evaporative coolers should not be interconnected with heating ductwork. Moist air passing over a furnace heat exchanger can rust it out, destroying the furnace.

7 INSULATION

TABLE OF CONTENTS

Page

► INTRODUCTION

With the exception of new super-insulated houses, virtually every house has room for improvement when it comes to insulation, ventilation, caulking and weatherstripping. These will improve comfort levels and conserve energy.

Financial Considerations

Perhaps the best motivation for retrofitting is to save money. It is important to weigh the costs of retrofitting against the potential savings in fuel costs. There are usually some areas of the house where it makes financial sense to upgrade. However, in many older houses, certain types of retrofitting, such as insulating solid masonry exterior walls, are not economically viable.

Misconceptions

Insulation is misunderstood by some people. Comments in the middle of the winter such as, "This house must be really well insulated because it is really warm in here." show a definite lack of understanding. Almost any house can be warm if the thermostat is set high enough. The house might be uninsulated, the heating system grossly inefficient, and the heating bills might be exorbitant, but the house can still be warm.

Insulation

Insulation is only part of the story; however, it is a good place to start. Insulation slows the rate of heat loss from a house. The best insulating materials are light weight. That is because still air is a very good insulator. The problem is that air moves around by convection and wind, and the heat travels freely in the air. A good insulation material is one that limits the movement of the trapped air.

Air Barrier

Most insulations, however, let some air pass right through them. An air barrier (usually a sheet of plastic) will prevent, or at least reduce, air movement.

Vapor Barrier

As the temperature of air goes down, the relative humidity goes up. Air which starts out at 70°F at 40% relative humidity will reach 100% relative humidity as it is cooled to 45°F Therefore, air in the insulation can cool to the point that it deposits moisture in the insulation (whether it be in a wall or attic). This water reduces the effectiveness of the insulation because water is a good conductor of heat. But more importantly, water which gets trapped in the building structure can lead to rot and peeling paint. Therefore, a vapor barrier is required on the warm side of most insulations (a few do not require it because they are not permeable). A properly installed polyethylene air barrier or a good coat of oil based paint, for example, will suffice as a vapor barrier.

Ventilation

Regardless of how hard one tries, it is not possible to create a perfect air barrier. Therefore, wherever possible, the cold side of insulation should be ventilated to remove the moisture laden air which leaks into the insulation. This allows any moisture which does get through to the cold side to be carried out of the building quickly.

Caulking and Weather- Stripping

Insulation, complete with an air/vapor barrier will not be very effective if the air (and, therefore, the heat) can simply bypass the insulation. Calking and weatherstripping go a long way towards preventing air leakage into and out of a home.

Of all the measures one can take to conserve energy (and money), and increase comfort (by reducing drafts), caulking and weatherstripping usually yield the highest return. It is relatively inexpensive, fairly easy to do and often has dramatic results.

► **A. ATTICS**

When insulating an unused attic area, the goal is to have the temperature in the attic the same as the outdoor temperature. This concept gives some people difficulty as they assume that to keep the house cozy, the attic should be as warm as the rest of the house. It is best to consider the attic space as part of the great outdoors and the sloped roof as nothing more than a large umbrella. Consequently, insulation should be provided on the floor of the attic rather than the underside of the roof.

Insulating the floor of the attic rather than the underside of the roof has several advantages. The first is gravity. It is much easier to install the insulation on the floor than tacking it to the underside of the roof, especially when considering large quantities. The second is heating costs. There is no percentage in heating unused attic space. The third reason is the prevention of condensation problems. Insulation on the floor of the attic allows for much easier ventilation of the attic space via roof vents and, in most cases, soffit vents. (Gable vents can also be used.) If there is lots of air movement through the attic space, any warm moist air from the interior of the house which has managed to find its way into the attic will be swept away. Refer to 15.0 "Ventilation" in this section.

Air/Vapor Barrier

An air/vapor barrier should be installed below (on the warm side of) the insulation. This is not easy on existing homes as usually there is some insulation in the attic already. As a general rule, a vapor barrier can be installed over existing insulation, if at least twice as much insulation is added on top (the cold side) of the vapor barrier. If there is not enough insulation on top of the vapor barrier, the vapor barrier will get cold and condensation could form immediately below it, damaging the house. Refer to 13.0, "Air/Vapor Barrier" in this section.

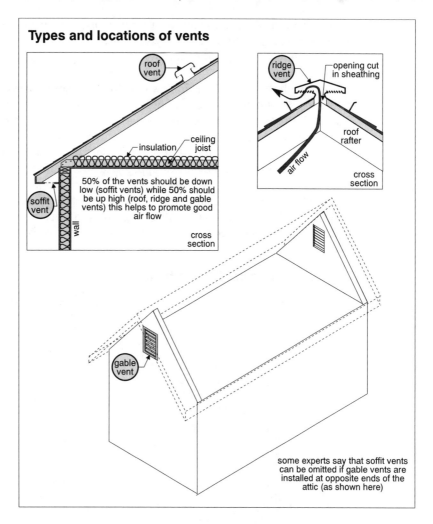

Figure 1. Attic Ventilation

► B. FLAT ROOFS

On a retrofit basis, the decision to insulate a flat roof cavity is a difficult one. It is hard to get the insulation in place. It can be blown in from above or below; however, this requires drilling holes through the ceiling or roof membrane. In some cases, it can be blown in at the eaves. Regardless of the approach, assessing the quality of the completed job is impossible without using sophisticated equipment. Batt-type insulation can be installed; however, it requires the removal of the ceiling finish or roof sheathing. This is usually not cost-effective. With either approach, the amount of insulation is limited by the size of the roof cavity.

Ventilation The next dilemma to be faced, is the question of ventilation. Unlike an attic space, where there is a significant amount of open space above the insulation, the flat roof cavity consists of a series of channels created by the roof joists which are sandwiched between the roof sheathing and the ceiling. To ventilate each channel would require at least two vents per channel and a reasonable air space above the insulation. This would further reduce the amount of insulation which could be installed and in some cases require a prohibitive number of roof

5

vents. Even at that, the vents would not work very well because the roof has little or no slope. Roof vents rely on convection to allow warm air to escape from the higher vents and cool air to enter through the lower vents.

To help with these problems in new construction, some flat roofs are constructed using trusses which are deep enough to allow for adequate insulation and ventilation. Air movement is not restricted to the channels created by the trusses because the trusses are not solid. The spaces between the webs of the trusses allow for better air flow through the entire roof cavity. As an alternative, if conventional roof joists are used, they are strapped with wooden members running at right angles to the joists which are secured to the top of the joists. The roof sheathing is installed on top of the strapping. This approach deepens the roof cavity to allow for more insulation and allows ventilation between the channels. Using either of these approaches on a retrofit basis is prohibitively expensive.

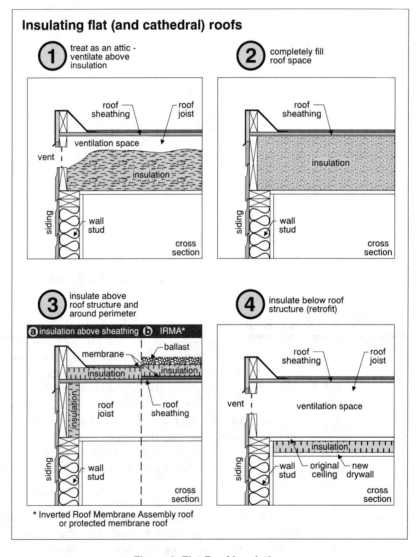

Figure 2. Flat Roof Insulation

Air/Vapor
Barrier

Even if the insulation and ventilation problems could be solved, there is still the question of an air/vapor barrier. It is impossible to install one without providing a new ceiling surface. Vapor barrier paints can be provided on the existing ceiling; however, they do not provide an air barrier. Air leakage can be reduced by sealing around ceiling penetrations such as light fixtures and plumbing stacks. Since there is no access for periodic inspections, moisture damage within the cavity usually goes undetected until it is severe.

Insulation
Above Roof
Sheathing

An alternative to all of the above would be to install the insulation above the roof sheathing. This approach only makes sense if a new roof covering is required and, even at that, the amount of rigid insulation which can practically be installed falls short of current residential standards. Without insulating the ends (at the eaves) of the channels created by the roof joists (or at least ensuring that they are reasonably weathertight), the new insulation above the sheathing can be "short-circuited" by cold air travelling through the roof cavity.

Insulation
Below Ceiling

This method of insulating flat roofs is fairly safe, but has other disadvantages. A rigid impermeable insulation board such as extruded polystyrene can be added on the underside of the ceiling and covered with new drywall. If the joints in the insulation and/or drywall are tight, there is better insulation, a good vapor barrier (the insulation itself), and a good air barrier.

The disadvantages are the loss of ceiling height (about one inch for each R-5 added), the relocation cost of ceiling light fixtures, and the cost of covering up perfectly good ceiling finishes. If the upper floor ceilings are in poor repair, perhaps this approach is workable.

Summary

In summary, a flat roof cavity is an area that was never intended to be insulated. The cost is prohibitive and the potential for severe condensation problems is great. These spaces are often best left alone.

► C. CATHEDRAL ROOFS / SLOPED CEILINGS

Cathedral roofs and sloped ceilings have similar problems to flat roofs when adding insulation on a retrofit basis. Installing the insulation itself is difficult; however, the installation of a proper air/vapor barrier and adequate ventilation is, in some cases, next to impossible. Please refer to "Flat Roofs" above.

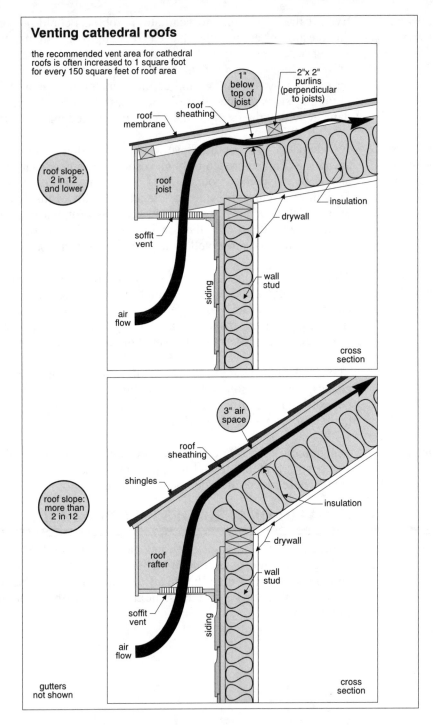

Venting cathedral roofs

the recommended vent area for cathedral roofs is often increased to 1 square foot for every 150 square feet of roof area

roof slope: 2 in 12 and lower

1" below top of joist

2"x 2" purlins (perpendicular to joists)

roof sheathing

roof membrane

roof joist

insulation

drywall

soffit vent

wall stud

siding

air flow

cross section

roof slope: more than 2 in 12

3" air space

roof sheathing

shingles

insulation

drywall

roof rafter

wall stud

soffit vent

siding

air flow

gutters not shown

cross section

Figure 3. Sloped Ceiling Ventilation (via Soffit Vents)

▶ D. SKYLIGHT WELLS

Skylight wells are also known as light shafts. Depending upon the configuration of the roof and the ceilings below, it is very common for the light shaft to pass through an unheated attic area. If this is the case, the walls of the light shaft should have a proper air/vapor barrier and insulation. Batt-type insulation or rigid insulation is commonly used for this purpose.

► E. KNEE WALLS

A knee wall is a vertical wall usually found in 1-1/2 or 2-1/2 storey houses. The knee wall separates the top floor living space from the side attic areas. The best way to insulate the area behind a knee wall is to insulate the unfinished rear side of the knee wall and to insulate the floor of the side attic in a similar fashion to the way the floor of a main attic would be insulated. Again, air / vapor barriers should be provided on the warm side of the insulation and the side attic spaces should be ventilated. No insulation is needed on the end (outside) walls of side attics, with this approach.

As an alternative, if the side attic areas are to be heated, insulation should be provided on the underside of the roof and across the portion of the floor which overhangs the exterior walls of the house (if any). The end walls of the side attic areas should also be insulated. With this arrangement, an air/vapor barrier is still required on the warm side of all insulation; however, ventilation is not practical.

► F. WOOD FRAME EXTERIOR WALLS

Pouring

Wood frame exterior walls can be insulated by pouring or blowing insulation into the cavity. Pouring insulation into wall cavities is usually only possible if the wall space is open in the attic and is continuous right down to the foundation walls. Even if this is the case, remember that some of the wall spaces will be interrupted by windows and doors and the areas below these will require blown-in insulation.

Blowing

If insulation is blown into the wall cavity, it must be blown into each stud space. This requires drilling more than one hole allowing access to each stud space or removing siding and sheathing at the top and bottom. Blown-in insulation can be installed from the inside or outside. In some cases, it is also possible to install from the basement or from the attic by drilling through the wall plates. Regardless of the approach, wall insulation should be installed by a qualified contractor. Installing a proper air/vapor barrier is also difficult without sandwiching the air/vapor barrier between the existing wall surfaces and new drywall. As an alternative, vapor barrier paint or vinyl or foil wallpaper can be used.

Blown or poured insulation in walls can settle leaving uninsulated spaces at the top.

Interior Approach

As an alternative to the above, interior finishes can be removed and a batt-type insulation can be installed in the stud cavities. An air/vapor barrier can also be installed. This approach only makes sense during major remodelling projects.

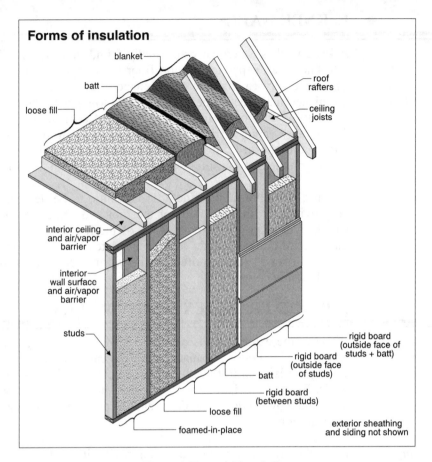

Forms of insulation

blanket

batt

loose fill

roof rafters

ceiling joists

interior ceiling and air/vapor barrier

interior wall surface and air/vapor barrier

studs

rigid board (outside face of studs + batt)

rigid board (outside face of studs)

batt

rigid board (between studs)

loose fill

foamed-in-place

exterior sheathing and siding not shown

Figure 4. Types of Insulation

Exterior Approach

Exterior finishes and sheathing can also be removed and insulation can be installed from the exterior; however this approach is not viable unless re-siding was planned anyway.

Installing strapping, insulation, and a new siding over the old is not advisable if the uninsulated wall cavity which still remains can "short-circuit" the new insulation by allowing cold air to circulate through it. Modifications needed to window and door trim as well as the cost of the new siding make this approach too expensive if the sole motivation is to reduce heating costs.

In summary, insulating existing wood-frame exterior walls is a tricky business that is often not cost-effective.

► G. MASONRY WALLS

Masonry walls usually consist of two thicknesses of brick or, a layer of brick and a layer of concrete block (or cinder block). There is sometimes a space between the two layers of masonry; however, the space is too small to provide any reasonable amount of insulation. There is also a small space between the inside layer of masonry and the interior wall finish. Again, this space is too small to insulate. Masonry walls can be insulated by providing a false wall on the interior or exterior of the existing wall. This will obviously change the outside appearance of the house or reduce interior room dimensions and affect such things as baseboards, windows, doors, electrical outlets, ceiling moldings, etc. In most cases, retrofitting wall insulation in masonry houses is not cost-effective.

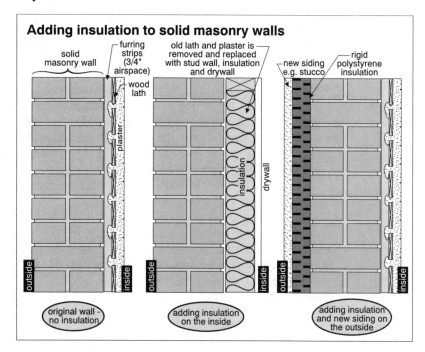

Figure 5. Insulation Improvements To Masonry Walls

► H. LOG WALLS

Log walls are solid and provide no means of insulating inside the wall itself. Additional insulation could conceivably be provided on the interior or the exterior of the existing walls; however, this will change the outside appearance of the house or reduce interior room dimensions. Most softwoods (which is what most log houses are constructed of) have an R value of about 1.25 per inch. Therefore, an eight inch thick wall would have an R value of approximately 10 which is below modem standards, but is not low enough to warrant major modifications.

Rather than conduction through the wall system, most heat loss in buildings of this type is by air infiltration. Sealing leaks is far more cost-effective than adding wall insulation.

▶ **I. BASEMENT WALLS-INTERIOR**

Insulating the inside of basement walls is often appealing, because it is fairly inexpensive, and relatively easy to do, especially if the walls are unfinished. If the basement walls are already finished, one must usually remove the existing interior finishes to properly insulate the walls.

There are risks and some difficulties associated with insulating basement walls from the interior. Firstly, if the basement has chronic moisture problems, interior insulation should not be attempted. It is best to insulate on the outside, correcting the moisture problem at the same time. This is, of course, a much more expensive approach, but does protect the foundation walls as well as upgrading the insulation. Secondly, if the foundation walls are frequently wet, interior insulation could result in frost damage to the foundation walls, as the walls will be significantly colder after the insulation job. The third dilemma when insulating from the interior is dealing with obstructions such as electrical panels, plumbing, oil tanks, etc.

Air/Vapor and Moisture Barriers

If, however, interior insulation is the approach taken, one should provide a wood stud wall on the inside of the foundation wall and fill the cavities with batt-type insulation. A moisture barrier should be provided against the foundation wall (before constructing the stud wall) and an air/vapor barrier should be installed on the warm side of the insulation. Under some circumstances, combustible plastic insulation can be glued to existing foundation walls; however, it must be covered with drywall or some other non-combustible material. No moisture barrier or air/vapor barrier is required.

New Construction

In new houses, insulation on basement walls in some northern climates need to be applied from the subfloor down to a maximum of 8 inches above the basement floor to comply with Current Standards, if less than 50 percent of the foundation wall is above grade. Many areas however, require no insulation on basement walls.

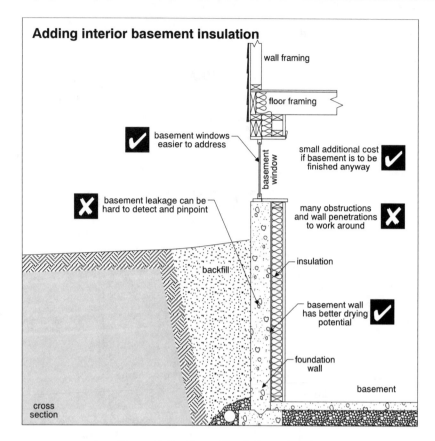

Adding interior basement insulation

- wall framing
- floor framing
- ✔ basement windows easier to address
- ✔ small additional cost if basement is to be finished anyway
- basement window
- ✗ basement leakage can be hard to detect and pinpoint
- ✗ many obstructions and wall penetrations to work around
- insulation
- backfill
- ✔ basement wall has better drying potential
- foundation wall
- basement
- cross section

Figure 6. Basement Insulation – Interior

Joist
Cavities

Regardless of the type of wall insulation, batt-type insulation should be added in joist spaces at the top of the wall. Depending upon the direction the joists run, this space may be a series of small spaces roughly fourteen inches wide (between the joist) or one long space parallel to the joists. Again, ideally, an air/vapor barrier is added on the warm side of the insulation (although it is difficult to install because of the nature of the space); however, no moisture barrier is needed on the cold side of the insulation. Caulking the foundation/sill, header/sill, and headed/subfloor connections will help reduce heat loss due to air leakage.

► J. BASEMENT WALL-EXTERIOR

Exterior wall insulation only makes sense if exterior digging is to be done for another reason, such as dampproofing the basement walls. Rigid or semi-rigid insulation which comes in boards is the best material. The insulation is fastened to the exterior of the foundation wall and the upper portion of the insulation (above ground level) should be covered within a protective material. A flashing should be installed at the top of the insulation to prevent water penetration in this location. Some insulations drain water very well. These can be used to reduce basement problems if the insulation carries water down to a functional perimeter drainage tile system.

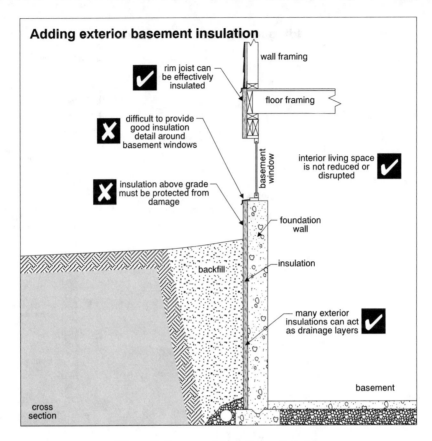

Adding exterior basement insulation

rim joist can be effectively insulated ✓

wall framing

floor framing

difficult to provide good insulation detail around basement windows ✗

interior living space is not reduced or disrupted ✓

insulation above grade must be protected from damage ✗

basement window

foundation wall

backfill

insulation

many exterior insulations can act as drainage layers ✓

basement

cross section

Figure 7. Basement Isulation – Exterior

► K. CRAWL SPACES

When dealing with crawl spaces, there are two options. The perimeter walls of the crawl space can be insulated so that the crawl space becomes a heated area, or the crawl space can be left cold and the floor above the crawl space can be insulated. If the crawl space walls are to be insulated, the same options are available as insulating basement walls.

If the crawl space is to remain unheated, refer to the following sections:

L) Floors Above Unheated Areas
M) Pipes in Unheated Areas
N) Ductwork in Unheated Areas
O) Exhaust Ducts in Unheated Areas
14) Add Moisture Barrier
15) Add Ventilation

As a rule, perimeter wall insulation, resulting in a heated space, is the preferred method; however, it is not practical in some instances. Crawl spaces under buildings constructed on piers, for example, do not lend themselves to perimeter insulation even if skirting has been provided between the piers. Crawl spaces which are chronically damp are best kept unheated and well ventilated.

► L. FLOORS ABOVE UNHEATED AREAS

Floors over unheated spaces (crawl spaces, garages, porches, cantilevers, etc) are usually insulated by installing batt-type insulation between the floor joists and securing it in place with a material such as chicken wire. The use of a plastic air/vapor barrier below the insulation to hold it in place is incorrect, and may cause rot. Again, this barrier should be on the warm side of the insulation.

In some cases, rigid plastic insulation can be used in lieu of batts; however, it must be covered by a non-combustible surface such as drywall. Rigid glass fiber insulation need not be protected.

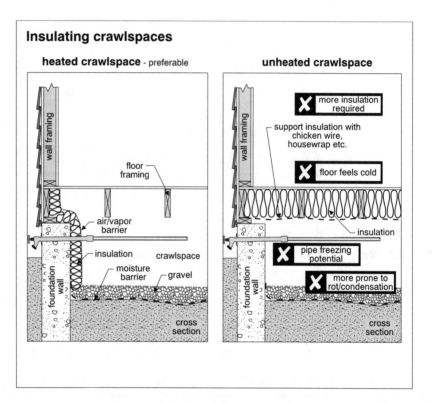

Figure 8. Insulation

If the unheated space is an attached garage, the areas which abut the house must prevent automobile exhaust fumes entering the house itself. In some areas, a fire separation is also required between house and garage.

Even when properly insulated, the space above an unheated area is usually cooler than the rest of the house; however, the following illustration showing a dropped ceiling is one approach if ceiling heights permit. This method only works well if a) the insulation does not obstruct air flow. b) the supply and return air ducts are balanced so that the space is not pressurized or depressurized. c) proper air barriers are installed to prevent the warm moist air from escaping into the wall cavities. A better method may be to insulate the floor with expanding isocyanurate or polyurethane foam insulation.

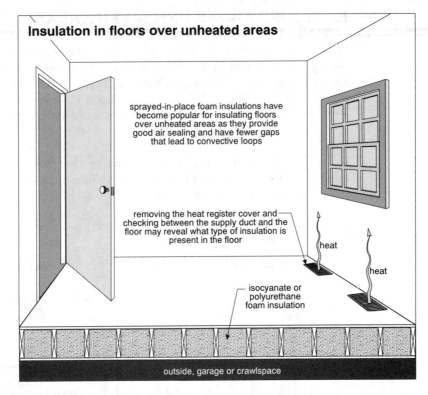

Insulation in floors over unheated areas

sprayed-in-place foam insulations have
become popular for insulating floors
over unheated areas as they provide
good air sealing and have fewer gaps
that lead to convective loops

removing the heat register cover and
checking between the supply duct and the
floor may reveal what type of insulation is
present in the floor

heat

heat

isocyanate or
polyurethane
foam insulation

outside, garage or crawlspace

Figure 9. Insulation Alternative for Warmer Floor Over Unheated Area

▶ M. PIPES IN UNHEATED AREAS

Plumbing pipes (supply and waste) and heating pipes which pass through unheated
areas should be insulated to a minimum of R-4, but higher if possible. It is important to remember, however, that even a well insulated pipe will eventually freeze if
the water in the pipe is not flowing. Insulation slows the rate of heat loss, but does
not stop it. Depending upon the configuration, it is often better to relocate the pipes
to a heated area or provide heating cables on the pipes under the insulation.

▶ N. DUCTWORK IN UNHEATED AREAS

Ductwork for cooling and/or heating which is located in unheated areas should
be insulated (minimum R-7) to prevent heat gain or heat loss. Some ductwork
comes pre-insulated. In some instances, the insulation is on the interior of the
ductwork and is not visible.

▶ O. EXHAUST DUCTS IN UNHEATED AREAS

Exhaust ducts in unheated spaces should be insulated to prevent condensation
from forming within the ducts. Often, bathroom exhaust fans are connected to
uninsulated ducts which pass through an attic. The warm moist air being
exhausted from the bathroom condenses on the inside of the ductwork. It runs
back down the duct and drips out of the exhaust fan. This is hazardous as the
water is dripping past the electric motor of the fan.

► 1.0 CURRENT STANDARDS

R-Value

RSI-Value

The numbers shown below are the current standards required by many northern codes. While these standards apply to new buildings only, they give an indication of the values one might insulate to if one were to upgrade. The numbers in this column are known as R-values. An R-value is simply a numerical representation of thermal resistance. The higher the number, the greater the resistance to heat transfer. RSI values are simply the metric equivalent of R-values. To obtain an RSI value, divide the R-value by 5.6.

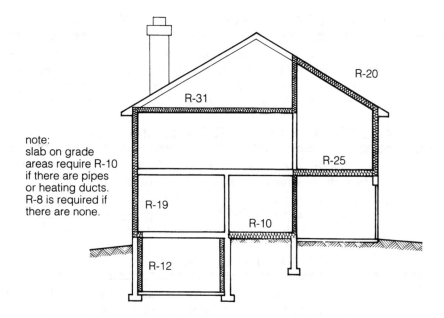

Figure 10. Recommended Insulation Values

Different types of insulation have different R-values per inch of thickness. Even the same type of insulation can have a different R-value, depending on its form. Glass fiber insulation, for example, has a higher R-value in batt form than in loose fill form.

► 2.0 EXISTING AMOUNT

This column represents the existing amount of insulation expressed as an R-value. It can be directly compared to the Current Standards outlined above to determine how the existing insulation stacks up against the minimum amounts called for in new construction.

▶ **3.0 GLASS FIBER INSULATION** (R-Value 2.9-4.2 per inch)

Glass fiber insulation is one of the most common types of insulation available and is made from threads of glass glued together with phenolic resins. It is available in batt form, rigid board and loose fill. It is resistant to moisture, mildew, fungus and vermin, and some types are non-combustible. It is, however, a skin and eye irritant and inhaling small threads of glass fiber is not good for the respiratory system. It should be understood that these irritations are only common during installation, and once the material is in place it is not considered to be a problem.

▶ **4.0 MINERAL WOOL (ROCK WOOL)** (R-Value 3.0-3.2 per inch)

Mineral wool is similar to glass fiber except that mineral waste is used to form the wool-like material. It, too, is available in batt form or as loose fill. Its insulating value is comparable to glass fiber and it has very good resistance to fire and rot. Further, it is slightly less irritating to work with than glass fiber.

▶ **5.0 CELLULOSE FIBER** (R-Value 3.4-3.6 per inch)

Cellulose fiber is essentially paper, finely shredded and treated with chemicals to make it somewhat resistant to moisture, fire, rot and vermin. It is usually blown in but can also be poured. It is prone to settling. Due to its relatively low cost, this material is very popular. Usually gray in color, it has a similar texture to lint. Cellulose fiber will absorb water which will lead to deterioration.

▶ **6.0 VERMICULITE** (R-Value 2.3 per inch)

Vermiculite is a mineral substance made from mica. This insulation is available as loose fill and can be identified by the small rectangular shape of the individual pieces. Vermiculite is relatively expensive. It is, however, non-combustible.

▶ **7.0 WOOD SHAVINGS** (R-Value 2.4 per inch)

Wood shavings used as insulation today are treated with fire retardant chemicals and can be made moisture resistant. This was not the case many years ago.

▶ **8.0 PLASTIC BOARD** (R-Value 3.7-6.0 per inch)

Most plastic board type insulations are made of polystyrene or polyurethane. Both pose fire hazards if left exposed. If applied on interior walls or ceilings, they should be covered with at least 1/2 inch drywall or plaster. While these materials have a very good R-value per inch of thickness, they are more expensive than most other types.

▶ **9.0 OTHER TYPES OF INSULATION**

There are many different types of insulation materials available on the market today.

INSULATION TYPES

Material	R-Value/Inch	Common Form
Glass Fiber	2.9-4.2	batt, loose fill, rigid board
Mineral Wool	3.0-3.2	batt, loose fill
Cellulose Fiber	3.4-3.6	loose fill
Vermiculite	2.3	loose fill
Wood Shavings	2.4	loose fill
Plastic Board	3.7-6.0	rigid board

► 10.0 NO ACCESS

In some areas of some homes, it is not possible to inspect the insulation as there is no access (e.g., attics without access hatches or crawl spaces with no means of safe entry).

► 11.0 ACCESS NOT GAINED

In some circumstances, access hatches have been provided to allow for an inspection of the insulation; however, for some reason, access could not be gained. Circumstances such as this might include an access hatch which has been nailed shut and would be damaged if the nails were removed. Access cannot be gained when shelving has been built into a closet space below the attic access hatch. Although the hatch is still there, it is impossible to reach. Sometimes loose insulation has been blown over the access hatch, in which case it will not be opened. This situation should be rectified after taking possession of the house.

► 12.0 SPOT CHECKED ONLY

Certain areas such as wall insulation can be spot checked only. Wall insulation can be checked by removing the electrical cover plates on exterior walls to probe into the wall cavity. During this process, furniture is not moved, nor are cover plates removed which have been painted in place. Many inspectors do not do this since it is not conclusive.

► 13.0 ADD AIR/VAPOR BARRIER

An air/vapor barrier is a continuous layer of material (usually plastic sheeting) that is impervious to the passage of water vapor and air. Air/vapor barriers should always be installed on the warm side of the insulation. They are used to prevent warm moist air, contained within the building, from migrating into insulated spaces. Air which gets into insulated spaces cools and forms condensation. The condensation can cause rot and reduce the effectiveness of the insulation. Barriers installed toward the cold side of the insulation may result in condensation damage as they trap the moisture. These barriers should be slashed or removed.

On a retrofit basis, there are many areas where an air/vapor barrier would be desirable; however, it is not practical to install one. Therefore, all areas which should ideally have an air/vapor barrier are not recorded in this section. Only areas that show signs of condensation problems or allow for the installation of an air/vapor barrier with relative ease, are mentioned. Vapor barrier paints, or vinyl or foil wallpaper are alternatives.

► 14.0 ADD MOISTURE BARRIER

While air/vapor barriers are designed to keep the moisture within a building, moisture barriers are designed to keep it out. A typical area for the application of a moisture barrier (plastic sheet) would be an earth floor in a crawl space. Damp earth floors can allow a significant amount of moisture absorption into the air in a house. One study revealed that the daily evaporation in a heated crawl space dropped from over sixteen gallons to less than a 1/4 of a gallon with the installation of a moisture barrier!

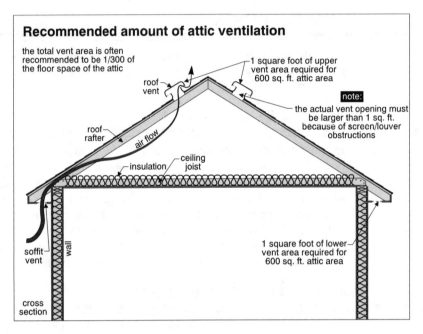

Recommended amount of attic ventilation

the total vent area is often recommended to be 1/300 of the floor space of the attic

1 square foot of upper vent area required for 600 sq. ft. attic area

roof vent

note:
the actual vent opening must be larger than 1 sq. ft. because of screen/louver obstructions

roof rafter

air flow

ceiling joist

insulation

1 square foot of lower vent area required for 600 sq. ft. attic area

soffit vent

wall

cross section

Figure 11. Attic Ventilation

► 15.0 ADD VENTILATION

Ideally, all of the moisture laden air within a house could be prevented from migrating through the insulation to cold areas by the presence of an air/vapor barrier. However, this is never practical. Therefore, it is wise to ventilate cold areas wherever possible.

Ventilation also removes warm air from the attic which keeps the house cooler in the summer and helps to prevent ice dams (see Roofing 1.14) in the winter. Cooler summer attic temperatures also help prolong the life of many roofing materials.

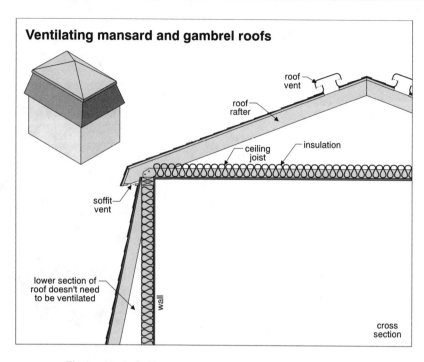

Figure 12. Attic Ventilation (Mansard and Gambrel Roofs)

Attic Ventilation Rate

Attics are the easiest areas to ventilate. The recommended ventilation rate is one square foot of ventilation for every three hundred square feet of attic space. Ideally, ventilation should be provided in such a way as to allow for good air flow from end to end of an attic space and from bottom to top. The best way to accomplish this would be to have continuous soffit vents (under the eaves) and a continuous ridge vent (at the top of the roof). On a retrofit basis, this is usually not practical.

Vent Location

Blocked Soffit Vents

Roof-top vents (the round or square metal vents seen on most roofs) and/or gable vents should account for approximately fifty percent of the total venting. They should have screens to keep insects and birds out of the attic. Where possible, they should be located high on the downwind side of the house to help create a draft up through the eaves. The remaining fifty percent of the ventilation should be provided under the eaves. These screened vents should be protected on the interior of the attic to prevent insulation from plugging them. Baffles are available which keep soffit vents clear. On some houses, soffit venting is not possible. Vents can be provided on the lower portion of the roof; however, they may allow leakage into the attic as snow and ice accumulates on the roof.

Turbine type vents (air powered vents) are not suggested as they only work on windy days, when they are not really necessary. On still days, when more ventilation is required, they do no more good than a regular roof-top vent. They are also very noisy if not well balanced and lubricated.

21

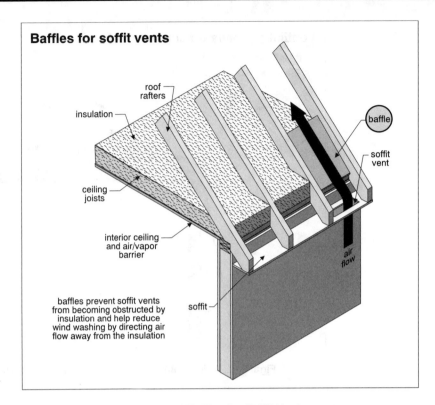

Baffles for soffit vents

roof rafters

insulation

baffle

soffit vent

ceiling joists

interior ceiling and air/vapor barrier

air flow

baffles prevent soffit vents from becoming obstructed by insulation and help reduce wind washing by directing air flow away from the insulation

soffit

Figure. 13 Baffles for Soffit Vents

Power Ventilators

Power ventilators are not suggested for winter use because they put the attic under negative pressure, which draws more warm moist air up from the house into the attic. Also, motors in attics tend to be neglected and eventually malfunction. (These fans are sometimes installed for summer use only. Removing hot attic air in the summer helps keep the house cooler.)

Crawl Spaces

Conventional wisdom has held that unheated crawl spaces should be ventilated to remove moisture. A common recommendation is one square foot of vent area for every 500 square feet of crawlspace area. This practice has recently been challenged in warm, humid climates, where moist air may be drawn into the cool crawlspace. In these areas, vents are usually no longer installed. There still may be a benefit to ventilation in drier climates. Most agree that heated crawlspaces require no ventilation

► 16.0 VENT EXHAUST FAN OUTSIDE

In many cases, exhaust fans from areas such as bathrooms, discharge into the attic space. This is not a good arrangement becuase the air in an attic should be dry. Air being exhausted from bathrooms is typically moisture laden. Therefore, all exhaust fans should discharge directly to the building exterior. The exhaust ductwork should be insulated. See paragraph "O" earlier in this section.

► 17.0 COVER PLASTIC INSULATION

Polystyrene and polyurethane insulations create a sever fire hazard when left exposed. When ignited, they burn rapidly and give off toxic fumes. Both types of insulation are considered safe when covered. Inside a house or garage, they should be covered with 1/2 inch drywall.

► 18.0 REMOVE INSULATION FROM RECESSED LIGHTS

Recessed lights which are covered with insulation can generate excessive heat and start a fire. Special barriers should be provided over recessed lights to allow for insulation and yet allow for suffiecient ventilation of the recessed lights. Alternatively, special lights designed for this application can be used. Some "pot" lights have different bulb wattage ratings, depending on whether they are in an insulated environment.

► 19.0 INCREASE INSULATION

Increasing insulation levels in a home should be considered an improvement rather than a repair. The optimum amount of insulation depends on local climate, fuel costs, the cost involved in adding insulation, the length of time one is planning to stay in the house, the level of comfort the homeowner expects, and a number of other factors. The decision to upgrade and the extent to which it's done, will be different for every homeowner.

In some cases, increasing insulation is economically viable. Where possible, the additional insulation should be of the same type as the original insulation. If a different type of insulation is used, it should be a type which will not compress the original unsulation. Cellulose and glass fiber insulations are most commonly used on a retrofit basis.

8 PLUMBING

THE
Home Reference
BOOK

► TABLE OF CONTENTS   Page

► INTRODUCTION

The purpose of a house plumbing system is twofold. On the supply side, the idea is to get water for drinking, washing and cooking to the appropriate areas of the house. The waste side of the plumbing system is intended to get rid of water and waste.

The supply water is under pressure and the waste water flows by gravity. Serviced communities provide the fresh supply water and carry away the waste. In rural properties, wells usually supply fresh water and septic systems handle the waste.

Since the beginning of the 20th century, plumbing systems have changed dramatically. There are now a myriad of fixtures and faucets available, and both supply and waste pipe materials have changed a great deal.

Plumbing components are expensive, and plumbing repairs or improvements are among the more costly projects homeowners undertake.

In a completed home, the majority of the piping, both supply and waste, is concealed within walls, ceilings and underground. Leakage, obstructions, or other problems may not be picked up during an inspection.

► 1.0 SUPPLY

1.1 Public Water Systems: Most homes in urban and suburban areas are provided with water by the town. Typically, the water mains in residential areas are 4 inches to 12 inches in diameter, and run several feet below the street level. Smaller pipes, usually 1/2 inch or 3/4 inch diameter, run from city mains into individual dwellings. The water is normally supplied at a pressure of 40 to 70 psi (pounds per square inch).

Problems

City water mains may be undersized or deteriorated in older neighborhoods, Some cities have poor pumping and/or distribution systems. In these cases, low water pressure problems are usually experienced at every home in the neighborhood. The only true solution is to petition the city to improve its system.

1.1.1 Service Piping: The service Piping carries the water from the street mains to the house. It is common to find that very little or none of the service piping can be seen.

Typical Materials

Lead: Lead piping was used between the street main and the house up until the mid-point of the century. A good deal of lead supply line is still in use, and the health authorities indicate that as long as it is used regularly, there is no difficulty with it. If the water has not been run for some time, some recommend that the water be flowed for several minutes before using it.

Copper: Copper piping is used today for virtually all supply lines from the city main to the house. From 1950 to 1970, 1/2 inch and 3/4 inch diameter piping were used commonly. Since roughly 1970, most source piping is 3/4 inch diameter. Copper usually has an indefinite life expectancy. Some water contains chemicals which can deteriorate copper piping.

Galvanized Steel: Galvanized steel is not commonly used as a residential service pipe, although some galvanized steel fittings can be found at the point of entry into the house. In some areas, galvanized service piping is used. although authorities usually require at least 1-1/4 inch diameter pipe.

Plastic: Plastic has not been used commonly for city source piping, although plastic piping is commonly used between a well, lake or cistern and a house. The performance of these pipe systems has been good, although it has only been used extensively since the 1960's.

Problems

Leaks

The underground water supply line from the property line into the house, is owned by the homeowner. Beyond the property line, the pipe is the responsibility of the city. A leak in the pipe requires excavation, and it is often difficult to know until one begins to dig, whether the leak is on the city's or the homeowner's side. The city is usually contacted and they excavate their section of the pipe, correcting the problem if they discover it. If no problem is found, the homeowner is left to correct the problem on his or her own. In some cases, the homeowner must pay for the city's work if the city pipe is not at fault.

Since the supply line from the street cannot be seen, no comment can be offered during a visual inspection. If there is a leak, it may go undetected for some time. The water meter inside the building is downstream of any leak in this pipe and thus, will not show the problem. In some cases, water can be heard running outside the basement wall. Water accumulating in the basement, or a wet spot on the lawn are often the first indications. Leaks may be caused by building settlement, excavation, poor connections, faulty valves or a flaw in the pipe itself.

Low Pressure

The more common problem with the supply piping from the street is poor water pressure in the house. This may be the result of a partially closed or obstructed valve in the street. It may also be because of blockage, such as a stone in the pipe. It is not unusual for fairly large foreign objects to get into supply plumbing systems. Normally they cause no problems, but occasionally they become lodged in shut-off valves and water meters, for example.

Pressure Regulators

Where municipal water pressure is above 80 psi, a regulator should be provided to prevent leaks at fixtures, stress on appliance hoses and possible broken pipe joints.

Small

In most new housing, the supply pipe from the street to the house is 3/4 inch diameter. In older houses, the piping was as small as 3/8 inch.

Modern life styles and additional plumbing fixtures usually require a larger line, capable of providing more water. Replacing this pipe is an expensive and disruptive job. It is often deferred as long as possible.

Crimped   With new piping, it is possible for the pipe to be crimped during installation or to be pinched under a rock, for example, during back-filling operations.

Freezing   It is unusual, although not impossible, for the supply line to be too close to the surface, and to freeze during very cold weather.

Lead   Up until World War II, most of the supply pipes in built-up areas were lead. While these generally provide good service, they do tend to be smaller and may have to be replaced. Also, lead is relatively soft, and if building settlement occurs, there is a chance of leakage or crimping the pipe. Leaks can also occur at older connections as a result of long term deterioration.

Shared   In some semi-detached (attached) and row houses built around the turn of the century, a single supply line would run under a front lawn, and then split to feed two houses. This often yields unsatisfactory water pressure for both houses and has to be replaced with two larger, separate lines.

Steel   Many of the old lead supply lines were connected to a galvanized nipple or short piece of steel pipe which contacted the soil. This pipe will corrode on the exterior as well as rust on the inside, and it may be susceptible to leakage or rupture in an older home. It is often wise to replace this as a precautionary measure. Galvanized steel service pipes can be expected to last roughly forty years. They are replaced with copper when pressure or leakage problems develop.

Under Basement Floor   Some older houses have supply lines that run under the basement floor, coming up into the basement near the middle of the house. In some cases, the water supply lines enter the basement in more than one spot. When problems (leakage or low pressure) are experienced, these under-floor lines are usually abandoned. The new pipe is connected to the supply line from the street at the front of the basement. The supply line is then run along the basement ceiling to the various take-offs.

Well   **1.2 Private:** Where a city water supply is not available, water must be provided by the homeowner. Typically, this is done by a well. Wells may be shallow (twenty-five feet or less) or deep (more than twenty-five feet).

Service Piping   The service piping is most often plastic and the comments in Section 1.1.1 are appropriate.

Pump   A pump is needed to move the water from the source into the house piping system. The pump may be located at the bottom of the well, at the top of the well, or in the home.

Reciprocating or piston type lift pumps were often used on older systems, while centrifugal pumps are used more typically in modern installations. Shallow wells may use reciprocating or centrifugal pumps. Deep well pumps are most often centrifugal, either jet type or submersible.

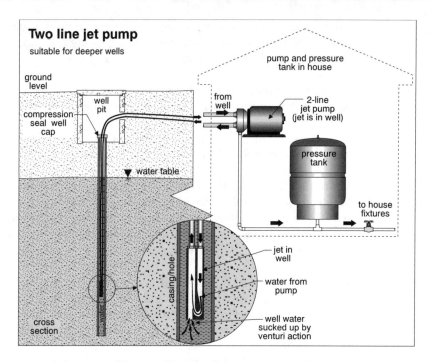

Figure 1. Two Line Jet Pump

A surface pump may be located in the basement of the house, or at the top of the well in a pump house. Pump houses are not common in buildings used year round, because the pump has to be protected from freezing in winter.

Well water should be tested on a regular basis, as recommended by the local health authorities. Typically, this involves sending a sample to the authority for testing. Many authorities provide test canisters.

Well draw-down tests can also be done by plumbers. This is a test of the pumping capacity of the well. The test is usually done over a period of hours and gives an indication of the water volume available. This may vary from season to season as the water table changes.

Pressure Tank

Where a pump is used, there is also a storage or pressure tank, typically located in the basement. This tank gets around the problem of having the pump come on the instant a faucet is opened in the home. This tank may be only a gallon or two, or it may be several gallons. The tank provides relatively even water pressure to the house.

Since water is incompressible, a portion of the tank should be filled with air. The air is easily compressed, and when there is a demand for water, the air pressure in the tank forces the water out. The tank pressure slowly reduces as the water leaves and the air expands. When the pressure gets to the lower setting of the pressure switch, the pump is activated, forcing more water into the tank and compressing the air again. As the air is compressed, the pressure builds up until the high limit switch is tripped, and the pump shuts off. The air above the water acts as a spring. Typical low and high limit settings for a pump are 25 psi and 50 psi.

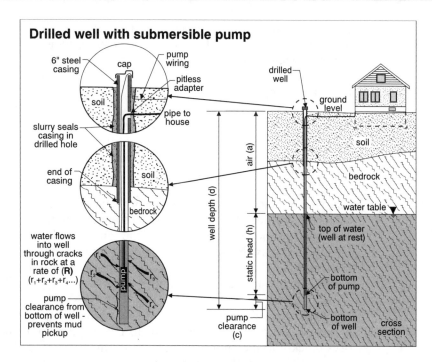

Figure 2. Submersible Pump

Waterlogged

Over time, the air in the tank will be absorbed into the water and the tank will become "waterlogged". This means that the tank is full or nearly full of water. Use of water in the house will often cause the pump to come on and off very quickly. This short cycling is very hard on the pump, and the system should be serviced promptly. It is not difficult to add air to the tank to correct the situation. Some tanks are provided with a diaphragm to separate the air and water, preventing the air from being dissolved into the water.

Lakes,
Rivers &
Cisterns

Private water sources may also include lakes, rivers or cisterns (large holding tanks). Cisterns may be filled by rain water or delivered water from a truck. Typically, pumping arrangements similar to wells are employed, and the water quality should be tested in the same fashion.

Pump

Problems

Problems with a supply pump include the following:

a) No power to the pump (switch shut off, fuse blown, poor electrical connection, etc.). If the problem is not obvious, an electrician should be called.

b) Pump does not work. (Pump seized or frozen, motor burned out, faulty pressure switch, bearings shot, etc.)

c) Pump short-cycles or runs continuously (foot valve leaking, pressure tank waterlogged, leak in piping system, pump has lost its prime, faulty pressure switch).

d) Excessive noise or vibration (poor alignment, worn bearings, etc.).

e) Water is dirty. The well may be running dry. A well draw-down test may be recommended by a plumber. Alternatives are to reduce water use (stop watering the lawn, for example) or improve the water supply.

f) Leak at pump or piping.

g) Pump operating, but pressure is poor. (Partially closed valve, obstructed pipe, leak in system, poor adjustment of pressure switches).

Most of these problems require a plumber.

Tank

The pressure tank is susceptible to corrosion and /or leakage. These tanks are subject to considerable condensation during the summer months, in particular. This condensation on the outside of the tank can ultimately corrode the tank. Ideally, the tanks should be insulated to minimize condensation, although very few are. A corroded tank is replaced when it begins to leak. A leak caused by a poor connection is easily repaired.

The tank is waterlogged (there is no air cushion in the tank) if, when the water is flowed, the pressure gauge drops to the cut-in point of the pump and then rises quickly to the cut-off point several times a minute. This is not a serious problem. The air cushion in the tank has to be restored. Some tanks have an air supply valve attached to them so that air can be pumped into the tank. Tanks with diaphragms should, in theory, never lose their air cushion. Eventually, of course, the diaphragms do fail.

1.3 Main Shut-off Valve Description and Function: The main shut-off valve should be located and tagged. This valve allows one to shut off all the house water at one location. The valve should be readily accessible, and it should be verified that it is operable. Since these valves are operated infrequently, it is not unusual for them to become stuck over time. They often leak when operated after a period of inactivity. For this reason, they are not tested during a home inspection.

Some main shut-off valves have bleed valves on them. These small auxiliary valves allow the water downstream of the shut-off valve to drain out of the system once the valve is closed. Some of these bleed valves can be shut off, although others discharge automatically, as the main valve is closed. This discharge of water can be disconcerting if one is not familiar with the bleed valve function. If the water which drains out of the pipe can do damage, a container should be provided under the valve while it is draining.

The valve cannot always be located during a home inspection, due to storage and/or finishes. Where this happens, the homeowner should locate the valve when the house is vacant. In mild climates the valve may be outside the house. In freezing climates, the valve should be in a heated area.

Problems

Missing, Damaged, Leaking

Where there is no main shut-off valve, one should be added near the point of entry into the house. Where the valve is damaged or inoperative, it should be repaired or replaced as necessary. Similarly, a leaking valve should be repaired promptly. This means shutting off the water at the street.

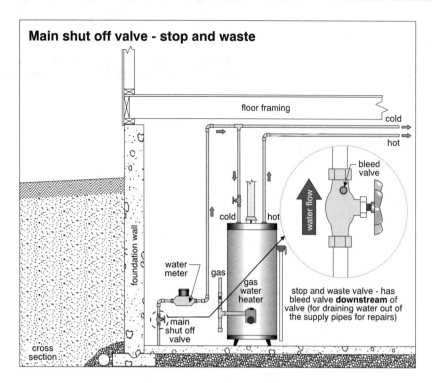

Main shut off valve - stop and waste

Figure 3. Main Shut-off Valve

*Partly
Closed*

Poor house water pressure is occasionally the result of partially closed main valves. This, of course, is easily corrected.

1.4 Supply Piping in House: A relatively small section of the supply piping can be seen during a typical home inspection. No comment can be offered on concealed plumbing.

Typical Materials

Galvanized Steel: Galvanized steel piping was used, almost exclusively, up to approximately 1950. Depending on the pipe diameter, the water composition, and the amount of use, this piping typically lasts forty to sixty years. Some lower quality pipes do not last as long, and there are some oversized pipes still in use after sixty years.

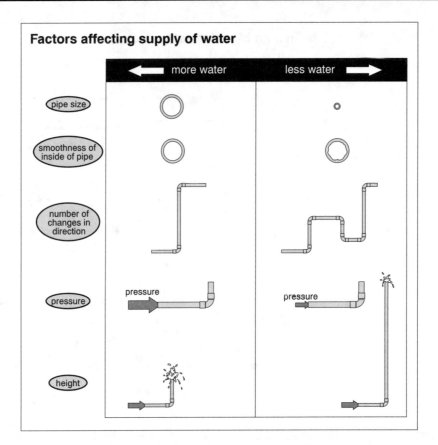

Figure 4. Factors Affecting Supply of Water

Galvanized steel pipes in a house are typically 1/2 inch inside diameter. The connections are threaded. When the pipe wears out, the rust accumulation inside the pipe chokes down the diameter of the pipe, resulting in poor water pressure. Eventually, the pipe will rust through, usually at the joints first, resulting in leakage.

Rust

As rust builds up inside the pipe, a brownish water color is often noted when a faucet is turned on, especially after several days of inactivity. This is rust accumulation which, after flowing water for several seconds, will disappear in all but the most severe cases.

Copper: Copper pipes have been in use residentially since approximately 1950. Since the mid 1950's, copper has been virtually the only material used. In the 1970's, plastic supply piping was approved, although it is still not commonly used.

Life Expectancy

Copper piping is typically 1/2 or 3/4 inch diameter. As far as we know, copper piping will last indefinitely, unless unusual water conditions (high corrosive mineral content) or manufacturing defects are present.

Types

Copper piping has soldered connections and the walls of the pipe are thinner than galvanized steel. (Note: In many areas, solder is now required to be lead free.) There are three types of copper piping used. Type M has the thinnest walls and is not used commonly by plumbers. Type L is the most common and is a medium wall thickness. Type K is the thickest, often used in underground service piping. It usually cannot be determined during a visual inspection which type of pipe has been used. This is not an issue in most residential situations.

Flexible
Flexible copper piping is available which can be bent around corners using special tools. This is not common since it is more expensive and can be awkward to work with in close quarters. It is often seen in amateurish installations.

Plastic: Plastic supply piping is most popularly used by the do-it-yourselfer. Connections can be made without soldering, and the pipe is easy to work with. There are two common types. Polybutylene pipe uses press-on fittings and care must be taken that the pipe does not contact heating ducts. If the pipe freezes, it is less likely to burst than copper piping and the pipe can be bent by hand on a seven inch radius. The pipe tends to sag and should be well supported by hangers.

Polybutylene (PB)
Polybutylene piping has been the source of some plumbing problems, including failed fittings, possibly resulting from faulty installation. PB piping was removed from the Uniform Plumbing Code in the U.S.A. in 1989, as an approved water distribution material. In some cases, the piping manufacturer will inspect, repair or replace the PB piping at no cost to the home owner.

CPVC
Chlorinated poly vinyl chloride (CPVC) pipe is not as flexible as polybutylene and the fittings are solvent welded (glued) rather than press-on. This pipe is likely to split if freezing occurs. Again, a good number of hangers should be provided.

Most plumbers prefer to work with copper and, although the plastic pipe is less expensive than copper, the fittings are expensive. Some codes do not allow plastic pipes, and there are several other types of plastic. Some are only suitable for waste, underground or cold water piping.

Brass: Brass piping has never been used extensively. It was used in the early 20th century in high quality homes and areas where water quality was such that steel piping may have been attacked. Brass piping is an alloy of copper and tin which can be identified by its threaded fittings and inability to attract a magnet.

Two different brass alloys were commonly used, one known as red brass and the other as yellow brass. The yellow brass lasted only 20 to 40 years, while the red brass can last 50 to 60 years. In either case, it is generally recommended that brass supply piping be closely monitored as it is likely to be near the end of its life. Brass piping becomes brittle toward the end of its life and may be subject to serious leakage problems. Generally speaking, brass is replaced with copper piping today.

City
1.4.1 Problems-Flow (Pressure): Water flow (in gallons per minute) is a function of several things, including the size and shape of the opening, and the pressure at the opening. The pressure available from the source (city or private pump) has an impact on water flow, of course. Typically, city water supplies are at 40 to 70 psi (static pressure).

Well
Most older private systems are set to maintain water pressure between 20 psi and 40 psi. This is too low for some lifestyles and plumbers can set systems higher, in some cases. This is only successful, of course, if the pump is capable of delivering higher pressure.

*Pressure
vs
Flow*

Static pressure is the pressure exerted by the water against the walls of the pipe with no water flowing. A horizontal pipe one hundred feet long connected to a huge reservoir with a constant pressure of 60 psi, will have a pressure of 60 psi anywhere along the pipe, if the valve at the other end is shut. As the valve is opened and water begins to flow, the pressure drops as water moves along the pipe. This is a result of friction loss along the pipe walls. If gages were put on the pipe every ten feet, the gage at the reservoir would still read 60 psi, and (depending on the pipe diameter and the amount of water flowing), the gage ten feet from the reservoir might read 58 psi; the gage twenty feet down would read 56 psi, and the next gage 54 psi, et cetera. At the end of the pipe, the pressure might be 40 psi. (This is a simplification of the process, and is not entirely accurate.)

As more water is flowed, the pressure would drop more at each point along the pipe. The water pressure at the reservoir would always be 60 psi. The reservoir is roughly equivalent to the city water main under the street. The amount of pressure lost as water flows through a pipe is largely a function of the pipe diameter and the amount of water flowing.

Improvement

The more plumbing fixtures flowing at once, the greater the pressure drop at all fixtures, and the lower the flow at each fixture. If we replace any ten foot section of pipe with a much larger pipe, the pressure drop across that section will essentially be eliminated. Replacing any section of pipe will result in somewhat better pressure (and flow), at the valve. This is very surprising to many people, who think that the most upstream section of pipe, or the entire pipe, must be changed in order to enjoy any benefit. The "bottleneck" principle does not apply in an absolute sense to plumbing systems. Water flow in a house can be improved to some extent by changing any pipe in the system.

Gravity

Gravity is another source of pressure loss in a residential plumbing system. Energy is required to push the water uphill. For every one foot of elevation increase in a pipe, approximately 0.434 psi is lost. Another way of saying this, is that it takes I psi to move water 2.31 feet higher. A house system will typically lose eight psi in a two story house, getting the water from the basement up to the second floor bathroom. With no water flowing, the static pressure available at the street main may be 60 psi, but the static pressure at the second floor basin would be 52 psi. Houses which are much higher than the street, or have third story plumbing fixtures, will suffer a pressure disadvantage.

*Galvanized
Steel*

Where the water pressure is poor in the distribution system, the most common cause is corroded galvanized steel piping. The common 1/2 inch diameter piping can close down so that the opening is only 1/8 inch in diameter or even less. The only solution is to replace this pipe, typically with copper. The diameter of the new pipe should never be smaller than the original piping. It is often wise to replace with a larger diameter pipe on the main feeds at least, to improve pressure further. A 3/4 inch pipe is recommended from the point of entry into the house to the water heater, at least. On large or multi-family dwellings, this should be larger.

Partial Replacement

When galvanized steel pipe is present, and pressure is low, it is common for the readily accessible pipes running across the basement ceiling to be replaced first. While there will also be some deterioration in the risers going up to the plumbing fixtures, the horizontal pipes tend to deteriorate slightly more quickly. The accessibility of the horizontal pipes in the basement makes it less expensive to replace these. Changing the basement pipes will help in the short term, but eventually the risers have to be done as well.

Replacing Hot Only

Another practice which is common, but is very short sighted, is to replace the hot water piping and not the cold. The hot water pipe pressure deteriorates somewhat sooner than does the cold. This is because the rust build-up on the inside of galvanized steel piping is the result of a chemical reaction (oxidization). Reactions such as this proceed more quickly with higher temperatures. Thus, the hot water piping deteriorates a few years before the cold.

When replacing pipes in a house, the labor is the major cost. When changing concealed pipes, a large part of the labor cost is breaking out the walls and ceilings to get at the pipes, and repairing and redecorating afterwards. It is expensive to break out and replace walls and ceilings twice within a five year period, the first time to change the hot pipes and the second to change the cold.

Lead Waste

It is also wise to replace any lead waste plumbing found at fixtures when replacing galvanized steel supply plumbing. The lead waste plumbing, although it may look fine, can be expected to leak soon in a bathroom old enough to have deteriorated galvanized steel piping.

Other Reasons

There are several other reasons for poor water pressure. The main shut-off valve in the basement may be partially closed or obstructed. The city valve near the property line may similarly restrict flow. The supply line from the street to the house may be undersized, damaged or leaking.

Long runs of relatively small (1/2 inch diameter) pipe within a house will result in considerable pressure drop, especially with more than one fixture flowing. Replacement with larger pipe or shortening the runs are possible solutions.

A sludge build-up in a water heater can lead to poor hot water pressure. The tank should be flushed every year or so. A water softener, especially if not well maintained, can adversely affect water pressure.

A partially closed or obstructed isolating valve in the system can result in poor pressure in one part of the house. Adding plumbing fixtures without enlarging pipes or adding new ones will often lead to pressure complaints. This is common in single family homes which are duplexed or triplexed.

A crimped, damaged or clogged pipe within the house will adversely affect pressure. This is common with amateurish work. On a private system, a defective, undersized or poorly adjusted pump will result in poor pressure.

Galvanized
Steel

1.4.2 Problems—Leaks: Galvanized steel piping will often leak first at the joints. Steel pipe has threads cut into it where it joins a fitting. The pipe wall is thinner at the threaded connections. As the piping rusts from the inside out, the pipe is most likely to rust through first at the threaded connections.

One of the phenomena with steel piping as it corrodes, is that it may rust through at one spot and begin to leak; however, the rust may form a scab over the leak and the leak may be intermittent as the rust progresses. This scabbing effect, if seen on the surface of the pipe will mean the pipe is close to the end of its life, even though it may not be actively leaking.

The interior of the pipe cannot be inspected. Observing the water pressure in the house is the only practical way to estimate the pipe condition. Since steel piping has not been used in single family homes since the early 1950's, it will be near the end of its life.

Leaking supply pipes can range from an annoying drip, to a major flood. In most cases, however, leakage appears first as a drip and progresses from there. With regular inspection, this can usually be picked up before serious flooding occurs.

Connections

Galvanized steel pipe is, of course, not the only pipe susceptible to leaks. Leakage as a result of a poor connection is often impossible to anticipate, and may be caused by vibration over a period of time. If a connection lets go suddenly, there will be a flood.

Damage

Mechanical damage will sometimes result in a leak immediately, although in other cases a joint is simply weakened and subsequent vibration will cause the leak sometime later. Concealed piping may be damaged by drilling or nailing into walls.

Copper/Steel
Contact

Leakage can occur in copper piping where steel clamps are used. Copper and steel undergo a galvanic reaction when in contact with each other. This rusting can easily be avoided. Copper piping should have either copper or plastic clamps. Copper should not touch steel ductwork or any other dissimilar metal. A piece of heavy paper separating the metals is enough to prevent the corrosion.

Dielectric
Connectors

Special connectors, designed to prevent galvanic reaction, are often used where steel and copper piping are joined. These dielectric connectors separate the metals and reduce the deterioration. The performance reported of these connectors is good in some cases, but poor in others.

1.4.3. Problems—Freezing: Leakage can be a result of pipes freezing. A one-time freeze may not result in leakage. In some cases, copper piping for example, will develop a bulge although the piping may not split on the first freeze. Frozen pipes, of course, do not leak. They leak only as the ice begins to thaw. Some types of plastic supply pipe have better resistance to freeze-up than copper.

It is easy to see how pipes can freeze if they are installed in an unheated area such as a garage or crawl space. Inside the house, it is more difficult to understand why pipes would freeze, especially in a building that has been through several winters. Pipes which have been in place for fifty years can freeze if, for example, an exterior wall is insulated from the inside of the house. If insulation is added on the interior (warm) side of the piping, the pipes which used to receive heat from the house are cut off from their heat source. Supply piping on exterior walls is always vulnerable to freezing.

In an old house, pipes running up to a kitchen sink may not have frozen in the past simply because the air under the sink circulated freely and kept the pipes warm. If the kitchen is remodelled, and a closed cabinet is provided under the sink, the same pipes may now freeze since they are cut off from the warm, circulating air.

Relocating a heat source may also lead to freezing pipes if the area around the pipes becomes colder as a result. This is common in remodelling projects where a bulky radiator is moved to make room for a cabinet. In many kitchen projects, the radiator is removed and not replaced with any heat source. The room may still be comfortable, but the pipes may not.

Solutions   Freezing pipe problems can be solved by providing electric heating cables. These electric cables are typically wrapped around the pipe or taped to the surface of the pipe. There are more sophisticated cables which can be run inside pipes, although these are not normally used residentially. Another solution is, of course, to relocate the pipes to a protected location.

Outdoor Faucets   Garden faucets have a valve on the outside for normal summer use, and an is lating valve inside the house. In the winter, the inside valve should be shut off, and the outside valve fully opened to allow any water to drain out. Some inside valves have auxiliary bleed valves to drain water which is downstream of the winter shut-off.

Many codes require back flow preventers on outside faucets to protect against cross connections. See 1.4.7.

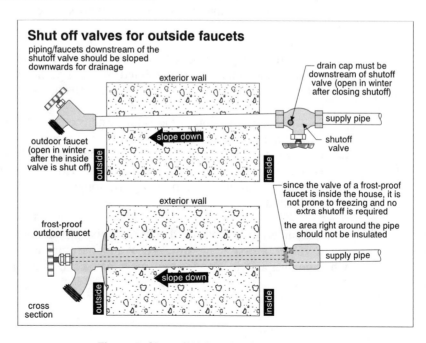

Figure 5. Shut-off Valves for Outdoor Faucets

There are special frost-proof outside valves which have long stems going through the wall, to shut off the water inside the building every time the faucet is used. These frost-proof valves do not require permanent shut off in the winter. Hoses must be disconnected and the values must be sloped to allow the valves to drain and prevent freezing.

1.4.4 Problems—Sweating:

In some homes, the cold water piping is insulated to avoid sweating of pipes. On a warm humid day, the water running through a pipe will cool the air immediate adjacent to the pipe. If the air happens to be almost saturated at 70' F., cooling the air to 60' F. will result in condensation on the pipes. This sweating of the pipes can be annoying, and if allowed to continue, can cause water damage to ceilings, floors, furniture or storage. If a basement is to be finished, the cold water piping above the ceiling should be insulated.

It is sometimes difficult to know whether a pipe is leaking or sweating. On horizontal piping there are some clues which help. Condensation beads appear on the pipe uniformly around the diameter of a pipe and along its length. If one looks closely, a leak can usually be traced to a source from which water will only be running along the underside of the pipe. On vertical piping, the same difference exists, but once water starts to run down the pipe, it can be difficult to be sure.

Condensation can be controlled with insulation, whereas leakage requires a repair.

1.4.5 Problems-Noise Control:

Noisy piping can be very irritating, although it is not often a serious problem. It is usually the result of pipes which are inadequately secured. When pipes are run up through walls, particularly when replacing older pipes with new, there is a tendency to feed pipes up through walls without breaking open any more wall than absolutely necessary. This may result in pipes which are not well secured as they pass through the walls.

As valves are opened and closed, vibration can be set up in the piping and it can rattle. Sometimes this can be corrected by pushing newspapers into the wall cavity to keep the pipes from contacting the walls or each other.

Where a pipe passes through the floor system or wood studs, for example, it may rub on the wood and squeak as the pipe changes dimension slightly. This is particularly noticeable on hot water piping, where the pipe will expand as it heats up. This can be corrected once the problem is isolated, by wrapping the pipe where it passes through the opening. In some cases, the opening has to be enlarged slightly.

*Water
Hammer*

Water hammer (or hydrostatic shock) is a noisy pipe problem that is experienced when valves are shut off quickly. Water hammer can also set up enough vibration over a period of time to damage pipe connections and result in leakage.

The mechanism of water hammer can be explained as follows: water passing through a pipe is moving quickly and has a certain momentum. When the valve is shut quickly, the momentum of the water carries it into the valve with some force. Since water is essentially incompressible, a large pressure is built up as a result, There is very high pressure at the end of the pipe against the valve, and relatively low pressure upstream in the pipe. The high pressure water wants to flow to the low pressure area to neutralize the imbalance. This happens so quickly that a small vacuum can be created against the valve as the water moves away from it. This can result in cavitation, and the water being pulled back against the valve a second time. This continues back and forth in slowly diminishing shock waves. Pressures up to 600 psi can result from water travelling up to 3,000 miles per hour, for very short periods.

Water hammer can result in very loud noises in supply plumbing pipes. Water hammer is identified by noises which occur only as valves are closed. If a valve is closed very slowly, and the noise does not occur, one can be sure that water hammer is the problem.

The solution is fairly simple, but sometimes difficult to get at. Consider a pipe running up the wall and coming out at a bathroom basin, for example. Simply extending the piping (roughly twelve inches) up the wall behind the basin will solve the problem. These additional pipes, known as air chambers, extend straight up inside the wall, past the take off for the faucet. See Figure 3. When the plumbing system is filled with water, these pipes will have air trapped in them. Since air is readily compressed, no matter how quickly the valves are shut off, the momentum of the water will be carried into the air, which acts as a cushion. The water is slowed down gradually, and water hammer will not occur.

Over a period of time, the air will be absorbed into the water and the air chambers will become ineffective. At this point the plumbing system has to be drained so that more air can be trapped in the air chambers. Simply draining and refilling the piping system will accomplish this.

There are special devices which can be purchased to control water hammer. These contain a diaphragm so that the air will not be absorbed into the water.

Water hammer is more of a problem with quick closing valves. and it is common with electrically operated valves on appliances such as washing machines and dishwashers.

Exposed to Damage

1.4.6 Problems-Location: Pipes which are hung too low from the basement ceiling, or surface mounted on walls, may be subjected to mechanical damage. As much as possible, the pipes should be protected, and should never be located so that they can be pinched by a door which is opened too far, or be pushed out of position by storage against them. Where necessary, wood blocks can be run along beside pipes to protect them from damage.

Hangers

All piping should he adequately supported with hangers. Copper piping should not be supported with steel hangers because of the corrosion which will take place. Copper pipes should not contact heating ducts for similar reasons. Plastic piping should also be kept away from heat ducts.

1.4.7 Problems—Cross Connections: A cross connection is the name given to a situation where waste water could enter and contaminate the supply water. This, of course, is a health hazard and should be avoided. A cross connection may occur where a laundry tub, for example, has a faucet below the top of the laundry tub. If the faucets enter through the side wall of the tub, it is possible that when the tub is filled with water, the faucet will be submerged. If this happens, the waste water in the tub could get into the drinking water through the faucet if the supply piping is being drained.

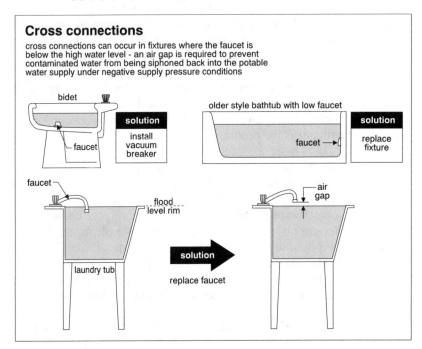

Figure 6. Cross Connections

The obvious solution is to raise the faucet set above the top of a tub or basin. This is common practice in modern plumbing, and cross connections do not occur under normal circumstances. Cross connections are also avoided through the use of an overflow. In bathtubs, for example, where the faucets may enter through the wall of the tub below the top, an overflow provided below the faucets will prevent a cross connection.

Bidet

Some plumbing fixtures necessarily create a situation which could lead to a cross connection. A bidet is a good example of this (see 3.9 and Figure 24 in this section). A bidet has a water supply at the bottom of the bowl. This allows water to be directed up in a spray from the bottom center of the bowl. There is, of course, the potential for waste water in the bowl to get into this supply water. A special device (vacuum breaker) located at the control valves for the bidet, prevents any water from flowing back into the supply plumbing.

Garden Hose While cross connections are normally avoided during original plumbing work, home handyman changes can defeat this. Careless use of the house plumbing system can also create a cross connection. Care should be taken, for example, to avoid placing a garden hose in a position to allow waste water to flow back into the supply plumbing system. For example, if the hose is used on the outside of the house while cleaning windows or gutters, and the hose is left in a pail of water, it is possible for the contaminated water to flow back through the hose into the drinking water. This may happen if the house water supply is shut off and partially drained for some reason, while the hose is in the pail.

Boiler
Connection On hot water heating systems, the plumbing is connected to the boiler so that water can be added to the boiler. Modern installations have a back-flow preventer to prevent the boiler water from coming back into the drinking water. This is another form of cross connection. Older systems do not have back-flow preventers to protect against this. Where no back-flow preventer is provided, a heating specialist may recommend one.

1.5. Isolating Valves: The purpose of an isolating valve is to allow someone to work on a part of the plumbing system without shutting off the entire house water supply. Almost every toilet has an isolating valve, and there should always be an isolating valve on the cold water supply to the hot water heater. Although not often installed, it is desirable to have isolating valves on every set of risers running up from the main feeds in the basement, and isolating valves under each sink and basin.

Leak **Problems:** The most common problem experienced with isolating valves is leakage through the valve connection, packing or washer.

Inoperative A problem that is often not noted until the valve is needed, is an inoperative valve. Many toilet isolating valves become stuck, and are therefore useless. This is very frustrating, since it is usually an emergency when the valve is tried. Replacing the isolating valve is not a large expense. If an isolating valve cannot be closed, the main water shut off to the house can be used in an emergency.

If an isolating valve does not turn with normal effort by hand pressure, a wrench should not be used unless one is prepared to shut off the main supply valve very quickly if the valve is damaged. Sometimes forcing a valve will not break it, but will result in leaking afterward.

Water
Heater It should be remembered that when the hot water system is to be drained to work on the system, an electric or oil-fired hot water heater must be turned off. A gas fired heater should be set to the pilot position.

1.6 Water Heaters: Water heaters may be gas, oil or electric. In some cities, it is possible to rent water heaters from the utilities or oil companies. This is usually less expensive than owning a heater. The life expectancy of a water heater is typically eight to twelve years, although there are exceptions on both sides. If the heater is a rental, or is owned but rentals are available, there is very little concern.

Life Expectancy

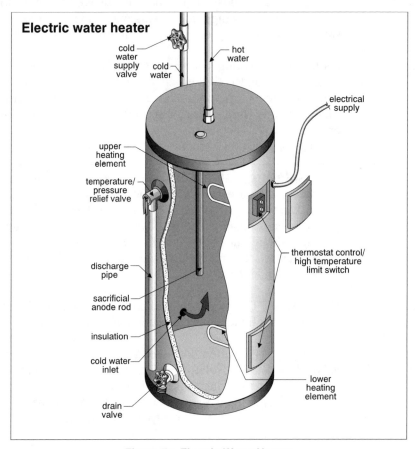

Figure 7a. Electric Water Heater

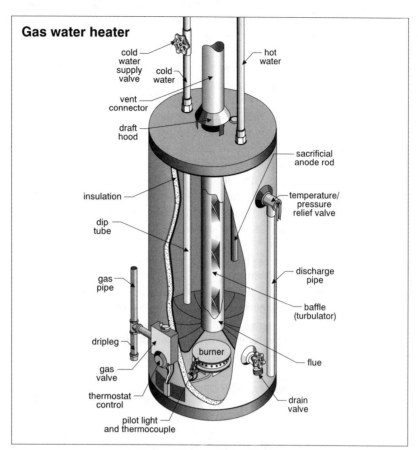

Figure 7b. Gas Water Heater

How They Work   Whether gas, oil or electricity, all water heaters operate in essentially the same way. The cold water enters the glass lined tank from the source, and heated water leaves the tank. The water temperature is typically 140° F. When hot water is removed from the tank (by opening a hot water faucet in the house), cold water enters the tank, triggering the thermostat. Eventually the tank will cool down, since heat cannot be added to the incoming water as quickly as the hot is drained off. The larger the tank, the longer it takes to run out of hot water.

Size   Water heaters should be of adequate size to satisfy the needs of the house. In a rental situation, it is easy to replace a small heater with a larger one, or to add a second hot water heater. A family of four will often find a 30 gallon gas or oil system or a 40 gallon electric system satisfactory.

Recovery Rate   When the hot water is depleted, the recovery rate of the heater becomes important. Generally speaking, oil has the fastest rate of recovery, with gas second and electricity third, depending on the size of burner or element. If water is drawn off slowly, the recovery rate may be such that the tank can be kept filled with 140° F water. The faster the recovery rate, the more water that can be used without running out of hot water.

Insulation   The tanks are insulated to slow the heat loss from the tank. More energy efficient tanks have better insulation. Some people also insulate their hot water piping.

Temperature
Settings

Thermostats control the water temperature. Dishwasher manufacturers often recommend that the water be 140° F. Some dishwashing detergents will not dissolve completely at lower temperatures. To save energy and avoid burns, 115 to 120° F is a better setting. Some dishwashers can now heat their own water, so the water heater setting can be lowered.

Tankless
Water Heaters

Tankless, coil, or instantaneous heaters can be used with hot water or steam boilers. Cold water is heated by passing through a coil in the boiler or a heat exchanger attached to the boiler. These units, which are often undersized, usually have no storage tank. The house boiler must be run year round. This wastes energy and reduces the boiler life. Since the boiler water temperature varies, a mixing valve (manual or automatic) should be provided. The coils frequently scale up, reducing hot water pressure. Replacement with a tank system is usually recommended.

Fuel

Problems: Whether gas, oil or electric, the water heater must have a continuous fuel and air supply. Gas piping should be steel, not aluminum, copper or brass. Any gas odor is a serious problem. Malfunctioning burners, pilot lights, controls or electrical elements will cause poor operation or may result in the system not working at all. Oil burners should be serviced annually. Many experts recommend draining one or two gallons out of the bottom of the tank monthly to prevent sludge build-up.

Exhaust
Venting

Most gas and oil water heaters have to be vented into a chimney with adequate draft. Poorly arranged or disconnected vents are safety hazards which should be corrected promptly. Aluminum vents are not permitted. Vent sections should be screwed together, and should slope up 1/4 inch per ft., minimum. Vents should extend 2 ft. above the roof and should be 2 ft. above anything within 10 ft. horizontally. Vents should extend at least 5 ft. above the draft hood. Exhaust gases spilling out at the draft hood or burner may present a life threatening situation. This problem requires immediate action. There are some modern mid-efficiency gas water heaters which employ induced draft fans to vent straight out through the house wall.

Location

Gas or oil water heaters should not be in sleeping areas. Gas fired heaters in garages should be 18 inches above floor level, and protected from mechanical damage.

Electric

It is not unusual to find one of the two elements in electric water heaters burned out. Replacing an element is not expensive. Most heaters are wired so that both elements cannot be on at the same time. Depending on which element fails, there may be some hot water, or none.

Leak and
Damage

Hot water heaters can, of course, leak, and the tanks can be mechanically damaged.

Sludge

Where sludge has accumulated in the bottom of the tank, water pressure from the hot water system may be limited. When water pressure problems are experienced on the hot water system only, it makes sense to drain the hot water heater to ensure that sludge accumulation is not the problem.

Hot/Cold Reversed

Since the piping connections into hot water heaters are often both at the top, it is easy to reverse the connections. The cold water connection on this type of tank has a long tube which extends down through the tank, so that the cold water is introduced at the bottom. The hot connection simply allows heated water to be drawn off the top of the tank. Reversing the connections on this pipe will lead to very inefficient performance.

Relief Valve

Discharge Tube

Rental

The temperature/pressure relief valve lets water escape if the temperature or pressure is too high. This valve should be connected to a tube which discharges 6 to 12 inches above floor level so hot water won't be sprayed on to anyone nearby. Some codes require that the tube discharge outside the build ing. The tube should be as large as the tank fitting and the tube end should never be threaded, capped or plugged. The tube should be able to withstand 250°F temperatures, should have no shut-off valve, and should be as short and as straight as possible. An alternative to the temperature part of the relief valve is a device which shuts off the fuel supply if the temperature is too high. With rental units, the utility, oil or gas company will look after the repair.

1.7 Hot Water Circulating System:

Some high quality homes have a system to constantly move the hot water through the heater and hot water distribution piping. This feature eliminates the need to wait for several seconds to get hot water out of a tap, for example, first thing in the morning.

In a conventional system, the water is heated at the hot water tank and then enters the distribution piping. The hot water in the pipe cools down to room temperature over time. When a faucet is opened, the cool water in the hot water pipe must be run through before heated water from the tank gets to the faucet.

The hot water circulating system forms a large loop, and the water is moved slowly through the system even when no faucets are flowing. The water does not have a chance to cool down, since it is passed through the water heater every few minutes.

Problems:

Like all electrically driven pumps, the motor can fail. The motor may also be warm or noisy, indicating problems. The pump can be seized, damaged, worn or leaking.

The hot water circulating pump systems are normally set up so that if the pump is inoperative, the hot water supply in the house can still be used in a normal fashion. This will not provide the hot water instantly, but beyond this, does not create a problem.

1.8 Inappropriate/Low Quality Materials:

Many materials used for supply plumbing were not intended for this use, and when installed may be expected to have a short and troublesome life. These materials include rubber hoses, garden hoses, and non-certified plastic piping. Connections made with the wrong materials or wrong devices cannot be expected to perform properly. Special connectors are provided for special types of piping.

► **2.0 WASTE SYSTEMS**

Only a small percentage of the waste piping system is visible. No comments can be offered during a home inspection on concealed piping.

2.1 Public: Most houses in built-up areas are connected to a municipal sewer system. This is a system in the street which allows waste from a house to flow by gravity into sewer piping. The waste is carried to a treatment facility where it is cleaned prior to being released.

Combination Sewers

In older neighborhoods, a combination storm and sanitary sewer was employed. In modern areas, and where sewer pipes have been replaced, there is a sanitary sewer to carry house waste and a separate storm sewer to carry rain and snow run off.

Shallow Sewers

Where the street sewers are not deep enough, the main drain pipe from a house must leave the house above the basement floor. This means that plumbing fixtures cannot be put in the basement without the waste being pumped up to the main drain level. A basement floor drain in this situation would also require special attention.

Risk of Back-up

A street with a storm sewer and sanitary sewers is more desirable than a combination sewer. Basement flooding as a result of storm sewer back-up is less likely in a house with separate sewers. With combination sewers, if there is a large volume of storm water, the sewers can be overloaded and water (including raw sewage) can back up through basement floor drains. In some areas, this problem is common and some homeowners install one-way valves in their floor drains which allows water down into the drain, but prevents water from coming back up. If pressures are high enough, sewage may back up through basement plumbing fixtures. In some cases, a check valve is put into the main drain line itself. These are obviously short term solutions at best and, ideally, the city should be petitioned to improve the sewer system.

Floor Drains and Downspouts

Where there are separate sewers, the floor drains should go into the sanitary sewer and gutters and downspouts should go into the storm sewer, or onto the ground several feet away from the building.

Overloaded Drain

Although it is rare, it is possible that a house with a city sewer system is refused permission to add more plumbing fixtures. There are a fixed number of fixtures which can drain into any given size of drainage pipe. This can be an unexpected stumbling block during a house expansion or renovation.

2.2 Private: The most common private sewer system is a septic tank and weeping tile bed. This system is employed in houses where city sewers were not available when the house was built.

The septic tank is a watertight container usually made of concrete, steel or fiber glass. It serves as a holding tank which allows heavy solids to settle to the bottom of the tank. Lighter materials which float are also in the tank. The heavy solids are known as sludge and the lighter floating materials are known as scum.

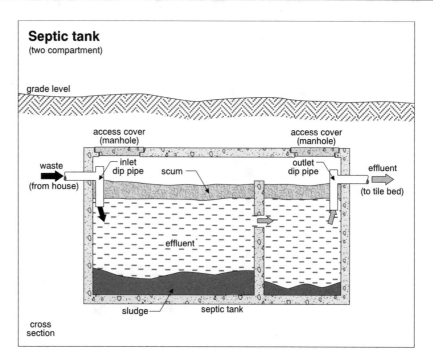

Figure 8. Septic Tank

Most of the material which enters the tank is in a liquid state. Within the tank, the majority of the solids are broken down to gases and/or liquids. The breakdown takes place as a result of bacteria action, both aerobic and anaerobic. The liquids are discharged from the tank into the tile bed. The gas escapes through the plumbing vents.

The tile bed is also known as a leaching bed, disposal field, soil absorption field or drain field. It consists of a network of perforated or open jointed pipes in trenches below the ground surface which allows the liquid waste (effluent) to percolate into the soil. The size of the leaching bed is dependent upon the ability of the soil to absorb the effluent, and the amount of waste the system receives.

There are variations on the conventional septic system, including closed holding tanks, which are pumped out on a regular basis. There are also more sophisticated systems wherein agitators and aerators are employed to accelerate the chemical decomposition of the solids in the tank. The bacterial action in these systems is aerobic only. These systems allow the use of smaller tile beds and are of particular value on smaller properties. While there is an advantage to this, the presence of electrical and mechanical parts creates the potential for higher maintenance.

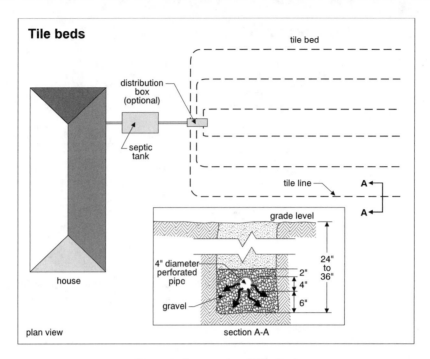

Figure 9. Conventional Tile Bed

Special sand can be used which allows very small tile beds to be installed. This is expensive, since the sand has to be brought onto the site, but it may be important to keep the tile bed small. These special tile beds are used with conventional septic tanks, or can be used with the mechanically assisted systems described above.

Septic systems should be kept well away from supply wells and other Sources of drinking water, for obvious reasons. Generally speaking, a well and a tile bed should be at least one hundred feet apart. A well and septic tank should be at least fifty feet from each other.

It is helpful to know the exact location of the tank and tile bed, the age of the system, and as many of the installation and service history details as are available. Where building expansion is planned, it is necessary to know where the tank and tile bed are. The tile bed location is often indicated by greener, healthier grass growing above the bed. The health and environment authorities may have a record of the location.

In some situations, it is not possible to determine whether the house waste system is public or private. Where there is any doubt, this should be checked with the vendor.

Problems

Odor and Pooling

A septic system which is not performing properly can pose a health hazard and should be treated as a high priority problem. The overall condition of a septic system and tile bed cannot be well evaluated during a visual inspection. The homeowner should watch for water pooling above the tile bed, or an odor coming from the bed. Homes which have been vacant for several months may show problems when the system is pressed back into service.

26

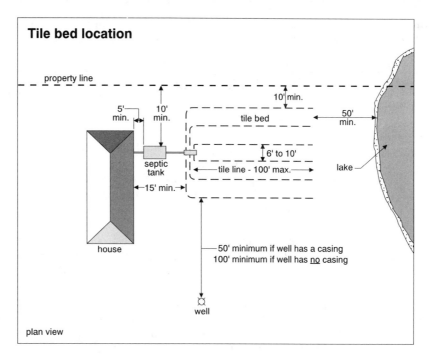

Figure 10. Tile Bed Location

Problems which lead to failure of septic systems include overloading of the tile bed, soil breakdown around the tiles, high water tables, clogging of the tiles, and broken or cracked tanks and tiles.

Solutions   Solution alternatives include repairs to broken or damaged components, relocation of the tile bed, bringing in special soil, and reducing the load on the system. Identifying the cause of failure and suggesting the correct solution is a job for a specialist.

Maintenance   Septic systems require regular maintenance. The system should be inspected annually and the tank should be pumped out every two to four years, as required. Tile beds do have a fixed life expectancy (often considered to be roughly twenty-five to thirty years). This depends on a great many factors and is very difficult to predict. Bleaches and strong detergents should be avoided where possible, since they may kill the bacteria in the tank. The amount of water entering the system should be minimized. Water saving toilets and shower heads are a good idea.

City Sewers   There are several areas where houses with original septic systems can now connect to street sewers. The connection to a municipal system can be well over a thousand dollars in municipal fees and connection charges alone. There are also plumbing costs to make the connections, which are the responsibility of the homeowner.

In most cases, abandoning a septic system which is in good working order is not cost-effective. Where the land is to be used to provide a building addition or swimming pool, of course, it is necessary to replace the septic system, despite its serviceability. Incidentally, it is very important to know the location and size of a septic system if any building expansion is planned.

Building
Addition

Local authorities may refuse to allow an addition to a home, depending on septic system capabilities. A new septic system, if required, will add significantly to the cost of the addition.

2.3 Waste Piping in House

Typical Materials

Galvanized Steel: Galvanized steel plumbing on the waste system is used in some areas solely for vent pipes. Vents carry air but do not carry water. The galvanized vent piping is not, therefore, subject to the same rusting problems as galvanized steel supply piping. Its life expectancy is very long, easily more than fifty years.

In other areas, galvanized drain and waste pipes were used. These have a relatively short life expectancy since the steel corrodes and the rough inner surface created by the corrosion can cause blockages as solids get hung up.

Copper: Copper waste plumbing was used commonly after World War II, up until the mid 1960's. Copper piping was used for branch drain lines, main stacks, and vent piping. It performs all of these functions very well. In single family residential use, it has become rare, since plastic waste plumbing is much less expensive to purchase and install. In multi-family construction, copper waste plumbing is sometimes used where authorities will not allow combustible plastic piping.

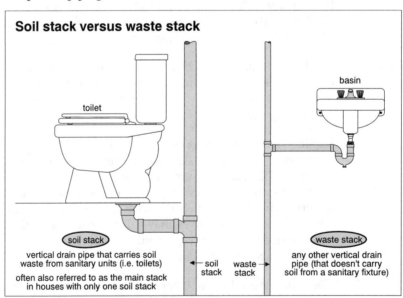

Soil stack versus waste stack

toilet

basin

soil stack

vertical drain pipe that carries soil
waste from sanitary units (i.e. toilets)

often also referred to as the main stack
in houses with only one soil stack

← soil   waste →
stack   stack

waste stack

any other vertical drain
pipe (that doesn't carry
soil from a sanitary fixture)

Figure 11. Soil Stack versus Waste Stack

The joints in copper piping are soldered and an indefinite life expectancy is projected under single family residential conditions.

Plastic: Since the 1960's, ABS plastic piping has become almost the exclusive waste plumbing material. It is used for drains, wastes and vents and is connected by using a plastic cement (glue). The piping is inexpensive, easy to work with and as far as we know, very durable. Its only disadvantage is that it is somewhat noisy when water is running through it. Efforts to control the noise include wrapping it with fiber glass insulation.

Cast Iron: Cast iron piping was used for the main stack in houses up until the 1950's. Its life expectancy is projected to be fifty years and up. It employs a bell-and-spigot connection traditionally with oakum packed into the joint and caulked with lead to seal it. There is also hubless cast iron pipe joined with neoprene sleeves clamped over the joint. Cast iron is expensive and awkward to work with, because it is very heavy.

Cast iron waste piping generally fails in one of two ways. The pipe can rust through, often in a pin hole pattern. It is also prone to splitting along a seam, particularly on horizontal runs.

Lead: Lead waste plumbing was used up until the 1950's, to connect plumbing fixtures to a main cast iron or copper drain. Lead was used because of its resistance to corrosion, and its workability. A piece of lead pipe can be bent fairly easily by hand.

Lead piping, because of its age, is prone to leakage, usually at the connections. It is typically replaced with ABS plastic pipe. Lead waste lines are usually replaced during any major plumbing work, whether problems are being experienced or not. Lead waste plumbing does not create a health hazard in terms of lead content, since it only contacts the waste water.

Lead Suspected: Since the sections of lead piping used are relatively small, they are often not visible. In houses built before the 1960's, where substantial updating has not been done, it is reasonable to assume that concealed lead waste plumbing exists. Where this is the case, the plumbing system is considered susceptible to leakage. The lead should be replaced, of course, when leaks appear or during any other work in the area.

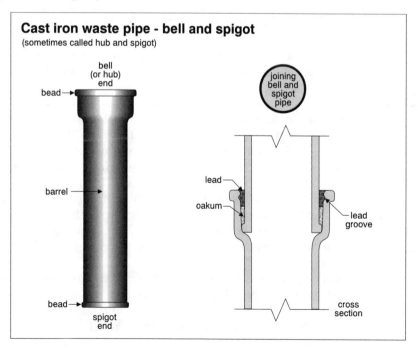

Figure 12. Cast Iron Waste Pipe

2.3.1 Problems—Leaks: Leakage from a waste plumbing system can, of course, be a health hazard and should be corrected immediately. Leakage may be the result of poor connections, mechanical damage or deterioration of piping. Since the majority of the waste plumbing system in a house cannot be seen, waste plumbing leaks can go undetected for some time, particularly if the amount of water flowing through the pipes is not great. Occasional use fixtures will often have small waste plumbing leaks which are not identified for months or even years.

Corrective action may be patching, or replacement, typically with ABS plastic. Old lead piping is prone to leakage and should be watched closely. It should be replaced if any plumbing work is done on nearby supply piping or fixtures. Similarly, when cast iron waste piping develops several pin hole leaks, or cracks at a seam, it is typically replaced with ABS plastic.

2.3.2 Problems—Slope: Waste plumbing pipes are often run almost horizontally. Since they depend on gravity for drainage, they must have at least some slope. The slope recommended is typically one-quarter inch per foot. Over time, with house settlement or pipe sag, the minimum slope can be lost. Low spots in waste plumbing may lead to a build-up of waste, effectively reducing the diameter of the pipe, and ultimately result in a blockage. This situation should be watched for and corrected where identified.

Too much slope on horizontal lines can cause siphoning at traps and poor drain performance. Codes specify maximum pipe slopes. The horizontal drain slope should be such that the fall front the trap water level to the vent is not greater than the pipe diameter. A good rule of thumb is five feet as a maximum distance between a trap and a vent. (See Section 2.6)

2.3.3 Problems—Freezing: Waste plumbing systems are susceptible to freezing, but to a lesser extent than supply plumbing pipes. The reason for this is that the waste piping normally has no water in it. Traps, however, do have water in them all the time and will freeze. Replacing the trap water with anti-freeze is common practice on seasonal buildings.

2.3.4 Problems—Obstructions: Clogs often develop at traps because the tight comers tend to collect foreign material. Traps should be arranged so that they can be removed easily to clear obstructions. Modem household traps often include a drain plug at the trap bottom. This is useful for removing objects such as rings which are dropped down drains, but may not be large enough to allow clearing of an obstruction. Obstructions are sometimes cleared with plungers or plumber's snakes. In some cases, the piping has to be dismantled. This work can create a health hazard, and great care should be exercised when dealing with any waste water problems. Tools, for example, should be washed after use.

Older homes have traps out in the front yard on the main waste system. These are common spots for obstructions. The waste line outside the house is also vulnerable to tree roots. Where the pipe has not been seriously damaged, a plumber's snake may clear a blockage. If the pipe is broken, digging and replacing are necessary.

2.4 Traps: Traps are provided below house plumbing fixtures and are designed to hold some water in the waste piping system. The purpose of a trap is to prevent sewer odors from coming back through the fixture drain when it is not in use. There are several different styles of traps (P traps, S traps, and Drum traps, for example). The P traps are considered the best residentially, as they are least vulnerable to siphoning or obstruction problems.

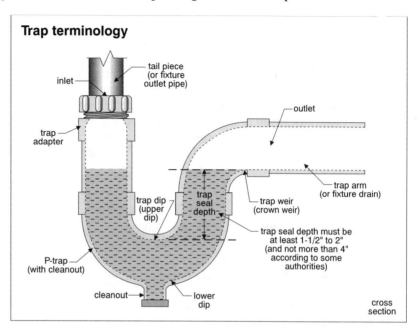

Figure 13. Components of Conventional P Trap

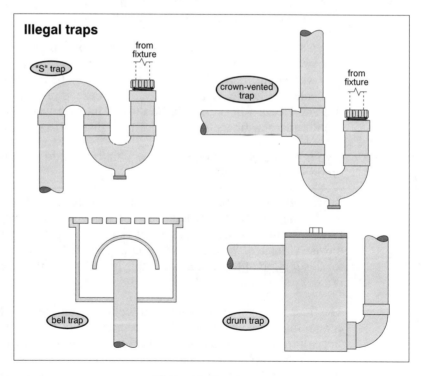

Figure 14. Illegal Traps

Most fixtures require traps, although a toilet does not, since the water in the toilet bowl creates a natural trap. Dishwashers are usually effectively trapped, although there is no formal fitting. The drain line from the dishwasher should be arranged to form a trap.

Trap Prime

Since the 1960's, it has become popular to provide a prime for traps in basement floor drains. This is usually accomplished through a one-quarter inch clear plastic tube which is connected to a regularly used plumbing fixture. This may be a laundry tub faucet or toilet, for example. Whenever the fixture is run, a small amount of water is taken off and is carried through the plastic tube into the floor drain. Water is added to the trap on a regular basis to replace any water lost through evaporation. The same thing could be accomplished by pouring a bucket of water down the drain every month or so. Another solution is to fill a floor drain trap with mineral oil. It will not evaporate and is environmentally safe. When the water level in a floor drain is noted to be low, it should be filled and the water level watched to see if there is a leak. A leak requires digging up and replacing the trap.

Problems

Missing and Leaking

Amateur plumbers' work may omit traps, and traps which leak are, of course, ineffective. Leaks in traps under sinks can usually be seen easily, but leaking traps under concealed fixtures such as bathtubs and shower stalls may not be noticed until considerable damage is done below.

Basement floor drain traps which crack are often not detected for some time. A sewer odor or movement of air up through the drain, may indicate a problem with the floor drain trap. (Air movement may simply be the result of down-spouts discharging into the floor drain above the trap. It is also possible that the water has simply evaporated out of the trap.)

Freezing

When a house is winterized, the supply plumbing pipes are drained. The waste pipes contain no water and they are not susceptible to freezing. The traps, however, could freeze. The traps cannot simply be drained, since sewer odors will enter the house. Consequently, anti-freeze is provided for the traps. Since this anti-freeze will ultimately be flushed into the waste system (either city or septic), the anti-freeze should be a type that will not harm the environment.

Double Traps

Two traps are not permitted on any plumbing fixture. This arrangement may produce chronic blockages.

2.5 Floor Drains: Floor drains should be provided at the lowest living level of any house. Floor drains can be inadvertently covered if the basement floor is resurfaced. If the basement floor is lowered, the floor drain may be unwisely deleted. Where an addition is provided, there may be no floor drain for this section of the basement. If this is lower than the original basement, this is a risky situation.

The floor drain should be located at the low point in the floor. This is always a compromise to some degree, since people do not like their basement floors to slope dramatically. The slope is often subtle, and in many cases the floor drain is not at the lowest point in the floor. In other cases, there is more than one low spot with a ridge separating them. Typically, only one of these areas will have a drain.

There should be a grate over the floor drain to prevent the introduction of foreign objects. The grate should not be allowed to become clogged.

It should be ensured that there is water in the floor drain trap. It is not uncommon to have trap leakage at floor drains. Sewer odors are often noted at floor drains as a result of unsealed traps.

Floor drains are reasonably expensive to add after the fact, and can often not be seen during a visual inspection. When possession is taken, the homeowner should ensure that floor drains are provided where needed. Floor drains are often located close to the boiler or laundry area, where leakage is most likely.

2.6 Venting: One of the least understood sections of a waste plumbing system is the venting. For water to drain freely out of a house waste system, there must be adequate venting. The venting performs three functions. It allows air in front of the water rushing through the waste pipe to be pushed out of the way, and it also allows air to be reintroduced to the waste piping after the water has gone by. Lastly, it allows sewer gases to escape outside through a vent stack.

Siphon

The second function is the most important. The trap at each plumbing fixture provides a water seal which prevents sewer odors from entering the house. After a fixture is used, there should be enough water left in the trap to provide a good seal. If a waste system is not properly vented, when the water runs through the drain line it will siphon the last bit of water out of the trap. As a column of water runs through a pipe, it is difficult to separate that column of water into two pieces (leaving the last part in the trap) because the space in the middle forms a vacuum. The water in the trap is siphoned out and down the drain.

It is important to have a vent connection just downstream of the trap. This allows air into the pipe, preventing a vacuum between the water which runs down the drain pipe and the water which remains in the trap. With the exception of floor drains under some circumstances, all fixtures should be vented.

As a rough rule, any fixture within five feet of the main stack does not need a separate vent. Where fixtures are more than five feet from the main stack and do require a separate vent, the vent must extend above every other fixture in the house. At this point it may join the main stack. It is, therefore, possible for a house to have several bathrooms, and only one vent stack going up through the roof.

Typical Materials

Vent piping may be cast iron, copper, galvanized steel or plastic.

Problems

Missing

Inadequate venting is typified by a siphoning or gurgling noise when water is drained out of a plumbing fixture. A sewer odor at a fixture usually indicates a trap or venting problem. The venting system is almost always concealed from view, except in a few small areas.

Location

Vents should terminate at least 3 feet above and 10 feet (12 feet in Canada) in any other direction from any door or window openings. Vents should extend at least 6 inches above the roof and be at least 12 inches away from a wall.

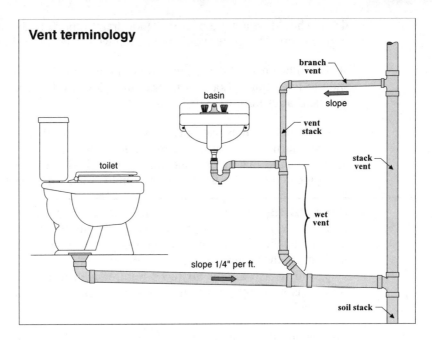

Figure 15. Vent Terminology

Too Short   The vent pipe should extend at least six inches up through the roof of the house. In some cases, the vent terminates in the attic which may allow odors to find their way into the house. Also, in cold weather, this can add very moist warm air into a cold attic, leading to condensation and frost damage of the wooden attic members.

Too Tall   The vent should extend only about twelve inches above the roof line. Vents which are very long may be subject to frost closure in the winter. The warm moist air passes up through the vent, and the air is cooled as it contacts the cold walls of the outdoor section of the vent pipe. The moisture in the air condenses and freezes on the walls of the vent pipe. In a prolonged spell of cold weather, this frost can build up to a point where it closes off the top of the vent. This, of course, negates the effectiveness of the venting system. Vents should be at least three inches in diameter where they penetrate the roof system in order to avoid frost closure.

Frost Closure   Vents which extend more than twelve inches above the roof should be watched for frost closure problems. In some cases, the vents can simply be cut shorter. In other cases, where the vent is extended to carry odors up past a window, it may be necessary to use a larger diameter vent. A frost closure problem can usually be solved temporarily by pouring a kettle full of just boiled water down the vent from the top.

Connection and Pipe Support   Since the venting system only carries air, leakage is usually not a big problem. Deterioration of the piping is also very unusual, although poor connection or poor pipe support is a possibility. The vent piping is usually exposed in the attic, and it is here that it may be vulnerable to mechanical damage.

Wet Vents   Wet vents (vents that also serve as drains) can become clogged or deteriorate as a result of the waste flowing through them.

Roof Leaks

Roof leakage around the vent stack flashing (where the stack penetrates the roof) is often mistaken for plumbing leakage. A vent stack passing through the roof membrane, creates an inherently weak spot in the roofing system. If leakage occurs here, the water may run down the outside of the vent stack, and appear near a plumbing fixture in the house. It is possible to look for a long time for intermittent leaks in the waste plumbing system which do not exist. By paying careful attention to when the leak occurs, it may be found that the apparent plumbing leakage occurs only during or after a rain.

Outside Vents

When a basement bathroom is added to a home, it is difficult to run a vent pipe up through the house and roof. Often, a vent is run out through the wall and up the outside of the building. This is acceptable although not attractive, and frost closure problems are more likely with this arrangement.

Automatic Air Vents

Where an individual fixture has been installed without appropriate venting, it is expensive to break into walls and ceilings to add proper venting. Mechanical devices which simulate conventional venting are available, although not approved by many plumbing authorities. These devices, known as automatic air vents, are essentially vacuum valves which allow air to be drawn into the waste plumbing system when negative pressure exists, but prevent any air escaping from the plumbing system under positive pressure. These devices provide a low cost alternative to conventional venting (See Figure 18) for all fixtures except toilets. Again, some plumbing authorities will not allow these.

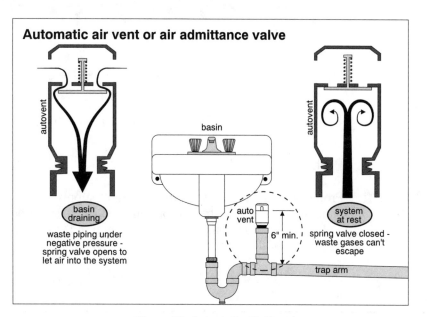

Automatic air vent or air admittance valve

basin draining

waste piping under negative pressure - spring valve opens to let air into the system

basin

auto vent

6" min.

system at rest

spring valve closed - waste gases can't escape

trap arm

Figure 16. Automatic Air Vent

2.7 Solid Waste Pumps: Solid waste pumps are used where conventional gravity flow cannot carry plumbing waste away. Fixtures in the basement of a house with a septic system usually need a solid waste pump to carry the waste up to the main sewer line. These systems are expensive and relatively complex.

These solid waste pumps are submerged in a tank with a sealed top. The house plumbing fixtures drain into the tank. When it is filled to a given level, the pump comes on, discharging the waste through a line which goes to a city sewer or septic system. The incoming line is typically three inches and the discharge line is usually two inches in diameter. A vent pipe is typically connected to the top of the tank. A float or diaphragm liquid level sensor activates the pump. Some have high liquid level alarms which notify the homeowner of a malfunction.

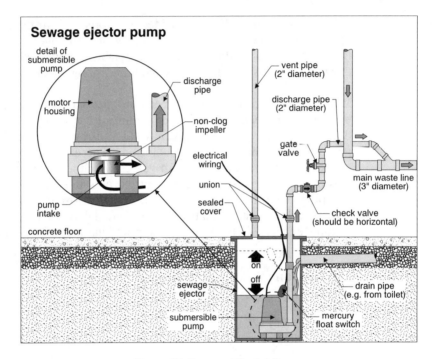

Figure 17. Sewage Ejector Pump

Problems

Problems can develop with the electrical supply, or the electric motor. The pump can become obstructed or damaged. Leaks can develop in the holding tank, or the connections. Clogs can develop in the piping systems which drain into or out of the tank.

Care must be taken with these systems, since raw sewage is, of course, a health hazard.

2.8 Sump Pumps: A sump pump is used to lift storm water from a low spot into a storm sewer or other discharge point, well away from the house. This electric pump is located in the sump (pit) below the basement floor level. Foundation drainage tiles or downspouts may discharge into the sump. A float switch activates the pump as the water level in the sump rises. Most systems use two floats.

The sump is a pit, typically with a concrete floor and walls. In some cases, earth walls and floors are used, although these may break down and clog the pump. There are plastic liners available intended for use in sumps.

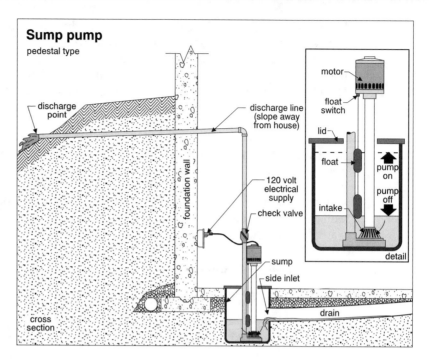

Figure 18. Sump Pump

Problems

Sump Deterioration

Problems occur if the sump deteriorates and allows debris or earth to enter the pump mechanism.

Electrical

If the electric supply to the pump is interrupted, during a power failure for example, the sump may flood. Since power failures often occur with heavy rains and storms, this can be a problem. There are pumps which can be driven by water pressure from the supply plumbing system, although these are not common and in some areas, are not permitted by plumbing authorities.

Pump and Motor

The pump mechanism or electric motor may become defective. Since the pumps are relatively inexpensive and easy to install, many people keep a spare pump on hand in case of failure. This, of course, will be a function of how critical the sump operation is. In many cases the sump operates only a few days per year; in other situations the pump may operate almost continuously.

Floats

Problems with the float system that controls the pump are very common. These are inexpensive to replace and adjust, but regular maintenance and inspection should include testing to verify that they are not entangled with the pump, the sump wall, or any foreign objects.

Discharge Pipe

The discharge piping for the pump is often a source of leakage. The piping is typically plastic which can easily be crimped or suffer from poor connections at joints. In severe cases, the discharge may be completely obstructed by a badly crimped line.

It is often difficult to find the discharge point of the piping. It may discharge into a city sewer system, a storm ditch at the front of the property, a French drain (a buried gravel pit designed to allow water to accumulate quickly and dissipate slowly by soaking into the soil), or simply onto the ground, several feet from the house. On a sloping lot, where the ground slopes down away from the house, this may be appropriate. In other cases, it can be a problem. Water in the discharge pipe may freeze if it does not have a good slope or is not well buried.

2.9 Laundry Tub Pumps: Where a laundry tub cannot drain by gravity into a waste system, a pump is usually provided below the tubs. This electrically powered pump carries water from the laundry tubs up into an appropriate waste system. This may discharge into a municipal sewer, a septic system, or a dry well. Different municipalities have different restrictions with respect to gray water (house waste water which does not contain human waste).

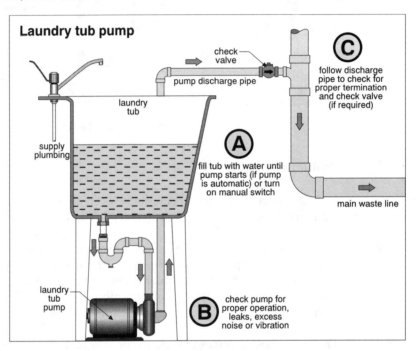

Figure 19. Laundry Tub Pump

Some pumps have an automatic control (typically a float system within the tub), although many are manually operated by a wall switch. The laundry tub is typically large enough to hold the water from a complete cycle of a washing machine. When the washing machine cycle is completed, the pump is turned on briefly to drain the laundry tub. Either arrangement is satisfactory.

Problems:

Problems can occur with the electric supply to the pump, to the pump motor, or to the pump itself. The float system or manual switch can be defective and the pipe carrying the water away can be leaking, crimped, or obstructed. Discharge pipes outside should have a slope so that water does not accumulate in the pipes. Where the pipe is not deeply buried and water can accumulate, it may freeze up in the winter. Manually operated pumps may have the motor burned out if left running with no water in the tub.

2.10 Inappropriate/Low Quality Materials: Many materials used for waste plumbing were not intended for this use, and may be expected to have a short and troublesome life. These materials include rubber hoses, garden hoses, and non-approved plastic piping. Connections made with the wrong materials or wrong devices cannot be expected to perform properly. Special connectors are provided for special types of piping.

Inappropriate materials raises questions about workmanship throughout the system. Traps and vents are commonly omitted on amateurish installations.

► 3.0 FIXTURES

3.1 Sinks: A sink is defined as a fixture used for cleaning things, rather than people. A basin, on the other hand, is used for personal washing. We refer to a kitchen "sink", but to a bathroom "basin" or "lavatory".

Sinks may be stainless steel, enamelled steel, enamelled cast iron, copper, porcelain, plastic, etc. None of these materials is indestructible, and all have their advantages and disadvantages. Some codes do not permit sinks made of wood, concrete or tile.

A sink which includes an integral countertop platform at the back, on which the faucets sit, is generally considered superior to a sink without such a platform. Since all faucets ultimately leak, the leakage is onto the sink platform, rather than directly onto the counter top. The damage is often prevented or less serious with the platform arrangement.

Leakage and Overflow

Leakage may be the result of a cracked or rusted sink, or a poor drain connection. Most kitchen sinks do not have overflows, so the sink cannot be left unattended while filling. Some codes do not allow overflows on kitchen sinks, for fear of trapped food particles accumulating in the overflow.

Sinks which are poorly secured will be prone to leakage, and faucets not well anchored to their sinks will also leak eventually. Sinks may rust or crack over time.

Cross Connection

Cross connections with sinks are possible. Please refer to the discussion of Cross Connections in 1.4.7 in this section.

Airgap Fittings

In some areas, approved airgap fittings are required on the discharge from a dishwasher. This is typically a chrome fitting which projects roughly three inches above the counter top adjacent to the kitchen sink. Waste water from the dishwasher travels up to the airgap fitting and back down through another line into a food waste disposal or drainage piping. The flood level of the fitting must be above the rim of the kitchen sink and the kitchen counter top. This fitting prevents water or other waste from flowing back into a dishwasher. If water discharges from the airgap fitting during dishwasher use, service is required.

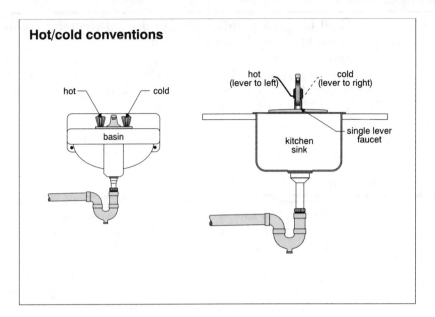

Hot/cold conventions

hot — — cold

basin

hot
(lever to left)   cold
(lever to right)

single lever
faucet

kitchen
sink

Figure 20. Hot/Cold Conventions

3.2 Basins (Lavatories): Basins, typically located in washrooms or bathrooms, may be made of stainless steel, enameled steel, enameled cast iron, copper, vitreous china, plastic, marble, simulated marble, etc. None of these materials will last forever, and all have their strengths and weaknesses.

Leakage and Overflow

Problems which are most common include leakage and overflowing. Most bath- room basins, but not all, contain overflows. Where there is no overflow, the basin cannot be left unattended while filling.

Rust

Many enamelled steel sinks have a welded steel overflow which is a common spot for rusting to occur. This rusting, visible from the underside of the sink, will eventually result in leakage and can appear just a few years into the life of the sink. Some post 1990 sinks rely on a siliconed joint rather than a welded seam. This may prove more durable.

Cracks

Cracking of cultured marble sinks around the drain connection is common. This does not normally lead to leakage in the short term, but is unsightly. Ultimately the basin has to be replaced. While the cause of this problem is disputed, it is suspected to be related to the pressure exerted by the expansion of the metal drainage components when exposed to hot water.

Cross connections with basins are possible, although not common. Please refer to the discussion of Cross Connections earlier in this section. (See Section 1.4.7)

Leakage

3.3 Faucets: There are several different types and styles of faucets with a wide range of qualities available. The traditional compression faucet employs a disk washer to shut off the water, when the washer is turned down against a seat. Leakage out through the faucet usually indicates a deteriorated washer. Leakage around the handle of a faucet usually indicates deteriorated packing. Both of these problems require minor repairs, and leaking packing is considered to be a greater threat than a leaking washer. A leaking washer will only allow water to run into the fixture, while leaking packing will allow water to run onto a counter top, for example.

Some modern faucets use a cartridge, valve, or ball to direct water flow. Single lever faucets have become common for sink, basin and bathtub use. These mixing valves allow the control of hot water, cold water and volume with a single handle.

There are sophisticated faucets available for showers, which will maintain the temperature selected, irrespective of pressure changes in the system. For example, if someone is having a shower, and two other cold water fixtures in the house are turned on, the cold water pressure to the shower will decrease. The person using an ordinary faucet may be scalded by the hot water which comes out of the shower head. The pressure sensitive mixing valve will adjust to this automatically, reducing the pressure on the hot water system to match the cold. Consequently, the volume of water available drops off significantly but the temperature remains the same. This is a much safer situation.

Damaged

Irrespective of the faucet type, leakage and difficulty in operating the valve are the two most common problems. Damaged faucet handles may be dangerous, if there are jagged edges. Where there is the possibility of someone cutting their hand using a faucet, the handle or entire faucet should be replaced as necessary.

Loose

It is common for faucet sets not to be well secured to the wall, counter top or fixture. This is a minor problem, although it can be difficult to access. If not corrected, it may result in leakage.

Faucets have moving parts and do require maintenance. Unfortunately, there is no regular preventative maintenance that is practical, and no easy way to predict leaks.

3.4 Toilets (Water Closets, Commodes, Hoppers): Most toilets are made of vitreous china, although other materials are occasionally used. There are several different styles of toilets and several different flush mechanisms. Some of the older toilets have relatively weak flush mechanisms and are more prone to clogging. Some toilets have a tank which is integral, although most toilets and tanks are two separate components.

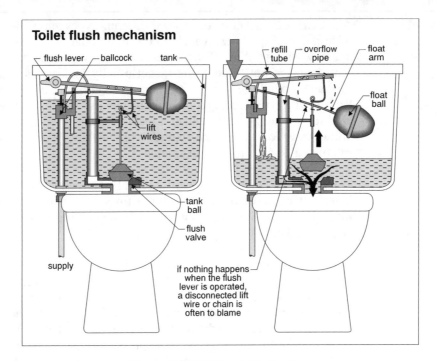

Figure 21. Toilet Flush Mechanism

Washdown

The old washdown toilet, identified by its large bulge on the front of the bowl, is a relatively poor toilet, with a very small wetted area inside the bowl. A large part of the bowl is nearly horizontal. This toilet type is no longer commonly available and is not allowed by some municipalities.

Reverse Trap and Siphon Jet

The reverse trap toilet is better, although somewhat noisy. A good wetted area is presented in the bowl. The siphon jet is an improved reverse trap; quieter and with a very good wetted area.

Siphon Action

The one-piece toilets are typically very expensive and very quiet. They are called siphon action and almost all the bowl surface areas are covered with water. The flush action can be somewhat lazy in these toilets.

Leakage

Problems can occur with leakage at the toilet supply line, at the storage tank, at the connection between the tank and the bowl, at the bowl itself (e.g. if the bowl is cracked), or at the connection between the toilet bottom and the drain pipe.

Loose

Toilets are often poorly secured to the floor system. This can result in leakage at the base of the toilet over the long term. It is usually easy to secure a loose toilet.

Inoperative or Continuously Running

If a toilet does not flush at all, there is usually no water in the tank. The problem is one of supply water to the tank. If the toilet runs continuously, this means there is leakage from the tank into the bowl. While this will not cause any water damage, per se, a continuously running cold water pipe bringing water into the toilet, and a continuously running drain may lead to condensation problems on the outside of these pipes, particularly during warm humid weather. The resulting water damage can be significant. A continuously running toilet also wastes a good deal of water. Repairs to the flush mechanism are called for in this situation. The flush mechanism is a relatively complicated mechanical device and problems may develop with the float, rod, plunger, ball cock, filler tube, refill tube, trip lever, tank ball, etc. These are typically inexpensive repairs.

Slow Flush

Slow flushing toilets are usually partially obstructed. In some cases, a plunger will clear the obstruction; in others, a plumber's snake is necessary. Occasionally, the toilet has to be temporarily removed to get at the problem.

Seat

Problems with the toilet seat are not functional from a plumbing standpoint. Seats can usually be replaced readily.

3.5 Bathtubs: Bathtubs may be free standing or built in, and may be enamelled cast iron, enamelled steel, fiber glass, plastic, etc. Custom bathtubs can be made of tile, marble or copper, just to name a few. Bathtubs are susceptible to chipped enamel, rusting, and leakage through supply or drain connections.

Overflow Connection

Bathtub overflows are a common source of leakage. Since they are not used on a regular basis, they are often installed poorly with the potential for leakage. When the bathtub does overflow in an emergency, water may escape around the over- flow connection. This is impossible to predict from a visual inspection.

Tub/Tile Intersection

When leakage is noted on a ceiling below a bathroom, the source is usually the bathtub area. In many cases, however, the leakage is not the fault of the bathtub, per se, but of the connection between the tub and tile enclosure. Conventional bathtubs have a one inch lip around the top of the tub, on the side and ends that go against the wall. When the wall is finished, the lip cannot be seen, since it goes up behind the ceramic tile. This lip is intended to minimize leakage at the tub/tile intersection. Early signs of a problem may be loose ceramic tiles.

Some bathtubs are designed to be free standing (away from the walls). These tubs do not contemplate the installation of a shower. Where these tubs are used with a conventional bathtub enclosure and a shower, they may be very susceptible to leakage around the edges. These tubs do not have the one inch lip around the outside of the tub shelf

Slope

The bathtub must be installed so water in the tub will flow naturally to the drain, and so that water that lands on the shelf around the perimeter of the tub will run into, not out of the tub. Spillage or splashing can defeat the best sloped installations.

Reglazing　　　Reglazing old bathtubs is a relatively new process. The advantage of this is that it can be done in place, and is much less expensive than replacing a tub. The results, however, do not seem to be long lasting and, if considering this, it may be wise to enquire about the life expectancy of the new finish.

The older cast iron bathtubs are credited with keeping the water hotter than the modem tubs, although this is not a matter of great import. Some builders provide fiber glass insulation around modem steel tubs, as a way of keeping the water hot.

3.6 Bathtub Enclosure: Bathtub enclosures may be ceramic tile, plastic, marble tile, simulated marble tile, glass tile, plastic tile or plastic laminates. All of these materials, if properly installed, are considered acceptable. Modem one piece acrylic or fiber glass enclosures are also considered effective if properly installed. Wood enclosures and hardboard materials with a simulated tile finish are not considered good long term materials, where a shower is to be used.

Tiles in Concrete　　　In houses built in the first sixty years of this century, it is common to find ceramic tiles set in concrete ("set in mud" is the tiler's term). This is a very good installation method and the life of the tile system can be fifty years or more. This system, however, is expensive to remove when demolition is necessary.

Tiles Glued On　　　Modem tile application typically uses an adhesive which bonds the tile to plaster, drywall, plywood or a lightweight concrete board. This method of securing tiles is less desirable since the adhesive can be weakened as water gets in behind the tile. Perhaps more importantly, concealed wall surfaces such as plaster, drywall or wood will also be damaged by the water.

Drywall Behind Tiles　　　Where drywall is used in a bathtub or shower stall enclosure behind the tile, it should be a special water resistant type (green drywall). This is not waterproof drywall, but does afford some protection against moisture.

Grout and Caulk　　　Water penetrates a tile enclosure two ways, typically. Openings in grout joints or poor grout mixes will allow water to pass through during showers. Secondly, the connection between the tile and the tub is a weak spot. No matter what quality caulking is used, over a period of time, an opening will develop between the tub and tile. Although there is a lip on the tub going up about one inch behind the tile, this does not prevent water damage. Since bathtubs will flex to some degree, when filled with water and a person, this movement contributes to deterioration of the caulking. Many tile experts recommend that when caulking a tub, the tub be filled with water and at least one person be in the tub.

Leaks Around Tile Openings　　　Leakage can occur in the bathtub enclosure through openings created for faucets, spouts and soap dishes, for example.

Loose Tile　　　When the tile is loose or buckling, the tile must be removed, and in many cases the support material (plaster, drywall or plywood) must also be replaced. The new low density concrete boards are better than drywall or plywood in terms of rigidity and resistance to moisture.

Windows   Windows above bathtubs can be a problem where there is a shower. This was a common window location in the first half of the twentieth century, before showers were common. A window may be damaged by rot over the long term if not protected from shower water accumulation. Where a window is in place, it should at least be protected by a waterproof curtain. Interior window sills should be avoided as much as possible, as should any other horizontal ledges which allow water to collect.

3.7 Shower Stalls: Traditionally, shower stalls were made of ceramic tile, glass or marble tile. Modem one, two or three piece shower stalls in fiber glass or acrylic are popular. Some of these are quite good quality. One of the problems with fiber glass and acrylic is that abrasive cleansers will scratch the surface, making it almost impossible to clean.

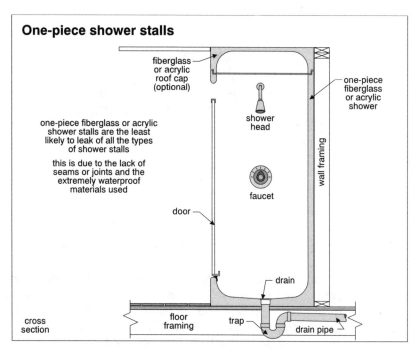

Figure 22. One-Piece Shower Stalls

Metal   Metal shower stalls are typically low quality and are prone to rusting around the bottom within the first few years.

Tile Leakage   Shower stalls are notorious for leakage through the tilework. Since there is a great deal of tilework in traditional shower stalls (all walls and the floor typically), any small openings in the grout or caulking may cause problems. Because shower stalls are often poorly lit, small tile flaws often go unnoticed until damage appears below. Leakage through the faucet and soap dish joints is common.

Bottom Pan   The construction of the tile shower stall includes a lead (traditional) or neoprene (modem) pan around the bottom of the stall. This one piece pan below the tile typically extends up about six inches above the bottom of the shower floor, on all four sides. This pan will catch minor leakage, although if it is not well secured around the drain, leakage will develop here. In the event of a serious leak, this pan will not be effective. Tile shower stalls are very expensive to rebuild, and are sometimes replaced with fiber glass or plastic shower stalls.

Weight

3.8 Whirlpool Baths: A whirlpool bath is essentially a conventional bathtub with a circulating pump, supply jets and a return intake added. Whirlpool baths can be very large, and contain a great deal of water when filled. In some cases, engineering consideration to the floor structure below should be given.

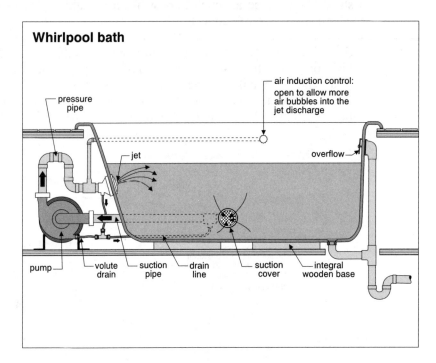

Whirlpool bath

- air induction control: open to allow more air bubbles into the jet discharge
- pressure pipe
- jet
- overflow
- pump
- volute drain
- suction pipe
- drain line
- suction cover
- integral wooden base

Figure 23. Whirlpool Bath

A conventional residential floor system is designed for thirty to forty pounds per square foot of live load. 'llypical floor loads imposed by whirlpools range from forty to sixty pounds per square foot. A visual inspection will not reveal the framing details below a whirlpool in most circumstances. Sometimes, evidence of deflection below the tub can be seen.

GFCI

The electric supply to the whirlpool should be protected by a ground fault circuit interrupter. This is a special, highly sensitive device which will shut off the electricity in the event of a very small electrical fault. This additional safety is important, of course, wherever water and electricity come together.

Pump and Motor

Problems may develop with the electric motor or the pump mechanism. Leaks or obstructions in the piping lines around the tub can appear, and may be difficult to access and repair. Connection points of the piping to the tub may be potential leakage areas as well.

Controls

The electrical control for the whirlpool should be located at least three feet from the tub. Many codes also require that the switch be a timer. There is a danger of people staying in the whirlpool for long periods of time. As a result, the whirlpool should only be able to be turned on for a fixed number of minutes. Some tubs have an air (pneumatic) switch with a timer right on the tub.

*Service
Access*

It is good practice to provide a readily accessible service door to work on the pump and motor. Where this is not available, repairs will be more expensive.

*Larger Water
Heater*

Larger whirlpools may require larger water heaters to ensure the tub can be filled with hot water. Some manufacturers recommend water temperatures not exceed 104°F, to avoid discoloration of the acrylic.

3.9 Bidets: Bidets are complex plumbing fixtures which are susceptible to cross connections. As a result, a vacuum breaker is provided at the supply piping connection to a bidet. This prevents waste water from flowing back into the supply water. Most bidets are china, and are subject to cracking or leakage. In areas of hard water, the small jets of a bidet can become clogged. Control valves and diverters may leak or break.

3.10 Saunas: A sauna room should be an insulated wooden structure. There should be no exposed metal components such as door hinges or handles in a sauna, for fear of burning someone who touches the metal component. A sauna may have a water faucet in it, in which case it should have a floor drain as well; however, it is not unusual to see a sauna with a supply faucet but no floor drain.

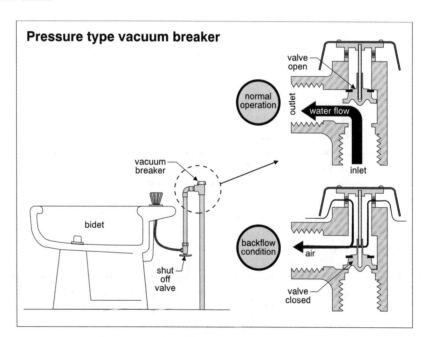

Figure 24. Vacuum Breaker

The electric sauna heater should have an outside control and should be specifically approved as a heater for a sauna room. The name plate sets out minimum clearances to combustibles, and these should be observed. The sauna heater should be securely fastened. It is not permitted to provide a shower or water spray device immediately above a sauna heater.

Due to the temperatures generated, electrical components in a sauna area (overhead light fixtures, for example) should be carefully arranged so that heat dissipation is not a problem.

Discharge Outside

3.11 Bathroom Fans: Bathroom fans are required by most codes where a bathroom does not have an operable window. The fan should discharge directly to the building exterior. In many cases, the fan terminates inside the house or roof space. This can add considerable moisture to a house, leading to condensation and rot problems.

Fans Desirable

Although fans are not required in bathrooms with operable windows, they are desirable in these rooms. In the winter months, one is not likely to open a window to dissipate the steam generated by a shower. This heavy concentration of moisture, particularly in a bathroom where showers are used regularly, can lead to premature failure of interior finishes such as paint and wallpaper, and result in mildew and rot in concealed areas.

Noisy

Bathroom fans are notoriously noisy. This is particularly true of lower quality fans. The fan may be operated by a separate switch, or by the room light switch. Some fan switches are on timers, and others are on rheostats (so the speed can be varied). Neither of these is considered particularly important.

Inoperative

Many bathroom fans are inoperative, because the motor or fan mechanism has failed. Often, the fan has simply been disconnected by a homeowner, irritated by the noise.

Capacity

The exhaust fan should provide at least twelve air changes per hour. For example, in a bathroom that is five feet by eight feet by eight feet high, the exhaust fan should have a capability of more than sixty-four cfm (cubic feet per minute).

Attics and Chimneys

Where the exhaust fan ductwork passes through unheated spaces such as attics, it should be insulated to prevent condensation. Exhaust fans should never discharge into chimneys.

3.12 Kitchen Fans: The kitchen fan may discharge directly to the building exterior, or may simply recirculate the air into the kitchen after passing it through a charcoal filter. Even fans which discharge to the building exterior typically have some sort of filter. In either case, the filters should be cleaned and/or replaced, following the manufacturer's recommendations. The hood-type kitchen fans are the most common provided today.

Older Style

Older kitchen exhaust fans are located directly in the exterior wall, and were often activated by opening the cover of the fan. These fans are typically good quality and although older, do provide effective exhaust ventilation.

Attics and Chimneys

Exhaust fan ductwork which passes through unheated areas such as attics should be insulated to prevent condensation. Kitchen fans should never discharge into chimneys.

Down-Draft

Some cook tops have built in fans with down draft, which exhaust air from the cook top area. On some appliances, these fans are of modest capacity, and where the exhaust ductwork to the exterior has to be lengthy or contains several bends, the fan performance may be weak.

Inoperative

An inoperative kitchen fan is usually the result of an interruption in the electrical supply, or failure of the electric motor. On occasion, the fan itself can be jammed or the bearings may have failed.

3.13 Outdoor Faucets: Outdoor faucets are conventional cold water supply valves, typically. During the winter months, the water supply should be shut off by another valve in the building interior. The outside valve is typically left open to allow any water in the pipe to escape. The inside winter shut off valve may be provided with an auxiliary bleed valve to allow any water between the two valves to escape.

Many codes now require backflow preventers on outdoor faucets to protect against cross connections. See section 1.4.7.

Frost-proof Special frost-proof valves provided on the building exterior do not require any interior shut-off in the winter. These valves have a long stem which penetrates through the building wall and effectively shuts off the water supply inside the building. These valves should be sloped to drain. They are, of course, more expensive.

Leakage and Damage Outdoor faucets are susceptible to washer and packing failure and resultant leakage. They are also more vulnerable to mechanical damage than inside valves. Because of their exposure to extremes of weather, it is possible for the valves to become inoperative. Replacement of these is not a major expense.

3.14 Laundry Tubs: The traditional concrete laundry tubs have been replaced, for the most part, recently by steel and plastic tubs. The concrete tubs although durable, are heavy and ultimately are prone to cracking. Where the old tubs are leaking, they can be patched, although usually they will soon develop more cracks. Replacing the tubs is not expensive. Removing the heavy concrete tubs is difficult, without breaking up the tubs. Where concrete laundry tubs are present, the waste plumbing is often lead. This lead waste plumbing is usually replaced with ABS plastic pipe when the tubs are replaced.

Cross Connections Older laundry tubs may be subject to cross connections. It should be ensured that the faucet set is installed above the laundry tub, so that there is no possibility of the faucet itself becoming submerged when the tub is full. Refer to the discussion of Cross Connections in this section. (See Section 1.4.7)

▶ 4.0 GAS PIPING

Houses which are supplied with gas have piping which runs underground to the house and then into the building. Depending on the local jurisdiction, gas shut off valves outside the building above grade are usually required on new installations.

Materials Gas piping indoors should be either iron or steel, yellow brass or copper. In some jurisdictions, copper is not permitted. Outdoor underground piping can be plastic.

Underground Piping Where iron or steel piping is used underground, it should be protected from rusting with coatings or wraps which cover the pipe underground and up to a point six inches above grade. Some areas also require cathodic protection (letting a sacrifice material rust to protect the gas piping).

Where plastic pipe is used underground, metal risers or chases should come up above grade. The plastic piping should not be visible or exposed to mechanical damage. A copper tracer wire is laid around the pipe to help the gas company find it later, when someone wants to dig in the area. The wire should be visible on the above grade section of the pipe.

Pipe Support   Piping should be well supported, and there should be no strain on the gas piping. The gas piping should not be used to support appliances.

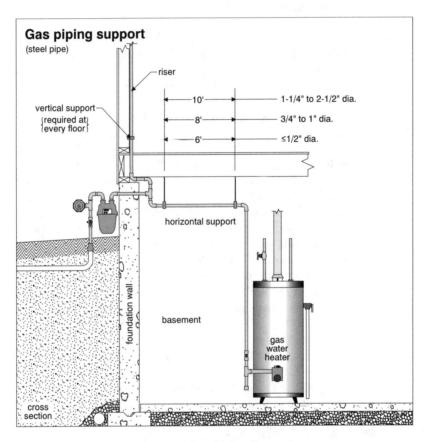

Figure 25. Gas Piping Support

Appliance Connections   Where appliances are connected, there should be a shut off valve in the same room for each appliance, as close to the appliance as is practical. Unions or swing joints should not be in concealed areas (walls, attic, et cetera).

In Canada, furnaces, boilers and water heaters must be connected directly to the piping. In the U.S., appliance connectors (flexible metal piping) can be used in some areas. The direct connection is considered superior, except perhaps, in areas where earthquake is a concern. Connectors, for the most part, should be three feet long, although range or dryer connectors can be six feet long. The connectors should not pass through walls, floors or ceilings, and should be immediately preceded by shut off valve. Aluminum connectors are permitted if they are not exposed to water, masonry, plaster or insulation. Gas hoses are not allowed indoors.

Where there are gas outlets for barbecues or fireplaces, the valves should be outside the hearth within four feet of the appliance, in the same room as the appliance.

Grounding

Gas piping should not be used for the grounding of electrical systems, however, in some jurisdictions, gas piping is bonded to supply piping (usually at the water heater) if the supply piping is grounded.

Leaks

Any gas leak is a potentially life threatening situation. If a leak is noted, all occupants should leave the house immediately and contact the gas company from a neighbor's house. No switches, telephones, door bells, or anything else which might cause a spark should be operated.

Drip Legs

Many jurisdictions require a vertical pipe extension (drip leg) below the elbow where the horizontal pipe feeds an appliance. Any foreign material in the gas coming toward the appliance will drop into the drip leg, rather than turn and head into the burner.

9 INTERIOR

THE
Home Reference
BOOK

TABLE OF CONTENTS   Page

► INTRODUCTION

The building interior is looked at for a number of reasons. The interior provides clues to structural problems and is often the area where water leakage is first detectable. The interior finishes themselves usually reflect the overall building quality and their condition helps indicate the level of overall maintenance.

The house interior contains the distribution points of the major systems. For example, each room should have an adequate heat supply and sufficient electrical outlets. The concern of the home inspector is function rather than appearance, and emphasis is placed on whether the room will work as it was intended. The home inspector does not comment on matters of personal taste.

► 1.0 MAJOR FLOOR FINISHES

Floors provide a durable surface for foot traffic and furniture. Good floors are level, have an even surface, and stand up for many years with little maintenance. Floors can be an architectural feature of the home. Different flooring materials have different properties. Some resist water damage; some are soft to walk on; some require no sealing or waxing; some are quiet; some are particularly long lasting.

Water Damage: Water damage is one of the most common problems on interior finishes. The water damage may be on walls, floors or ceilings. There are five areas of interest, typically, with any evidence of water damage. It is helpful to know a) the source of the damage, b) whether it is still active, c) whether there is any concealed damage, d) what the cost is to cure the problem, e) and subsequently, what the cost is to repair the damaged building materials.

Common sources of water damage include roof leaks, flashing leaks, ice damming, window and skylight leaks, plumbing leaks, leaks from hot water heating systems, and condensation. Water damage may also result from such things as aquariums, room humidifiers or dehumidifiers, over-watering of plants, melting snow and ice from boots during wintertime, etc.

Roof leaks are usually localized and the source of the problem will often be an intersection or a flashing in the roof. Roof leaks can be difficult to trace because the water does not always appear on the interior immediately below the leak above. This may be the result of water running along framing members, or vapor barriers which prevent water coming through in specific locations. Many roof leaks appear first around ceiling tight fixtures, for example.

Water damage often looks more serious than it is. Short term exposure to water will not harm most building structure materials. Plaster and drywall, however, are damaged very quickly by water. Similarly, many floor finishes can be damaged or stained quickly by water. In one sense, this is good. The material which can be easily seen is the first material to deteriorate. It is unusual to have extensive building damage done by water which appears at an interior finish, as long as the problem is solved promptly.

1.1 Concrete: Concrete floor finishes are typically only used in basements and garages. In new construction, the concrete basement floor is at least three inches thick. The floor should slope down to a floor drain. The slope is dramatic in some cases and barely perceptible in others.

In modern construction, a four to six inch gravel base is provided below the slab to minimize water moving up through the slab. The gravel allows water to drain away freely, rather than holding water against the slab. Moisture barriers (plastic sheets) may also be provided under the slab, and in energy efficient construction, or slab-on-grade construction, rigid insulation is sometimes used below the floor.

In older construction, concrete floor slabs were as thin as 1/2 inch. Very often these were not underlaid with a gravel base, and are prone to impact damage, heaving and break-up.

It is important to understand that concrete floors are not part of the structure. They are typically installed after the structure is up, although, ideally before finish flooring or millwork is done. A good deal of moisture is given off as concrete cures, and the basement should allow good air movement to dissipate this moisture.

Concrete floors can be overlaid with finished flooring, as desired. However, since almost every house has water on the basement floor sometime during its life, the choice of finishes should anticipate this.

Cracked or Broken

Problems: A cracked and broken concrete floor may only be a problem if it is not safe to walk across, or if there is moisture coming up through the floor. Since it is not a structural component, replacement of this floor is rarely a priority item.

The solution is to remove the broken flooring and provide a new floor. Ideally, a four to six inch gravel base should be provided before the new three inch thick concrete slab is poured. Often, this will reduce basement ceiling height to an unacceptable level. Eliminating the gravel base, or reducing its thickness, and reducing the thickness of the concrete will slightly increase the risk of future break up or water problems.

Poor Slope

A concrete floor which does not slope down to a floor drain can lead to water accumulation on the floor if there is significant leakage, either from outside water or from plumbing or heating water. Adding more concrete to an existing slab is difficult, since the chances of the new concrete bonding to the old are very slim. A better solution is probably to add another floor drain. This is expensive in that it does require breaking up some of the concrete floor. If the concrete floor is deteriorated overall, it may make sense to remove the entire floor and replace it.

Cold

If the basement is to be used as living space, the concrete floor is often cold. One solution is to place a raised wood floor over the concrete prior to adding a finish flooring material. Disadvantages to this approach include the expense, the loss of headroom and the fact that rot and/or termite activity may go undetected for some time. In most cases, a comfortable situation can be created with an underpad and carpet. Both should be synthetic and as moisture resistant as practical. Where the floor slab is to be replaced, the underside of the floor slab can be insulated with a material designed for this application.

1.2 Hardwood: Hardwood floors are typically oak, although other woods such as birch, beech and maple, are also used. Hardwood flooring may be in the form of strips, typically tongue-and-groove, or parquet. Parquet floors often consist of six inch squares with each square made up of six one-inch strips. The squares are laid with the grain in adjoining squares at right angles, giving a checkerboard effect to the floor. Parquet flooring may be nailed or glued down. There are several different types and installation techniques.

Hardwood flooring in modern construction is typically 3/8 inch thick and 1-3/4 inches wide. This adds very little to the rigidity of a floor system. In higher quality older homes, the hardwood strips were sometimes 3/4 inch thick and 2-1/4 inches wide.

In some cases, hardwood flooring was used without any subflooring. This is an acceptable approach as long as the hardwood is 1/2 inch thick or more. The width of the hardwood strips varies, but is typically 1-1/2 inches to 2-1/2 inches. Hardwood flooring boards wider than three inches are called planks.

The hardwood flooring should not be laid parallel to board subflooring. If the subflooring is installed on the diagonal, the hardwood flooring can be installed in either orientation (45' offset from the subfloor). If the subflooring is perpendicular to the joists, the hardwood flooring should be parallel to the joists.

With tongue-and-groove flooring, the underside is usually slightly hollowed, and the top edge of the board is slightly wider than the lower edge. The idea is that the top edges of the board should fit snugly and there can be a small gap at the bottom edge. A gap at the top would be undesirable, of course. The hardwood strips are nailed in place by toe-nailing through the tongue. Nails are driven in at a 45' angle. When the floor is finished, no nails should be visible.

Problems: Hardwood flooring is a high quality and durable floor system. It can be mechanically damaged, attacked by termites, rot and fire, or damaged by water. Wood flooring is not ideally suited to kitchen and bathroom areas, since it is susceptible to water damage. It is possible to replace individual boards that are damaged, but matching can be tricky.

The 3/8 inch thick hardwood flooring can usually be sanded once to provide a new wood surface. 3/4 inch hardwood flooring can be sanded several times. Wood flooring can be covered with carpeting or other flooring materials.

Hardwood flooring glued to concrete often comes loose. The glue is broken down by water in the floor, and pieces of flooring pop out. After the floor is dried, the floor can be reattached. If the wood is warped or water stained, it should be replaced.

Squeaky Floors: Squeaky floors are not a structural problem. A floor usually squeaks when walked on because the flooring finish or subfloor is not tightly secured to the floor joists below. The subfloor sitting directly on the joists must be secured tightly to the joists, and the finished flooring material (e.g. hardwood) must similarly be tightly fastened to the subfloor. This is done with nails, screws and/or glue.

When the flooring is not tightly secured, it sits just off the support in some spots. When someone steps on the flooring in this area, it is pushed down onto its support. When the foot is taken off the floor, it springs back up. The squeaking is usually the result of the nails sliding in and out of the nail holes, or adjacent wood surfaces rubbing.

Resecure

The solution, of course, is to better secure the hardwood to the subfloor, or the subfloor to the joists. This can be done with nails or screws. It is difficult to glue a floor down after it has been installed. It can be very difficult to get at the floor system. Sometimes the finish flooring material is removed, or the floor is resecured from below (if the ceiling below is unfinished). In some cases, where the floor is carpeted, it is possible to nail through the carpet to secure the flooring. Nails with very small heads are used.

When nailing or screwing a subfloor to the joists from above, it is sometimes difficult to find the joists. Nails or screws which do not enter the joists are of no value. Wood shims or blocking are sometimes used from below.

Talcum Powder

Surface nailing into hardwood flooring is not desirable from a cosmetic stand point, and where the floor system cannot be pulled down tightly from below, a dry lubricant such as talcum powder is sometimes used. The lubricant is spread onto the floor and worked into the cracks. If enough of the lubricant reaches the nails, the squeaking noise may be eliminated as the nails slide in and out of the holes. While this method will often result in some improvement, it is rarely completely effective in eliminating squeaks.

1.3 Softwood: Pine is the most common softwood flooring. Pine floors were typically used either as finish flooring in a "1x4" tongue-and-groove configuration, or as a subfloor. When used as a subfloor below hardwood, the softwood was typically laid in 1x4 or 1x6 planks, perpendicular to, or on the diagonal to the floor joists. In this case, the subflooring was nailed straight down into the joists. The boards were typically separated slightly to allow for expansion.

Softwood subflooring used under linoleum or other thin kitchen floor coverings was usually tongue-and-groove and tightly fit to provide a smooth, strong surface upon which to put the flexible flooring system. Modern practice is to use 1/4 inch plywood underlayment between the subfloor and finish flooring.

Damage

Problems: When softwoods such as pine, fir or cedar are used as finish floorings, they present a relatively soft surface which can be damaged by high heeled shoes, for example. Furniture marking and denting is another common problem on softwood floors.

Sanding   It is more difficult to sand softwood floors than hardwood, because low spots can be created very quickly by the sanding machine. Generally speaking, a softwood floor can only be satisfactorily sanded once. Because this material has no subfloor below, it cannot be safely sanded to less than roughly 5/8 inch thick. It should be noted that with a tongue-and-groove flooring system, the sanding limitation is not working right through the floor, but working down through the floor far enough to expose the tongue or weaken the groove between the boards.

It has become popular to expose pine subflooring in kitchens. While the honey color of pine is considered very attractive, it should be understood that this is not an ideal kitchen floor system. Apart from being relatively soft, it is very difficult to keep the joints well sealed, and liquid spills are difficult to clean up completely. Polyurethane finishes commonly used do not, over the long term, provide a watertight membrane. It is common, when softwood floors are sanded, to mix the sawdust which is generated with a glue, and work the mix into the open joints to provide a filler material. This filler material can work loose and pop out of the floor.

Softwood floors can be damaged by rot, termites and fire.

Squeaky Floors:
Squeaky floors are not a structural problem. A floor usually squeaks when walked on because the floor is not tightly secured to the floor joists below.

When the flooring is not tightly secured, it sits just off the support in some spots. When someone steps on the flooring in this area, it is pushed down onto its support. When the foot is taken off the floor, it springs back up. The squeaking is usually the result of the nails sliding in and out of the nail holes, or adjacent wood surfaces rubbing.

The solution, of course, is to better secure the floor to the joists. This can be done with nails or screws. It is difficult to glue a floor down after it has been installed. Sometimes the floor is resecured from below (if the ceiling below is unfinished). In some cases, where the floor is carpeted, it is possible to nail through the carpet to secure the flooring. Nails with very small heads are used.

When nailing or screwing a floor to the joists from above, it is sometimes difficult to find the joists. Nails or screws which do not enter the joists are of no value. Wood shims or blocks are sometimes used from below.

Surface nailing into flooring is not desirable from a cosmetic standpoint, and where the floor system cannot be pulled down tightly from below, a dry lubricant such as talcum powder is sometimes used. The lubricant is spread onto the floor and worked into the cracks. If enough of the lubricant reaches the nails, the squeaking noise may be eliminated as the nails slide in and out of the holes. While this method will often result in some improvement, it is rarely completely effective in eliminating squeaks.

1.4 Wool Carpet: Wool is an expensive carpeting material favored for its look, feel and durability. As synthetic products have improved and remain less expensive, wool is becoming rare as a broadloom carpet material. It is used in many carpets, blended with a synthetic material. Wool is a natural product and is less resistant to water damage than synthetics. It also has less resistance to stains than some synthetics.

Problems: Even the best quality carpet will eventually wear out in high traffic areas first. Carpet which is stained can sometimes be cleaned or dyed, although this is often not completely successful. Carpet which stretches and develops ridges and buckles can be pulled tight to lie flat again by a carpet installer.

Carpet installed in an area which is chronically damp (e.g. some basements) will eventually rot. Carpeting is not an ideal flooring material in kitchen and bathroom areas, since it is difficult to clean up spills. Wool carpet is susceptible to burns, as is synthetic carpet.

Squeaky Floors: Squeaky floors are not a structural problem. A floor usually squeaks when walked on because the hardwood or subfloor below the carpet is not tightly secured. The subfloor sitting directly on the joists must be secured tightly to the joists. This is done with nails, screws and/or glue.

When the flooring below the carpet is not tightly secured, it sits just off the support in some spots. When someone steps on the flooring in this area, it is pushed down onto its support. When the foot is taken off the floor, it springs back up. The squeaking is usually the result of the nails sliding in and out of the nail holes, or adjacent wood surfaces rubbing.

The solution, of course, is to better secure the hardwood (if any) to the subfloor and the subfloor to the joists. This can be done with nails or screws. It is difficult to glue a floor down after it has been installed. Sometimes the floor is resecured from below (if the ceiling below is unfinished). In some cases, it is possible to nail through the carpet to secure the flooring. Nails with very small heads are used.

When nailing or screwing a subfloor to the joists from above, it is sometimes difficult to find the joists. Nails or screws which do not enter the joists are of no value. Wood shims or blocks are sometimes used from below.

1.5 Synthetic Carpet: Synthetic carpeting is the most common and is recommended in areas where the carpeting may become wet. Where the backing material is not moisture resistant, synthetic carpet will be quickly damaged if wet. Jute backed carpets, for example, should be kept dry. Many types can be cleaned more easily than wool. Common materials include polypropylene, nylon and acrylic. The quality of a carpeted floor depends upon the type, weight and construction of carpeting, the type of underpad, and the installation work.

Synthetic carpet will wear out and may be stained. Some stains can be removed with cleaning materials or dyes, although the results are not always satisfactory. Although synthetic carpets are better than wool in damp environments, if enough moisture is present, mold and mildew will become problems and the carpet will deteriorate.

Synthetic carpeting in kitchens and bathrooms is better than wool, but is still very difficult to clean. In general, this is not a recommended floor finish in these areas. Indoor/outdoor carpeting is more resistant to moisture than conventional carpets, although in kitchens and bathrooms it may hold the stains, spills and odors.

If the carpeting develops ridges or buckles, it can be pulled tight by a carpet installer. Poor seams can usually be improved by a good installer. Most carpeting has a grain and adjacent pieces of carpeting should be installed with the grain oriented the same way. Synthetic carpeting is susceptible to burns.

Squeaky Floors: Squeaky floors are not a structural problem. A floor usually squeaks when walked on because the hardwood (if any) or the subfloor is not tightly secured. The subfloor sitting directly on joists must be secured tightly to the joists. This is done with nails, screws and/or glue.

When the flooring is not tightly secured, it sits just off the support in some spots. When someone steps on the flooring in this area, it is pushed down onto its support. When the foot is taken off the floor, it springs back up. The squeaking is usually the result of the nails sliding in and out of the nail holes, or adjacent wood surfaces rubbing.

The solution, of course, is to better secure the hardwood (if any) to the subfloor and the subfloor to the joists. This can be done with nails or screws. It is difficult to glue a floor down after it has been installed. It can be very difficult to get at the floor. Sometimes the floor is resecured from below (if the ceiling below is unfinished). In some cases, it is possible to nail through the carpet to secure the flooring. Nails with very small heads are used.

When nailing or screwing a subfloor to the joists from above, it is sometimes difficult to find the joists. Nails or screws which do not enter the joists are of no value. Wood shims or blocks are sometimes used from below.

1.6 Resilient: Resilient floor coverings include vinyl-asbestos, solid vinyl, vinyl faced, rubber, cork, asphalt and linoleum, installed in sheets or tiles. The material is glued down. Some of these materials are inexpensive, while others are very costly, especially if the product includes a cushioned backing material and a no-wax surface.

In modern construction, these materials are typically applied over an underlayment such as a 1/4 inch plywood. Since most of these materials are very thin, they will show through any irregularities in the floor surface.

Some of the modern tile systems employ a peel-and-stick adhesive. A paper backing is removed to expose the adhesive as the tile is laid.

Problems: Where flooring is improperly installed, lifting or loose sections can be a problem. Most resilient floorings are susceptible to cutting and burning. Localized repairs are very difficult to make. Flooring laid over uneven surfaces may not stay fastened, will show the irregularities and will usually fail prematurely.

Some of the backing material on tiles or sheet goods is quite susceptible to moisture. Where the back of a flooring is likely to be wet, even intermittently, these materials should not be used. Floor replacement may be necessary where this has been done, particularly with tile floors, since the number of seams makes it fairly easy for water to get through. Some of the materials are vulnerable to color change if exposed to direct sunlight over time. While this does not affect the usability, appearance is usually an issue.

Squeaky Floors: Squeaky floors are not a structural problem. A floor usually squeaks when walked on because the subfloor is not tightly secured to the floor joists below. Resecuring is done with nails, screws and/or glue. It is also possible for the underlayment to be poorly secured to the subfloor.

When the flooring or underlayment is not tightly secured, it sits just off the support in some spots. When someone steps on the flooring in this area, it is pushed down onto its support. When the foot is taken off the floor, it springs back up. The squeaking is usually the result of the nails sliding in and out of the nail holes, or adjacent wood surfaces rubbing.

The solution, of course, is to better secure underlayment to the subfloor or the subfloor to the joists. This can be done with nails or screws. It is difficult to glue a floor down after it has been installed. It can be very difficult to get at the floor. Sometimes the finish flooring material has to be removed, or the floor is resecured from below (if the ceiling below is unfinished).

When nailing or screwing a subfloor to the joists from above, it is sometimes difficult to find the joists. Nails or screws which do not enter the joists are of no value. Surface nailing into resilient flooring is not acceptable. Wood shims or blocking are sometimes used from below.

1.7 Ceramic/Quarry Tile: Generally considered to be high quality materials, ceramic or quarry tiles are hard fired clay products which may be glazed or unglazed. These materials stand up well to heat, water and normal wear and tear, and have good resistance to stains and cuts. These are brittle floor systems, subject to cracking if not well supported. A conventional wood flooring system generally has too much flex to permit ceramic or quarry tile. Better installations include a concrete base for the tile, typically one inch to five inches thick. Ideally, the tiles are pressed into the concrete while it is still setting. Joints are then grouted. Tiles are typically 1/4 inch to 1/2 inch thick and may be any size from one inch by one inch to twelve inches by twelve inches. Several shapes, colors, patterns and finishes are available.

In modern construction, a very thin mortar base or adhesive is used over a thicker subfloor than would ordinarily have been used. If well installed, this can be satisfactory. Again, joints have to be appropriately grouted. It is common for ceramic or quarry tile floors to be cracked in areas where floor joists are susceptible to the most deflection, or where heavy traffic patterns occur. Tiles can be damaged by dropping tools or other heavy objects.

Traditionally, ceramic tile floors were used in bathrooms and vestibules, because of their natural resistance to moisture. Ceramic or quarry tile floors are used in kitchens, for the same reason, although they are unforgiving if one drops glass onto them, and they are also somewhat more tiring to stand on because of their very hard surface.

Current building codes generally require that ceramic tile be set in at least 1-1/4 inches of mortar, (when mortar is used) and that a 2x2 inch galvanized wire mesh be used in the mortar bed. If laid on a wood subfloor, sheathing paper or another suitable water resistant material should be laid on top of the wood subfloor before the mortar is added.

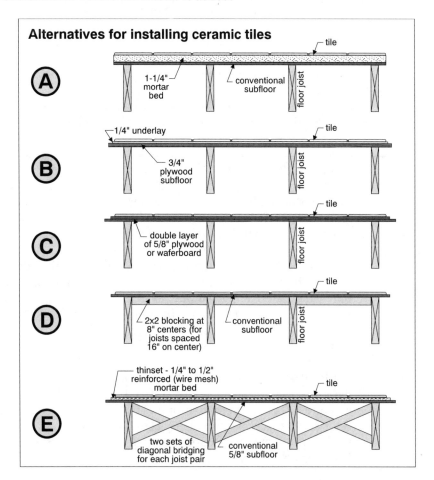

Alternatives for installing ceramic tiles

(A) tile · 1-1/4" mortar bed · conventional subfloor · floor joist

(B) 1/4" underlay · tile · 3/4" plywood subfloor · floor joist

(C) tile · double layer of 5/8" plywood or waferboard · floor joist

(D) tile · 2x2 blocking at 8" centers (for joists spaced 16" on center) · conventional subfloor · floor joist

(E) thinset - 1/4" to 1/2" reinforced (wire mesh) mortar bed · tile · two sets of diagonal bridging for each joist pair · conventional 5/8" subfloor

Figure 1. Support for Ceramic Tiles

If the tiles are adhered to a conventional wood subflooring, one of the following reinforcement techniques should be used:

1. Subflooring should be at least 3/4 inch plywood or waferboard with the edges supported by two by two's. The joists should be on sixteen inch centers, maximum. A 1/4 inch plywood underlay should also be used.

2. A 5/8 inch underlay should be provided over the subfloor. The seams of the underlay should be staggered, relative to seams in the subfloor.

3. Two by two blocking can be used under the subfloor, running perpendicular to the joists. The blocking should be spaced no more than eight inches apart for floor joists sixteen inches on center.

Problems: The most common problem with these floor tiles is cracking. This is usually the result of a floor system which is not stiff enough to support the tile. The solution, of course, is to improve the floor rigidity. Tiles can also be cracked by impact damage. Heavy items dropped on the tiles will sometimes crack or break them. Replacing individual tiles is not difficult, although color change and grout matching may be a problem.

Occasionally, incorrect grouts are used, the grout is improperly mixed, the grout is poorly installed, or grouts deteriorate due to unusual conditions. Regrouting is not terribly difficult, although matching colors can be a problem.

Some ceramic tiles are intended for wall use only. When used on floors, they will deteriorate quickly. They should, of course, be replaced with an appropriate tile.

1.8 Slate/Stone/Marble/Terrazzo: Slate, stone and marble are naturally occurring materials which are cut to size for use as flooring tiles. Terrazzo is made up of marble chips set in concrete, usually laid in squares defined by lead beading. The surface is polished to give a smooth floor. This high quality flooring is common in hospitals and schools, for example.

These materials are not terribly common residentially, although they are used in some high quality houses. In terms of their strength, appearance and durability, they are among the best available. Installation techniques have to be similar to ceramic and quarry tile, in that the weight of the material itself may cause deflection of conventional flooring systems. Joints on slate, stone, and marble must be properly grouted.

Problems: Cracked or broken flooring is the most common problem with these materials. The source of difficulties is usually a floor system with too much flex for this type of surface. The solution is, of course, to reinforce the floor and replace the damaged pieces. Improper grout mix or installation can lead to problems. Regrouting is time consuming, but not terribly difficult. Grouting does not apply to terrazzo floors.

Marble and some stone floors are susceptible to staining.

► 2.0 MAJOR WALL FINISHES

Wall finishes provide a decorative skin to conceal building components. Wall finishes hide structural members, insulation, ductwork, pipes, and wires. Good wall finishes are plumb and straight. Surfaces may be smooth or textured and better wall finishes are durable. Some wall finishes are versatile, taking decorative finishes such as stain, paint or wallpaper readily. Walls may make a decorating statement, or may be simply background. In some cases, the combustibility of wall finishes may be of interest. In kitchens and bathrooms, resistance to water damage is an asset.

Water Damage: Water damage is one of the most common problems on interior finishes. The water damage may be on walls, floors or ceilings. There are five areas of interest, typically, with any evidence of water damage. It is helpful to know a) the source of the damage, b) whether it is still active, c) whether there is any concealed damage, d) what the cost is to cure the problem, e) and subsequently what the cost is to repair the damaged building materials.

Common sources of water damage include roof leaks, flashing leaks, ice damming, window and skylight leaks, plumbing leaks, leaks from hot water heating systems, and condensation. Water damage may also result from such things as aquariums, room humidifiers or dehumidifiers, over-watering of plants, melting snow and ice from boots during wintertime, et cetera.

Roof leaks are usually localized and the source of the problem will often be an intersection or a flashing in the roof. Roof leaks can be difficult to trace because the water does not always appear on the interior immediately below the leak above. This may be the result of water running along framing members, or vapor barriers which prevent water coming through in specific locations. Many roof leaks appear first around ceiling light fixtures, for example.

Water damage often looks more serious than it is. Short term exposure to water will not harm most building materials. Plaster and drywall, however, are damaged very quickly by water. The material which can be easily seen is the first material to deteriorate. It is unusual to have extensive building damage done by water which appears at an interior finish, as long as the problem is solved promptly.

2.1 Plaster/Drywall: Plaster and drywall are essentially the same material. Drywall is premanufactured while plaster is mixed and applied by trowel on site. Plaster and drywall are made largely of gypsum. In some cases, aggregate or fibers are added to the gypsum as stabilizers and strengtheners. Horse hair was one of the materials commonly added to older plaster to help strengthen it. Lime may be added to improve workability.

These interior finishes are very common because they are inexpensive, relatively easy to apply and afford good fire resistance.

Wood Lath   Older plaster systems typically employ a wood lath which is comprised of boards roughly one inch wide by one-quarter inch thick. These "yardstick" type boards were nailed to the studs or strapping horizontally, with roughly one-quarter inch spaces between each board. The plaster was then trowelled on in two or three coats. The first layer of plaster would ooze through the spaces between the wood lath, sag, and harden to form a "key" which held the plaster onto the lath. This first layer is called a "scratch" coat. Where a three step process is used, the second coat is called the "brown" coat and the third is a "finish or putty" coat, In a two step process, there is still a scratch coat and a brown coat, but they are applied one immediately after the other. The finish coat is applied after the brown coat has set.

Gypsum Lath   In the late 1930's, gypsum lath became popular. These premanufactured plaster sheets replaced the wood lath because they were quicker and less expensive to install. The gypsum lath was paper covered, similar to drywall. It came in various sizes, but was typically sixteen inches by forty-eight inches. The gypsum lath was covered with one or two coats of plaster and the total thickness of the system would be approximately 1/2 to 5/8 inch. The lath itself is typically 3/8 inch thick.

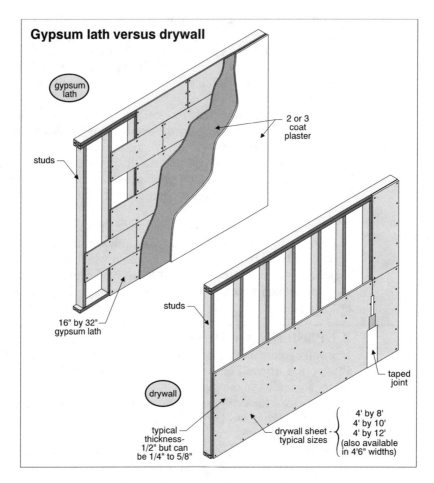

Figure 2. Gypsum Lath versus Drywall

Wire Lath   Wire mesh lath is sometimes used in areas where reinforcing is necessary, for example, on door frames and comers. Wire lath was also used in some bathroom areas in some cases where ceramic tile was to be provided.

Drywall   Drywall became popular in the early 1960's, and is used almost exclusively today. There is very little difference between a properly executed drywall and plaster job. Poor drywall work is usually identified at the seams. Sections of drywall are typically four feet by eight, ten, twelve, or fourteen feet. Drywall is typically available in 3/8 inch, 1/2 inch and 5/8 inch thicknesses.

The seams between boards must be taped and filled with drywall compound. If the taping and finishing work is poor, the seams can often readily be seen. Special drywalls, resistant to water or fire are available.

14

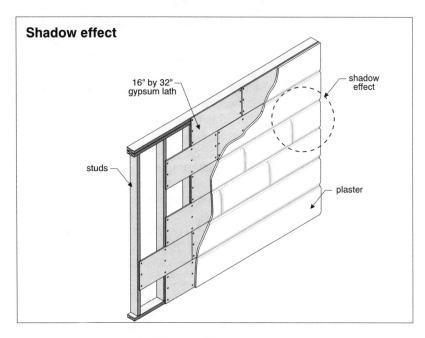

Figure 3. Shadow Effect

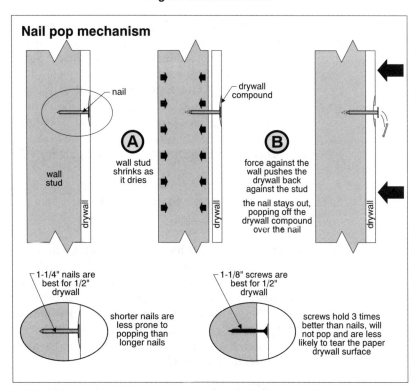

Figure 4. Nail Pops

Damage

Problems: Both plaster and drywall can be readily patched where small damaged areas are noted. Re-drywalling over old plaster or drywall is sometimes done where large areas are damaged.

Shadow Effect

A common problem with plaster applied over gypsum lath is the shadow or bulge effect. This was created when the plaster was applied too quickly. The finish coat was sometimes applied before the first coat dried completely. The moisture was driven back into the gypsum lath which sagged. The result is a pattern visible in the wall or ceiling that shows seams every sixteen inches in one direction. Sometimes seams are also visible perpendicular to these, at thirty-two or forty-eight inch intervals. This pattern is often only visible with a bright light shining across the plaster surface.

The problem is not progressive. No repairs are necessary. If improved appearance is desired, a skim coat of plaster can be added, depending on the condition of the surface. A plasterer should be consulted.

Loose

Where plaster has lost many of it keys, due to the vibration and wear and tear of everyday living, large sections of walls or ceilings may become loose. Where there is danger of plaster falling, this should be corrected promptly. People can be seriously hurt by falling plaster.

Solutions

Removal of the old plaster, and replacement with new plaster or drywall is the preferred approach. However, removing old plaster and lath is messy, disruptive, and time consuming. Adding new drywall over old plaster is common and may be acceptable. It is critical to attach the drywall through the old plaster to the studs or strapping. Attaching the drywall to the plaster alone may only accelerate the plaster coming off. Adding new plaster or drywall over walls and ceilings may result in baseboards, trim and decorative moldings looking recessed into the wall. This may or may not be acceptable cosmetically. Electrical boxes also sink back into the wall when drywall is added over plaster.

Another option is to replaster over old plaster. This is often accomplished by fastening wire lath over the old plaster and then applying plaster in the common two or three step process.

Applying a new finish over loose cracked plaster may accelerate the deterioration, due to the added weight.

2.2 Paneling: Paneling may take the form of veneered plywood, asbestos-cement board, veneered particle board, or solid wood. It is available in many forms and appearances, varying from a simple and inexpensive 1/8 inch sheet of 4 x 8 plywood, to an intricate, highly finished hardwood system, typical of dining rooms and libraries in high quality homes.

Problems: Paneling is often more durable than a plaster or drywall finish, although wood materials, of course, undergo more movement as a result of expansion and contraction. These finishes can be considerably more expensive than drywall. In some applications, the combustibility of this material may be an issue. Most paneling does not take paint or wallpaper as readily as drywall or plaster. Redecorating paneling can be difficult without removing it. Some paneling is difficult to patch without leaving any evidence.

2.3 Brick/Stone: These are not common wall finishes, and may be unfinished walls in many cases. However, some renovation work includes removal of original plaster to expose brick construction on either interior or exterior walls. This brickwork was usually not intended to be viewed, and may show a large number of small, damaged or off-colored bricks. Mortar joints are often quite irregular.

Removing plaster from an exterior brick wall reduces the insulating value of the wall, and can make the room colder. Removing plaster from an interior brick wall does not pose the same problem, although it does reduce the acoustic insulating properties of the wall. This may be an issue, for example, on a semidetached house with a common brick wall. Sealing exposed brick walls helps control the dust from the bricks and mortar.

Thin slices of brick approximately one-half inch thick, or imitation brick can be applied to a wall using an adhesive or embedding the brick in mortar. This is sometimes done around fireplace openings to create the illusion of a solid masonry fireplace. Full bricks are not used because the weight involved would require resupporting the floor below.

2.4 Concrete/Concrete Block: These materials are associated with unfinished walls, typically in a basement. They can be painted to provide a more finished appearance. Concrete is strong and these walls are unlikely to be damaged as a result of normal usage. Waterproofing products are often applied to the interior faces of basement concrete or block walls in an effort to reduce moisture penetration. This is rarely completely effective.

2.5 Stucco/Textured/Stipple: interior stucco is essentially plaster, and is typically installed in a two or three coat process. The finish is often sculpted or worked to provide a decorative appearance. The texturing is done with trowels, sponges, brushes, or other tools to give the desired effect. In modern construction, a sprayed on one-coat stipple finish is often used over drywall.

Problems: The modern stipple finish is inexpensive and quick to apply. It does not, however, cover poor drywall work, as flaws will show through. It should also not be used in kitchen or bathroom areas since the uneven surface is very difficult to clean.

Localized repairs to any textured surface are usually noticeable because the texturing is difficult to match. Painting is more difficult than a flat surface, and wallpapering is usually not possible. The strength and durability is similar to plaster or drywall, although small projections are easily worn off the surfaces, if people or animals brush against the wall.

► **3.0 MAJOR CEILING FINISHES**

Water Damage: Water damage is one of the most common problems on interior finishes. The water damage may be on walls, floors or ceilings. There are five areas of interest, typically, with any evidence of water damage. It is helpful to know a) the source of the damage, b) whether it is still active, c) whether there is any concealed damage, d) what the cost is to cure the problem, e) and subsequently what the cost is to repair the damaged building materials.

Common sources of water damage include roof leaks, flashing leaks, ice damming, window and skylight leaks, plumbing leaks, leaks from hot water heating systems, and condensation. Water damage may also result from such things as aquariums, room humidifiers or dehumidifiers, over-watering of plants, melting snow and ice from boots during wintertime, etc.

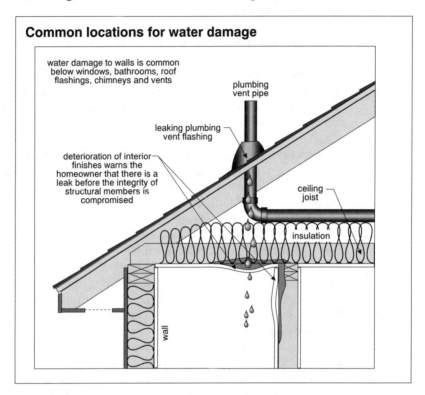

Common locations for water damage

water damage to walls is common below windows, bathrooms, roof flashings, chimneys and vents

plumbing vent pipe

leaking plumbing vent flashing

deterioration of interior finishes warns the homeowner that there is a leak before the integrity of structural members is compromised

ceiling joist

insulation

wall

Figure 5. Water Damage

Roof leaks are usually localized and the source of the problem will often be an intersection or a flashing in the roof. Roof leaks can be difficult to trace because the water does not always appear on the interior immediately below the leak above. This may be the result of water running along framing members, or vapor barriers which prevent water coming through in specific locations. Many roof leaks appear first around ceiling light fixtures, for example.

Water damage often looks more serious than it is. Short term exposure to water will not harm most building materials. Plaster and drywall, however, are damaged very quickly by water. The material which can be easily seen is the first material to deteriorate. It is unusual to have extensive building damage done by water which appears at an interior finish, as long as the problem is solved promptly.

3.1 Plaster/Drywall: Plaster and drywall are essentially the same material, Drywall is premanufactured while plaster is mixed and applied by trowel on site. Plaster and drywall are made largely of gypsum. In some cases, aggregate or fibers are added to the gypsum as stabilizers and strengtheners. Horse hair was one of the materials commonly added to older plaster to help strengthen it. Lime may be added to improve workability.

These interior finishes are very common because they are inexpensive, relatively easy to apply, and afford good fire resistance.

Wood Lath   Older plaster systems typically employ a wood lath which is comprised of boards roughly one inch wide by one-quarter inch thick. These "yardstick" type boards were nailed to the joists or rafters, with roughly one-quarter inch spaces between boards. The plaster was then trowelled on in two or three coats. The first layer of plaster would ooze through the spaces between the wood lath, and harden to form a "key" which held the plaster onto the lath. This first layer is called a "scratch" coat. Where a three step process is used, the second coat is called the "brown" coat and the third is a "finish" or "putty" coat. In a two step process, there is still a scratch coat and a brown coat but they are applied one immediately after the other. The finish coat is applied after the brown coat has set.

Gypsum Lath   In the late 1930's, gypsum lath became popular. These premanufactured plaster sheets replaced the wood lath because they were quicker and less expensive to install. The gypsum lath was paper covered similar to drywall. It came in sizes that varied, but was typically sixteen inches by forty-eight inches. The gypsum lath was typically provided with one or two finish coats of plaster and the total thickness of the system would be approximately 1/2 to 5/8 inch. The lath itself is typically 3/8 inch thick. Wire mesh lath was used in areas where reinforcing was necessary.

Drywall   Drywall became popular in the early 1960's, and is used almost exclusively today. There is very little difference between a properly executed drywall and plaster job. Poor drywall work is usually identified at the seams. Sections of drywall are typically four feet by eight, ten, twelve or fourteen feet. Drywall is typically available in 3/8 inch, 1/2 inch and 5/8 inch thicknesses. The seams between boards must be taped and filled with drywall compound. If the taping and finishing work is poor, the seams can often readily be seen.

Damage   Problems: Both plaster and drywall can be readily patched where small damaged areas are noted. Re-drywalling over old plaster or drywall is sometimes done where large areas are damaged. Where plaster has lost many of it keys, due to the vibration and wear and tear of everyday living, large sections of ceilings may become loose. Where there is danger of plaster falling, this should be corrected promptly. People can be seriously hurt by plaster falling, especially from a ceiling.

Removal of the old plaster, and replacement with new plaster or drywall is the preferred approach. However, removing old plaster and lath is messy, disruptive, and time consuming. Adding new drywall over old plaster is common and may be acceptable. It is critical to attach the drywall through the old plaster to the joists or rafters. Attaching the drywall to the plaster may only accelerate the plaster coming off. Adding new plaster or drywall over ceilings may result in decorative mouldings appearing recessed into the ceiling.

Another option is to replaster over old plaster. This is often accomplished by fastening wire lath over the old plaster and then applying plaster in the common two or three step process. Applying a new finish directly over cracked, loose plaster may accelerate the deterioration, due to the added weight.

*Shadow
Effect*

A common problem with plaster applied over gypsum lath is the shadow or bulge effect. This was created when the plaster was applied too quickly. The finish coat was sometimes applied before the first coat dried completely. The moisture was driven back into the gypsum lath which sagged. The result is a pattern visible in the wall or ceiling that shows seams every sixteen inches in one direction. Sometimes seams are also visible perpendicular to these, at thirty-two or forty-eight inch intervals. This pattern is often only visible with a bright light shining across the plaster surface.

The problem is not progressive. No repairs are necessary. If improved appearance is desired, a skim coat of plaster can be added, depending in the condition of the surface. A plasterer should be consulted.

3.2 Acoustic Tile: These tiles, typically made of fiber board and perforated to improve their acoustic performance, have been popular since the 1950's. Typically, they are twelve inches by twelve inches and are stapled or nailed to strapping. This type of ceiling tile was often installed when finishing a basement, or was installed over a damaged plaster ceiling.

Problems: The tiles do have better acoustic properties than plaster and drywall, although they are subject to mechanical damage and water damage, similar to drywall or plaster. Repairs are easy if matching tiles can be found. The tiles can be painted, with some loss of acoustic performance.

3.3 Suspended Tile: Suspended tile became popular residentially in the 1960's, and can be made of fiber board or fiber glass, for example. Some have a plastic coating. Combustible plastics, such as polystyrene, should not be used as ceiling tiles. This system utilizes a metal T-bar grid supported by wires from the original ceiling. One disadvantage of this type of system residentially, is that it does require lowering the ceiling at least two to three inches. Advantages include relatively good acoustic properties, case of removal to access anything above the ceiling, and individual tiles can be replaced readily.

3.4 Metal: Metal ceilings were typically made of tin and most often were installed in kitchen areas residentially, during the late 1800's and early 1900's. Their design was often a decorative square pattern intended to simulate the look of ornate plaster ceilings. This was a fairly durable ceiling system and in some areas has become fashionable again. The metal is normally painted.

3.5 Stucco/Textured/Stipple: interior stucco is essentially plaster, and is typically installed in a two or three coat process. The finish is sculpted or worked to provide a decorative appearance. The texturing is done with trowels, sponges, brushes, or other tools to give the desired effect. In modern construction, a sprayed on one-coat stipple finish is often used over drywall. This textured finish is inexpensive and quick to apply. It does not, however, cover poor drywall work, as flaws will show through. It should also not be used in kitchen or bathroom areas since the uneven surface is very difficult to clean. Localized repairs are usually noticeable because the texturing is difficult to match. Painting is more difficult than a flat surface, and wallpapering is usually not possible. The strength and durability is similar to plaster or drywall.

► 4.0 TRIM

Baseboard and Quarter Round

Most houses have some interior trim including baseboard, quarter round and door and window casings. Baseboard and quarter round are usually wood members which are installed at the intersection of the walls and the floors. Baseboard protects the bottom of the walls from things like brooms and vacuum cleaners, and also serves to provide a finished joint between the walls and floor. Baseboard can be anything from a two inch high piece of plain lumber to an intricate two or three piece architectural moulding, ten or twelve inches high. Quarter round is usually relatively small (approximately 3/4 inch radius) and covers the joint between the floor and the baseboard. Most often, it is the same material as the baseboard. Some modern architectural treatments omit quarter round, and occasionally baseboard is omitted as well.

In some high quality homes, other materials, such as tile or marble, are used for baseboard. This is an expensive treatment, of course. A commercial treatment occasionally found in homes is broadloom turned up the wall to form a carpet baseboard.

Casings

Door and window casings provide a finished look to the junction of a wall and door or window opening. Again, the casings are most often wood and may be quite simple or very elaborate. Some modern architectural styles include no trim work around doors and windows.

Cornice Moldings

Moldings at the junction between walls and ceilings are typically referred to as cornice moldings. They may be made of wood, plaster or foamed plastic. Depending on the age and quality of the house, these can be very elaborate. In modern conventional housing, these are not used to any great extent.

Medallions or Rosettes

Ceiling medallions or rosettes are usually plaster details found around light fixtures on ceilings. These details were common only in principal rooms such as living rooms or dining rooms. They can be fabricated on site, or pre-manufactured systems can be purchased and installed in any home. Reproduction medallions in foamed plastic are now available.

Trim Functions

These trim details perform few functions other than to protect exposed joints or comers. They add architectural appeal to a home, and better quality moldings and trim may mean better quality construction. They may provide clues as to the original quality of the house and can help to date additions or renovations

Missing Loose and Damaged

Problems: Wood trim can, of course, be missing, damaged or loose. Where there is elaborate or specialized, replacement with an exact matching system may not be practical. Custom millwork is very expensive. Also, some of the woods used in the past are not available today. It is sometimes more cost effective to replace the entire trim in a room rather than try to match a section of old trim which has been damaged beyond repair.

When wall to wall broadloom was installed in some houses, quarter round was often removed and not replaced. Removing the broadloom usually necessitates at least some trim work.

When replacing windows or doors in a home, it may be necessary to replace trim work as well.

Plaster trim such as cornice moldings, ceiling medallions, et cetera, is difficult to repair if damaged (for example, by water). Rebuilding or repairing a damaged molding is time consuming and requires some plastering skills. There are, however, still people available to do this sort of work, if one is willing to pay for it.

Water Damage

Water damage is one of the most common problems on interior finishes. Please refer to Section 3.0.1.

► 5.0 STAIRS

Stairs and stairwells form part of the interior finish of a home. Structural problems related to stairwell openings are addressed in the Structure section.

Components

The stairs themselves are typically made up of stringers, treads and risers. The stringers are the long diagonal supports for the stairs which rest on the floor of the lower story and are usually secured to the side of a floor joist on the upper story. The stringers are almost always made of wood (e.g. 2 x10), although they can be metal. There are usually two stringers, although there can be one or three. The treads are the components on which people step and the risers are the vertical members at the back of each tread. Again, treads and risers are most often wood. Open staircases do not have risers.

Rise, Run, and Tread Width

Stairwell terminology includes "rise and run". The run is the horizontal distance from one riser to the next, measured along the tread. The run is usually less than the tread width because the tread has a nosing which projects beyond the riser below. For example, it is typical to have a tread width of ten inches and a run of nine inches. The rise is the vertical distance from the top of one tread to the top of the next. The rise and run for each step must be the same in any staircase.

Minimums and Maximums

Good stair design has a maximum rise of 8 inches, a minimum run of 8-1/4 to 9 inches and a minimum tread width of 9-1/4 inches. Generally speaking, the lower the rise and the wider the tread, the more comfortable the staircase is to use. Dimension rules are often broken on basement and loft stairwells. It is very difficult to rearrange a poorly built staircase and, in most cases, the occupants simply learn to live with it. The rules of thumb vary somewhat, area to area.

Width and Headroom

A stairwell used on a regular basis should be at least 34 to 36 inches wide. Wider stairs are more pleasant and make it easier to move furniture. The headroom above each tread should be at least 6 foot, 5 inches to 6 foot, 8 inches. More is better, but less is common on basement stairs. Again, it is rarely worth changing.

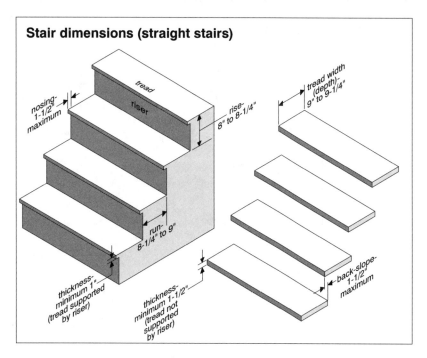

Stair dimensions (straight stairs)

Figure 6. Stair Dimensions

Doors and Landings

Where there is a door at the top of the set of stairs, it should open away from the stairs. If it opens towards the stairs, there should be a landing so that someone coming up the stairs won't be knocked down by another person opening the door. If an unsafe situation exists, it is usually less expensive to rearrange the door than to add a landing. This situation is sometimes created on older homes where a storm door has been added. The original front steps come up to a door which opened into the house. The storm door has to open out and, when added, creates an unsafe situation. Ideally, the stairs should be rebuilt with a landing.

Curved Stairs and Winders

Curved stairs or stairs with winders are not considered as safe as straight stairs. The treads often get very narrow on one side. Many codes accept some runs on curved stairs as narrow as six inches. Winders are pie shaped treads which disappear to a point at the inside edge. These are not desirable, but are common. Winders usually appear in groups of three and should not turn through more than 30° each. The total set of winders should not turn through more than 90°. Spiral staircases are built entirely of winders and, in many areas, are not permitted as the only way to get from one floor to another. The thinking is that in a fire these staircases are dangerous because they are difficult to get down quickly.

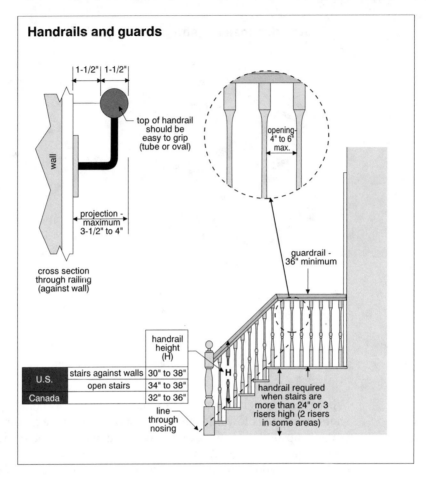

Handrails and guards

| 1-1/2" | 1-1/2" |

top of handrail should be easy to grip (tube or oval)

opening- 4" to 6" max.

wall

projection - maximum 3-1/2" to 4"

cross section through railing (against wall)

guardrail - 36" minimum

handrail height (H)

		handrail height (H)
U.S.	stairs against walls	30" to 38"
	open stairs	34" to 38"
Canada		32" to 36"

H

handrail required when stairs are more than 24" or 3 risers high (2 risers in some areas)

line through nosing

Figure 7. Handrails and Guards

Railings

Railings are recommended on at least one side of each staircase with more than two risers. Railings on stairs in new construction are usually required to be thirty-four to thirty-eight inches high in the U.S.A. and thirty-two to thirty-six inches high in Canada. Railings around the top of open stairwells should be at least thirty-six inches high. On older homes, railings are often lower and, rather than rebuilding an elegant railing, most people live with the lower one. Where children's safety, for example, is in question, a higher temporary railing can be added.

Many codes do not limit the size of openings in railings in single family homes.

Where there are small children or other reasons for concern, a good rule is no opening larger than four inches in diameter. Some codes use a six inch rule. Most modern railing systems comply with this. In the same sense, stairs with open risers may be unsafe where a small child can crawl through the opening between two treads.

Problems: Stairs may be poorly supported if the floor system is weak or if the stringers are underdesigned, damaged or have shifted. Where a side stringer has pulled away from the treads, the treads may lose their support and fall out. Loose, worn or poorly supported treads are a safety concern.

Stairwells which violate size or uniformity rules are difficult to negotiate and may lead to an accident. Missing, weak or poorly arranged railings are a similar concern. Unfortunately, these situations are common in older homes and may not be cost-effective to rearrange.

► 6.0 WINDOWS

Windows provide light and ventilation for homes, at the expense of some heat loss (windows let more heat escape than even an uninsulated wall). They also allow air leakage, and can allow water leakage if poorly installed or maintained. Well designed windows add to the aesthetic appeal of a home.

Anatomy: There are several types of windows, but some components are common to most. Some of the main components are described here. The pieces of glass in a window are called "panes" or "lites". The panes are held in a sash, which may move as the window is opened. The sides of the sash are called the stiles, and the top and bottom pieces are the rails. When the window within the sash is divided up into several small panes, the dividing pieces are muntins. The sides of the window frame are the jambs, the sill is the bottom assembly of the frame, and the head is the top. The casing or trim covers the edge of the frame where it meets the wall finish. There may or may not be a casing on the inside and outside of the building.

Putty or glazing compound is used to hold the glass in the sash in traditional window systems.

Conventional window glass is 3/32 inch to 1/8 inch thick. Thicker glass is sometimes used where increased strength or thermal insulating value is desired.

Glass may be strengthened by tempering. Fully tempered glass is made three to five times stronger than ordinary glass by heating it and then cooling it very quickly. Tempered glass is also safer than ordinary glass because it breaks into small rectangular particles. Tempered glass is used in sliding doors and skylights, for example.

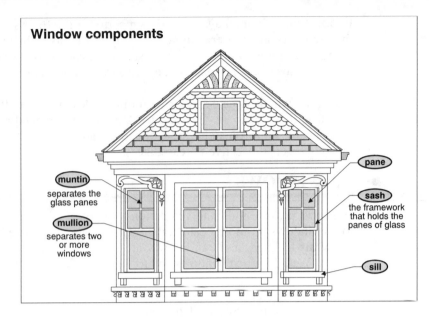

Figure 8. Window Components

Glass can be tinted to reduce glare or absorb heat. Heat can also be reflected with coated glass. Wired glass provides additional fire resistance, but may actually be weaker than conventional glass. Some experts feel it is more dangerous to humans if broken. Someone putting their hand through any pane of glass will usually be cut. Because the wire holds the pieces of glass in place, the person may be cut more severely pulling their arm back through wired glass.

Laminated glass is a sandwich made up of two or more layers of glass and a plastic film between. Depending on what is desired, laminated glass can improve strength, safety and/or sound insulation. When the term "safety glass" is used, it may mean the glass is tempered, wired, laminated or a combination.

For privacy or architectural appeal, glass can be etched chemically, sand-blasted, painted, tinted, stained or given a reflective coating.

6.1 Major Window Types - Primary

6.1.1 Double Hung:
A double hung window is made of two moving parts, with an outer part in the top half of the opening and an inner part on the bottom half of the opening. The windows move up and down in their guides. Traditionally, both the top and bottom halves could be moved up and down.

Typically, the top half becomes inoperative with painting and is rarely used. The bottom half should be kept operative. Early double hung windows were held open by the use of a counterweight system. A sash cord is attached to each side of the window. The sash cord goes up and over a pulley near the top of the side frames. The weight travels up and down in a channel in the frame. The weight holds the window in place when it is raised to the desired height.

Some modern double hung windows use a spring loaded mechanism concealed in the side of the sash. A spring is wound up as the window is raised and lowered, holding the window in place. A spring loaded coil tape is another way of holding a double hung window open.

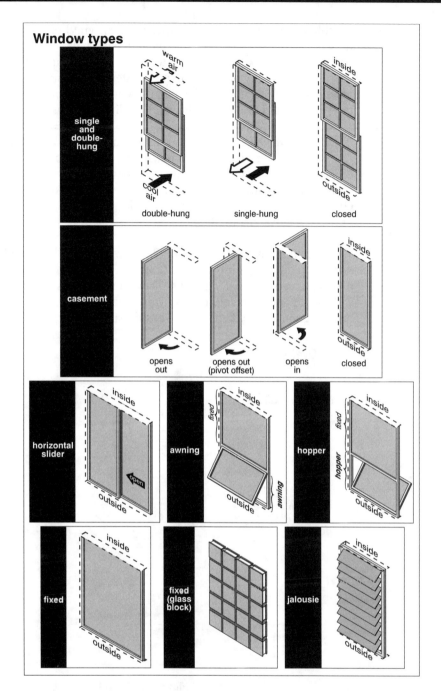

Figure 9. Window Types

Some modern high quality double hung windows are pivoted at the bottom, and when release pins at the top are moved, the window can be rotated out of its normal operating plane, into the room so that the outside of the glass can be easily cleaned without going outdoors.

Double hung windows may be wood, metal, vinyl or a combination. The glass may be a single, double or triple pane in each half of the window. Wood, metal or plastic muntins may be used to create several smaller panes. Modern windows often employ artificial muntin systems set inside the window to give the appearance of several smaller panes. A lower quality version of this includes tape applied directly to the glass to look like muntins.

6.1.2 Casement: Casement windows are hinged at the side and open inward or outward. There is usually a handle on the side of the window opposite the hinge, and in some cases, a guide bar along the bottom of the window. An operating crank is often included at the bottom of modern casement windows. Glazing may be single, double or triple. Materials may include wood, metal, vinyl, or a combination thereof.

Wood muntins may be used to break the glass up into smaller panes. This is done on older or traditional style houses. Casement windows have become very popular as replacement windows. They can provide very good ventilation and, if well made and installed, can be very weathertight. Larger casement windows require good quality hardware to ensure smooth operation.

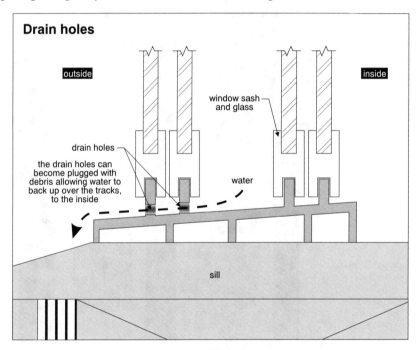

Figure 10. Drain Holes

6.1.3 Sliders: Horizontal sliding windows have become popular in the latter half of the 20th century. Several low quality sliders have given this style of window a somewhat tarnished reputation. Some of the windows are nothing more than simple panes of glass with knobs attached on the surface of the glass. They typically travel in a wood or vinyl track. These are poor quality windows, subject to considerable air and water leakage. Better sliders are provided with sashes (metal, vinyl or wood) around the glass. Sliders are relatively inexpensive, and have very simple locking hardware as a rule. If well made, their performance can be as good as any other type of window. Glazing may be single, double or triple.

Problems include low quality hardware subject to breakage, tracks at the bottom which don't drain water to the outside, poorly fit slides, and poor joints at corners of the frames. Leaks often result in water damage to wall finishes below the windows, most often at corners. Exterior caulking may help in some cases; in others, storm windows added on the outside improve weathertightness. Where the problem is chronic, replacement windows may be the best answer.

6.1.4 Awning: Awning windows are hinged at the top and typically swing out. In most cases, there is an operating crank at the bottom of the window. Typical materials include wood, vinyl and metal. Glazing may be single, double or triple. These windows are not terribly common, although in one sense, are desirable. These windows, if left open during the rain, are less likely to allow water penetration into the house than most other types. The amount of ventilation they permit is good, although unless the hardware is well made and the windows well fit, operating can be difficult.

A variation on the awning window is the hopper window. This is hinged at the bottom and may open in or out. These are not a popular design as they catch rain and debris if they open outward, and interfere with furniture placement if they open inward.

6.1.5 Fixed: Fixed windows, sometimes called picture windows, are simply a pane of glass fit into a window opening and held in place with stops. The glass can be anything from a single pane of minimum thickness glass to double or triple glazing, to a full six inch thick glass block. There is obviously no ventilation capability for fixed windows. Large windows are expensive to replace and handling picture window glass can be difficult and dangerous because of its size.

Replacement Windows

6.1.6 Window Problems: windows are relatively complex systems and can suffer several problems. Where difficulties are experienced with several windows in a home, it may make sense to replace the windows. However, this is rarely cost-effective. Replacement windows are expensive and, in most cases, will not pay for themselves in reduced heating costs over a reasonable number of years. Where replacement windows are installed, it should be appreciated that some of the price being paid is for the improved appearance, reduced maintenance and ease of operation. Some improvement in room comfort and energy consumption will also be enjoyed, although these items cannot, on their own, justify new windows in most cases.

Glass

Panes of glass may be missing, broken or cracked. In some cases, panes of glass work loose and will rattle on windy days. On older houses where windows have been painted a number of times, the glass may be heavily covered with paint. Removing this paint often scratches the glass, impairing visibility. Older glass has more bubbles and distortions, although this cannot be considered a defect. Manufacturers' flaws include discoloration, clouding and rust streaking of the windows. In some cases, distortion may also be a problem. Double or

Lost Seal

triple glazed windows may lose their seal, resulting in intermittent or permanent condensation or clouding between the panes of glass. It may not be possible to identify a failed seal during a home inspection. The corrective action for these problems is replacement of the glass. Unless the glass is missing or broken, replacement of the glass is not a priority item.

Putty   The putty or glazing compound holding a window in place may be deteriorated, loose or missing. This is normally improved during regular repainting.

Muntins   Muntins between panes of glass may be broken or cracked. Loose muntins should be resecured. Where the muntins are lead (typical of homes built in the first half of the 20th century, often with diamond shaped panes of glass), the windows tend to bulge inward or outward. This is thought to be a result of impact or the thermal expansion of the lead, and may be related to the addition of storm windows. Depending on severity, this can sometimes be repaired by a glass specialist, although, in some cases, the window has to be replaced. Specialty shops can reproduce leaded glass windows.

Sashes   Wood sashes may be deteriorated as a result of mechanical damage, rot, or failed joints. It is not unusual to find the stiles and rails of wood double hung windows coming apart. This is often a result of people opening the window by lifting up on the top rail. Hardware attached to the bottom rail should be used for opening and closing double hung windows. Where this hardware is missing, it should be replaced. Metal and vinyl sashes may also fail, but this is less common than on wood.

                 On some vinyl horizontal sliding windows, it is common for the vinyl sashes to be pulled away from the glass. This is often because the sash is used to pull a window closed. It is better practice to push a horizontal slider closed than to pull on it, even though the manufacturer may provide pulling hardware.

Sash Cords   Sash cords on double hung windows are often broken or missing. The pulleys at the top of the jamb are often inoperable, because they have been painted. Sash cords, incidentally, should not be painted; nor should the window guides in the frame. While cotton sash cords can last for many years, some people prefer to replace them with nylon or metal sash cords. The chain sash cords are somewhat noisier, of course.

Springs   The spiral spring hardware used to hold up some double hung windows is prone to jamming, particularly if paint is introduced. It is also common for the springs to become detached from either the window or the jamb. Springs can break on this type of sash support. Similarly, springs on the coiled tape system can break. Again, painting of any of the operating hardware on windows may render it inoperative.

Condensation   Sashes and frames on early metal windows are susceptible to condensation problems. Because metal is a good thermal conductor, the inside face of the metal can be very cold, promoting condensation on the interior of the building. Warm moist house air contacting the metal cools quickly, losing its ability to hold moisture. Modern systems have a thermal break, which keep the inside metal surface warmer. Vinyl frames can suffer similar problems. Some experts say it is important to have more of the thermal mass of a sill or frame on the inside (warm) side of a window to minimize condensation.

Sills

Sill assemblies can be loose, rotted or improperly sloped. Manufactured window systems with a primary and a storm window typically have drain holes below the outer pane so that any water which accumulates between the inner and outer panes can escape. In some cases, these windows are installed backwards, with the drain holes on the inside and the sill sloping into the house. This, of course, results in damage to the walls below the sills on the inside of the house. Blocked drain holes are a related problem, but these are easily cured by removing the obstructions.

A common problem with manufactured window systems is a poor connection at the sill/jamb intersection. Water will accumulate on a window sill system from driving rains or condensation, for example. Although the sills should be sloped to drain water out, and there should be drain holes available to carry the water away, any imperfections in this system (or a very fast build up of water) will result in water pending on the sill for some time. If the comers of the sill are not tightly sealed to the bottom of the jambs, the water will leak out through the comers of the window. It is very common to see water staining or wall damage below the corners of windows. Sometimes caulking of this joint is adequate, although, in severe cases, the window has to be taken out and replaced or reassembled at the comers. The problem is aggravated if the outer pane is left open and only the inner pane is closed. While more convenient for the occupant, this allows wind driven rain to accumulate between the inner and outer panes.

Casings

Window casings or trim may be loose, missing of damaged. While this is largely a cosmetic problem, some additional air leakage and resulting heat loss will often be noted where the trim fit is poor.

Heads

The most common problem with the head of a window is a sagging lintel. If the lintel (beam) above the window opening is not strong enough, the window may be deflected. This can result in a window which will not operate, and ultimately the glass will break. In some cases this problem is progressive; in others, the window lintel will sag into position and then remain fixed. This problem is common where the opening is large, such as in the case of picture windows or sliding doors, for example.

Hardware

Window hardware may be missing, broken or inoperative. In many cases, it is cheaper to replace hardware rather than try to repair or clean heavily painted hardware.

Caulking

Caulking of windows should be considered in two separate areas. Caulking on the outside of the window should be done to prevent water penetration. Caulking on the inside of the windows should be done to prevent air leakage out of the house. There are several different types of caulking materials suitable for each application, and the manufacturers' recommendations or the recommendation of a specialist should be followed when choosing a caulking for a given application. Caulking is not a lifetime material and modest quality caulkings have to be replaced every one to two years.

Screens

Window screens may be aluminum, steel, bronze, fiber glass or nylon, for example. Metal screens may be rusted and all screens can be torn or pushed out of their frame.

Inoperable   Inoperable windows are very common and may be the result of paint or dirt in the operating mechanisms or tracks. Building settlement or swelling of wood components may also result in inoperative windows. Jammed, broken or missing hardware may also prevent easy operation.

6.1.7 Skylights: Skylights or roof windows have become popular residentially since the 1960's. Typically they use tempered glass or plastic and may be flat or bubble shaped. Older units or special-use skylights may have wired glass. Some skylights are operable, although most are not. Skylights are often installed after the house is built, and installation can be tricky. In addition to cutting a hole in the roof, (and the structural considerations brought on by doing that) leakage must be prevented where the skylight joins the roof covering. This can be difficult, as the skylight almost always presents a curb which will collect water. The skylight should have a flashing detail which makes a good watertight connection between the roof and the skylight.

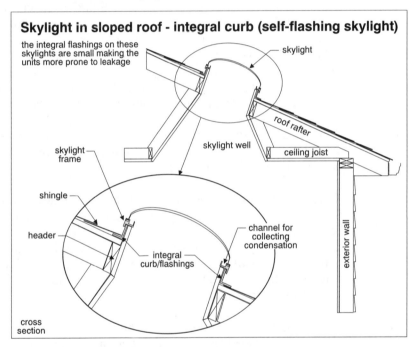

Figure 11. Self Flashing Skylight

Low quality and poorly installed skylights are very common and it is safe to say that most skylights have leaked at some point. Home-made skylights rarely perform well. Manufactured skylights should be installed following the manufacturer's recommendations. Flashing kits available from the factory should be used, where appropriate.

Glazing   Skylights and solariums often use acrylic or other plastic materials for panes instead of glass. These materials have better resistance to breakage than conventional glass, although they are subject to scratching. Abrasive cleaners should not be used on plastics, and overhanging tree branches should not contact the pane. Skylight glazing may be single, double (most common) or triple. Leakage is a common problem, although usually it is a result of poor installation rather than a poor quality fixture. It is often difficult to identify the source of the leakage without dismantling the system.

6.1.8 Solariums: Solariums are structures with the walls and roof made mostly of glass. They are also called sun rooms, Florida rooms, plant rooms and greenhouse rooms. The framing for the solarium may be wood, metal, vinyl, or a combination, and the glazing may be glass or plastic. Glass used in anything other than a vertical plane should be strengthened by tempering, or laminating. Glass used in roofs may have to withstand a falling tree branch or hail stones, for example.

Solariums are typically added onto a house and very often have three exterior glass walls. It should be understood that solariums are an indulgence in terms of energy, since glass is not a good insulator. These areas are expensive to heat and cool, and glass walls form an expensive building system, and one that is difficult to seat against water leakage. Even high quality solariums, if not perfectly installed, will leak around the roof and, in some cases, through the windows as well. Leakage is most common at the bottom of the glass roof areas, where good flashing details are difficult to achieve.

6.2 Predominant Glazing

6.2.1 Single: Until approximately 1950, virtually all windows were single glazed. This means that only one pane of glass was used in a window. In some cases, a thicker glass pane (up to one-quarter inch) was used in an effort to improve heating efficiency, although this makes very little difference. The additional thickness of the glass will give it some additional strength. Single glazed windows can be retrofit with a second pane added to the sash itself, although more conventionally, a storm window is added. The insulation value of a single conventional pane of glass is approximately R-1.

6.2.2 Double: Double glazing has become very popular, with the earliest common use residentially in the 1950's. Initially, double glazing was used primarily for picture windows, although now it is used on all windows. Double glazing may be either one of two types. Both are considered satisfactory.

Factory Sealed
The factory sealed double glazing is designed to have no air infiltration or exfiltration between the panes of glass. When these panes do lose their seal, they may develop condensation between the two panes, which makes it difficult to see through the glass. This reduces their insulating value only slightly. Replacement is not a priority from a functional standpoint. The condensation may disappear temporarily if sunlight warms the air between the panes sufficiently.

Vented
There are also ventilated double glazing systems wherein small holes between the outside air and the space between the two panes of glass allow for air movement. While condensation can develop here, it usually dissipates quickly. The ventilation holes can become clogged, which may trap condensation between the panes.

*Space
Between
Panes*

The space between the panes of glass does to some degree, affect the insulating performance of the glass. Generally speaking, an air space of 1/2 inch or less is common. An optimum air space is usually considered to be roughly 5/8 to 3/4 inch, although there is some disagreement among the experts. This space should be small enough to prevent convection currents, but large enough to allow a sufficient amount of air between the panes to act as an insulator. Some double glazed window systems include such things as venetian blinds between the panes of glass. These are expensive systems and are not seen commonly.

A typical double-glazed window has an R value of approximately 2.

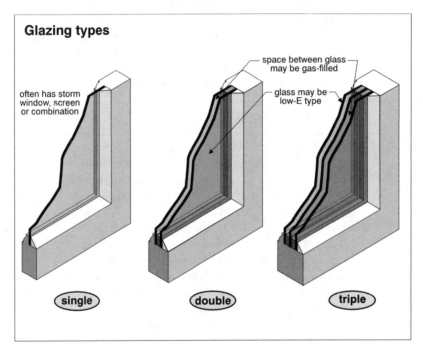

Figure 12. Glazing Types

6.2.3 Triple: Triple glazing is becoming more common as energy costs increase. There are two air spaces between three panes of glass which do afford more insulating value. A seal which is lost may result in condensation between the panes. This obstructs visibility, and to some extent reduces the energy efficiency of the window system. A lost seal does not mean a window has to be replaced immediately. Most triple glazed systems have hermetically sealed air pockets between the glazing, rather than ventilated air spaces.

The insulating value of a triple glazed window is approximately R-3.

6.2.4 Primary Plus Storm: Many window systems include a primary (inner) window, and a separate storm (usually outer). The storm windows may be original to the house, or added later. It should be understood that the major benefits of storm windows are reduced drafts and reduced condensation.

The insulating value of a primary plus storm window is not significantly more than a primary window alone. Modern building codes require walls to be insulated to R-12 or more. A single pane of glass has an insulating value of roughly R-1. Interestingly, a double pane has an R value of 2. Adding a storm window does not make a window opening particularly well insulated. Triple glazing yields roughly R-3.

The air space between the primary window and the storm is often several inches. If it is more than four inches, the insulating value will be significantly reduced. A minimum air space between two panes of glass is generally one-half inch, with a three-quarter inch air space often considered to be about the optimum.

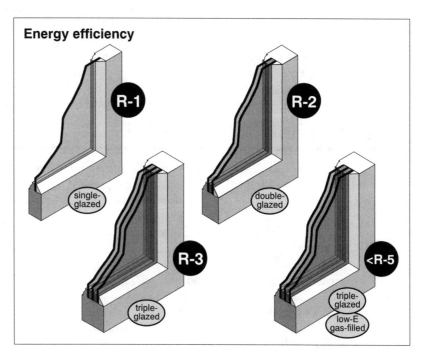

Figure 13. Energy Efficiency

Condensation The additional seal afforded by the storm window does reduce air movement in or out of the house around the window opening. This leads to reduced energy costs as well as improved comfort. Adding a storm window has another benefit. During the winter months, a single glazed window has a very cold glass surface, inside the house, and out. Warm moist air in the house contacting the glass, will deposit condensation on the glass. This runs down the glass and can damage the window itself, and ultimately the wall below. The addition of a storm window makes the inner pane of glass warmer, preventing condensation under normal circumstances. In very cold weather, condensation may be noted on interior glass surfaces, even with double or triple glazing. This is a sign that the humidity levels in the house should be lowered.

Removable Storms

Until World War II, most of the storm windows were wood systems installed from the outside. Typically held in place with clips or brackets, they were put up every fall and removed in the spring. In some cases, screens replaced the storms during the summer months. Many older houses have no storms, and since there are no standard window sizes, add-on storm windows have to be custom made. Their fit is often less than perfect, and the storm window performance is compromised as a result.

Self-Storing Storms

Around the time of the Second World War, metal self-storing storms and screens became popular. Vinyl storms are also popular today. These are also called combination storms and screens, triple track storms and screens, or permanent storms and screens. They are typically comprised of a frame which contains two panes of glass and one screen. Most often there are two tracks. In the outer track, the screen sits in the bottom and a fixed pane of glass sits on top. On the inside track, there is a second pane of glass which is at the bottom, in front of the screen. This inner pane can be raised to open the window, providing ventilation. The screen and upper pane of glass do not move. These systems can usually be removed from the interior, which makes cleaning very easy. Other than that, however, these systems remain in place year round.

► 7.0 DOORS

Doors provide a way to enter and exit the house, of course, and can add to the architectural appeal of homes. Doors present a security problem in most houses. Most doors are a source of heat loss, due to poor insulating properties of common door materials (e.g. wood). Air and water leakage around door openings is also common. Some doors add natural light and ventilation (e.g. sliding glass doors) to a home. Exterior doors should be sturdy enough to offer some security, should stand up to weathering, should be fit tightly to minimize air and water leakage, and should include provision for locking hardware.

7.1 Typical Exterior Doors

7.1.1 Solid Wood: This is a traditional exterior door material. Wood has some natural insulating properties although weathertightness is always enhanced with the addition of a storm door. The heaviest wood door does not provide as much insulation value as even a poorly insulated wall.

From a security standpoint, a solid wood door is relatively good, depending on the amount of glass area and, of course, the hardware and installation quality.

7.1.2 Hollow Wood: Hollow wood doors are generally not for exterior use. From energy, security, and durability standpoints, hollow wood doors are a distant second to solid wood. A common problem with hollow wood doors is deterioration of the wood veneer on the surface exposed to the exterior.

7.1.3 Metal (Insulated Core): This is a very common type of exterior door in modern construction. With a metal exterior skin and insulating material (typically polystyrene or polyurethane) inside, this can make a good insulating door. Another advantage of a metal door is that magnetic weatherstripping can be used to create a good air seal.

Metal doors often have decorative plastic moldings on the surface. Problems have been experienced when a storm door is added to an insulated metal door. The space between the doors can become overheated, and the plastic moldings may be affected. In the worst cases, the metal door panel may even buckle. Many manufacturers recommend against the use of storm doors with insulated core metal doors.

7.1.4 Garage Doors: Some municipalities allow doors connecting the house and attached garage. Where these are permitted, they should be treated as exterior doors. They should be weatherstripped to prevent automobile fumes entering the house, and should have an auto-closer so the door will not be left open. There should be a six inch step (minimum) going down from the house into the garage. Some jurisdictions require a fire-rated door.

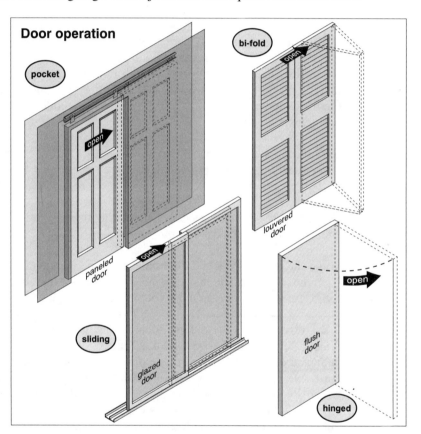

Figure 14. Door Operation

7.1.5 Storm Doors: Storm doors have become very popular where the main door is solid wood. Most storm doors are metal although wood storms are also available. Many include a removable glass pane that can be replaced with a screen. Others have a self storing storm and screen system, similar to conventional storm windows. No matter how good a single exterior door is from a weathertightness standpoint, a storm door will usually improve the situation. The second door, if properly fit, will significantly reduce air leakage around the single door. Most storm doors are equipped with a self closer, and it is important that the closer be adjusted to close the door tightly to achieve a snug fit.

7.1.6 French: French doors are popular on traditional style homes, both old and new, and are becoming popular as a renovation feature. Historically, French doors have been weak in terms of their energy efficiency, although they are expensive systems and generally considered aesthetically pleasing.

Storm doors can be provided on French doors. This will improve the energy efficiency. The traditional materials are wood, although metal and vinyl doors are now available. Panes of glass are broken by muntins into small sections, or false muntins are provided to make it look like several smaller panes.

7.1.7 Sliding Glass: Sliding glass doors have been popular since the 1950's. They provide a large glass area with excellent visibility, and can provide a very large door opening, depending on the size of the unit. Sliding glass doors are available in wood, metal and vinyl or a combination thereof.

Early sliding doors that were made of metal were very poor insulators. A common problem with the early doors was the development of condensation and ice on the inside of the metal door frame. More recent treatments include a thermal break between the inner and outer halves of the metal frame. This keeps the inside metal part of the frame warmer, and reduces condensation and icing problems.

Sliding doors am typically two thicknesses of glass. Each pane can be in a separate sliding door component, or there may be one door sash with a double glazed or even triple glazed pane.

Better quality sliding glass doors are distinguished by more expensive hardware and sophisticated means of adjustment.

Some sliding glass doors do not have a locking mechanism that can be operated from the outside of the house by a key. This may be of concern where access to the house is most convenient through the sliding glass door.

7.2 Door Problems: Functional problems with doors include damage to the door material (rotted wood, buckled metal, et cetera). Door hinges which are damaged or poorly secured make doors difficult to open and close and, if not corrected, will lead to damage of the door and the frame. Latching mechanisms which do not work properly impair security. If the door is not properly weather-stripped, unnecessary heat loss is experienced. Frames which are damaged or out of square result in heat loss and doors which may be hard to open and close. Door thresholds which are loose or damaged are unsafe and should be repaired or replaced as necessary.

Storms   Storm doors which do not close properly are ineffective from an energy efficiency standpoint, and may be damaged in strong winds. Auto-closers should be adjusted as necessary. In some cases, the door frame has to be straightened or the door re-hung. Damaged glass should be repaired for safety, security, and heat loss reasons. Damaged screens and storm doors can also be safety concerns and should be repaired or replaced promptly.

Sliding Doors

Sliding glass doors often suffer hardware damage or the track becomes dirty and the doors will not operate easily. On older metal sash sliding doors, the damage to the building interior at floor level can be significant, as a result of condensation and ice build up. The absence of a thermal break in the metal frame leads to a very cold interior metal surface. The cold metal contacts warm moist air in the house. As the moist air is cooled, condensation develops as droplets on the metal frame. The water runs onto the floor, or forms ice temporarily and as it thaws, will melt and run onto the floor. This damages the door sill, floor boards, subfloor and, in severe cases, the joists and header below. Providing an additional sliding door on the exterior will minimize the problem, although this creates a door opening which requires a number of motions to open and close. The preferred solution is, of course, to replace the sliding door system. Typically on these older systems, the hardware is not in good shape in any case.

Damage to the frame is common on sliding doors. This is often caused by excessive force used in opening and closing the door, often necessitated by damaged or poorly adjusted hardware, or a dirty track. Where the guides or rollers have been mechanically damaged, the door will not ride freely.

The weatherstripping on early sliding doors was not high quality, and a good deal of air leakage can be experienced.

When sliding glass doors are installed in a newly created wall opening, a substantial lintel is required above the opening. Where undersized lintels are used, it is common to notice a sag over the sliding doors. Where the lintel is not extended far enough on to the wall beyond the opening at either end, it is possible for the lintel to slide off one end or to crush itself or the studs at the ends. If enough deflection in the lintel takes place, the doors will not operate freely.

Step Up

Ideally, all doors should have at least a six inch step up from the outdoors to the door sill. This is often omitted on sliding doors leading onto a deck, for example. Where this step is not present, snow accumulation on the exterior can leak through the bottom of the door system readily. Where no six inch step-up is noted, good inspection practices and regular maintenance (including snow clearing) are often necessary to prevent serious water damage.

The loss of a seal between double glazed panes on a sliding door is common. This results in a clouding of the glass which may be permanent. Because of the large panes of glass usually involved, this is a relatively expensive problem. Replacement is not a high priority as only a very small loss in energy efficiency is suffered. Replacement is usually undertaken because of the unsightly appearance of the clouded glass. Some door sashes are arranged so that they can he dismantled. Others are manufactured in such a way that this cannot be done. Replacement is, of course, more expensive in the latter case.

► 8.0 FIREPLACES

Fireplaces have been used historically for heating homes and preparing food. Today, fireplaces are primarily recreational. Most fireplaces take more heat away from a home than they provide and, in this sense, they are truly a luxury item. Fireplaces provide radiant heat into a room, but use the warmed house air for combustion. The air that goes up the chimney typically represents more heat loss than the radiant heat gain from the flames. A roaring fire can draw three hundred to four hundred cubic feet of air out of a house every minute. Heatilators, glass doors and outside combustion air intakes all work to reduce the heat loss.

Chimney Draw

There are many types of fireplaces, each with their own advantages. It is not possible to predict which fireplaces will draw well and which will be problems. Some draw well most of the time, but are troublesome under certain wind conditions. There are a number of solutions for poor draw discussed in this section. A rule of thumb to achieve good draw is that the chimney flue area should be one-twelfth the size of the fireplace opening. Where the top of the chimney is less than fifteen feet above the hearth, this is often adjusted to one-tenth.

Safety

Fire safety is a much greater concern than the quality of draw. Fireplace and chimney systems may be unsafe because of poor construction or installation, building settlement, improper usage or poor maintenance. Many safety related items are not visible. Where there is reason for doubt, it is best to engage a fireplace specialist. In any case, fireplace and chimney systems should be inspected and cleaned at least annually.

Foundations and Hearths

8.1 Masonry: Traditional fireplaces include a footing and foundation system which is of the same material as the house foundation. The hearth (the floor of the fireplace) is typically four inches of poured concrete covered with at least one inch of firebrick, stone, slate or tile. The covering on the hearth outside the firebox can be thinner. The hearth itself should extend at least sixteen inches beyond the front of the fireplace and at least eight inches beyond either side.

Masonry Fireboxes

The firebox walls are usually brick, stone or concrete block with a firebrick liner. The liner is typically at least two inches thick on the sides and back, and the total wall thickness should be about eight inches. Where the back of the fireplace is the outside wall of the building, the wall need only be about six inches thick. The mortar joints in the firebrick should be a special refractory mortar and should be as thin as possible. No mortar is required in the firebrick on the hearth, since the bricks are not likely to move out of position.

Some early masonry fireplaces did not include a special firebrick liner. The common brick which was used will eventually break down and this should be replaced with firebrick when necessary,

Metal Fireboxes

Some masonry fireplaces have a metal firebox. In these cases, the walls of the firebox are steel plate. These can be satisfactory, although some fail by bowing or buckling. This is usually a result of inadequate clearance between the metal and the masonry. (A metal firebox, incidentally, should not be confused with a zero clearance fireplace or a fireplace insert. These are discussed elsewhere in this section.) The metal fireboxes have a masonry wall behind them.

Dampers   Masonry fireplaces should include a metal damper. The damper may be operated from outside the fireplace by a handle on the mantle face, or by a lever located inside the firebox. The first arrangement, although not common in modem fireplaces, is slightly more desirable. If a fire is lit with a damper closed inadvertently, the damper can be opened easily when the handle is outside the firebox. The damper handle itself should be two inches from any combustible materials on the surface of the mantle.

To ensure good draft, the damper should be at least six inches above the front of the fireplace opening. The damper opening should be as wide as the firebox, and the damper is usually closer to the front of the firebox than the back. Many dampers are designed so that when the damper is open, the damper itself will deflect down-drafts away from the fireplace.

Problems with dampers include rusting through, becoming jammed or mis-aligned. Perhaps the most serious problem is a missing damper. It is fairly expensive to install a damper where none was allowed for on original construction. Glass doors may be an acceptable alternative.

Smoke   The smoke shelf is located behind the damper and provides a deflection pad for
Shelf   down-drafts and rain or snow. Fireplaces designed for burning coal and most zero clearance fireplaces, for example, do not have a smoke shelf.

Smoke   The smoke chamber is located above the damper and below the chimney. The
Chamber   smoke chamber and chimney are typically brick, stone or concrete block. The smoke chamber is often covered with a special cement parging to provide a smooth surface. The side walls of the smoke chamber are sloped to direct the smoke from the wide damper opening into the narrow chimney flue. The slope of the smoke chamber wall should not be more than forty-five degrees off vertical and should slope evenly from both sides. Brick corbelling is not recommended in a smoke chamber. The smoother the walls of the smoke chamber, the more likely the smoke is to move freely through it,

Chimney   The chimney itself is usually made of the same masonry unit as the fireplace and, since approximately 1950, clay tile liners, roughly 5/8 inch thick, have been provided on the inside of the chimney. The clay tile liners are usually assembled in two or three foot long sections and the joints should be mortared together. It is common practice near the top of the chimney to have a section of clay tile liner suspended on nails two or three inches above the section below. This gap is created so the top piece of clay tile will project the desired distance above the chimney cap. This gap in die liner is not a good practice and will lead to deterioration of the chimney masonry.

Mantles   Fireplace mantles should not have combustible materials within six inches of the fireplace opening. Where there is combustible material above the fireplace opening, and it projects 1-1/2 inches or more out from the surface of the mantle, it should be at least twelve inches above the opening. Many wood mantle shelves violate this rule and may be subject to overheating.

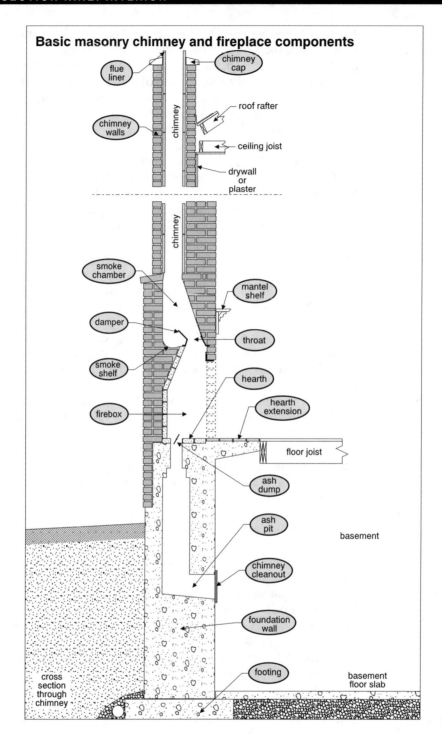

Basic masonry chimney and fireplace components

flue liner

chimney cap

roof rafter

chimney walls

chimney

ceiling joist

drywall or plaster

chimney

smoke chamber

mantel shelf

damper

throat

smoke shelf

hearth

firebox

hearth extension

floor joist

ash dump

ash pit

basement

chimney cleanout

foundation wall

cross section through chimney

footing

basement floor slab

Figure 15. Masonry Fireplace

8.1.1 Ash Dumps: Some fireplaces have a trap door in the hearth to allow cool ashes to be dumped into a pit below the fireplace. The ash pit can be emptied from below. This eliminates the need to sweep ashes into a container and carry them through the house. Ash pits should be separated from combustibles by at least four inches of solid masonry. Missing ash dump doors in fireplace hearths should be replaced prior to using the fireplace.

8.1.2 Outside Combustion Air: Fireplaces have traditionally used warm house air for burning the wood or coal. This is wasteful, since the air has been heated by the furnace or boiler, and the fireplace can draw three hundred to four hundred cubic feet of air out of the house every minute. This air loss may also compete with the furnace or boiler for air, resulting in a dangerous back draft situation. When this happens, air moves down the furnace chimney bringing exhaust gases back into the house. Some of these exhaust gases are poisonous.

A solution which has become popular (and is now required by some codes) is to bring in some outside air for the fireplace. This is accomplished using a screened vent on the building exterior. A length of four inch diameter metal ductwork, insulated to approximately R-7, is used with a damper which can be operated from inside the house. A register is located in front of or inside the fireplace floor. If the register is inside the firebox itself, it should be hooded so that hot embers cannot enter the ductwork. The section of metal ductwork within three feet of the fireplace should be at least two inches away from any combustibles.

This arrangement provides outside air for the fireplace and minimizes the amount of house air lost up the chimney. The use of glass doors, in addition to this outside combustion air intake, essentially cuts the fireplace off from the house altogether.

Problem   Problems with this system include obstruction of the ductwork or outside air intake, especially if the intake is too close to the ground. If the screen is missing or broken on the inlet, it is not unusual for birds or other pests to set up house-keeping in the ductwork. If the damper is inoperative or ill-fitting, considerable heat loss may occur when the fireplace is not is use. On the other hand, if the damper is stuck in the closed position, the system is defeated.

Ductwork which is combustible or is too close to combustible materials is a fire hazard, of course, and uninsulated ductwork will result in added heat loss and possible condensation problems on the outside of the duct. If the register in the fireplace is not hooded, hot embers may enter the ductwork and create a serious fire hazard.

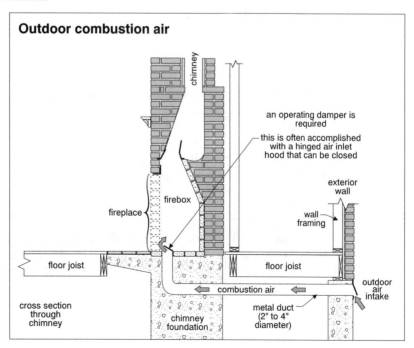

Figure 16. Outside Combustion Air

8.2 Prefabricated Or Zero Clearance Fireplaces: Zero clearance fireplaces have been popular since the 1970's. These are insulated metal units which are very light in comparison to masonry fireplaces. They can be located almost anywhere in a house, since a special foundation is not required.

Despite the name, care must be taken during installation to ensure appropriate clearances from combustibles, as recommended by the manufacturer.

Chimneys

These fireplaces are typically connected to metal chimneys specially designed for this use. A safe installation needs a good connection between the fireplace and chimney, good connection of the chimney sections, and proper extension of the chimney above the roof. The system should be well secured and combustible clearances for the chimney should be maintained.

Dampers and Glass Doors

Zero clearance fireplaces have a damper, but usually have no smoke shelf. Many include a built in heatilator system and some are approved for use with glass doors. Only the glass doors stipulated by the manufacturer may be used.

Inspection

Whether the fireplace is masonry or metal, it is impossible to conduct a complete inspection visually. Some faith must be placed in the manufacturer and installer. Manufactured units which have been approved by the appropriate authorities provide some assurance and, under the best circumstances, the installation is inspected before it is closed in.

8.3 Fireplace Inserts: Many conventional masonry fireplaces have a metal insert added in an effort to increase energy efficiency. These usually include a door on the front and operate much like a wood stove. The units are more energy efficient than open fireplaces and, if property installed, can be quite satisfactory. Many difficulties have been experienced, however, with poor connections between the insert and the original chimney. Very often the damper on the orig- inal chimney has to be removed or permanently opened to install the insert. None of the original masonry of the fireplace may be removed when installing an insert. Inserts are not allowed in zero-clearance fireplaces.

Once the insert is installed, it is very difficult to perform a good inspection, or to clean the chimney properly. Many experts recommend that the insert be removed annually for cleaning, although this is not an easy job.

8.4 Fireplaces Designed For Gas: Many fireplaces installed in the late 19th and early 20th century were designed for use with natural or manufactured gas. These systems typically employ a very small firebox and often have decorative marble, cast iron or ceramic borders around the fireplace opening. These are generally not suitable for conversion to wood-buming fireplaces without major improvements.

New natural gas fireplaces are also available, some of which do not even require a chimney. A natural gas fireplace can sometimes be installed in a masonry fire- place. In some cases, a chimney liner may be necessary. A natural gas fireplace cannot be used for burning wood.

8.5 Fireplaces Designed For Coal: Coal-burning fireplaces were common in the late 1800's and early 1900's. They typically employed cast iron grates with a pull-out drawer in the bottom to remove the ashes. Most units had two dampers and the firebox was both narrow and shallow. Some units had slotted, heavy, cast iron covers available to put over the entire opening.

These fireplaces are often used for burning wood, although most specialists recommend that this not be done without a careful examination of the fireplace and chimney system. Because these units are very small, they are not suitable for most wood fires. The coal-burning system usually included an insert which has to be removed to perform a proper examination. This is beyond the scope of a visual home inspection. These fireplaces are invariably old and should always be inspected by a specialist prior to using them, even for burning coal.

8.6 Roughed-in Fireplaces: Roughed-in fireplaces are common inclusions in modem construction. Often a roughed-in fireplace is provided in the basement. Some municipalities do not allow these to be left open, since a few home owners have tried to use them without building a proper firebox and damper system. A roughed-in fireplace generally means that an opening has been left with a connection to the chimney. It may require $2,000 or more to install an operating fireplace here.

8.7 Non-functional Fireplaces: Many decorative fireplaces look, at first, and even second glance, like working fireplaces. These were particularly popular in houses built from the 1920's to the 1940's. The presence of a decorative fireplace does not mean that a fireplace can be added inexpensively. Decorative fireplaces are not suitable for conversion, although, in some cases, a decorative mantle can be saved and reused. There is usually no chimney associated with a decorative fireplace.

8.8 Wood Stoves: Freestanding wood stoves and fireplaces are common in cottage areas and are often seen in family recreation rooms. A well manufactured and properly installed stove can be a safe and energy efficient system. However, many problems have been experienced with inappropriate installations.

Problems arise with inadequate clearance from combustible materials, and poor connections of the exhaust flue and chimney system. Each manufacturer has specific requirements for their particular product, and it is best to consult the manufacturer's installation guide. Manufacturers will usually provide installation and operating directions, even if the system is already in place.

Many insurance organizations are concerned with wood stove safety, and it may be desirable to have a specialist inspect a wood stove installation. Because of the controlled and relatively slow bum of a wood stove, creosote deposits in chimneys can be a problem. All chimneys should be cleaned regularly, but special attention should be paid to wood stove chimneys.

Listing
Organizations
Wood stoves may be listed by Underwriters Laboratories (UL),Underwriters Laboratories of Canada (ULC), Canadian Standards Association (CSA) or Warnock Hersey, for example. Installation clearances are set out in the listings for these units. Where a listing cannot be found on a unit, the following guidelines are typically used.

Chimney
A masonry chimney or a metal chimney, specially designed for solid fuels should be used. Under normal circumstances, the stove should not share a flue with any other appliance. Under no circumstances should a stove share a flue with an appliance on a different story.

Flue
Flue pipes or breechings (the pipes that join the stove to the chimney) should have no more than ten feet of horizontal run, no more than two ninety degree elbows, supports every three feet, and should have joints which allow condensate to drain into the stove. This last item means that where joints have one sleeve that fits inside another, the lower sleeve should be outside the upper sleeve. The minimum flue slope up from the stove to the chimney is 1/4 inch / foot. The flue/chimney connection should be tightly made with a thimble or flue ring.

The exhaust flue pipe should not extend into the chimney flue opening. Flue pipes should have a melting point above 2,000 degrees F., and should not be made of galvanized steel. The flue pipes should be kept at least eighteen inches from combustibles, including wood-frame walls covered with plaster or drywall.

Floor
Protection
Wood stoves should sit on a concrete floor or a protected wood floor. The wood floor should be protected with a noncombustible pad (sheet metal, for example) which extends eighteen inches beyond the stove door and eight inches beyond the other sides. On top of this should be eight inches of hollow masonry. Usually, two courses of four inch units are used, arranged to allow air circulation. Stoves which sit off the floor can rest on special metal plates with spacers. Masonry units can be omitted.

Combustible
Clearances
Wood stoves should at least be five feet from an oil tank for a furnace. Stoves should be forty-eight inches from combustibles (even if covered by plaster or drywall) on all sides and sixty inches above. Clearances can be reduced if special protection is provided. It should be noted that a four inch brick wall built against a plastered wood-frame wall does not adequately protect the wall and no reduction in required clearances is permitted.

It should be understood that many installations will not meet the clearances indicated above. The original installation instructions may have called for less clearance. Standards have also become more stringent in recent years.

Side and rear clearances can be reduced by two-thirds if the wall is protected by metal sheets spaced out one inch from the wall. A reduction of one-half is acceptable if brick or ceramic is spaced out from the wall one inch.

Some certified wood stoves have combustible clearances as small as eighteen inches on all sides. Add-on heat reclaimers are not permitted on wood stoves.

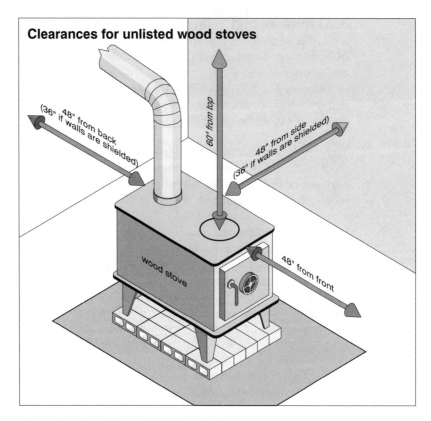

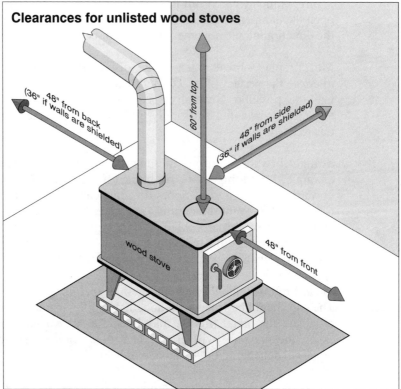

Figure 17. Clearances Required for an Unlisted Stove

8.9 Fireplace and Wood Stove Problems: Fireplaces may be unsafe for a number of reasons. Common problems include cracked hearths (often a result of building or fireplace settlement), deteriorated firebrick, inadequate clearance from combustibles (walls, mantles, lintels, etcetera), openings in the fireplace or chimney (as a result of building settlement, poor construction technique or deterioration of materials). Wherever safety related problems are suspected, a specialist should be engaged.

Hearths

Many fireplace hearths are undersized. They should project sixteen inches out in front of the firebox and eight inches beyond either side. Improvements may or may not be cost-effective, although with small hearths, close attention must be paid to sparks and embers.

Poor Draw

Poor draw on a fireplace may be the result of a chimney which is too short, a flue which is too small, a fireplace opening which is too large, a poorly shaped firebox, a damper which is too small, too low or too far back, a rough surfaced or poorly shaped smoke chamber, an excessive offset in the chimney flue (more than forty-five degrees), the absence of a smoke shelf, or inadequate combustion air. Another simple cause for a smoking fireplace is the fire being too close to the front of the fireplace. Moving the fire back will solve this problem. If the fireplace is too shallow to permit this, the fireplace may have to be rebuilt.

A chimney breast which is too thick may also result in a smoking fireplace. Ideally, the breast should be no more than four inches thick.

A dirty chimney can result in a smoking fireplace because it is difficult to fully open the damper, or the accumulation of debris on the smoke shelf will change the direction of air movement in the chimney.

Most fireplaces break at least some of the rules of good design. The trick is not to create the perfect fireplace, but to correct the most serious flaws as economically as possible. Generally speaking, simple solutions should be tried first, and more substantial work only undertaken if the inexpensive approaches are unsuccessful.

Straightforward solutions include reducing the fireplace opening size (for example, by adding more firebrick on the hearth), extending the chimney upwards, or adding glass doors. In some cases, adding a rain cap on the chimney top will prevent down drafts and cure the problem. Adding combustion air may solve a smoking problem and may also improve the safety of the house, while at the same time, reducing heat loss. Where these do not work, a specialist should be engaged and more extensive work will be required.

Metal Fireboxes

Metal fireboxes should be kept one-half inch to one inch away from masonry. The gap should be filled with noncombustible insulation. Where this gap is not provided, the metal firebox may buckle as it expands during a fire. In some cases, the masonry will crack. The metal and/or masonry may have to be replaced, depending on the advice of a specialist.

Ash Dumps

Fireplaces with ash dumps should have covers. If the cover is missing, hot embers may accumulate in the ash pit. The pit is not intended to be a fireplace and combustible materials near the pit could be ignited. It is not an expensive undertaking to replace the cover.

Zero-Clearance   Unsafe installations of zero clearance fireplaces are common, due to poor connections between components, failure to provide insulation where required, provision of insulation where none is allowed, and/or failure to maintain the needed clearance from combustibles (even zero-clearance fireplaces require clearance from some surfaces). As mentioned earlier, it is often difficult to see these problems once the system has been installed. The absence of a hearth in front of the fireplace is a common problem with these systems. Other hearth problems include undersized or poorly installed hearth systems.

Shared Flues   A fireplace cannot share a chimney flue with any other appliance, including another fireplace. Some older houses were built with shared flues, and it is strongly recommended that in these cases, one of the two appliances be abandoned. A specialist should be consulted to investigate the arrangement and recommend the most inexpensive corrective action. Possible solutions include closing off a second floor fireplace which is not used regularly, replacing the heating system with one which does not require a chimney connection (an electric furnace or a high efficiency gas furnace, for example), or providing a new chimney for one of the appliances.

This situation exists in many attached houses, where back-to-back fireplaces share a chimney flue. This can be an awkward arrangement to detect initially, and to resolve amicably. Another place where this arrangement is commonly seen includes a furnace in the basement, a fireplace in the living room directly above, and a second floor parlor fireplace directly above the living room. Often the chimney will have two flues, despite the presence of three appliances. From a simple visual inspection, it cannot be determined which two appliances share a flue.

The amount of flexibility one has may be limited because heating systems typically have smaller flues than fireplaces. Relocating or changing the heating system may not allow connection of a fireplace into a small flue. Professional advice is required in a situation like this.

Facade Movement   A common problem on modern fireplaces is a masonry facade pulling away from the wall itself. This usually takes the form of rotation of the mantle in towards the room, with the greatest amount of movement at the top. The cause is usually a floor system too weak to carry the weight of the concentrated masonry load without sagging. In most cases, the problem is not serious, but where the tightness of the firebox is compromised, repairs are necessary. Repairs typically include resupporting from below.

► 9.0 PARTY WALLS

Introduction: Party walls or common walls separate two different homes in the same building.

Masonry: Masonry party walls provide relatively good fire protection between the two houses, although very little in the way of acoustic insulation.

Wood-frame: Wood-frame partition walls provide less fire protection, although if properly installed and insulated, can be better from an acoustic standpoint. A great many walls are masonry part of the way up through the house, and wood-frame in the attic.

None in Attic: In some attached houses, there is no wall between the attic areas. This openly communicating space is a less desirable situation in terms of fire protection, of course, than a masonry wall right up to the underside of the roof. Modern construction codes do not permit this arrangement.

► 10.0 BASEMENT LEAKAGE - INTRODUCTION

Basement leakage is the most common problem found in houses; 98% of all basements will leak at some point during their life. While structural damage caused by leakage is very rare, water in the basement can be a major inconvenience and often causes damage to interior finishes and storage. In addition, odors caused by mold, mildew, and lack of ventilation are particularly offensive to some people.

Unfortunately, wet basements cannot be assessed for their severity, frequency, and inconvenience factor during a one time visit. There may or may not be clues that indicate a history of basement dampness. Even if visible, the clues usually do not give an indication of the severity or frequency.

Section 10.1 lists some of the clues that indicate basement dampness. However, the clues are usually inconclusive and can sometimes be misleading. For example, efflorescence forms on basement walls as water migrates through and evaporates, leaving minerals behind. Most people assume that the greater the efflorescence, the more severe the problem. In reality, the drier the air in the basement, the greater the rate of evaporation and hence, the greater the mineral deposits. Therefore, the amount of efflorescence can be increased simply by using a de-humidifier.

Rust, mold and mildew can be caused by moisture penetration into the basement, but can also be caused by condensation forming on foundation walls as hot, humid summer air comes in contact with the cool walls.

Moisture problems are also intermittent. In some houses, water penetration will occur after virtually every rain. In other houses, it will occur only after periods of prolonged rain, and in still others, it will only happen with wind driven rain or during a spring thaw. In most cases however, the resultant damage gives no indication of frequency.

10.1 Identification of Problems

Wall
Repairs

A. Repairs noted on the interior and exterior which may suggest wet basement problems include patching with bituminous materials, cement parging, or any-one of a myriad of waterproofing products. On the exterior, freshly excavated areas may also indicate moisture problem repairs. New sod along the edge of a house would similarly be an indication that exterior water control work may have been undertaken.

Efflorescence
B. Efflorescence is a whitish mineral deposit often seen on the interior of foundation walls. The presence of efflorescence indicates moisture penetration, although it does not tell a great deal about the severity of the problem or whether the problem is active. As water passes through the wall, it dissolves salts in the masonry, concrete or mortar, so that when the water arrives at the wall surface, it contains a good deal of minerals in solution. The crystalline salt deposit, known as efflorescence, is left as water is evaporated off the wall surface. This may be the result of outside water passing through the wall, or water rising up through the wall by capillary action.

Rust
C. Rusty nails in baseboards or paneling, rusted electrical outlet boxes or rusted metal feet on appliances may indicate wet basement problems.

Mildew Stains, Etc.
D. Other indicators include mildew; water stains; sagging cardboard boxes stored on the floor; crumbling plaster or drywall; lifting floor tiles; rotted or discolored wood at or near floor level; storage on skids or boards raised off the floor; dehumidifiers; peeling paint; crumbling concrete.

Lowered Basement Floors
E. When basements are lowered, the exterior drainage tile becomes largely ineffective, because it ends up above the floor level. Houses with lowered basements are much more prone to leaking basement problems. This is anticipated in some cases, and interior drainage tile may be provided below the new basement floor. More information may be found in the "Lowering Basement Floors" discussion and Figure 6 in Section 2.0 of the Structure chapter.

Water Source
When a wet basement problem is identified, it should be determined that the source is not from within the house. A leaking plumbing system, water heater, washing machine, or hot water heating system, may all be confused with basement leakage. Sewers may back up through floor drains, causing basement flooding. During the summer months, condensation on cold water piping can make a localized section of a basement surprisingly wet. Condensation on cool foundation walls can also be mistaken for leakage. This often results in a damp basement odor. These sources obviously require specific and appropriate corrective action.

10.2 Approach: As explained in the Introduction, basement leakage clues, or lack thereof, are not a good indication of the severity or frequency of the leakage problems. Since virtually all basements leak at some point, the question is probably not, "Will the basement leak?" but, "When?".

If one is willing to invest some time and effort, most wet basement problems can be cured or significantly reduced, relatively inexpensively. The dilemma is that some cannot.

Most contractors hired to solve wet basement problems are not prepared to bear this responsibility. They do not want to suggest solutions that usually work, but sometimes don't, even if those suggestions would result in significant savings for the home owner. Therefore, many contractors offer solutions which reduce their likelihood of receiving call-backs. Unfortunately, these solutions tend to be the most disruptive and expensive.

If one cannot afford to experiment (because, for example, the basement is going to be rented out, or is about to be finished), the higher cost but lower risk approach makes sense. However, a less radical and more systematic approach will usually yield a far less expensive solution.

Less than 10% of basement leakage problems are caused by ground water (underground streams and high water tables). Since more than 90% of wet basement problems are caused by surface water (rain or snow) collecting around the building, the surface water issues should be addressed first.

Rather than providing a barrier to water penetration and a collection system for the water, it makes sense to make the water flow away from the building. Even houses with porous foundation walls and no drainage tiles will not leak if the surface water flows away from the house and is not allowed to saturate the soil around the building.

The same philosophy holds true with the water that runs off roof surfaces. If it can be collected and discharged away from the house, it will not contribute to basement dampness.

Once the source of the water has been reduced as much as possible, attention should be directed towards localized cracks and holes in foundation walls which provide little resistance to water penetration. Large scale digging, dampproofing and the installation of drainage tiles should only be contemplated after improving gutters and downspouts, grading, and obvious points of penetration.

The remainder of this chapter deals with these repairs in order of priority. If the steps are taken systematically, most basement dampness problems can be cured or significantly reduced, relatively inexpensively.

10.3 Gutters and Downspouts: Eliminating or minimizing the source of the water is very important with respect to keeping any basement dry. The gutters and downspouts must be complete and free from leakage or overflowing. Downspouts must be well connected and continuous. The downspouts should either discharge into a waste plumbing system below ground, or above grade at least six feet away from the building, depending on land slope, soil porosity, etc.

It is common for downspouts which discharge into an underground waste plumbing system to become obstructed or broken below grade level. This can lead to a large concentration of water just outside the foundation wall which almost inevitably results in leakage. Excavating and repairing or replacing this section of piping is expensive. Often, rearranging the downspout to discharge above grade several feet from the building is a less expensive and equally satisfactory alternative. Where above grade discharge is not practical, the underground drainage system must be repaired.

Localized low areas including basement stairwells, window wells, et cetera, may allow water to collect. Drains should be provided in the bottom of these, and the drain should be kept clear of debris. If necessary, these openings can be covered to prevent water accumulation. There are clear plastic dome covers, for example, available for basement window wells. These do allow light into the basement, although, of course, ventilation is cut off. Grading around window wells is critical.

10.4 Grading Improvements: Regrading the exterior to drain water away from the building rather than toward it is one of the most effective solutions to wet basement problems. Ideally, the ground should slope down away from the house at a rate of one inch per foot for the first six feet. Impervious surfaces like asphalt driveways can slope less, with almost any positive slope being effective.

This work can be expensive where driveways, patios or sidewalks have to be lifted, although in lawn and garden areas, adding some inexpensive topsoil is all that is required. Gravel is not a good material to use, since water will flow through this easily. Well compacted soils which force most of the water to run across the surface are preferred.

Even when basement leakage is not an active problem, good drainage should be ensured during any landscaping or driveway work. Where good grading cannot be achieved, catch basins should be used. Water should be directed toward the basins which should carry water to a drainage system. Catch basins are prone to clogging and frost heaving. Good maintenance is necessary to ensure a dry basement.

Where the grading problem is initiated by a neighboring property, the local building authorities can be of assistance in resolving any problem. City building departments are generally aware of the importance of good grading.

Where drainage cannot be away from the building for six feet or so (because of a neighbor's house, for example) the best compromise is a low area between two buildings which directs water along a trough to a point away from both buildings. If this is not possible, a catch basin may be necessary.

Poor grading is a common problem on newer houses. The backfill around new houses is often not well compacted (for fear of damaging new foundation walls). Over the first few years, the soil will settle, and the grading may have to be improved.

From Inside

10.5 Patching Cracks: Cracks in poured concrete basement walls can sometimes be successfully repaired from the inside. There are several products available to the homeowner in the hardware and building supply stores. Some require the crack to be dry, while others can be applied to wet walls. For these products, it is generally best to widen out the crack into a "V" shape to allow the patching material to bond to the wall.

Epoxy And Polyurethane

Epoxy is usually installed by a contractor and is considered by some to be the best patch material for poured concrete walls. It is, however, only as good as the person who mixes and installs it. Epoxy is different than most patching materials in that it does have structural integrity. A properly installed epoxy patch will never crack again. The wall will fail elsewhere first. If the forces that caused the crack are still present, a crack parallel to the original crack will reform. For this reason, some contractors prefer polyurethane injection, as it stays flexible.

For Minor
Problems Only
It should be understood that patching cracks does not remove the water problem; it only traps it outside the basement. Patching cracks is usually only successful. for minor problems. In many cases, the water will simply find another way in. It is better to prevent water accumulation outside the basement, rather than to try to make a boat out of the basement. The big appeal of patching cracks inside the basement is that it is inexpensive. Interior patching is very seldom effective for hollow block walls.

Outside
Patching
Better
Patching from the outside is more expensive, but more often successful. Covering a patch with a good draining material, such as glass fiber insulation board designed for below grade use, will help protect the patch and keep water away. If the basement is only wet in areas adjacent to obvious cracks, patching may be a practical approach.

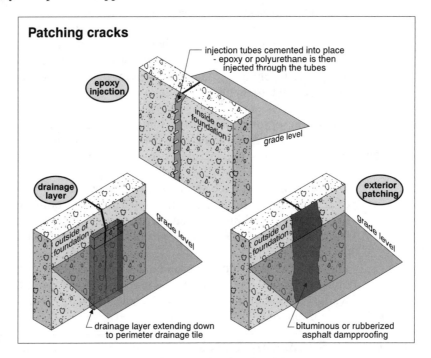

Figure 18. Patching Cracks

10.6 Excavation, Dampproofing and Drainage Tile: When basement leakage cannot be eliminated or minimized by controlling the surface water or by patching, more extensive measures are required.

At this point, it is necessary to excavate on the building exterior, to dampproof the outside walls, and to provide or replace the perimeter drainage tile system.

Drainage Tile   Perimeter drainage tile systems, sometimes incorrectly called weeping tiles, were introduced to residential construction after the first World War. They did not become popular until some time after this. On an older house, even if they are present, they are often obstructed. This drainage tile system was traditionally a four inch clay tile pipe. The piping was laid outside the footing around the perimeter of the house, below the basement floor level. Individual sections of pipe were not connected, with roughly a 1/4 inch space left between each section of pipe. This allowed water to run into the piping if the soil in this area was saturated. The joints were covered at the top with building paper to prevent soil and other debris from getting into the piping system.

This approach was somewhat effective, although over the long term tree roots and debris inevitably found their way into the pipe. The pipes were usually surrounded and covered with gravel to allow water to penetrate quickly to the pipes and be carried away. In older homes, the piping system would discharge into the combination sewer.

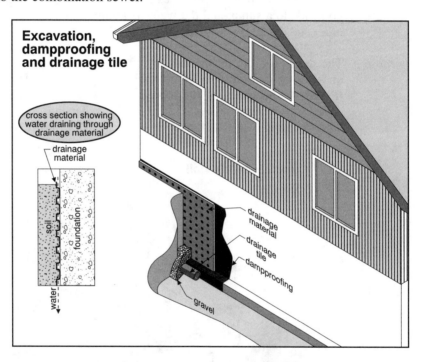

Figure 19. Foundation Drainage Tile

In modern construction, the piping used is perforated plastic, and it is arranged to discharge straight into a storm sewer. The perforated plastic piping which has replaced the clay tile piping is corrugated and very flexible. The perforations are in half of the diameter of the pipe only. The piping should be laid with the holes down.

Often only one or two walls of the basement have to be excavated and so treated, although in severe cases, the entire perimeter must be addressed.

The drainage tile should be laid so that the top of the tile is below the bottom of the floor slab. The drainage tile should be surrounded at the top and sides with at least six inches of gravel or crushed stone. Filter paper above and below the tile will help prevent clogging.

The drainage system should discharge into a storm sewer where possible. Where no sewer is available, the drainage can be above grade well away from the house, if the natural slope allows a gravity flow down to such a point. Where dry wells are permitted, the foundation drain can discharge into a dry well. This is a gravel pit, typically located below the foundation drainage system, at least fifteen feet from the building. This is also called a french drain, and is only suitable where soil conditions will allow drainage out of the well. The water table, of course, must be below the bottom of a dry well. See Figure 20 in the Plumbing section.

Where none of these approaches is possible, the foundation drain system must go inside to a sump, and the water is pumped up and out, into a sewer system or a good distance away from the house.

Dampproofing The dampproofing on the exterior typically involves parging the wall with a one-quarter inch layer of mortar which ideally extends down to the footing. (Parging is not required on poured concrete.) The foundation/footing joint is coved to improve the seal and direct the water into the drainage tile. Next, a dampproofing coat which may be bituminous or plastic, is applied to the wall.

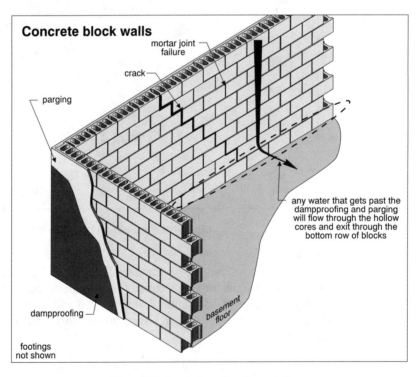

Figure 20. Dampproofing Foundations

*Exterior
Basement
Insulation*

Many experts recommend exterior basement insulation. Rigid glass fiber insulation board designed for use below grade provides good insulation and helps keep the basement dry. Water entering the insulation flows quickly down through it to the drainage tile.

*Drainage
Layer*

As an alternative, a drain layer/membrane can be placed against the exterior walls below grade to allow water to flow freely to the drainage tile.

10.7 Interior Drainage Systems: Because excavating on the exterior is expensive, and almost always leads to disruption of patios, driveways, and landscaping, a less expensive alternative is sometimes employed from the building interior. A roughly ten inch wide strip of the concrete floor is broken up around the inside of the foundation wall. A drainage tile system is installed below the basement floor inside the footings. The water can then be run into a waste sewer system, if gravity permits, or a sump.

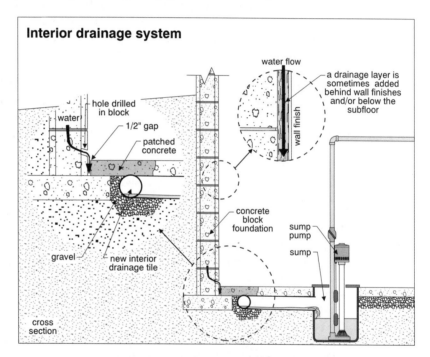

Figure 21. Interior Drainage System

This approach is somewhat less desirable than the exterior approach, since water has no natural inclination to find this drainage tile. Water may accumulate on the outside of the foundations for some time and may leak through the exterior walls before it is carried away by this drainage system on the inside. The water, of course, must pass through the foundation or footing system, or go under the footing to reach this tile. In rare cases, this can undermine the footings.

Also, with no exterior excavation, dampproofing or waterproofing the outside of the foundation wall is not possible. In some cases, holes are drilled through the foundation wall just above the footing to allow water to drain into this tile system.

Incidentally, the tile is typically surrounded by gravel. The cost of this approach is typically one third to one quarter of the cost of exterior work, depending on the difficulties encountered on the outside. There are many cases where this proves satisfactory, although on a case by case basis, it is very difficult to know whether it will work.

10.8 Ground Water Problems: In the very few cases where the problem is ground water rather than surface water, more extensive solutions are required. Normally, houses are not built below the water table. However, the water table may rise intermittently in areas with heavy seasonal rainfall. Changes in neighborhoods as development increases, for example, may lead to changes in the natural water table.

Where the basement floor is below the water table, water constantly pouring into the basement will often be experienced. A drainage tile system and a sophisticated pumping system, perhaps employing dual pumps, is often used. Since the water is constantly present, and pumps are susceptible to either mechanical or electrical failure, a house with this arrangement is always vulnerable to wet basement problems.

Where the presence of water in the soil impairs the ability of the soil to carry a foundation for a new home, a mat or raft foundation may be built. These are one piece heavily reinforced concrete floating foundations. Another option is to build on piles driven deep into the ground. Please refer to the Structure chapter.

Where the water table is higher than a normal basement floor, building without a basement or with only a shallow crawl space is desirable.

10.9 Basement Floor Leakage: Water leakage up through a basement floor slab is usually a result of saturated soil in and around the foundation. This is often accompanied by leakage through the foundation walls, or through the intersection of the foundation wall and the basement floor slab. In severe cases, the hydrostatic pressure can cause the floor slab to heave, although this is more often a result of frost when the house is left unheated during winter.

The corrective actions for basement wall leakage are also appropriate for water penetration through a floor slab. Ideally, the source of the water is eliminated. If this is not possible, the water has to be controlled and diverted to a sump. Original basement floors which were very thin (one inch or less, for example) are sometimes broken up so badly that they are replaced. Gravel fill, four to six inches thick, is usually added before the new slab is poured, and a waterproof membrane (often plastic) may be laid under the new floor. The new floor thickness is ideally three inches, although often the basement headroom in old houses is so restricted that losing another three inches of height is a big sacrifice. As a result, the concrete floor is often thinner.

10.10 Summary: Once the problem is identified as exterior water penetration, the corrective action process would be a step by step approach as follows. First, provide or improve gutters and downspouts as necessary. Second, reslope exterior grading to provide natural drainage of water away from the building. Third, patch any obvious cracks or gaps from the interior. Fourth, excavate and patch the foundations where leakage is localized. While this is being done, it makes sense to see whether perimeter drainage tile is in place and, if so, to determine its condition. A plumber's snake can be fed through the tile to ensure it is clear.

The next step would be to engage a professional to comment on whether an interior drainage tile system below the basement floor may be appropriate, or whether excavation, dampproofing and an outside foundation drainage tile system is appropriate.

The exterior excavation, dampproofing and perimeter drainage tile system may also require the addition of a sump and pump, depending on local drainage characteristics.

If chronic flooding is a problem, it may be wise to contact the city and neighbors to see whether the problem is area wide, or specific to one house. Where the problem is a neighborhood situation, the city will often make efforts to improve surface drainage or to control storm water.

City officials and neighbors can often advise whether the problem is related to surface water or ground water. Areas of high water tables are often well known to the city authorities. (High water table areas, of course, make it difficult for utility people to lay water supply and sewer lines below grade level.)

People offering quick and easy solutions to wet basement problems are to be approached with some skepticism. Some companies utilize an injection process around the house wherein an expandable material such as bentonite clay is used in an effort to fill the voids in the soil around the foundations and prevent water accumulation. Generally speaking, this is not an effective long term solution and, in some cases, there is no noticeable improvement.

By the same token, people jumping to the conclusion that the solution is always expensive and always requires digging, should also be approached with some skepticism.

SAMPLE
REPORT FORMS

► AUTHORIZATION FORM / RECEIPT

Subject Property

Address: _____

_____

Date: _____

Time: _____

Client Information

Name: _____

_____

Mailing Address: _____

_____

Home: _____

Business: _____

Fax: _____

Email: _____

Fee

Base Fee: $ _____

Tax: $ _____

Total Fee: $ _____ payable at the time of the inspection.

Authorization

The Client requests the inspection of the Subject Property **subject to the following limitations and conditions** (including those on the reverse):

The inspection is based on a visual examination of the readily accessible features of the building, and is performed in accordance with the Standards of Practice of the American Society of Home Inspectors enclosed herewith.

The written report provided after the inspection is an opinion of the present condition of the property. The inspection and report are not a guarantee, warranty or an insurance policy.

I have read, understood and accepted the terms of this agreement including the limitations and conditions on the reverse of this page.

Date: _____

Signature of Client or Representative: _____

If representative, please print name: _____

Please refer to the following pages for additional information regarding the scope and limitations of the inspection.

Note: *The inspection report is for the exclusive use of the client named above. No use of the information by any other party is intended.*

Receipt

_____

Payment Received in Full: (signature)

_____

Inspector: (Print Name)

Company

_____

Request

Dear Client: We'd like to know how we did. Please complete and return the short questionnaire on the following page. Thank you.

► ADDITIONAL LIMITATIONS AND CONDITIONS

These items are in addition to limitations and exclusions in the ASHI®
Standards or in the written report

1. The inspection is not technically exhaustive. More comprehensive inspections are available at much greater cost.

2. Without dismantling the house or its systems, there are limitations. Clues and symptoms often do not reveal the severity of problems. Some problems present no clues during the inspection. These will not be identified. For example, we will not find shower stall leaks that occur only when someone is taking a shower. Other conditions are only visible when furniture is moved or carpets are lifted.

3. The purpose of a home inspection is to examine buildings to evaluate the condition of the components and determine whether systems are performing their intended functions. We do not evaluate the quality of indoor air or determine if there are irritants, pollutants, contaminants or toxic materials or organisms in the home including such things as mold or mildew. We may use the visible presence of mold to aid in our evaluation of the building itself, since the moisture that supports mold growth may damage the building components or systems. However, we will not comment on the implications of the presence of mold itself.

4. Emphasis is placed on major expenses. While some minor problems are found when looking for major items, an all-inclusive list of deficiencies will not be provided.

5. Comments on repair costs provide an order-of-magnitude only. Contractors should be contacted for specific quotations.

6. The report is not complete without the Bottom Line, report forms and reference text.

7. We will have no liability to the Client for any claim or complaint if conditions have been disturbed, altered, repaired or replaced or otherwise changed before we have had a reasonable period of time to investigate.

CLIENT QUESTIONNAIRE

We truly appreciate feedback – both good and bad. We would be most grateful if you would take a few minutes to complete this questionnaire and return it. Thank you.

1. Why did you choose us to perform the inspection? Please place two check marks (✓✓) beside the main reason you chose us and one check mark (✓) beside any additional reasons.

a) We have worked for you before ☐

b) We inspected the house you are selling ☐

c) Our yellow pages advertisement ☐

d) Our response to your telephone enquiry ☐

e) Our ability to respond quickly ☐

f) Our brochure ☐

g) Our website ☐

h) You have read one of our books or articles ☐

i) Attended a seminar ☐

j) Saw our advertisement ☐

  Where? _____

k) Newspaper/magazine article ☐

l) Television/radio show ☐

m) Our money-back guarantee ☐

n) Professional status:
  ASHI ☐

o) Referral from:
  friend or relative ☐
  real estate agent ☐
  lawyer ☐
  banker ☐
  other ☐

  Name and Firm

  _____

  _____

2. Please rate the following 1-5 (1 = poor, 5 = excellent)

General satisfaction with us	1	2	3	4	5
Confidence in inspector's ability	1	2	3	4	5
Inspector's communication skills	1	2	3	4	5
Value of service vs. fee	1	2	3	4	5
Our telephone ability	1	2	3	4	5
Usability of The Home Reference Book	1	2	3	4	5
Likelihood of using us next time	1	2	3	4	5

3. Was there anything about our service that you especially liked? *(use reverse side if needed)*

_____

_____

_____

_____

_____

_____

4. Was there anything about our service that you didn't like? *(use reverse side if needed)*

_____

_____

_____

_____

_____

5. Any suggestions for improving our service? *(use reverse side if needed)*

_____

_____

_____

_____

_____

_____

_____

6. Did you buy the house? ☐ Yes ☐ No

7. Optional: fill in or leave blank, as you wish.

Name _____

Phone _____

Email Address _____

Inspection Address _____

_____

Date of Inspection _____

Inspector's Name _____

☐ **I would be happy to serve as a reference if others inquire about the service.**

► SIGNIFICANT ITEMS

Potentially significant expenses (greater than $500/$1000/$_____)over the short term are identified below. This page must not be considered as the complete report. Please read all other forms and appropriate text. Any items marked "0" under time frame should be treated as priority items.

ROOFING

EXTERIOR

STRUCTURE

ELECTRICAL

HEATING

COOLING/HEAT PUMPS

INSULATION

PLUMBING

INTERIOR

► OVERALL RATING

The following rating reflects both the original quality of construction and the current condition of the home, based on a comparison to similar homes.

☐ ☐ ☐ ☐ ☐ ☐ ☐ ☐ ☐

Below Average   Typical   Above Average

_____

_____

_____

_____

_____

Location References:

☐ **NOTE: For the purpose of this report, the front of the house is considered to be facing:**

OR

☐ **NOTE: For the purpose of this report, assume you are standing on the street facing the front door.**

N   S   E   W

F is the front   **LH** is the left
R is the rear   **RH** is the right

EXPLANATION OF CODES FOR REPORT FORMS

REFERENCE	This column identifies the appropriate sections of the text.

TASK

P	provide	I	improve
R	repair or replace	M	monitor
F	further evaluation required		

LOCATION

B	basement	LR	living room
1	first floor	DR	dining room
2	second floor	K	kitchen
3	third floor	Bath	bathroom
CS	crawl space	G	garage
N	north	WR	washroom
E	east	ENS	ensuite
S	south	BR	bedroom
W	west	FR	family room
M	master	LA	laundry area
A	attic	C	central
V	various	T	throughout
F	front of house	LH	left side of house
R	rear of house	RH	right side of house
EX	exterior	O	office or study

Note: the direction the house is assumed to face is noted on the page entitled **Significant Items**.

TIME

0	immediate	2	less than two years
1	less than one year	"X"	less than "X" years
U	unpredictable *(This component could last a few months or several years.)*	D	discretionary item *(Improvements can be made, but are not critical.)*
M	regular maintenance or ongoing	?	if necessary

COST

B	buyer is to perform the work	<	less than
S	third party is to perform the work	>	more than
M	minor cost or regular maintenance item	²	approximately
D	dependent *(Cost will depend on extent of work and approach taken. In some cases, the best approach cannot be determined during a one-time visual inspection.)*		
L	consult local resources or contractor(s) for life cycle and cost information.		

Note: Any figures given are very rough estimates. Several quotations from contractors should be obtained. Our experience has shown that quotes often vary by 300%.

ROOFING, FLASHINGS AND CHIMNEYS

DESCRIPTION

REFERENCE	Asphalt 1.1	Wood 1.2	Slate 1.3	Concrete / Clay 1.4	Asbestos Cement 1.5	Metal 1.6	Corrugated Plastic 1.7	Built Up 1.8	Roll Roofing 1.9	Modified Bitumen 1.10	Other 1.11	Strip When Reroofing 1.12	Vulnerable Areas 1.13	Risk of Ice Damming 1.14
Main Slope														
Second														
Third														
Main Flat														
Second														
Dormer(s)														
Bay(s)														
Porch(es)														
Garage														

3.0 Chimneys:
- ☐ Metal
- ☐ Wood over Metal
- ☐ Stucco over Metal
- ☐ Masonry over Metal
- ☐ Cement Asbestos
- ☐ Masonry
- ☐ Mutual
- ☐ Partially Removed
- ☐ Abandoned
- ☐ None

4.0 Probability of Leakage:
- ☐ High
- ☐ Medium
- ☐ Low

IMPROVEMENT RECOMMENDATIONS   ☐ *NONE AT PRESENT*

Reference | **Limitations**

Roof Inspection By: ☐ Binoculars ☐ Ladder at Edge ☐ Walking on ☐ _____

Roof Inspection Limited / Prevented By: ☐ Snow/Ice ☐ Wet ☐ Gravel ☐ Deck ☐ Solar Panels ☐ Another Building ☐ Trees ☐ Height ☐ No Access ☐ Fragile ☐ Slope ☐ _____

Chimney/Flashing Inspection Limited By: _____

Task | **Location** | **Time**

Ref	Description	Task	Location	Time
1.0	**ROOFING** -1.13 Vulnerable Areas, 1.14 Ice Dams, 1.15 Tree Branches			
	Main Slope - old, damage, patched, cracked, curled, missing, rot, loose, leak			
	Second - old, damage, patched, cracked, curled, missing, rot, loose, leak			
	Third - old, damage, patched, cracked, curled, missing, rot, loose, leak			
	Main Flat - old, damage, patched, blistered, gravel, ponding, seams, scuppers, drains, leak			
	Second - old, damage, patched, blistered, gravel, ponding, seams, scuppers, drains, leak			
	Dormer(s) - old, damage, patched, cracked, curled, missing, rot, leak			
	Bay(s) - old, damage, patched, cracked, curled, missing, rot, leak			
	Porch(es) - old, damage, patched, cracked, curled, missing, rot, leak			
	Garage - old, damage, patched, cracked, curled, missing, rot, leak			
2.0	**FLASHINGS** - replace when re-roofing			
2.1	**Valley** - damage, suspect, rust, patched, holes, leak, overshoots gutter			
2.2	**Hip & Ridge** - damage, suspect, poor, nail heads, split, leak			
2.3	**Sloped/Flat** - damage, suspect, rust, patched, leak			
2.4	**Roof/Wall** - damage, suspect, patched, loose, wood clearance, counter flashing, bay, leak			
2.5	**Chimney** - saddle, damage, suspect, loose, poor, rust, patched, counter flashing, leak			
2.6	**Parapet Wall** - damage, suspect, cap flashing, counter flashing, leak			
2.7	**Plumbing Stack/Mast/Flue** - damage, suspect, pitch pan, patched, rust, leak			
2.8	**Dormer(s)** - damage, suspect, wood clearance, counter flashing, leak			
2.9/10	**Skylight(s)/Solarium** - damage, suspect, curb, counter flashing, caulking, leak			
2.11/12	**Drip Edge/Gravel Stop** - incomplete, rust, improper, add when re-roofing, loose			
2.13	**Roof/Ridge Vent(s)** - damage, suspect, patched, loose, nailheads, leak			
3.0	**CHIMNEY(S)**			
	Main - mortar, spalling, cracked top, 3.1 cap, 3.2 brace, 3.3 height, 3.4 screens, rust			
	Second - mortar, spalling, cracked top, 3.1 cap, 3.2 brace, 3.3 height, 3.4 screens, rust			
	Third - mortar, spalling, cracked top, 3.1 cap, 3.2 brace, 3.3 height, 3.4 screens, rust			

COMMENTS

☐ See Supplementary Section ☐ Inappropriate Materials or Installation

EXPLANATION OF CODES FOR REPORT FORMS

REFERENCE — This column identifies the appropriate sections of the text.

TASK

P	provide	I	improve
R	repair or replace	M	monitor
F	further evaluation required		

LOCATION

B	basement	LR	living room
1	first floor	DR	dining room
2	second floor	K	kitchen
3	third floor	Bath	bathroom
CS	crawl space	G	garage
N	north	WR	washroom
E	east	ENS	ensuite
S	south	BR	bedroom
W	west	FR	family room
M	master	LA	laundry area
A	attic	C	central
V	various	T	throughout
F	front of house	LH	left side of house
R	rear of house	RH	right side of house
EX	exterior	O	office or study

Note: the direction the house is assumed to face is noted on the page entitled **Significant Items**.

TIME

0	immediate	2	less than two years
1	less than one year	"X"	less than "X" years
U	unpredictable *(This component could last a few months or several years.)*	D	discretionary item *(Improvements can be made, but are not critical.)*
M	regular maintenance or ongoing	?	if necessary

COST

B	buyer is to perform the work	<	less than
S	third party is to perform the work	>	more than
M	minor cost or regular maintenance item	2	approximately

D — dependent *(Cost will depend on extent of work and approach taken. In some cases, the best approach cannot be determined during a one-time visual inspection.)*

L — consult local resources or contractor(s) for life cycle and cost information.

Note: Any figures given are very rough estimates. Several quotations from contractors should be obtained. Our experience has shown that quotes often vary by 300%.

EXTERIOR

1.0 Gutters & Downspouts:
- ☐ 1.0 Integral/Built-in
- ☐ 1.1 Aluminum
- ☐ 1.1 Galvanized Steel
- ☐ 1.1 Plastic
- ☐ 1.1 Copper
- ☐ 1.1 Wood
- ☐ 1.2 Discharge Below Grade
- ☐ 1.2 Discharge Above Grade

2.0 Lot Topography:
- ☐ Flat
- ☐ Towards House
- ☐ Away From House
- ☐ Ravine

4.0 Wall Surfaces:
- ☐ 4.1 Brick
- ☐ 4.2 Stone
- ☐ 4.3 Block
- ☐ 4.4 Stucco/EIFS
- ☐ 4.5 Wood Siding
- ☐ 4.6 Metal Siding
- ☐ 4.7 Vinyl Siding
- ☐ 4.8 Wood Shingles
- ☐ 4.9 Asphalt Shingles
- ☐ 4.10 Asbestos Cement Shingles
- ☐ 4.11 Clay Shingles
- ☐ 4.12 Slate
- ☐ 4.13 Insulbrick
- ☐ 4.14 Artificial Stone
- ☐ 4.15 Hardboard or Plywood

9.0 Retaining Walls:
- ☐ Wood
- ☐ Concrete
- ☐ Stone
- ☐ Masonry
- ☐ Other_____

IMPROVEMENT RECOMMENDATIONS ■ NONE AT PRESENT

Limitations:
- ☐ Carpeting/Snow Over Steps/Decks/Porches
- ☐ Restricted/No Access Under Steps/Decks/Porches
- ☐ Grading Not Visible Due To Snow
- ☐ Absence Of Historical Clues Due To New Finishes/Paint/Trim
- ☐ Vines, Shrubs, Trees, etc., Against Building Restricted Inspection
- ☐ Exterior Inspection From Ground Level
- ☐ Storage Against/Inaccessible Wall
- ☐ No Access/Car/Storage In Garage
- ☐ Garage Door Opener Not Tested
- ☐ _____

Reference		Task	Location	Time	
1.0	†**GUTTERS** - old, leak, damage, slope, rust, loose, paint, clogged, end caps, onto roof				
1.2	†**DOWNSPOUTS** - discharge above grade 6ft from house, splash block(s)				
	- loose, connections, clogged, tile, damage, split, extend to lower gutter				
2.0	†**LOT GRADING** - slope away from house, swale, drain, low areas				
2.1	†**Window Wells** - needed when re-grading, damage, wood/soil				
6.0	†**WALKS/PATIOS/DRIVEWAYS** - drain, slope away from house, seal gap at house,				
	- broken up, trip hazard				
6.0	†**LANDSCAPING** - trim trees/shrubs away from building				
3.0	**SOFFIT & FASCIA** - loose, rot, vermin damage, paint, leaks				
3.0	**DOORS, WINDOWS & TRIM** - loose, rot, paint/stain, caulk, rust, threshold, leak, weather strip				
4.16	**Door/Window Flashings** - ineffective, joints, caulk, incomplete, sill				
4.0	**WALL SURFACES** - vines, spalling, mortar, cracks, damage, caulking, utility entrances				
	- pipes, vents, loose, rot, paint/stain, delaminating, EIFS				
4.17	**Wood/Soil Contact** - 8 inch clearance				
4.18	**Foundation Walls** - pointing, parging, spalling, cracks, height above grade				
5.0	**PORCHES, DECKS,** - 5.1 steps, 5.2 railings, 5.3 columns, 5.4 beams,				
	BALCONIES, - 5.5 joists, 5.6 floors, 5.7 roof structure, 5.8 skirt,				
	ENTRANCES - damage, rot, termite, sag, loose, settlement, connection to house				
	& CARPORTS - trip hazard, cracks, paint/stain, spalling				
7.0	†**BASEMENT WALK-OUT** - 7.1 frost, 7.2 steps, 7.3 railing, 7.4 drain,				
	- 7.5 threshold, 7.6 walls, 7.7 cover				
8.0	**GARAGES** - 8.1 detached garage - typical low quality, disrepair				
	- 8.2 fire or gas proofing, 8.3 man-door closer, 8.4 combustible insulation,				
	- 8.5 floor, 8.6 drainage, 8.7 vehicle door, opener, adjustment, auto reverse, rot, damage				
9.0	**RETAINING WALLS** - movement, cracked, rot, weep holes				

COMMENTS

☐ See Supplementary Section ☐ Inappropriate Materials or Installation ☑ See Windows and Doors in Interior Section

---

† Any or all of these items may contribute to **Basement Leakage**. Please see Interior Form.

The Home Reference Book ©

EXPLANATION OF CODES FOR REPORT FORMS

REFERENCE	This column identifies the appropriate sections of the text.

TASK				
P	provide	I	improve
R	repair or replace	M	monitor
F	further evaluation required		

LOCATION				
B	basement	LR	living room
1	first floor	DR	dining room
2	second floor	K	kitchen
3	third floor	Bath	bathroom
CS	crawl space	G	garage
N	north	WR	washroom
E	east	ENS	ensuite
S	south	BR	bedroom
W	west	FR	family room
M	master	LA	laundry area
A	attic	C	central
V	various	T	throughout
F	front of house	LH	left side of house
R	rear of house	RH	right side of house
EX	exterior	O	office or study

Note: the direction the house is assumed to face is noted on the page entitled **Significant Items**.

TIME				
0	immediate	2	less than two years
1	less than one year	"X"	less than "X" years
U	unpredictable *(This component could last a few months or several years.)*	D	discretionary item *(Improvements can be made, but are not critical.)*
M	regular maintenance or ongoing	?	if necessary

COST				
B	buyer is to perform the work	<	less than
S	third party is to perform the work	>	more than
M	minor cost or regular maintenance item	²	approximately
D	dependent *(Cost will depend on extent of work and approach taken. In some cases, the best approach cannot be determined during a one-time visual inspection.)*		
L	consult local resources or contractor(s) for life cycle and cost information.		

Note: Any figures given are very rough estimates. Several quotations from contractors should be obtained. Our experience has shown that quotes often vary by 300%.

STRUCTURE

3.0 Foundations:
- ☐ Poured Concrete
- ☐ Masonry Block
- ☐ Stone
- ☐ Brick
- ☐ Clay Tile
- ☐ Piles and Grade Beams
- ☐ Piers
- ☐ Wood
- ☐ Not Visible/None

4.0 Configuration:
- ☐ Basement
- ☐ Crawl Space
- ☐ Slab-on-Grade

5.0 Floor Construction:
- ☐ Joists
- ☐ Trusses
- ☐ Concrete
- ☐ Not Visible

6.0 Exterior Wall Construction:
- ☐ Masonry
- ☐ Wood Frame
- ☐ Wood Frame, Brick Veneer
- ☐ Log
- ☐ Post and Beam
- ☐ Not Visible

7.0 Roof and Ceiling Framing:
- ☐ 7.1 Rafters/Roof Joists
- ☐ 7.4 Trusses
- ☐ Not Visible

IMPROVEMENT RECOMMENDATIONS ☐ *NONE AT PRESENT*

Limitations — Restricted/No Access To: ☐ Crawl Space ☐ Roof Space ☐ Knee Wall Areas ☐ Attic ☐ Slab-on-grade ☐ _____% Of Foundation Wall Not Visible

☑ Finishes, Insulation And/Or Storage Concealing Structural Components

☐ Crawl Space/Roof Space/Knee Wall Areas/Attic/Inspected From Access Hatch/Entered But Access Was Limited

Reference	Item	Task	Location	Time	
2.0	**FOOTINGS** - settled, too shallow, basement stairwell, suspect, floor lowered				
3.0	**FOUNDATIONS** - cracked, bowed, water damage, height, spalling, settled				
	- further evaluation, prior repairs, typical flaws				
5.0/1	**FLOORS Sills** - not anchored, below grade, rot, damage, suspect				
5.2	**Beams** - sag, end bearing, poorly secured to columns, rot, damage, lateral support, notches				
5.3	**Posts / Columns** - out of plumb, adjust, rot, rust, spall, footing?				
5.4	**Joists** - sag, end bearing, concentrated load, rot, damage, cracks, notches, holes				
5.5	**Stairwell Openings** - header/trimmer undersized, poor connection, support				
5.6/7	**Sub-Flooring / Bridging / Bracing** - poorly secured, sag, edges unsupported, incomplete, rot				
5.8	**Cantilevers** - water damage, excessive span				
5.9	**Floor Trusses** - span, cut				
5.10	**Concrete Floors** - broken up, improperly sloped, suspended, heaved				
6.0/1	**WALLS Masonry** - lean, bow, mortar, cracks, prior repairs				
6.6/7	**Arches / Lintels** - cracks, mortar, masonry, leaning, span, end bearing, rust, prior repairs, spalling				
6.3	**Brick Veneer** - bow, mortar, cracks, weep holes, prior repairs				
6.2	**Wood-Frame (Studs)** - warped, concentrated loads, bracing, rot, sagging lintels, leans				
6.4/5	**Log / Post & Beam** - gaps, settling, rot, damage, checking, buckling				
7.0/1	**ROOFS Rafters** - span, spreading, sagging, split, rot				
7.2/3	**Collar Ties / Knee Walls** - lateral support, securement, location				
7.4	**Roof Trusses** - span, braces missing, uplift, cut				
7.5	**Roof Sheathing** - edge support, delaminating, sag, rot, mildew, condensation, water stains				
8.0	**CHIMNEYS** - leaning, mortar, cracks, incomplete, firestops				
9/10.0	**TERMITE / INSECT DAMAGE** - treatment/further investigation recommended				
	- wood/soil contact, prior treatment				
12.0	**FIRE DAMAGE** - floor, wall, attic				

COMMENTS

☐ See Supplementary Section ☐ Inappropriate Materials or Installation

EXPLANATION OF CODES FOR REPORT FORMS

REFERENCE	This column identifies the appropriate sections of the text.

TASK				
	P	provide	**I**	improve
	R	repair or replace	**M**	monitor
	F	further evaluation required		

LOCATION				
	B	basement	**LR**	living room
	1	first floor	**DR**	dining room
	2	second floor	**K**	kitchen
	3	third floor	**Bath**	bathroom
	CS	crawl space	**G**	garage
	N	north	**WR**	washroom
	E	east	**ENS**	ensuite
	S	south	**BR**	bedroom
	W	west	**FR**	family room
	M	master	**LA**	laundry area
	A	attic	**C**	central
	V	various	**T**	throughout
	F	front of house	**LH**	left side of house
	R	rear of house	**RH**	right side of house
	EX	exterior	**O**	office or study

Note: the direction the house is assumed to face is noted on the page entitled **Significant Items**.

TIME				
	0	immediate	**2**	less than two years
	1	less than one year	**"X"**	less than "X" years
	U	unpredictable *(This component could last a few months or several years.)*	**D**	discretionary item *(Improvements can be made, but are not critical.)*
	M	regular maintenance or ongoing	**?**	if necessary

COST				
	B	buyer is to perform the work	**<**	less than
	S	third party is to perform the work	**>**	more than
	M	minor cost or regular maintenance item	**^{2}**	approximately
	D	dependent *(Cost will depend on extent of work and approach taken. In some cases, the best approach cannot be determined during a one-time visual inspection.)*		
	L	consult local resources or contractor(s) for life cycle and cost information.		

Note: Any figures given are very rough estimates. Several quotations from contractors should be obtained. Our experience has shown that quotes often vary by 300%.

ELECTRICAL

DESCRIPTION

2.1/2/3 Service Entrance Cable:
- ☐ Copper ☐ Overhead
- ☐ Aluminum ☐ Underground
- ☐ Not Visible

2.4/5 Service Size:
____/____/____ Amps (240Volts)

2.6 Main Disconnect/Service Box:
Rating____/____/____Amps
- ☐ Fuses ☐ Breakers
- Location:_____

2.7 System Grounding
- ☐ Water Pipe ☐ Copper
- ☐ Ground Rods ☐ Aluminum
- ☐ Ufer/Other ☐ Not Visible

3.0 Distribution Panel
Rating____/____/____Amps
- ☐ Fuses ☐ Breakers

3.2 Auxiliary Panel(s)
- ☐ Fuses ☐ Breakers
- Location(s):_____

4.0 Distribution Wire:
- ☐ Metallic Sheathed
- ☐ Non-metallic Sheathed
- ☐ Copper ☐ Aluminum
- ☐ Aluminum to Major Appliances
- ☐ Knob-and-Tube Copper
- ☐ Copper Clad Aluminum

5.2 Outlets:
- ☐ Grounded ☐ Ungrounded

Number:
- ☐ Minimal ☐ Typical ☐ Upgraded

5.3 Arc/Ground Fault Circuit Interrupter:
- ☐ Panel
- ☐ Outside
- ☐ Bathrooms
- ☐ Garage
- ☐ Whirlpool
- ☐ Kitchen
- ☐ Basement
- ☐ Other_____
- ☐ None

IMPROVEMENT RECOMMENDATIONS ☐ *NONE AT PRESENT*

Power Off: ☐ Throughout ☐ In Some Areas
☐ Restricted/No Access To_____
☐ System Ground Not Visible/Accessible ☐ Fuse Block(s) Not Pulled
☑ Concealed Electrical Components Not Inspected ☐ Main Disconnect Cover Not Removed

Reference	Limitations		Task	Location	Time	
2.1/2/3		**SERVICE Entrance** - damage, clearance, seal at wall/meter, height, loose				
		- drip loop, frayed, exposed neutral				
2.4/5		**Larger Service** - if lifestyle requires it				
2.6		**Service Box** - undersized, corrosion, overheated, damage				
2.7		**SYSTEM GROUNDING** - ineffective, meter bypass, spliced, clamp, electrode(s)				
3.1		**SERVICE PANEL** - damage, loose, obsolete, rust, double-taps, crowded, location				
3.1		**Panel Overcurrent Protection** (undersized panel)				
3.2		**Auxiliary or Larger Panel** - doubled-taps, feed wire, crowded, grounding, ground/neutral joined, miswired				
3.3/1.11		**Fuses / Breakers** - damage, loose, overfused, 15 amp for branch circuits, fuse block				
3.4/5		**240 Volt Circuits/Linking**				
3.6		**Panel Wires** - damage, overheated, loose				
3.7/8		**Panel (Dead Front) Cover Plate / Unprotected Panel Openings** - covers, fuses				
3.9/11		**Abandoned Wire in Panel / Connections in Panel**				
3.10		**Access to Panel**				
4.1		**BRANCH CIRCUIT WIRING** - damage, loose, exposed, support, strain relief				
		ducts/piping, undersized, extension cord, abandoned, exterior wiring				
4.2		**Overloaded Circuits** - more branch circuits				
4.3		**Dedicated Circuits** - furnace, fridge, water heater, range, dryer, A/C				
4.4		**Knob-and-Tube** - connections, damaged, brittle, suspect, replace when renovating				
4.5		**Aluminum** - special connectors, overheating, outlets, panel, loose, antioxidant				
5.1		**Lights / Ceiling Fans** - inoperative, pot lights, damage, loose, exposed wires/bulbs				
5.2		**Outlets** - number, loose, damage, inoperative, miswired, worn, overheating				
5.2.2		**Ungrounded Outlets** - 3-prong, fill ground slot, GFCI				
5.2.3		**Split Receptacles** - link				
5.2.4		**Reversed Polarity Outlets**				
5.3		**Arc/Ground Fault Circuit Interrupters** - test faulty, inoperative, desirable				
5.4		**Switches** - damage, loose, obsolete, inoperative, location				
5.5		**Junction Boxes** - missing, loose, exposed wires, crowded				
5.6		**Cover Plates** - damage, outlets, switches, boxes				

COMMENTS

☐ See Supplementary Section   ☐ Inappropriate Materials or Installation

☑ All recommendations are safety issues – Treat them as high priority

EXPLANATION OF CODES FOR REPORT FORMS

REFERENCE		This column identifies the appropriate sections of the text.

TASK

P	provide		**I**	improve
R	repair or replace		**M**	monitor
F	further evaluation required			

LOCATION

B	basement		**LR**	living room
1	first floor		**DR**	dining room
2	second floor		**K**	kitchen
3	third floor		**Bath**	bathroom
CS	crawl space		**G**	garage
N	north		**WR**	washroom
E	east		**ENS**	ensuite
S	south		**BR**	bedroom
W	west		**FR**	family room
M	master		**LA**	laundry area
A	attic		**C**	central
V	various		**T**	throughout
F	front of house		**LH**	left side of house
R	rear of house		**RH**	right side of house
EX	exterior		**O**	office or study

Note: the direction the house is assumed to face is noted on the page entitled **Significant Items**.

TIME

0	immediate		**2**	less than two years
1	less than one year		**"X"**	less than "X" years
U	unpredictable *(This component could last a few months or several years.)*		**D**	discretionary item *(Improvements can be made, but are not critical.)*
M	regular maintenance or ongoing		**?**	if necessary

COST

B	buyer is to perform the work		**<**	less than
S	third party is to perform the work		**>**	more than
M	minor cost or regular maintenance item		**≈**	approximately
D	dependent *(Cost will depend on extent of work and approach taken. In some cases, the best approach cannot be determined during a one-time visual inspection.)*			
L	consult local resources or contractor(s) for life cycle and cost information.			

Note: Any figures given are very rough estimates. Several quotations from contractors should be obtained. Our experience has shown that quotes often vary by 300%.

HEATING

Fuel: ☐ Gas ☐ Electricity   **7.0 Chimney Liner:**   **8.0 Efficiency:**
☐ Oil ☐ Wood   ☐ None ☐ Metal   ☐ Conventional ☐ High
(for Wood Stoves, see Interior 8.0)   ☐ Clay ☐ Not Applicable   ☐ Mid ☐ _____

2.0 ☐ **Electric Heaters**   ☐ Cement ☐ Not Visible
3.0 ☐ **Furnace**   ☐ Required ☐ Required for   **9.0 Capacity:**
4.0 ☐ **Boiler**   **17.0** ☐ **Steam Boiler**   ☐ Not Required   Conversion/   (input/output) ____/____/____ x 1000 BTU/hr
5.0 ☐ **Conversion to Forced Air**   Upgrade   Approx. Age: ____/____/____ yrs. old
6.0 ☐ **Conversion from Oil to Gas**
15.9 ☐ **Hot Water Radiant Heat**
15.10 ☐ **Electric Radiant Heat**   **10.0 Failure Probability:**
18.0 ☐ **Combination Heating System**   ☐ High   ☐ Medium   ☐ Low
Main Fuel Shut Off Value at _____

14.24 ☐ **Heat Recovery Ventilator**

IMPROVEMENT RECOMMENDATIONS   ☐ *NONE AT PRESENT*

		Data Plate: ☐ Missing ☐ Not Legible ☐ Incomplete ☐ Chimney Clean-out Not Opened			

Data Plate: ☐ Missing ☐ Not Legible ☐ Incomplete   ☐ Chimney Clean-out Not Opened
16.1 ☐ System Shut Off/Inoperative ☐ Oil Tank Not Visible   ☑ Radiator/Zone Valves Not Tested
16.2 ☐ Summer Test Procedure   ☑ Heat Loss Calculations Not Done
16.3 ☐ A/C or Heat Pump Operating   ☑ Safety Devices Not Tested
☐ Heat Exchanger Not Visible/Inaccessible   ☐ Circulating Pump Not Tested

Reference		Task	Location	Time	
	COMBUSTION SYSTEM				
11.0	**Gas Piping** - leaks, material, support				
14.20	**Oil Tank** - leak, abandoned, oil piping, filter, location				
14.3/4	**Oil Burner / Primary Control** - adjustment				
14.2/15	**Gas Burner / Gas Valve** - adjustment, rust, flashback, leak				
14.6/7	**Pilot & Thermocouple / Pilotless Ignition**				
14.16/12	**Heat Shield / Refractory** - damage, exhaust gases				
14.1/10	**Exhaust Flue / Barometric Damper** - rust, connections, slope, inoperative, exhaust gases, plastic				
14.17/18	**Chimney / Liner / Clean-out** - dirty, obstructed, further investigation				
14.5/11	**Combustion Air / Clearance from Combustibles** – inadequate				
14.8/9	**Vent Damper / Induced Draft Fan** - inoperative, service				
14.13/14	**Condensate Line / Pump** - leak, dirty				
14.19	**Thermostat** - damaged, location, adjustment, loose				
10.0/12.1	**FURNACE** - heat exchanger, rust, suspect, old, inoperative, service, retrofit				
12.3	**Blower / Motor** - noisy, dirty, adjust belt				
12.4	**Humidifier** - location, adjustment, leak, dirty, damper, inoperative, drained, not tested				
12.5/6	**Air Filter / Electronic Filter** - dirty, inoperative, service, damaged				
12.7	**Fan / Limit Switch** - adjustment				
12.8	**Electric Plenum Heater** - inoperative				
15.7	**Motorized Dampers** - adjustment, inoperative				
15.1/2	**Supply / Return Ducts & Registers** - number, location, connections, rust, obstructed - balance, damaged, see 13.0 in Cooling/Heat Pumps				
13/17.0	**BOILER - Hot Water / Steam** - old, inoperative, service, leak				
13.3/4	**Expansion Tank / Relief Valve** - leak, waterlogged, discharge				
13.5/6	**Pressure Reducing Valve / Back-flow Preventer** - leak, adjustment				
13.2/7	**High Temp. Limit / Low Water Cut-out** - leak, adjustment				
13.8/9	**Isolating Valves / Circulating Pump** - leak, noisy, inoperative				
15.3/4	**Radiators / Baseboards / Valves** - leak, corrosion				
15.5/6	**Bleed Valves / Piping** - leak, corrosion				
15.8/9	**Zone Valves / Radiant Heat**				
18.0	**Combination Heating System** - undersized, leaks, water temp				
14.23	**ELECTRIC Heaters** - inoperative, rust				
14.21/22	**Elements & Wiring / Fuses & Breakers** - safety, overfusing, exposed, burned, melted				
15.10	**Electric Radiant Heat** - inoperative				
14.24	**Heat Recovery Ventilator** - dirty, duct connection, intake, exhaust, flow collars				

COMMENTS

☐ See Supplementary Section   ☐ Inappropriate Materials or Installation

Supply Temp: _____/_____/_____   Return Temp: _____/_____/_____   ΔT: _____/_____/_____

EXPLANATION OF CODES FOR REPORT FORMS

REFERENCE	This column identifies the appropriate sections of the text.

TASK

P	provide	I	improve
R	repair or replace	M	monitor
F	further evaluation required		

LOCATION

B	basement	LR	living room
1	first floor	DR	dining room
2	second floor	K	kitchen
3	third floor	Bath	bathroom
CS	crawl space	G	garage
N	north	WR	washroom
E	east	ENS	ensuite
S	south	BR	bedroom
W	west	FR	family room
M	master	LA	laundry area
A	attic	C	central
V	various	T	throughout
F	front of house	LH	left side of house
R	rear of house	RH	right side of house
EX	exterior	O	office or study

Note: the direction the house is assumed to face is noted on the page entitled **Significant Items**.

TIME

0	immediate	2	less than two years
1	less than one year	"X"	less than "X" years
U	unpredictable *(This component could last a few months or several years.)*	D	discretionary item *(Improvements can be made, but are not critical.)*
M	regular maintenance or ongoing	?	if necessary

COST

B	buyer is to perform the work	<	less than
S	third party is to perform the work	>	more than
M	minor cost or regular maintenance item	$\approx$	approximately
D	dependent *(Cost will depend on extent of work and approach taken. In some cases, the best approach cannot be determined during a one-time visual inspection.)*		
L	consult local resources or contractor(s) for life cycle and cost information.		

Note: Any figures given are very rough estimates. Several quotations from contractors should be obtained. Our experience has shown that quotes often vary by 300%.

COOLING/HEAT PUMPS

DESCRIPTION ☐ NONE

1.0 Air Conditioning:
- ☐ 1.1 Air Cooled
- ☐ 1.2 Water Cooled
- ☐ 1.3 Independent System
- ☐ 1.4 Gas Chiller

2.0 Heat Pump:
- ☐ 2.1 Air Source
- ☐ 2.2 Auxiliary Heat
- ☐ 2.3 Ground/Water Source
- ☐ 2.4 Independent Unit

3.0 Cooling Capacity:
_____/_____/_____ x 1,000 BTU/hr

4.0 Failure Probability:
- ☐ High
- ☐ Medium
- ☐ Low

5.0 Approx. Compressor Age:
_____/_____/_____ yrs old

19.0 House Fan: ☐

20.0 Evaporative Cooler: ☐
Motor:
- ☐ One Speed
- ☐ Two Speed

Roof Jack Condition:
_____

Damper Location:
_____

IMPROVEMENT RECOMMENDATIONS ☐ NONE AT PRESENT

Data Plate: ☐ Missing ☐ Not Legible ☐ Incomplete ☐ Not Found ☐ System Shut Off/Inoperative ☐ Restricted Access ☐ Outdoor Coil Covered

Outdoor Temperature Prevented Testing in: ☐ Cooling Mode ☐ Heating Mode ☑ Heat Gain and Heat Loss Calculations Not Done ☐ House Fan Not Tested ☑ Window A/C Excluded

Reference	Limitations		Task	Location	Time	
1.0	**AIR CONDITIONING** - undersized?, old, service					
2.0	**HEAT PUMP** - undersized?, old, service					
2.3	**Ground/Water Source** - buried piping, supply well, discharge well, suspect					
5.0	**Compressor** - old, inoperative, noisy					
6.0	**Plenum / Indoor Coil** - dirty, corroded, frost, temperature drop - too great, too small					
7.0	**Outdoor Coil** - dirty, iced up, not level, fin damage					
8.0	**Water Cooled Coil** - leak					
9.0	**Outdoor Fan** - noisy, inoperative, damage, obstructed					
10.0	**Condensate Tray / Line / Pump** - leak, stains, blocked, inoperative, trap					
11.0	**Refrigerant Lines** - leak, damage, corrosion, insulation missing, seal at plenum/wall					
12.0	**Indoor Fan** - dirty, noisy, undersized?, vibration, adjustment					
13.0	**Ductwork** - undersized?, disconnected, obstructed, dirty, rust, support, incomplete, humidifier damper, balancing, damaged					
14.0	**Attic Ductwork Insulation** - damage, incomplete					
15.0	**Supplemental Cooling** - if necessary					
16.0	**Attic Drip Pan** - leaking, missing, common drain - **drain line** - missing, disconnected					
17.0	**Water Lines** - supplied from pool, leak, damage					
18.0	**Thermostat** - damaged, location, adjustment, loose					
19.0	**HOUSE FAN** - old, inoperative, vent outside, wiring					
20.0	**EVAPORATIVE COOLER - motor, connection, wiring, pump**					
	- spider tubes, clips, bleeder, water line, air gap					
	- fan, tray, housing, roof jack, damper					
	- old, leak, loose, inoperative, rust					

COMMENTS

☐ See Supplementary Section ☐ Inappropriate Materials or Installation

_____

_____

_____

_____

_____

_____

Supply Temp: _____/_____/_____   Return Temp: _____/_____/_____   ΔT: _____/_____/_____

EXPLANATION OF CODES FOR REPORT FORMS

REFERENCE	This column identifies the appropriate sections of the text.

TASK

P	provide	**I**	improve
R	repair or replace	**M**	monitor
F	further evaluation required		

LOCATION

B	basement	**LR**	living room
1	first floor	**DR**	dining room
2	second floor	**K**	kitchen
3	third floor	**Bath**	bathroom
CS	crawl space	**G**	garage
N	north	**WR**	washroom
E	east	**ENS**	ensuite
S	south	**BR**	bedroom
W	west	**FR**	family room
M	master	**LA**	laundry area
A	attic	**C**	central
V	various	**T**	throughout
F	front of house	**LH**	left side of house
R	rear of house	**RH**	right side of house
EX	exterior	**O**	office or study

Note: the direction the house is assumed to face is noted on the page entitled **Significant Items**.

TIME

0	immediate	**2**	less than two years
1	less than one year	**"X"**	less than "X" years
U	unpredictable *(This component could last a few months or several years.)*	**D**	discretionary item *(Improvements can be made, but are not critical.)*
M	regular maintenance or ongoing	**?**	if necessary

COST

B	buyer is to perform the work	**<**	less than
S	third party is to perform the work	**>**	more than
M	minor cost or regular maintenance item	^{2}	approximately
D	dependent *(Cost will depend on extent of work and approach taken. In some cases, the best approach cannot be determined during a one-time visual inspection.)*		
L	consult local resources or contractor(s) for life cycle and cost information.		

Note: Any figures given are very rough estimates. Several quotations from contractors should be obtained. Our experience has shown that quotes often vary by 300%.

INSULATION

DESCRIPTION

Note:
Adding insulation to a home is an improvement rather than a repair. Please read Section 19.0.

REFERENCE	Main Attic	Second Attic	Third Attic	Main Flat	Second Flat	Cathedral / Sloped	Knee Walls	Wood-Frame Walls	Wood-Frame Walls (Addition)	Masonry Walls	Masonry Walls (Addition)	Basement Walls	Crawl Space (Walls)	Crawl Space (Floor Above)	Floor Above Porch / Garage	Log Walls
	A	A	A	B	B	C	E	F	F	G	G	I/J	K	K/L	L	H
2.0 Existing Amount (R-Value / Depth)																
3.0 Glass Fiber																
4.0 Mineral Wool																
5.0 Cellulose																
6.0 Vermiculite																
7.0 Wood Shavings																
8.0 Plastic / Foam Board																

13.0 Air / Vapor Barrier
- ☐ Plastic
- ☐ Kraft Paper
- ☐ Not Visible
- ☐ None Found
- ☐ _____

15.0 Roof Ventilation
- ☐ Ridge Vent
- ☐ Roof Vent
- ☐ Gable Vent
- ☐ Soffit Vent
- ☐ Fascia Vent
- ☐ None Found
- ☐ Power Ventilator
- ☐ _____

15.0 Crawl Space Ventilation
- ☐ Wall Vents
- ☐ Into Basement
- ☐ None Found
- ☐ _____

IMPROVEMENT RECOMMENDATIONS ☐ NONE AT PRESENT

☐ 10 / 11.0 Access Not Gained to: Attic/Roof Space /Wall Space/Crawl Space Knee Wall Areas/Floor Space

☑ Walls Spot Checked Only   ☑ Continuity of Air/Vapor Barrier Not Verified   ☐ Power Ventilator Not Tested
☐ Attic/Crawl Space Viewed from Access Hatch/Entered But Access Was Limited

Reference	Limitations		Task	Location	Time	
	A	**ATTIC - insulation** - amount, wet, compressed, voids				
13.0		- **air/vapor barrier** - incomplete, wrong place, damage				
15.0		- **ventilation** - amount - roof, soffit, ridge				
		- obstructed - roof, soffit, gable, baffle				
		- condensation, mildew, rot, ice dams, condensation				
		- power ventilator inoperative, suspect				
		Access Hatch - insulation, weather strip, fit				
B/C		**FLAT / CATHEDRAL ROOF - insulation** - amount, wet, condensation				
		- **ventilation** - suspect				
D		**SKYLIGHT WELLS - insulation** - loose, incomplete				
E		**KNEE WALLS - insulation** - incomplete, falling, damage				
13.0		- **air/vapor barrier** - wrong place, damage, incomplete				
F/G/H		**WALLS - insulation**				
I/J/K		**BASEMENT / CRAWL SPACES - insulation** - amount, incomplete, damage, falling, rim joists				
14.0		- **moisture or air/vapor barrier** - incomplete, damage, wrong place				
15.0		- **ventilation** - obstructed, leak, rot, mildew				
L		**FLOORS ABOVE UNHEATED AREAS - insulation** - loose, fallen, incomplete, damage				
14.0		- **air/vapor barrier** - wrong place				
M		**PIPES IN UNHEATED AREAS - insulation**, location, heating cables				
N/O		**DUCTWORK IN UNHEATED AREAS - insulation**, condensation, rust, damage				
16.0		**Vent Exhaust Fan Outside**				
17.0		**Exposed Plastic/Foam Insulation** - fire hazard, cover, remove				
18.0		**Recessed (Pot) Lights** - check/remove insulation - fire hazard				

COMMENTS

☐ See Supplementary Section   ☐ Inappropriate Materials or Installation

☑ See Comments on Page 3 of text re: Caulking and Weatherstripping. Please read Section 1.0 - Current Standards.

EXPLANATION OF CODES FOR REPORT FORMS

REFERENCE		This column identifies the appropriate sections of the text.		

TASK	P	provide	I	improve
	R	repair or replace	M	monitor
	F	further evaluation required		

LOCATION	B	basement	LR	living room
	1	first floor	DR	dining room
	2	second floor	K	kitchen
	3	third floor	Bath	bathroom
	CS	crawl space	G	garage
	N	north	WR	washroom
	E	east	ENS	ensuite
	S	south	BR	bedroom
	W	west	FR	family room
	M	master	LA	laundry area
	A	attic	C	central
	V	various	T	throughout
	F	front of house	LH	left side of house
	R	rear of house	RH	right side of house
	EX	exterior	O	office or study

Note: the direction the house is assumed to face is noted on the page entitled **Significant Items**.

TIME	0	immediate	2	less than two years
	1	less than one year	"X"	less than "X" years
	U	unpredictable *(This component could last a few months or several years.)*	D	discretionary item *(Improvements can be made, but are not critical.)*
	M	regular maintenance or ongoing	?	if necessary

COST	B	buyer is to perform the work	<	less than
	S	third party is to perform the work	>	more than
	M	minor cost or regular maintenance item	^{2}	approximately
	D	dependent *(Cost will depend on extent of work and approach taken. In some cases, the best approach cannot be determined during a one-time visual inspection.)*		
	L	consult local resources or contractor(s) for life cycle and cost information.		

Note: Any figures given are very rough estimates. Several quotations from contractors should be obtained. Our experience has shown that quotes often vary by 300%.

PLUMBING

DESCRIPTION

1.1.1 Service Piping into House:
- ☐ Lead
- ☐ Copper
- ☐ Plastic
- ☐ Galvanized Steel
- ☐ Not Visible

1.4 Supply Piping in House:
- ☐ Galvanized Steel ☐ Plastic
- ☐ Copper ☐ Brass
- ☐ Not Visible

1.4.1 Water Flow (Pressure): ☐ Functional
- ☐ Above Average ☐ Below Average
- ☐ Typical for Neighborhood _____

1.6 Water Heater:
- ☐ Combination System (see Heating 18.0)
- ☐ Conventional ☐ Induced Draft ☐ Tankless/Indirect
- ☐ Electric ☐ Gas ☐ Oil ☐ _____
- Estimated Age: _____ / _____ yrs
- Failure Probability ☐ high ☐ med. ☐ low
- Tank Capacity _____ / _____ gallons

1.7 ☐ Hot Water Circulating System

2.3 Waste Piping in House:
- ☐ Galvanized Steel ☐ Cast Iron
- ☐ Plastic ☐ Lead
- ☐ Copper ☐ Not Visible

2.7 ☐ Solid Waste Pump
2.8 ☐ Sump Pump
2.9 ☐ Laundry Tub Pump

Main Shut Off Valve at_____

IMPROVEMENT RECOMMENDATIONS ☐ *NONE AT PRESENT*

Limitations
- ☐ Water Shut Off/Winterized ☐ Main Valve Not Located ☐ Gas Shut Off ☐ Septic System Not Inspected
- **Fixtures Not Tested/Not in Service:** ☐ Water Heater ☐ Toilet ☐ Sink ☐ Basin ☐ Bathtub ☑ Hot Tub
- ☑ Tub/Sink Overflows Not Tested ☐ Whirlpool Bath ☐ Sauna ☐ Shower ☐ Bidet ☐ Laundry Tub
- ☑ Water Treatment Equipment Not Inspected ☐ Restricted/No Access to:_____
- ☑ Concealed Plumbing Not Inspected ☑ Isolating/Relief Valves & Main Shut-Off Valve Not Tested

Reference		Task	Location	Time	
1.1	**SUPPLY- Public** - piping to house, leak, pressure regulator, pressure/flow, lead				
1.2	**Private - pump, tank** - leak, waterlogged, rust, relief valve				
1.3/5	**Main Shut Off Valve / Isolating Valve** - leak, damaged, handle, meter				
1.4	**Piping** - leaks, freezing, noise, rust, cross connections, support, pressure/flow				
	- steel, lead, polybutylene				
1.6	**Water Heater** - wiring, combustion air, controls, valve, leak, drip pan, old				
	- Tank - rust, leak, soot, relief valve, discharge tube - reduced, extend, location				
	- Exhaust Flue / Damper / Draft Hood - slope, rust, connections, size, support				
	- location, clearance from combustibles, exhaust gases, aluminum				
1.7	**Circulating System** - inoperative, pump				
4.0	**Gas Piping** - leaks, material, support, rust, bonding, installation				
2.1/.2	**WASTE - Public / Private** - odor, backup, clean out, unsealed openings				
2.3	**Piping** - leaks, slope, freezing, obstructions, replace lead/steel when renovating, rust, support				
2.4/5	**Trap/Tail Piece/Floor Drain** - leak, prime, dry, S-trap, corroded, not visible				
2.6	**Venting** - auto-vent, too short/tall, frost, suspect, siphon, diameter				
2.7/9	**Solid Waste Pump / Laundry Tub Pump** - inoperative, leak				
2.8	**Sump Pump** - inoperative, leak, backflow valve, clogged, lid, discharge, not visible				
3.1/2	**FIXTURES - Sink / Basin** - leak, cracked, rust, chipped, slow drain, airgap, eventual updating likely				
	- Sink / Basin - leak, cracked, rust, chipped, slow drain, airgap				
3.3	**Faucet** - leak, inoperative, loose, stiff, drip, handle, diverter, vegetable sprayer				
	Faucet - leak, inoperative, loose, stiff, drip, handle, shower head, diverter				
3.13	**Outdoor Faucet** - leak, damage, shut off, loose				
3.4	**Toilet** - leak, inoperative, loose, running, slow flush, cracked, floor damage, mechanism				
	Toilet - leak, inoperative, loose, running, slow flush, cracked, floor damage, mechanism				
3.5/6	**Bathtub / Bathtub Enclosure** - leak, tile, caulk, grout, window, damage, rust, drain slow, doors				
	Bathtub / Bathtub Enclosure - leak, tile, caulk, grout, window, damage, rust, drain slow, doors				
3.7	**Shower Stall** - leak, tile, caulk, grout, loose, door, possible concealed damage				
	Shower Stall - leak, tile, caulk, grout, loose, door, possible concealed damage				
3.8	**Whirlpool Bath** - hand held shower, GFCI, pump, leak, settlement, noisy, motor-access, switch				
3.9/10	**Bidet** - leak, cracked, loose / **Sauna** - inoperative				
3.11/12	**Bathroom / Kitchen Fan** - inoperative, discharge outside, noisy, desirable, ductwork				
3.14	**Laundry Tub** - leak, damage, cracked, concrete, loose, slow drain				

COMMENTS

☐ See Supplementary Section ☐ Inappropriate Materials or Installation

EXPLANATION OF CODES FOR REPORT FORMS

REFERENCE	This column identifies the appropriate sections of the text.

TASK

P	provide	I	improve
R	repair or replace	M	monitor
F	further evaluation required		

LOCATION

B	basement	LR	living room
1	first floor	DR	dining room
2	second floor	K	kitchen
3	third floor	Bath	bathroom
CS	crawl space	G	garage
N	north	WR	washroom
E	east	ENS	ensuite
S	south	BR	bedroom
W	west	FR	family room
M	master	LA	laundry area
A	attic	C	central
V	various	T	throughout
F	front of house	LH	left side of house
R	rear of house	RH	right side of house
EX	exterior	O	office or study

Note: the direction the house is assumed to face is noted on the page entitled **Significant Items**.

TIME

0	immediate	2	less than two years
1	less than one year	"X"	less than "X" years
U	unpredictable *(This component could last a few months or several years.)*	D	discretionary item *(Improvements can be made, but are not critical.)*
M	regular maintenance or ongoing	?	if necessary

COST

B	buyer is to perform the work	<	less than
S	third party is to perform the work	>	more than
M	minor cost or regular maintenance item	$\approx$	approximately
D	dependent *(Cost will depend on extent of work and approach taken. In some cases, the best approach cannot be determined during a one-time visual inspection.)*		
L	consult local resources or contractor(s) for life cycle and cost information.		

Note: Any figures given are very rough estimates. Several quotations from contractors should be obtained. Our experience has shown that quotes often vary by 300%.

INTERIOR

DESCRIPTION

1.0 Major Floor Finishes:
- ☐ 1.1 Concrete
- ☐ 1.2 Hardwood
- ☐ 1.3 Softwood
- ☐ 1.4/1.5 Carpet
- ☐ 1.6 Resilient
- ☐ 1.7 Ceramic/Quarry Tile
- ☐ 1.8 Slate/Stone/Marble/ Terrazzo

2.0 Major Wall Finishes:
- ☐ 2.1 Plaster/Drywall
- ☐ 2.2 Paneling
- ☐ 2.3 Brick/Stone
- ☐ 2.4 Concrete/ Concrete Block
- ☐ 2.5 Stucco/Texture/ Stipple

3.0 Major Ceiling Finishes:
- ☐ 3.1 Plaster/Drywall
- ☐ 3.2 Acoustic Tile
- ☐ 3.3 Suspended Tile
- ☐ 3.4 Metal
- ☐ 3.5 Stucco/Textured/Stipple
- ☐ 2.2 Wood

6.0 Windows:
- ☐ 6.1.1 Single/Double Hung
- ☐ 6.1.2 Casement
- ☐ 6.1.3 Sliders
- ☐ 6.1.4 Awning
- ☐ 6.1.5 Fixed
- ☐ 6.1.7 Skylights
- ☐ 6.1.8 Solariums

6.2 Glazing:
- ☐ 6.2.1 Single   ☐ 6.2.2 Double
- ☐ 6.2.3 Triple
- ☐ 6.2.4 Primary Plus Storm

7.0 Exterior Doors:
- ☐ Solid Wood
- ☐ Hollow Wood
- ☐ Metal
- ☐ Garage
- ☐ Storm
- ☐ French
- ☐ Sliding Glass
- ☐ Plastic/Fiberglass

8.0 Fireplaces:
- ☐ 8.1 Masonry
- ☐ 8.2 Zero Clearance
- ☐ 8.3 Insert
- ☐ 8.4 Gas
- ☐ 8.5 Coal
- ☐ 8.6 Roughed-In
- ☐ 8.7 Non-Functional
- ☐ 8.8 Wood Stove
- ☐ None

9.0 Party Walls:
- ☐ Masonry
- ☐ Wood Frame
- ☐ None In Attic
- ☐ Not Visible

10.0 BASEMENT/CRAWL SPACE LEAKAGE
- ☐ Evidence of leakage
- ☐ Cannot predict how often or badly crawl space or basement will leak
- ☐ Read Section 10.0 in the text before taking action

IMPROVEMENT RECOMMENDATIONS   ☐ *NONE AT PRESENT*

Limitations
- ☐ Absence Of Historical Clues Due To New Finishes/Paint
- ☐ Storage/Furnishings In Some Areas Limited Inspection
- ☑ Quality Of Chimney Draw Cannot Be Determined
- ☑ No Comment Made on Cosmetic Finishes   ☐ Fireplace in use
- ☑ CO detectors, security systems, intercoms, central vacuum, chimney flues and elevators were not inspected
- ☐ Restricted/No Access To: _____
- ☐ _____ % of foundation wall not visible
- ☐ Drainage Tile not visible

Reference		Task	Location	Time	
1.0	**FLOORS** - water stains, loose, cracked, slope, bouncy, patched, damage, worn				
2.0	**WALLS** - water stains, loose, cracked, patched, damage — typical flaws				
3.0	**CEILINGS** - water stains, loose, cracked, sag, patched, damage				
	- smoke detectors				
4.0	**TRIM/COUNTERS/CABINETS** - water damage, loose, rot, obsolete, damaged, hardware				
5.0	**STAIRS** - uniformity, rise, run, tread width, headroom, railings, pitch				
6.0	**WINDOWS - Primary - glass, sash, frame, sill, screen, hardware, caulking, putty, weatherstripping**				
	- water damage, loose, cracked, broken, paint/stain, rot, condensation, lost seal, leak				
	slope, operability, original lower quality units				
	Storms - glass, sash, screen, hardware, caulking				
	- water damage, loose, cracked, broken, condensation, inoperative, incomplete, weepholes				
6.1.7	**Skylight/Solarium** - water damage, condensation, leak, rot, cracked, lost seal				
7.0	**DOORS - main, garage (man-door), storm, french, sliding**				
	- glass, sash, frame, sill, screen, hardware, weatherstripping				
	- damage, leak, adjust, trim, rot, operability, lost seal				
8.0	**FIREPLACES / WOOD STOVES - inspect / sweep chimney before using**				
	- foundation, hearth, firebox, damper, mantle, mortar, lintel, liner				
	- chimney draw, combustible clearance, shared flue, size, rust, gaps, settlement, support				
	- gas leaks, lighter valve, fan, combustion air vent, doors, screens, damage				
9.0	**PARTY WALLS**				
10.0	**BASEMENT / CRAWL SPACE LEAKAGE** - efflorescence, stains, dampness, prior repairs				
	1. - gutters, downspouts, grading, driveways - attempt these improvements first				
	2. - cracks/form ties				
	3. - excavation, damproofing, tile - consider as a last resort				
	- suspect, evidence of prior repairs				

COMMENTS

☐ See Supplementary Section   ☐ Inappropriate Materials or Installation

EXPLANATION OF CODES FOR REPORT FORMS

REFERENCE	This column identifies the appropriate sections of the text.

TASK				
	P	provide	**I**	improve
	R	repair or replace	**M**	monitor
	F	further evaluation required		

LOCATION				
	B	basement	**LR**	living room
	1	first floor	**DR**	dining room
	2	second floor	**K**	kitchen
	3	third floor	**Bath**	bathroom
	CS	crawl space	**G**	garage
	N	north	**WR**	washroom
	E	east	**ENS**	ensuite
	S	south	**BR**	bedroom
	W	west	**FR**	family room
	M	master	**LA**	laundry area
	A	attic	**C**	central
	V	various	**T**	throughout
	F	front of house	**LH**	left side of house
	R	rear of house	**RH**	right side of house
	EX	exterior	**O**	office or study

Note: the direction the house is assumed to face is noted on the page entitled **Significant Items**.

TIME				
	0	immediate	**2**	less than two years
	1	less than one year	**"X"**	less than "X" years
	U	unpredictable *(This component could last a few months or several years.)*	**D**	discretionary item *(Improvements can be made, but are not critical.)*
	M	regular maintenance or ongoing	**?**	if necessary

COST				
	B	buyer is to perform the work	**<**	less than
	S	third party is to perform the work	**>**	more than
	M	minor cost or regular maintenance item	**≈**	approximately
	D	dependent *(Cost will depend on extent of work and approach taken. In some cases, the best approach cannot be determined during a one-time visual inspection.)*		
	L	consult local resources or contractor(s) for life cycle and cost information.		

Note: Any figures given are very rough estimates. Several quotations from contractors should be obtained. Our experience has shown that quotes often vary by 300%.

There may come a time that you discover something wrong with the house, and you may be upset or disappointed with your home inspection.

Intermittent Or Concealed Problems

Some problems can only be discovered by living in a house. They cannot be discovered during the few hours of a home inspection. For example, some shower stalls leak when people are in the shower, but do not leak when you simply turn on the tap. Some roofs and basements only leak when specific conditions exist. Some problems will only be discovered when carpets were lifted, furniture is moved or finishes are removed.

No Clues

These problems may have existed at the time of the inspection but there were no clues as to their existence. Our inspections are based on the past performance of the house. If there are no clues of a past problem, it is unfair to assume we should foresee a future problem.

We Always Miss Some Minor Things

Some say we are inconsistent because our reports identify some minor problems but not others. The minor problems that are identified were discovered while looking for more significant problems. We note them simply as a courtesy. The intent of the inspection is not to find the $200 problems; it is to find the $2,000 problems. These are the things that affect people's decisions to purchase.

Contractors' Advice

The main source of dissatisfaction with home inspectors comes from comments made by contractors. Contractors' opinions often differ from ours. Don't be surprised when three roofers all say the roof needs replacement when we said that, with some minor repairs, the roof will last a few more years.

Last Man In Theory

While our advice represents the most prudent thing to do, many contractors are reluctant to undertake these repairs. This is because of the "Last Man In Theory". The contractor fears that if he is the last person to work on the roof, he will get blamed if the roof leaks, regardless of whether the roof leak is his fault or not. Consequently, he won't want to do a minor repair with high liability when he could re-roof the entire house for more money and reduce the likelihood of a callback. This is understandable.

Most Recent Advice Is Best

There is more to the "Last Man In Theory". It suggests that it is human nature for homeowners to believe the last bit of "expert" advice they receive, even if it is contrary to previous advice. As home inspectors, we unfortunately find ourselves in the position of "First Man In" and consequently it is our advice that is often disbelieved.

Why Didn't We See It	Contractors may say "I can't believe you had this house inspected, and they didn't find this problem". There are several reasons for these apparent oversights:
Conditions During Inspection	1. It is difficult for homeowners to remember the circumstances in the house, at the time of the inspection. Homeowners seldom remember that it was snowing, there was storage everywhere in the basement or that the furnace could not be turned on because the air conditioning was operating, et cetera. It's impossible for contractors to know what the circumstances were when the inspection was performed.
The Wisdom Of Hindsight	2. When the problem manifests itself, it is very easy to have 20/20 hindsight. Anybody can say that the basement is wet when there is 2 inches of water on the floor. Predicting the problem is a different story.
A Long Look	3. If we spent 1/2 an hour under the kitchen sink or 45 minutes disassembling the furnace, we'd find more problems too. Unfortunately, the inspection would take several days and would cost considerably more.
We're Generalists	4. We are generalists; we are not specialists. The heating contractor may indeed have more heating expertise than we do. This is because we are expected to have heating expertise and plumbing expertise, roofing expertise, electrical expertise, et cetera.
An Invasive Look	5. Problems often become apparent when carpets or plaster are removed, when fixtures or cabinets are pulled out, and so on. A home inspection is a visual examination. We don't perform any invasive or destructive tests.
Not Insurance	In conclusion, a home inspection is designed to better your odds. It is not designed to eliminate all risk. For that reason, a home inspection should not be considered an insurance policy. The premium that an insurance company would have to charge for a policy with no deductible, no limit and an indefinite policy period would be considerably more than the fee we charge. It would also not include the value added by the inspection.

We hope this is food for thought.